The People's Liberation Army and

China in Transition

The People's Liberation Army and China in Transition

edited by Stephen J. Flanagan *and* Michael E. Marti

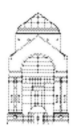

NATIONAL DEFENSE UNIVERSITY PRESS
WASHINGTON, D.C.
2003

Opinions, conclusions, and recommendations expressed or implied within are solely those of the contributors and do not necessarily represent the views of the Defense Department or any other agency of the Federal Government. Cleared for public release; distribution unlimited.

Portions of this book may be quoted or reprinted without permission, provided that a standard source credit line is included. NDU Press would appreciate a courtesy copy of reprints or reviews.

Library of Congress Cataloging-in-Publication Data

The People's Liberation Army and China in transition / edited by Stephen J. Flanagan and Michael E. Marti
     p.cm.
  ISBN 1–57906–061–7
  1. China. Zhongguo ren min jie fang jun. 2. China—Armed Forces. 3. China—Armed Forces—Political activity. 4. Civil-military relations—China. I. Flanagan, Stephen J. II. Marti, Michael E.
  UA835 .P58 2002
  355'.033051—dc21

2002015193

First Printing, August 2003

NDU Press publications are sold by the U.S. Government Printing Office. For ordering information, call (202) 512–1800 or write to the Superintendent of Documents, U.S. Government Printing Office, Washington, D.C. 20402. For GPO publications on-line access their Web site at: http://www.access.gpo.gov/su_docs/sale.html.

For current publications of the Institute for National Strategic Studies, consult the National Defense University Web site at: http://www.ndu.edu.

Contents

Part V—U.S.-China Military Relations

Part VI—Options for U.S.-China Relations

Illustrations

Foreword

The global war on terrorism has provided a new context for relations between the United States and China. As the September 2002 *National Security Strategy of the United States of America* makes clear, cooperation with China on a range of economic, political, security, and military issues increasingly serves U.S. interests. At the same time, this relationship retains elements of competition and the potential for confrontation, compounded by a legacy of periodic crises and mutual wariness. Achieving a national consensus on an appropriate balance in U.S.-China relations, especially in military-to-military affairs, remains a central challenge for those who analyze, formulate, and implement America's China policies.

The distinguished contributors to this volume offer fresh and sometimes divergent assessments of major trends in Chinese society, national security policy, and military affairs as the "fourth generation" of national leaders settles into the seats of power. The essays examine leadership shifts under way in the People's Liberation Army and how the Chinese armed forces are coping with dramatic changes in economic and social life, the Chinese Communist Party's search for relevance, developments in the global security environment, and the revolution in military affairs. Also explored are trends in civil-military relations, growing Chinese nationalism, evolving PLA military capabilities, Beijing's approach to key regional and global issues, the prospects for U.S.-China relations and military-to-military cooperation, and the implications of these developments for U.S. defense planning.

The People's Liberation Army and China in Transition provides insights into critical issues that will impact China, the Asia-Pacific region, and world, and advances balanced assessments of U.S. policy options. I trust readers will find that it makes a valuable contribution to the ongoing national debate.

Paul G. Gaffney II
Vice Admiral, USN
President

Acknowledgments

Michael Marti and I are indebted to the distinguished contributors to this volume for revising and updating for publication their papers from an October 2001 National Defense University (NDU) conference. David Shambaugh graciously provided sound organizational suggestions and a new essay for the book that assesses the sweeping changes in the high command of the PLA over the past few years.

Dr. Marti orchestrated the conference and the initial preparation of the book. He was ably assisted in these efforts by the China Center's research assistants, John Kemmer, then a student at the State University of New York at Binghamton, and Melanie Ziarko, then a student at Wittenberg University. Linda Vaughn of the staff of the Institute for National Strategic Studies (INSS) provided outstanding graphic and administrative support for the conference. After Dr. Marti returned to his position with the Department of Defense in the summer of 2002, I took up the effort to complete the editing of the book. Howard Krawitz, distinguished visiting fellow in INSS and a contributor to the volume, provided valuable advice in readying several chapters for publication.

Special thanks go to the editorial staff at NDU Press, who were indispensable to the production of this volume. Jeffrey Smotherman and Lisa Yambrick edited and proofread several drafts of the entire manuscript with great skill and dedication under the supervision of George Maerz and William Bode. Robert Silano, Director of Publications, oversaw the process from beginning to end. William Rawley of the U.S. Government Printing Office created the cover and managed the typography and design of the book.

We have benefited greatly from our collaboration with a number of the leading American scholars of China and Chinese military affairs. However, in the end, we alone bear responsibility for the final product.

Stephen J. Flanagan
Director, Institute for National Strategic Studies
    and Vice President for Research
National Defense University

The People's Liberation Army and

China in Transition

Chapter 1

The PLA in a Changing China: An Overview

Stephen J. Flanagan and Michael E. Marti

The People's Liberation Army (PLA) is striving to cope with dramatic changes in Chinese society, shifts in the global security environment, and the revolution in military affairs. The factors affecting this process are many and varied: the social and economic revolutions under way within China; the search by the Chinese Communist Party (CCP) for a relevant role in a more complicated political milieu; the installation of the "fourth-generation" leadership at the November 2002 16th Congress of the CCP and the March 2003 10th National People's Congress; China's evolving diplomacy; the growth of the country's relative military strength; and the ambitions of a politically oriented military establishment that is also undergoing a leadership shift as it seeks to create a new image and identity for itself. The outcome of this process will profoundly affect China, the Asia-Pacific region, and, perhaps, the entire world.

This book includes a collection of revised and updated papers prepared originally for an October 2001 conference entitled *The PLA and Chinese Society in Transition*, which was sponsored by the Center for the Study of Chinese Military Affairs in the Institute for National Strategic Studies at the National Defense University. The analyses explore the context and processes governing PLA ambitions to remake itself. The six parts of the book assess likely developments in civil-military relations under the fourth-generation leaders, the impact of growing nationalism in China, evolving PLA military capabilities, key regional and global issues, the prospects for U.S.-China relations and military-to-military cooperation, and the implications for U.S. defense planning.

The contributors to this volume are a diverse group of leading American experts on Chinese military affairs from universities, research centers, government, and the private sector. Their assessments and policy recommendations are wide-ranging and reflect many of the divergences among China watchers. Several important points are worth highlighting:

- During 2002–2003, the People's Republic of China successfully and peacefully completed the largest single transfer of civilian and military power in its history. As expected, the fourth-generation leadership, headed by former State Vice President Hu Jintao, ascended uneventfully to seats of power in Beijing. Hu became both state president and CCP general secretary. Yet the third generation of leaders, led by former State President Jiang Zemin, did not leave the stage entirely. Jiang still commands potentially significant amounts of power behind the scenes. He retained his position as Central Military Commission (CMC) chairman, the nexus of party and military leadership, and placed a number of his protégées and loyal followers in other key positions, ensuring his continued influence over the course of China's evolution.

- To some extent, China's fourth-generation leaders represent unknown quantities. Still we know that many of them differ from their predecessors in several important ways. China's new leaders tend to be pragmatic technocrats. They lack extensive military and revolutionary experience. They tend to be more inwardly focused, perhaps less sophisticated in international affairs, than the previous generation. Most importantly, unlike the generation that has just stood down, this new generation was largely unaffected by the ravages of the Cultural Revolution.

- The PLA military leadership is playing an important, but not necessarily the decisive, role in its transformation. China's political apparatus continues to have significant control over the process. In this regard, the powerful position of the PLA in the CCP Central Military Commission, a key party organ, remains an important source of influence.

- The PLA is undergoing a military leadership secession of equal importance with China's civilian political transition. A new group of senior military officers has already assumed major responsibilities in military regions, general staff departments, and service branches.

- The PLA is pursuing a vigorous and multifaceted military modernization program supported by significant real annual increases in defense spending. It is expanding missile force capable of striking Taiwan, even from longer ranges. It is acquiring new multirole combat aircraft with long-range strike capabilities, improving its command, control, communications, and intelligence, and augmenting naval capabilities for perimeter defense and local amphibious operations. There are two major uncertainties in assessing future defense trends: how long can China sustain the remarkable economic expansion that has supported this defense buildup, and how much will other priorities curtail military modernization requests?

■ The PLA military strategy sees the United States as its principal adversary. As a result, the PLA increasingly emphasizes preemptive, asymmetric strikes against critical American military targets, as well as active and passive defenses against U.S. long-range precision strike systems.

■ Nationalism is a growing force within Chinese society as a whole and the PLA in particular. Together with continued economic prosperity, nationalism has become a major factor affecting regime legitimacy and the overall basis of state power. Nationalist issues have spurred the PLA to focus more attention on irredentist claims, as well as longstanding geostrategic claims along China's periphery.

■ Even as the war on terrorism has created a new context in which Washington and Beijing could begin developing military cooperation in pursuit of mutual security interests, significant political and cultural obstacles and an overarching atmosphere of mutual mistrust continue to hamper such cooperation. Establishment of a permanent commission to support the development of bilateral defense cooperation programs is essential to building even a moderately successful relationship. Opportunities exist for realigning counterpart relationships between the PLA and the U.S. defense community. Realignment would ensure that policymakers in each government deal directly with one another rather than through intermediaries or their respective intelligence communities. Expansion of the number and types of military exchanges and dialogues could help build confidence, understanding, and practical cooperation.

How the Book Is Organized

Part I considers the political and military transitions in China during 2002–2003 and their implications for Chinese civil-military relations and U.S. foreign and defense policy. Part II examines the impact of growing nationalism on Chinese politics and the PLA. Understanding the PLA role in Chinese society requires consideration of PLA doctrine, strategy, and force structure, so Part III provides critical assessments of current and projected capabilities that are essential for informed speculation about future intentions. Part IV examines China's national security concept and military doctrine and strategy to understand the main determinants of military planning and operations. Part V assesses the record and prospects for U.S.-China military-to-military relations. Finally, Part VI advances two divergent paths for U.S.-China relations.

Part I—China's Fourth-Generation Leadership

In the opening chapter, Bates Gill notes that the transition has brought sweeping change to the CCP, the Chinese state apparatus, and the PLA. Gill characterizes the fourth-generation leaders as pragmatic technocrats with little military experience and a bad taste for the extremism of the Cultural Revolution, which disrupted their formative years. He notes that the top leadership contenders—Hu Jintao, Li Changchum, Wu Bangguo, Wen Jiabao, Zeng Qinghong, and Lou Jiwei—and other party chieftains share an overwhelming concern for maintaining conditions that will sustain internal growth and stability, which are the principal bases for continued CCP leadership in China. He notes that these goals must be achieved at a time when a number of difficult social, economic, and political problems are coming to a head. Gill envisions four issues dominating the attention of the Chinese leadership during this period: the politics of transition, entry into the World Trade Organization (WTO), socioeconomic difficulties, and party reform.

In addition to the equities of various factions and generations within the party, Gill notes that the leadership is increasingly sensitive to the public mood. He foresees the era of collective leadership continuing. While Jiang Zemin tried to establish himself as a paramount leader, he still must lead by building consensus. Gill sees Jiang and the third generation of leaders using their networks to retain considerable power even after the formal transitions. Thus, he recommends keeping lines open to both the retiring elders and expanding contacts with fourth-generation leaders.

Gill, like several other contributors to this volume, sees China's integration into WTO as a critical challenge. While WTO is likely to boost trade, stimulate the economy, and spur enterprise restructuring, some sectors and many individuals will suffer dislocation. In addition, the leadership will have to grapple with internal corruption, income disparities between different regions, and dire health and environmental problems. Backlash related to all these problems will cause domestic turmoil during and after the leadership transition period. Finally, there is the identity crisis within the CCP, which no longer has any compelling and cohesive ideological message for the people. As Gill notes, the party leads by "a mix of coercion, delivery of economic growth, and the absence of a viable alternative." Jiang Zemin's "Three Represents" call on party members to be more representative of the advanced productive forces of society (private entrepreneurs), of advanced culture in China, and of the fundamental interests of the majority of the Chinese people. Gill sees Chinese leaders focused on two external concerns during the transition. The first is balancing its cooperation with the United States on global counterterrorism efforts with its concerns for how this effort could expand U.S. regional and global influence. The second is managing cross-strait relations, where Gill sees the transition contributing to a tough but cautious approach to Taiwan's political assertiveness.

Gill notes that Washington can have little influence over transition politics. However, he advocates that U.S. policies toward China be attuned to the tumultuous economic and social challenges that the fourth-generation leaders face, with the goal of fostering broad outcomes favorable to U.S. interests. Gill urges American officials to maintain channels to all elements of Chinese leadership, to understand the troubled domestic environment the Chinese leadership is facing, and to leverage counterterrorism cooperation in ways that encourage progress on other issues, such as proliferation and human and political rights, that constrain development of a productive U.S.-China relationship.

David Shambaugh explores the changing nature of civil-military relations in China. He notes that the PLA is undergoing a leadership succession of equal importance with the political transition. He reviews the sweeping turnover of top personnel in the PLA that occurred before, at, and after the 16th Party Congress. While Jiang Zemin remained as chairman of the CMC at the Congress and Hu Jintao stayed on as vice-chair, there was much more change than continuity in the military leadership. Shambaugh argues that this transition without a purge or crisis reflects the growing professionalism of the PLA. He notes that the new CMC was streamlined from 11 to 8 members, and none of its members (other than Hu Jintao) were appointed to a position on the Politburo Standing Committee. More broadly, it is interesting to note that PLA representation on the CCP Central Committee has fallen to nearly an all-time low of 21 percent. The continuation of Jiang Zemin as chairman of both the party and state CMC creates two procedural anomalies, the subordination of the PLA to party and state command. He notes that Jiang's retention of power has clouded an otherwise smooth succession and did encounter some opposition. He also notes that Hu Jintao has no previous military credentials of his own and has not been engaged in military affairs. While the PLA will respect Hu as a party and state leader, Shambaugh argues, Hu will need to court the regional military leadership to build support for his eventual assumption of the CMC.

Shambaugh notes that while we do not possess extensive biographical data on those second-echelon officers beneath the CMC, a number of changes in leading PLA personnel took place in the military regions, general departments, and services in the year prior to the Congress. This cohort not only represents the fourth generation of PLA leaders but also the fifth. It is from this pool of officers that the senior military leadership will be drawn in the years ahead. Still dominated by the ground forces, the group has substantial field command experience and is well educated. However, they are not well traveled abroad and have little actual combat experience. Shambaugh predicts that this cadre is likely to focus on comprehensive modernization of the PLA, is unlikely to intervene in high-level politics, and wants to avoid performing internal security functions.

All this reflects further institutional bifurcation of party and army. The military played no apparent role in the civilian leadership succession before or at the 16th Congress and vice versa. Not a single senior party leader has one day of military experience, and none of the new military leaders have any experience in high-level politics. This trend was evident in the third generation of leaders but is a marked departure from the former fusing of civilian and military leaderships. This bifurcation reinforces the ongoing trend toward corporatism and professionalism and a diminishment of ideological considerations in the PLA. In this context, one can begin to speak of *civil-military* rather than *party-army* relations in the PRC, with the PLA developing *limited autonomy* from the ruling party and possibly entering an intermediate stage in a transition from a party-army to a national army. Shambaugh has no doubts that the PLA will defend China against external enemies. However, whether it will move against internal enemies that may threaten the rule of the Communist Party will be the ultimate test of the redefined relationship of the army to the party and state in China.

Part II—The Impact of Growing Nationalism

Nan Li examines the growth of PLA nationalism, which he refers to as conservative nationalism. In the post-ideological world and competitive global economy, the central role of the state apparatus is to ensure that China can develop and prosper relative to other countries. The primary role of the PLA in this context has become to maintain China's territorial integrity, expand the depth of the country's security zone, and protect critical lines of communication. Li contends that the PLA withdrawal from the class-based politics of the Cultural Revolution and, more recently, from its extensive commercial activities further reinforced this nationalist agenda. According to Li, PLA nationalism is conservative in scope—focused mainly along China's periphery—and in pace—seeking a gradual consolidation of what the Chinese call comprehensive national power. While noting that there are liberal internationalist voices in the PLA that support multilateralism and peaceful resolution of disputes, Li contends that conservative nationalism is the dominant paradigm in the PLA today.

This mindset, Li argues, engenders military support for forceful efforts to prevent Taiwanese independence, advance certain territorial claims, and realize other regional interests. He contends that PLA conservative nationalism has influenced recent political trends, including Jiang's theory of the Three Represents that broadened membership in the CCP to "advanced productive and cultural forces." Li sees the PLA as playing a subtle but important role in the leadership transition, with a clear profile of the kind of figures who would support their agenda. He argues that Hu Jintao fits this profile fairly well, given his strong record in fighting Tibet separatism when he served as first party secretary in that province. He notes that the PLA has also sponsored sizable media, propaganda, and popular entertainment programs with themes designed to bolster wider support for its strong national security agenda. Li concludes that growth, which would stave off a major socioeconomic crisis and support further defense modernization, could exacerbate PLA nationalism, as would further U.S. moves that were seen as backing Taiwan independence. In contrast, an economic recession, democratization, or a U.S. policy that combines a balance of military resolve and engagement could potentially constrain PLA nationalism.

Moving to Chinese society in general and the growth of nationalism, Edward Friedman argues that the goal of contemporary Chinese nationalism is to establish hegemony in Asia but that this tendency need not lead to conflict with the United States if forces that favor economic growth and international integration can prevail. He contends that a U.S. policy of cautious and vigilant engagement can, at the margin, help these peaceful forces prevail against the dominant chauvinists in Chinese politics. According to Friedman, Chinese nationalism developed as a response to the perceived fear that, following the fall of the Soviet Union, China would be targeted for containment or elimination by the United States.

This concern, combined with Chinese economic growth and official efforts to stoke anti-Americanism, has contributed to the growth of nationalism. Friedman argues that the government could be riding a tiger in stirring this nationalist fervor because it could turn against the leadership in a time of crisis when their actions are not seen as sufficiently strong in defending the national interest. At the same time, Friedman notes that this nationalist, anti-American sentiment in China is not an informed opinion and hence is subject to rapid change. This argues for a cautious engagement to strengthen forces in China that favor peaceful cooperation and to demonstrate U.S. willingness to work constructively with Beijing in areas of common interest.

Part III—Military Trends

While much is written about PLA force goals and aspirations, a key uncertainty in assessments and projections remains the question of resources. Chinese defense spending is grossly underreported, and there are great uncertainties as to whether the government can maintain the steady budget increases essential for realization of force goals.

James Mulvenon surveys PLA evolution since 1949 and assesses PLA aspirations to become a modern army after a difficult two decades of restructuring, downsizing, doctrinal experimentation, and diminished institutional standing at home. He notes that prior to the 1970s, the PLA was focused inward on continental defense in accordance with the doctrine of People's War. Naval and air forces were seen as providing little more than a speed bump to likely invading high-technology armies—the United States from 1949 to the mid-1960s and the Soviet Union from the mid-1960s to the mid-1980s. In the late 1970s and early 1980s, Deng Xiaoping initiated a transformation in military doctrine and force structure, turning the PLA focus outward to deal with local wars along the periphery of China. However, the army has seen only one real test of this concept since these changes were implemented, the 1987 operations along the Vietnam border. The largest mobilization of the ground forces took place during the 1989 Tiananmen crackdown on internal dissent. Since 1989, the focus of all PLA forces has been on a single dominant planning scenario: a Taiwan crisis. But this shift has also given the navy and air force increased importance and higher priority in resources for modernization.

Mulvenon explains that the army retains a critical role in defending the party and the people from internal and external enemies. However, he notes that these missions have also suffered attrition. Given the improbability of a ground invasion of China, the ground forces have exercised this function with existing equipment and have received low priority in the struggle for procurement resources. At the same time, the army role in internal security has been diminished considerably since 1989 with the transfer of a number of PLA units to the People's Armed Police. In addition, the army has not played a prominent role in the internal debate on the revolution in military affairs, thus limiting service influence over the future shape of the PLA. Mulvenon and other analysts conclude that the majority of the 100 army divisions are likely to remain low- to medium-tech forces that lack weapons with the range and precision to be used in an offensive mode against modern armies. If the army is to realize its goal of developing selected forces capable of acting swiftly to deal with contingencies along the country's periphery, Mulvenon concludes, it will have to make further reductions in force structure, continue its significant communications enhancements, procure a number of modern weapons, increase reserve capabilities, and expand training.

Bernard Cole reviews the evolution of China's maritime strategy of active offshore defenses, use of the island chains as strategic delineators, and quest for blue-water naval capabilities. He argues that while the People's Liberation Army Navy (PLAN) will increase its capabilities for active offshore defenses in a broad area around its periphery, this will not lead to development of a blue-water fleet capable of global operations. Cole traces how General Liu Huaqing, head of the PLAN from 1982 to 1987, pressed for expansion of naval operations from coastal defense to offshore active defense. Liu set a course for a three-stage naval development process focused on two maritime areas of strategic concern to the nation—the first and second island chains. The first island chain extends 200 to 700 nautical miles from the mainland to include the Yellow Sea, the western East China Sea, and the South China Sea, including Taiwan and other land features claimed by Taiwan. The second island chain is even more ambitious, encompassing maritime areas out to 1,800 nautical miles for the mainland along a north-south line stretching from the Kuriles to Indonesia, including most of the East China Sea and the East Asian sea lines of communication. The third phase of Liu's putative maritime strategy envisions the PLAN as a global force in the middle of the 21st century, built around aircraft carriers or missile-carrying submarines.

While Beijing's current naval modernization is almost always discussed in the context of Liu's theory, Cole argues that development plans and doctrinal shifts focus primarily on development of a mobile navy capable of using surprise and initiative to protect China's periphery against superior forces. He notes that the PLAN surface fleet is modernizing at a measured pace. The most notable surface developments are the acquisition of four *Sovremenny*-class guided missile destroyers with supersonic anti-surface ship cruise missiles and about a dozen modern Chinese-built destroyers and frigates armed with subsonic cruise missiles. However, these modern ships lack capable area air-defense missile systems and have limited antisubmarine systems. The rest of the surface fleet is of 1950s vintage. He notes that the PLAN Air Force has far fewer aircraft than the regular air force and most of these are older models, with the exception of 28 Russian- and French-designed helicopters. The PLAN Air Force has also been slow to acquire the systems and to conduct training for aerial refueling—a critical step in extending the reach of airpower. Cole indicates that the PLAN does not have and is not building a significant amphibious assault capability in the navy or the merchant fleet. The most formidable arm of the PLAN is the submarine force, led by four very quiet and lethal *Kilo*-class boats, including 23 Chinese-designed *Ming*- and *Song*-class diesel-electric boats. He concludes by noting that while the PLAN is the largest navy in East Asia and one of the largest in the world, it would have to rely on speed, mobility, and surprise in confronting a strong opponent, particularly the United States. He suggests that the PLAN is capable of undertaking limited sea denial operations and active offshore defense operations in waters within the first island chain (a few hundred miles off its coast). While capable of some blue-water presence, Cole sees global reach as a distant, uncertain PLAN goal.

Richard Fisher contends that the PLA Air Force (PLAAF) is pursuing the first large-scale modernization of its forces in an effort to acquire capability for offensive and defensive operations in all weather conditions and in a modern, high-tech environment. Fisher cites Department of Defense reports to Congress on the PLA that note that, absent any compensatory actions by Taiwan, the airpower balance in the Taiwan Strait could favor the PLAAF by 2005. Fisher also estimates that the PLAAF will pose a significant threat to a U.S. carrier battlegroup by that point. Fisher describes how PLAAF equipment modernization is being supported by important doctrinal shifts, including interest in offensive and multiservice (joint) operations. He argues that plans to expand multirole combat aircraft are designed to complement the expansion of ballistic and cruise missile forces. Fisher also sees indications that airborne troops are being developed for strategic strikes and that air defense forces, which are being expanded substantially, are considered a critical component in support of offensive operations.

Fisher highlights several key trends in PLAAF equipment modernization: a new interest in modern training aircraft and simulators; plans to procure 300 to 400 new or modified multirole combat aircraft; acquisition of new types of antiair and ground attack munitions, including precision-guided bombs, missiles, and antiradar antiship missiles; greater emphasis on support platforms (tankers, electronic warfare capabilities, and both development and foreign acquisition of airborne warning and control systems [AWACS]); and plans for procuring expanded air transport assets. Fisher notes that the PLAAF has also acquired a fourth-generation fighter aircraft, the Russian Su-27, but the Chinese have had problems incorporating these aircraft into their forces. The PLAAF still has no modern, dedicated close-air support aircraft with precision-guided munitions and heavy machineguns akin to the U.S. A–10 or the Russian Su-25 and appears content to rely on older aircraft with gravity bombs and attack helicopters. However, Fisher cites reports that the Chinese plan to outfit about 25 of the 100 H–6 bombers in the PLAAF with television-guided land-attack cruise missiles to give these 1950s aircraft new offensive capabilities that could be used against Taiwan in tandem with short-range ballistic missiles in the Second Artillery. Fisher notes that while the Chinese reportedly were developing an indigenous successor to the H–6 or might acquire a new bomber from the Russians—Tu-22M (Backfire) or the Su-34—neither development has materialized. As with other services, the PLAAF needs access to modern intelligence and information to engage in effective offensive operations. Fisher notes that the PLA may be planning to procure an array of eight imaging and eight radar satellites to improve reconnaissance capabilities.

While granting the myriad of challenges that the Chinese must address to assemble, train, maintain, and pay for this modernization, Fisher concludes that the PLAAF is making serious investments and realizing important strides. He argues that the growth of the PLAAF and other forces could lead Beijing to assume in a crisis a few years hence that it has the capabilities to take decisive military action against Taiwan, particularly if the United States were seen as distracted by the war on terrorism or other global security problems. To deter the mainland, Fisher advocates a robust effort to increase Taiwan's active and passive defenses. He also argues that the United States should accelerate introduction of advanced combat aircraft, relocate certain American forces in the region closer to Taiwan, increase the survivability of certain reconnaissance and communications satellites, and accelerate deployments of theater missile defenses and land-attack cruise missiles.

Although large gaps remain in Western knowledge of the resources the Chinese are actually devoting to defense, PLA modernization plans clearly will be costly. Western analysts differ as to whether China's projected economic growth is adequate to support the ambitious PLA plans. Richard Bitzinger seeks to sort through this debate by explaining what is known and unknown (and what probably will never be known) about Chinese defense spending to clarify the limits of using this analysis to ascertain Chinese military priorities and capabilities. He argues that Western efforts to fill the gaps in official Chinese expenditure figures, while scientific and well intended, have reached a methodological dead end.

Bitzinger notes that one fact foreign analysts have known since 1950 is the official top line of Chinese military expenditures. In 2001, the Chinese announced a defense budget of $17 billion, a 17-percent increase over the previous year, which continued a 12-year trend of real growth. China's official defense budget doubled between 1989 and 2000 and increased by 58 percent between 1995 and 2000. This increase was justified as necessary to "adapt to changes in the military situation in the world" and to "prepare for defense and combat in a high-technology environment." Bitzinger cites reports that Beijing plans to fund yearly double-digit defense budget increases, such that official spending could more than double current levels by 2005. He argues that one can conclude from these trends that Beijing is seriously committed to modernizing the PLA into an advanced military force and is signaling potential adversaries that it wants these forces to gain certain strategic objectives.

Bitzinger points out that the defense budget has constituted about 9 to 10 percent of the overall state budget and less than 2 percent of gross domestic product over the past decade. Both figures have fallen significantly since the 1980s, indicating that defense spending is actually a declining burden on the Chinese economy. Similarly, the Chinese do offer a public breakdown of rough spending categories. Analysis of these trends reveals that while Beijing contends that the bulk of recent defense increases have gone to improve salaries and benefits of PLA soldiers, in fact, procurement and operations and maintenance accounts have actually grown at significantly higher levels.

However, it is well known that the official Chinese defense budget accounts for only a fraction of overall defense spending. Military research and development costs and the costs of the People's Armed Police are funded by other parts of the state budget. Arms imports are extra-budgetary purchases, militia and reserve forces are partly borne by provincial accounts, and official subsidies of the military-industrial complex do not appear in the defense top line. In addition, the defense budget does not reflect income from certain businesses that the PLA still owns or controls indirectly, despite official divestiture of most PLA businesses since 1998. Moreover, some form of purchasing power parity formula needs to be applied to Chinese defense expenditures since personnel expenses and most goods cost less than they would in the West. Among the other gaps in Western knowledge are allocations of spending to various services, numbers and types of weapons procured, and spending on training and logistics.

Bitzinger offers alternative approaches to analysis of Chinese defense budgets, including a method that focuses on assessing likely future procurement costs as a way to assess if there is a mismatch between capabilities and spending. Using this methodology, which he cautions is still fraught with caveats, he concludes that the Chinese could readily afford a modest buildup with a 5 percent increase in official defense spending and a fairly robust one with 10 percent annual growth for 10 years. At the same time, he notes that if the economy continues to grow at current rates, the defense burden on the state budget is likely to remain low. He concludes that analysts should avoid a focus on the bottom line of total defense spending and instead look for reliable indicators of where the money is going and why.

Part IV—Key Policy Challenges

David Finkelstein examines China's "New Security Concept," first advanced at the March 1997 Association of Southeast Asian Nations Regional Forum as a Chinese vision for a multilateral security environment in the post-Cold War era that rejected the need to strengthen alliances and the use of force. Finkelstein concludes that the new concept is primarily a political and economic construct that has had little impact on its target audience in Southeast Asia but has helped advance China's Shanghai Cooperation with the countries of Central Asia. He sees the concept as having had little direct impact on defense planning.

A Chinese leadership in transition, growing nationalism, and uncertain economic prospects complicate the handling of several key issues in U.S. policy toward China, including Taiwan, the direction of military-to-military exchanges, WTO membership, Russian arms purchases, and dual-use commercial equipment.

Taiwan remains the most sensitive and explosive issue in U.S.-China relations. Cynthia Watson explores how the PLA may approach this strategic issue in the coming years. Watson notes that the PLA has a unique responsibility to protect the CCP rather than the state per se. As a result, the PLA leadership sees its primary mission as protecting not only the country's physical security but also CCP legitimacy. However, she postulates that professionalization is changing the character of the army and may make it more nationalistic. As the CCP becomes dominated by leaders with no military experience, such as Jiang Zemin and Hu Jintao, and the PLA becomes more professional, Watson forecasts that the CCP leadership may be concerned about diverging assessments of national interests between the party and the armed forces, as well as its ability to control the PLA. Watson concludes that the changing party-army relationship and a more assertive PLA with differing policy preferences between the two institutions could complicate Beijing's decisionmaking process in a future Taiwan crisis.

Watson notes that many mainland and Taiwanese observers seem convinced that time is on Beijing's side with respect to reunification as a consequence of Taiwan's economic stagnation, PLA modernization, and Beijing's new cooperative relationship with Washington in the war on global terrorism. Another factor mitigating cross-strait and U.S.-Chinese tensions, Watson contends, is the relatively restrained approach that the Bush administration has taken with respect to arms sales to Taiwan. Nevertheless, she argues that PLA leaders see reunification of Taiwan with the mainland as so essential to national sovereignty that they would be prepared to endure likely setbacks to economic development—and attendant risks to social order—that would surely follow military action to secure reunification. She sees any wavering on Taiwan by a future CCP leadership concerned with the economic downsides as leading to civil-military tensions. Watson concludes that the PLA is likely to be a more assertive and influential actor in Chinese domestic deliberations on Taiwan and other key issues after the 16th Party Congress.

John Tkacik illuminates the contours of Taiwan domestic politics and concludes that while they are becoming more dynamic and democratic, they will remain sharply divided along ethnic lines for the foreseeable future. The main ethnic cleavages in Taiwan's political culture are between mainlanders, Hoklo Lang Taiwanese, Hakka Taiwanese, and Malayo-Polynesian aborigines. Tkacik argues that these ethnic and factional divisions will preclude the Taipei government from making dramatic moves toward or away from Beijing. Tkacik discusses how these ethnic cleavages played in voting for the three major candidates in the March 2000 presidential elections: Chen Shui-bian (Democratic Progressive Party [DPP]), James Soong (People First Party [PFP]), and Lien Chan (Kuomintang [KMT]). Chen carried down-island Hoklo areas (representing 40 percent of the vote), Soong won among mainlanders, Hakka, and aborigines (36 percent), leaving Lien with ethnic Taiwanese voters loyal to the KMT (23 percent). Former President Lee Teng-hui's tepid support for his party's candidate, Lien, led to his distant third-place showing and a subsequent shattering of the once-dominant KMT.

Tkacik predicts that the KMT–PFP electoral alliance for the 2004 presidential elections will be tenuous, while the DPP will remain handicapped by its loose organizational structure and factionalism. He concludes that because national identity is at the heart of cross-strait tensions, Taiwan politics will not permit an accommodation of the mainland demand that Taiwan become a political entity subordinate to Beijing's authority. Absent some shift by Beijing, Tkacik is pessimistic about cross-strait rapprochement. At the same time, he foresees that the inclination of the majority Hoklo-Taiwanese to declare independence will be restrained by uneasiness of the minority Hakka, mainlander, and aboriginal communities.

Eugene Rumer contends that while Sino-Russian relations improved over the past decade, these ties are being recast in light of both countries' reassessment of their foreign policy priorities after September 11, 2001, differing relationships with the United States, and related domestic considerations. While the two countries have some common interests and a shared wariness of American power, Rumer dismisses the notion of a Russian-Chinese alliance or strategic partnership as an exaggeration even before September 11. He characterizes the Sino-Russian relationship as, "at best, a marriage of convenience and, and, at worst, a latent geopolitical fault line in Eurasia."

Rumer traces how the war on terrorism has opened new channels between Russia and the United States. Vladimir Putin's decisive support for U.S. actions in Afghanistan and willingness to compromise on key arms control issues—hardly welcome in Beijing—demonstrate that good relations with Washington are a higher priority than ties with Beijing. China remains a key market for the financially strapped Russian defense industry. The two neighbors have common interests in the stability of Central Asia and in limiting U.S. influence there. However, the Russian foreign policy elite continues to harbor concern that burgeoning Chinese military and economic power could threaten Russian control of the Far East regions. Rumer concludes that Putin cannot afford to antagonize Beijing or suspend its arms sales. However, if the rapprochement between Moscow and Washington continues, the Sino-Russian strategic partnership will likely become hollow.

Kevin Nealer reviews the broad economic context and the impact of trade with the United States for PLA modernization efforts. He concludes that declining exports and the impact of complying with WTO obligations will place additional demands on government resources, making it difficult to sustain projected defense budget increases. Nealer predicts that China will see increased unemployment, social dislocation, pressures on its legal system, and growing disparities in wealth between the coastal regions and the interior. He dismisses as overly simplistic the notion that Chinese access to U.S. capital markets frees up Chinese assets to support military expansion. He reminds us that the PLA must compete with other governmental components for funds in budget battles. Moreover, Nealer notes that the disclosure requirements of international capital markets have given Western observers much greater insights into the structure and functions of Chinese companies than ever before. With regard to the problem of diversion of critical civilian technology for military applications, Nealer argues for fewer but higher fences around the systems and capabilities that matter most to the United States.

Howard Krawitz explores the implications of China's trade opening for regional stability. Krawitz agrees with Nealer that WTO accession will force China to grapple with many economic and social challenges on a massive scale. He posits two scenarios for China's evolution under WTO membership. First, China could adjust well by adapting to the inflow of Western capital, management practices, and technology to strengthen the competitiveness of its enterprises. Such a confident and circumspect China could be more readily integrated into the global economic system and would likely see peace and stability as key to maintaining the country's prosperity. Second, in a worst-case scenario, implementation of WTO-mandated changes could exacerbate domestic political, economic, and social differences and make the country more ungovernable. If the Chinese public also perceived that they were not benefiting from integration into the international economic community, Krawitz postulates that conservative and nationalist backlash would likely stimulate military aggressiveness and attempts at regional hegemony.

Under the first scenario, particularly if it is accompanied by the stabilizing impact of a growing Chinese middle class, Krawitz sees the U.S.-China relationship as cooperative, productive, and mutually beneficial. Krawitz grants that a more prosperous and militarily capable China could also pursue an aggressive, nationalist course. However, he sees this as unlikely, arguing that the new generation of leaders are technocrats focused on economic development and disinclined to military adventurism. That said, he notes that the worst-case scenario is certain to lead Beijing toward a tense and confrontational relationship with the United States and neighboring countries. Krawitz concludes that helping China implement economic reforms serves long-term U.S. interests. He argues for a strategy that includes the following elements: realistic expectations about the U.S. ability to influence China; clarity and consistency, which have often been lacking in the policies and communications of both sides; and patience in spanning the gap between the cultures and worldviews of the two countries.

Part V—U.S.-China Military Relations

Paul Godwin notes that evolving PLA doctrine and strategy see the United States as China's most dangerous potential adversary with considerable ability to project and sustain high-intensity warfare on China's periphery and deep into its interior. Godwin explores the role mutual apprehension plays in this relationship. Where the United States perceives China as the single state in Asia likely to challenge its preeminence in the region, China assumes that America seeks to contain it and will intervene militarily in any conflict that may erupt over Taiwan. Consequently, the PLA must brace itself for a long-term confrontation with the United States in the Asia-Pacific region. Godwin reviews the military doctrine, strategy, and concepts of operations that PLA planners draw from as they think through the formidable challenges presented by the capabilities of U.S. forces and their operational doctrine. According to Godwin, Chinese military doctrine now stresses the need for retaining a minimum nuclear deterrent, preemptive strikes against command, control, communication, computers, and information assets, carrier battle-groups, and foreign bases, as well as passive and active defenses against long-range, precision strike systems.

Alfred Wilhelm argues that expanding U.S.-China military-to-military contacts and security cooperation is essential to overcoming mutual suspicions and building a foundation for peaceful relations between the two countries. Wilhelm, who served as a defense attaché in Beijing, recounts how bilateral security cooperation after 1979 evolved on the basis of setting aside differences and working together in pursuit of mutual interests, particularly containment of Soviet influence. In support of these common interests, the military-to-military relationship included high-level visits, functional military exchanges (including education), and military technology cooperation. He notes that the Chinese entered these interactions with suspicion of Washington's motives and took a practical, narrowly defined approach designed to extract knowledge and technology. This approach led most officers on the U.S. side to conclude that the PLA derived much more from these interactions than the United States. However, Wilhelm contends that these tentative interactions improved channels of communication between the U.S. military and the PLA, enhanced transparency, and contributed to further amiable relations, which lasted until the late 1980s. The warming of Sino-Soviet relations and strains in U.S.-China relations following the Tiananmen massacre in 1989 led to a rupture in military-to-military contacts. Attempts by the Clinton administration to revive contacts in the early 1990s were derailed by Congressional alarm with the PLA buildup and Chinese espionage, coupled with the Taiwan Strait crisis in 1997. The EP–3 incident in April 2001 both put a hold on further contacts and brought into question the ability of military-to-military ties to enhance crisis communications.

Wilhelm agrees that the war on terrorism has created an immediate need and a new context for Washington and Beijing to develop durable military cooperation in pursuit of mutual security interests. He cautions that such a relationship will have to overcome important political and cultural obstacles and an overarching atmosphere of mutual mistrust. Wilhelm grants that PLA opacity in military contacts and dialogues inhibits reciprocity and the deepening of these ties. However, these impediments were overcome in the 1980s and, he argues, can be hurdled again if both sides show sufficient political will. He contends that the CCP decision in the 1990s to allow party officials to have contacts with nonsocialist foreign officials opens the door to realigning counterpart relationships between the PLA and the U.S. defense community to ensure that policymakers in each government are dealing directly with one another rather than through intermediaries or their respective intelligence communities. For example, the counterpart of the Secretary of Defense is not the Minister of Defense but the most senior military member of the CMC after the chairman, the General Secretary of the CCP. In addition, he urges that President Bush and other senior U.S. officials seek to build personal working relationships with Chinese officials in comparable positions. Wilhelm urges the two governments to create a standing defense commission with a full-time staff to support the development of a bilateral agenda and to monitor and advise the commission on bilateral defense programs. In that regard, he recommends significant expansion of the number and types of military exchanges and dialogues to build confidence and understanding through practical cooperation.

Part VI—Options for U.S. China Relations

Richard Thornton criticizes U.S. policy toward China over the past three decades for being instrumental in the growth of Chinese power. He contends that China cannot be a strategic partner with the United States and that continued American economic engagement, originally designed to help China become a counterweight to Russia, will help China realize what he characterizes as its hegemonic ambitions. Thornton contends that U.S. policies toward China should reflect the desirable strategic environment for the United States rather than American aspirations for China. Thornton holds that expansion of U.S. trade and investment in China after 1992 has greatly advanced the country's military power, but the overall economic system remains quite fragile. He sees Beijing's current strategy as making China into a great power using investment from East Asia and the United States to become stronger in order to achieve an intimidating military capability that would enable them to restructure the balance of power in East Asia to their advantage. Thornton asserts that Chinese policy toward Taiwan represents a general challenge to the United States in the Far East.

Thornton proposes a new U.S. policy designed to thwart Chinese expansion by exploiting the country's economic vulnerability. This strategy, which he likens to the Reagan administration approach to the Soviet Union, would constrict trade, limit the flow of technology, and inhibit China's ability to acquire hard currency. Thornton urges that, in tandem with this approach to restrict capital flows, the United States should maintain superior military capabilities, with an emphasis on missile defenses, to counter this key element of Chinese strategy. Thornton notes that the global economic recession, the war on terrorism, and Chinese entry into the WTO could unfold in ways that would advance his goal of precluding China from challenging the U.S. position of dominance in East Asia.

In contrast, David Lai contends that conflict between a status quo Unites States and a rising China can be avoided if the relationship is managed properly. He notes that the three policy schools for handling China—engagement, containment, and *congainment*, a hybrid of the two that blends economic engagement with military containment—all seek to change China into the image of the United States. He contends that the three approaches differ primarily in their means of achieving this goal. He notes that China's leaders view current U.S. policy of circumspect economic engagement and military containment with considerable suspicion.

Lai agrees that the global war on terrorism offers new opportunities to advance common Sino-American interests. He argues that many past and current elements of U.S. policy indicate a misunderstanding of China that is reflected in several areas: overstating the Chinese military threat, overestimating China's economic development, overlooking changes in China including Americanization of elements of Chinese lifestyle, and underestimating the ability of Chinese leaders to move their country forward. Lai argues for a balanced and restrained U.S. approach to relations with China that eschews labeling China as either a strategic partner or competitor. Lai also argues that U.S. intervention in internal Chinese affairs generally strengthens Chinese resistance to change. Lai contends that Chinese leaders have to stop viewing the United States as an archenemy, overcome self-imposed ideological barriers to cooperation, and limit the role of the military in domestic affairs. Lai concludes that while these changes in mindsets will take time, bilateral relations will improve, particularly if helped by the emergence of a multilateral regime for enhancing diplomatic dialogue and managing security in East Asia.

Conclusion

The analyses offered by the contributors to this volume illustrate that American China watchers are still far from consensus on the effects that growing nationalism, economic expansion, further integration into the global economy, and political transition will have on Chinese strategic behavior and military capabilities. All agree that China is a rising power. Questions relating to how quickly the country will grow, how it will apply its power, and how its leaders will choose to deal with the United States and its neighbors remain subjects of highly contentious debate. The analyses in this volume offer valuable baseline assessments of PLA force structure, doctrine, and strategy. They also demonstrate that there is a great deal of information in Chinese sources about PLA aspirations, intentions, force structure, and capabilities for those who care to mine it.

The contending assessments articulated herein reflect and have influenced significant shifts in U.S. policy toward China since 2001. The Bush administration came to office intent on undoing the Clinton administration's notion of a strategic partnership and on treating China as more of a strategic competitor. This initial policy thrust called for a much more circumspect approach to trade and investment, coupled with a military strategy designed to dissuade Beijing from seeking to challenge the U.S. position in East Asia. Then came September 11, 2001. The September 2002 U.S. National Security Strategy document noted that the war on terrorism has created a new context for Sino-American relations and opportunities to pursue new forms of cooperation toward mutual security interests. The November 2002 Crawford Summit and subsequent bilateral exchanges have all emphasized the prospects for further cooperation on trade, terrorism, managing stability in East Asia, and renewal of military-to-military contacts. Given the contradictions inherent in U.S.-China relations, it seems certain that there will be several more shifts in the tone and substance of American policy toward the Middle Kingdom over the coming decade.

Part I

China's Fourth-Generation Leadership

Chapter 2

Chinese Leadership Transition

Bates Gill

Over the course of 2002–2003, the leadership of the Chinese Communist Party (CCP), the state, and the military in the People's Republic of China (PRC) has undergone sweeping change. As is typical of PRC political affairs, many familiar persons—such as Jiang Zemin, Li Peng, and Zhu Rongji—will retain critical behind-the-scenes power because of loyalty networks built over long political careers.

The *shang tai* process of inducting the new "fourth generation" of leaders began well before it was formalized during the 16th CCP Congress in November 2002, at which new members of the Political Bureau Standing Committee, the Political Bureau, the Central Committee, and the Central Military Commission were selected. At the 10th National People's Congress in March 2003, the leaders of China's government, including the premier, vice premiers, state council members, and heads of government ministries also changed significantly.

Given China's enormous importance as a major regional power, one of the globe's largest economies and trading nations, and the world's most populous country going through a remarkable socioeconomic and political change, U.S. policymakers will need to monitor and gauge the implications of the ongoing leadership shifts in the PRC carefully. There is little that Washington can specifically do with confidence to support the rise or fall of one individual or another—a business that would best be avoided in any event.

However, U.S. policy toward China must first be attuned to the sensitivities and nuances of this leadership change and then be developed with an eye to fostering broad outcomes favorable to American interests if possible. With these thoughts in mind, three major questions are offered for the United States to address in its dealings with China during this period of leadership transition in Beijing:

- *Who are some of the new leaders?* Brief backgrounds are offered, with a special focus on Hu Jintao and other younger leaders at the top of Chinese political and government circles.
- *What will be China's domestic concerns during this period?* These include leadership transition; economic restructuring and smooth World Trade Organization (WTO) integration; control of internal unrest and the ills of socioeconomic change; and party reform.
- *What will be China's external concerns during this period?* Three major interests are the new counterterrorist framework, perceptions of continued U.S. hegemony, and managing relations with Taiwan.

The chapter concludes with brief recommendations of how U.S. China policy might take these issues into account in the context of Chinese leadership change and foster outcomes more favorable to American interests over time.

The New Leaders

Several individuals now on the rise in Chinese politics who likely will play leading roles in the future are well worth noting. Many uncertainties remain, however, and much backroom battling and political infighting is yet to come. The United States would be well served to remember that point as it formulates its policies toward China.

Those discussed below do not represent an exhaustive list, but they are worth watching. The sorry experience of past designated successors—such as Lin Biao, Hua Guofeng, Hu Yaobang, and Zhao Ziyang—must have given pause to Hu Jintao, who was widely touted to be the next "first among equals" in Chinese leadership circles, before he secured his hold on chairmanship of the party and the state presidency. The subjects of discussion were selected for their relative youth (all 60 years of age or younger in 2001), their hold on important posts within party, state, or military apparatuses, and their connections to key elders in the Chinese political system.

These figures and other potential leaders of the fourth generation exhibit some interesting commonalities. First, they joined the Communist Party well after the founding of the People's Republic of China and cannot claim to be part of the revolutionary old guard or founding generation of the "new China." What they know of pre-1949 China, the Chinese civil war, and the struggle and victory of the Chinese Communist Party, they have learned mostly from history texts.

Second, they directly experienced the excruciating political and economic growing pains of the Maoist era, particularly the Cultural Revolution, which swept up and deeply affected almost all members of this generation in their formative years. That they since have pursued advanced scientific studies and succeeded in politics during the reform years after 1978 suggests their understanding of the need for China to follow a more pragmatic and cautious—rather than ideologically determined—course.

Third, most members of the fourth generation, like the generation before them, are technocrats, trained in the sciences and economics, with little or no military experience.

Hu Jintao, born in eastern Anhui Province in December 1942, turned 60 in 2002. Before assuming chairmanship of the CCP, he concurrently held four major positions in the Chinese leadership hierarchy: member of the Standing Committee of the Political Bureau of the 15th Central Committee of the Chinese Communist Party (he w~, also listed first among members of the Secretariat of the 15th Ce~ al Committee); vice chairman of the Central Military Commissio~, state vice president; and president of the Central Party School. Like most of China's current top leaders, Hu is a technocrat, having studied hydroelectric engineering at Qinghua University.

He joined the party in 1964, and his political career was subsequently marked by his work in some of China's most remote and backward provinces, leadership positions with the Communist Youth League and the All-China Youth Federation, and his comparatively youthful ascent to the top-most leadership of China. He spent much of his early career rising through the ranks of one of China's poorest provinces, Gansu, to which he had been "sent down" during the Cultural Revolution in 1968.

Many credit Hu's rapid rise to power to his keen political instincts. In 1982 at age 39, he was the youngest member of the Party Central Committee. He was the youngest provincial governor in power (at age 42) when he took the party chief position in Guizhou in 1985. In 1988, Hu was appointed to head Tibet, where, in early 1989, he oversaw the violent suppression of Tibetan unrest and then held the lid on during the Tiananmen crisis that spring. He was promoted to the Political Bureau Standing Committee in 1992 and rose to become the fifth most powerful person in China, after Jiang Zemin, Zhu Rongji, Li Peng, and Li Ruihuan.

Hu has traveled abroad often in recent years, including official tours to Asian neighbors, such as Japan, South Korea, and Vietnam, and to the Middle East, Africa, and South America. However, he has not spent an extended period in foreign countries, such as Jiang Zemin (who passed almost a year training at the Stalin Autoworks in Moscow in 1955–1956) and Deng Xiaoping (who spent 6 years as a student in France, 1920–1926). Until late

2001, Hu had not traveled to either the United States or Europe and kept contact with officials from those countries to a minimum. Hu made his first foray to Western countries in a 2-week tour that began October 27, 2001, traveling to Russia, the United Kingdom, Spain, France, and Germany. On this journey, he met many prominent Western leaders, including Vladimir Putin, Tony Blair, Jacques Chirac, Lionel Jospin, and Gerhard Schroeder. He hosted President George W. Bush during his visit to Qinghua University in February 2002, and 2 months later made his first visit to the United States in late April and early May. In addition to meeting with senior officials and members of Congress in Washington, Hu also made stops in Honolulu, New York, and San Francisco.

Li Changchun was born in 1944 in Dalian, Liaoning Province. He joined the party in 1965 while at Harbin Polytechnical University, where he graduated in 1966 with a specialization in electrical engineering. He was elected a member of the 15th Central Committee Political Bureau, his current position, in 1997. Li is also a vice premier under the State Council. Unlike either Wu Bangguo or Wen Jiabao, Li can claim some direct association with the military: He is believed to be first secretary of the Guangdong Military District Army Party Committee, as well as the first political commissar of the Guangdong Military District. As many analysts expected, he rose to the Standing Committee of the Political Bureau in 2002.

Wu Bangguo was born in 1941 in Anhui Province. A party member since 1964, he worked in Shanghai after graduating from Qinghua University with a degree in radio electronics in 1967. He rose through the ranks of Shanghai politics, became close to both Jiang Zemin and Zhu Rongji, and succeeded Jiang to become the municipality party chief in 1991 at age 50. In 1992, he was brought on to the Political Bureau of the Central Committee, a position he still holds today. He is also a vice premier on the State Council, ostensibly working for Zhu Rongji; however, many see him as Jiang's man on that body.

Wen Jiabao was born in 1942 in the east coast city of Tianjin. Wen studied geology at the undergraduate and graduate levels from 1960 to 1968 in Beijing and joined the party while a student in 1965. His subsequent work as a geologist and low-level politician in Gansu Province until about 1981 coincided with time that Hu Jintao spent there. He became a full member of the Political Bureau in 1997 at the 15th Party Congress, a position he holds today. He concurrently holds a position as a vice premier under Zhu Rongji and is the youngest of his colleagues at that post.

Wen's rise was in part due to his association with reform-minded leaders Hu Yaobang and Zhao Ziyang, but he has apparently avoided trouble in the wake of their downfalls in the late 1980s. Some analysts speculate he may take his reformist credentials to the premier post, succeeding Zhu in 2003.

Zeng Qinghong deserves mention, though he is over 60 years old (64 in 2003). He became an alternate member of the Political Bureau in 1997 and is a secretary (seventh among seven in the officially published order) on the Secretariat of the 15th Party Central Committee. He is also director of the Party Central Committee Organization Department, a key position that charges him with overseeing personnel matters within the party.

However, Zeng's potential future power comes more from his association with China's principal leader, Jiang Zemin. He is widely recognized as a close associate of and political strategist for Jiang and is part of the "Shanghai clique," having risen to vice-party chief in Shanghai. Importantly, he has been credited with conceiving the *sange daibiao* (the "Three Represents"), Jiang Zemin's much-touted contribution to the CCP theoretical canon. Zeng regularly travels with Jiang at home and abroad, and he accompanied the Chinese president to the United States as his chief of staff during the fall 1997 U.S.-China summit.

For these reasons, all eyes have been on Zeng to achieve ever-higher status in the Chinese political leadership. Nevertheless, Jiang has unsuccessfully tried three times—most recently in September 2001—to have Zeng promoted to full membership on the Political Bureau. As long as Jiang Zemin retains his influence, Zeng will remain an important figure to watch given his promotion to a full seat on the Political Bureau in 2002.

Internal Concerns

During its leadership transition over 2002–2003, the overwhelming concern for the party chieftains will remain maintaining the conditions for internal growth and stability on the one hand and for party legitimacy on the other. Simply put, the overriding concern will be to assure continued stable socioeconomic reform and growth—delivering the economic and social goods—that are principal bases for continued Communist Party leadership in China. But this goal must be achieved at a time of increasing fragility and uncertainty both within Chinese leadership circles and within the broader Chinese society. Over the coming 2 to 5 years, an array of social, economic, and political forces will converge in thorny and complicated ways for the Chinese leadership.

At least four prominent issues of internal concern will consume much of Chinese leadership time over the 2002–2003 period: politics of transition; smooth WTO entry and integration; dealing with a host of socioeconomic and political difficulties; and party reform.

Politics of transition. While not readily apparent to most observers, the upper reaches of the Chinese body politic are divided over issues of ideology, party reform, national economic and security strategy, loyalty networks, and the politics of personal self-interest and ambition. Outside observers point to various, often-overlapping factions within the Chinese hierarchy, such as conservatives, reformists, nationalists, internationalists, the Shanghai clique, and leaders with provincial interests. Although these leaders are not elected by popular vote, Chinese party bosses appear increasingly sensitive to the mood of the *laobaixing* (common man) on the street. All of these interests and more will come into play during the transition process as elders, heirs apparent, and ambitious prospects of the fourth and fifth generations all jockey for legacy-building, opportunity, influence, and power.

Some structural certainties of the transition do bear mentioning. First, the era of collective leadership will likely continue. Even as the 16th Party Congress approached, Jiang struggled in attempts to establish himself as paramount leader in the tradition of Mao or Deng. Hu Jintao or another candidate may be seen as Jiang was—that is, at the core of a collective leadership but not all-powerful, at least in the early years of the succession. As expected, Hu gained the party leadership and the presidency but not the head of the Central Military Commission. What this means in practice is that Hu will need to play consensus politics at the top and will be unable to take bold measures unilaterally.

Second, Jiang Zemin will retain a significant degree of behind-the-scenes influence—particularly in party politics and over foreign policy, two areas in which he has invested significant personal political resources. Indeed, the very diffusion of influence among various new leaders, with no single person able to claim absolute authority, may mean that party elders will need to stay engaged to resolve differences that arise over key decisions. Several of the key likely leaders—such as Li Changchun, Wu Bangguo, and Zeng Qinghong—owe their positions to Jiang, and he will exercise influence through them. Similarly, while he stepped down from his party posts in 2002 and his premiership in 2003, Zhu Rongji will likely maintain his influence through persons in his loyalty network, such as Wen Jiabao and Wang Zhongyu (age 70 in 2003).

But in the near term, Chinese leaders, both current and future, will focus enormous amounts of attention to the political transition process over the coming months. Much of what they do, at home and abroad, will be with an eye to solidifying their preferred outcomes in the political leadership transition. At a minimum, this probably puts a premium on "risk-averse" behavior.

WTO accession and integration. A goal coveted by Jiang Zemin and Zhu Rongji—formal entry into the WTO—was achieved by the end of 2001, but the hard work of integration, implementation, and adherence has begun. Analysts have different views of how well this process will unfold, but almost no one sees it being easy for China.

China's top leaders are counting on the WTO to expand trade and improve the economy further. From the mid-1990s to 2000, China's year-on-year gross domestic product growth rate, while impressive, had steadily declined to about 7 percent in 2000. China's leadership seems to have accepted that WTO entry will help expand trade, bolster the economy, and stimulate the private sector in China, in the process absorbing redundant labor, particularly from the uncompetitive state-owned sector, attracting foreign investment and technology inputs, and forcing much-needed reform and restructuring of the Chinese economy. Most studies foresee a dramatic increase in China's trade numbers overall and suggest the leaders' wager on the WTO will pay off over time.

But the 3 to 5 years following WTO entry will not be all easy ones for the entire Chinese economy. Some sectors—such as producers of textiles, light industrial goods, and toys; telecommunications; and foreign-invested, export-oriented producers in general—that are already engaged and competitive in the international economy will benefit from WTO entry, but others will profit less.

Some harsh light will be thrown on a system in which banks have propped up ailing industries with loans, and state-owned enterprise employees and retirees have come to expect certain social benefits from the state. WTO entry will prompt a surge in agricultural exports to China, especially from the United States, which will easily outmatch China's inefficient agricultural sector. In addition, China's concessions on banking, insurance, financial services, and retail/wholesale distribution services will result in a flood of new, proficient foreign businesses in these sectors. Some of China's "smokestack" industries, especially automobile production, will likely suffer from WTO entry. The global economic decline of 2001–2002 also put added pressures on the Chinese economy as some of its export markets shrunk just as the country entered the WTO.

In addition to potential economic dislocation and its socioeconomic consequences, China's leaders will need to monitor WTO implementation and adherence, which over the longer term may be the more difficult challenge. In particular, a range of barriers to market entry, such as local fees, licenses, and distribution bottlenecks (long a part of doing business in China) probably will persist and slow the expected pace of economic restructuring among inefficient industries.

The bottom line for Chinese leaders is the need to focus on careful management of WTO entry and implementation. This process will absorb their energies for its importance to stimulating the economy, avoiding internal dislocations and external tensions, and continuing to deliver the economic good times to most Chinese. Alternative outcomes could spell serious trouble for the Chinese economy and, ultimately, the Chinese Communist leadership.

Socioeconomic and political ills. Beyond the issues of WTO entry lie far larger domestic policy questions that will be infused into the ongoing political transition. China's remarkable transformation over the past 20 years has presented the leadership with new and difficult socioeconomic challenges. Such problems inevitably would accompany rapid modernization, but questions arise over whether the nature of the Chinese political system permits it to respond adequately to these challenges. Poor leadership response undermines the legitimacy of local and central government officials and further erodes popular confidence in the current crop of CCP leaders. China's leaders seem to have no illusions about this and have tried, with varying degrees of success, to counter some of the egregious ills where they can, such as dealing with corruption within the military and party.

But other problems will prove even more intractable and will have to be the focus of leaders' attention in the coming years. In addition to dealing with rampant corruption within its own ranks, the Chinese leadership has also taken steps—such as the major "go West campaign" for development of China's westernmost regions—to address the yawning gap between rich and poor in China and between the more advanced coastal provinces and the far poorer and more backward regions of the inland provinces. China's industrialization of the past 50 years, coupled with the spectacular growth and modernization of its urban areas, has led to serious environmental problems nationwide, even to the point of potentially constraining economic growth in some areas. Chinese leaders only belatedly offered more honest acknowledgments of their human immunovirus/acquired immune deficiency syndrome (HIV/AIDS) and severe acute respiratory syndrome (SARS) epidemics. These crises reflect both a lack of transparency in public health information and a larger breakdown in China's healthcare system. Many of China's most pressing socioeconomic problems fuel the growth of the country's itinerant floating population, which in turn further exacerbates social ills at the local level.

In recent years, economic and social tensions have led to an increase in the incidence of protests, riots, and other, more aggressive expressions of alienation and discontent in the Chinese population. Local unrest among urban workers and countryside farmers is not uncommon and usually occurs in response to economic slights and local government excesses and corruption. Disaffection and a sense of moral decay have led some to seek spiritual solace in ways banned by the state—in unsanctioned houses of worship or with groups such as the Falun Gong. But China also faces more troublesome unrest in the form of separatist groups—such as in the far western province of Xinjiang—some of which have turned to terrorism as a political tool.

In short, over the 2 years of political transition and beyond, Chinese officials have a raft of domestic problems to address, problems which are both a target and a result of China's modernization plans. Leaders will need to watch vigilantly developments in these troubled and fraying spots in the country's social and political fabric.

Party reform and political change. While addressing these most immediate domestic concerns, which are mostly outside the party, the Chinese leadership will also need to grapple with reform from within. No one but the staunchest ideologues in China today believes that the party has any compelling and cohesive ideological message to offer the people. The party leads not by example but by a mixture of coercion, delivery of economic growth, and the absence of a viable alternative. As a result, the party has struggled to establish a new relevancy in a transformed China before its very successes in the socioeconomic spheres totally undermine what little political legitimacy it still has.

These issues and the problems that they pose form a core set of issues for the leadership to address. In particular, Jiang Zemin and his supporters have worked to reshape the party's ideological image, in many ways rendering it hardly recognizable to the conservative communist old guard. The goal is apparently to find a way to bolster party leadership and legitimacy in new and more complex times, while sloughing off the stale irrelevancies of Marxist-Leninist-Maoist thought.

The party has taken a number of interesting steps to deal with this dilemma. Most prominent in this effort has been Jiang Zemin's promotion of the Three Represents as his principal contribution to the Chinese Communist ideological canon. The thrust of the Three Represents is to call on party members to be more representative of the advanced productive forces of society, of advanced culture in China, and of the fundamental interests of the majority of the Chinese people. Interpretations of this campaign suggest that it is Jiang's effort to make the party more relevant and flexible in changing times.

Another aspect of this effort was Jiang's announcement in July 2001 that henceforth private entrepreneurs (namely, capitalists) would be welcomed into the party. In another interesting move, in 2000, the Central Party School, under the leadership of president Hu Jintao, was tasked with the job of examining how to transform the party from a "revolutionary" one to a "national" or "governing" one.

In short, the Chinese Communist Party is going through a serious identity crisis, the outcome of which remains uncertain. Because it can affect the very legitimacy and survival of the party and its elite, it will be a topic of enormous importance and sensitivity for China's highest leaders in the coming months and years.

External Concerns

While the lengthy and complex menu of domestic challenges noted above will be the main focus of Chinese leaders' energies for the next several years, important external concerns cannot be ignored. To the degree U.S.-China relations will affect the leadership transition, at least two key concerns bear closer scrutiny: balancing counterterrorism and counterhegemony and managing cross-Straits relations.

Counterterrorism vs. counterhegemony. Thus far, China's response to the September 11, 2001, attacks in the United States have been better than expected. China backed the relevant United Nations (UN) Security Council resolutions for the use of force against terrorism by the United States and its coalition partners, sent a delegation of counterterror and intelligence experts to consult with counterparts in Washington, and supported the idea of issuing a declaration condemning terrorism at the Asia Pacific Economic Cooperation summit meeting in Shanghai in October 2001. It may be possible to elicit further cooperation from China, mostly in the form of continued diplomatic and political support. China's voice is important in certain quarters of the international community, such as on the UN Security Council, and among its friends in Central and South Asia, such as Pakistan and Iran. It may also be possible for China to offer more in the way of intelligence sharing, though expectations on this score may be limited.

Obviously, China has its own reasons for supporting the counterterror campaign. First, Beijing is not about to block the groundswell of international support for the effort. Indeed, China has its own problems dealing with radicalized separatists in the Turkic-speaking regions of the country's far northwest province of Xinjiang, where Islamic fundamentalism is making inroads. China too shares the U.S. interest in seeing that Central and South Asia remain stable in this dynamic period for the region's security, perhaps doubly so in the case of Pakistan, a quasi-ally that Beijing has assisted in becoming a nuclear weapons state armed with ballistic missiles. China will bear an enormous responsibility if these weapons fall into terrorist hands. Clearly, China has a stake in the right outcome in its neighbor, Afghanistan, and in the restive Central Asian region more broadly.

But Chinese leaders have reasons for ambivalence as well, and a number of pitfalls may complicate their continued cooperation. For example, many aspects of the U.S.-led effort to combat terrorism are precisely those that in recent years have made China increasingly concerned about its security situation vis-à-vis the United States. Indeed, the antiterror campaign may make Beijing even more nervous. For example, Beijing can only watch with concern as the U.S.-Japanese and U.S.-Australian alliances are revitalized and strengthened to deal with terrorists and the states that harbor them. Likewise, a growing U.S. military presence in Central Asia and improved relations with Moscow strengthen America's global reach and will likely constrain or even reverse years of meticulous Chinese diplomatic efforts with Russia and Central Asia. In addition, as a staunch defender of traditional notions of state sovereignty, Chinese strategists probably will not acquiesce so readily to a more active or expanded interventionist military policy on the part of the U.S.-led coalition following Afghanistan.

In short, the Chinese leadership can do little at the moment but watch as the international counterterror effort unfolds. On the one hand, it spells opportunity for improved U.S.-Chinese relations, an outcome Jiang Zemin and most other Chinese leaders eagerly seek for their own benefit and for that of China. On the other hand, the expansion of the campaign in certain ways will require deft Chinese diplomacy at home and abroad to strike the right balance between attaining Chinese interests and not conceding all the initiative to a hegemonic United States. Finding and sustaining that balance will be a core feature of Chinese foreign policy and its dealings with Washington for the foreseeable future and color the debates over leadership choices in Beijing over 2002–2003.

Managing cross-Strait relations. Of all external issues, none has a greater ability to affect leadership credibility in China than managing the relationship with Taiwan. Stakes are extremely high; there is so much to gain from success and even more to lose from failure. As an issue of constant concern and enormous political sensitivity to the Chinese leadership, management of the Taiwan question will be an important factor in determining who will lead the mainland in the years ahead. As such, little to no political capital is to be gained through conciliatory approaches toward Taiwan. To the degree Taiwan-related issues will affect a fourth-generation candidate's credentials for leadership, a tough or hardheaded view probably will be preferred.

That said, a more nuanced, multifaceted, but still tough Chinese approach toward Taiwan has emerged in recent years that appears to have support among China's leaders and that seems likely to continue through the political transition of 2002–2003. That the Chinese leadership apparently believes it is working is one important vote in its favor. But in the current risk-averse environment of transition politics, the more subtle policy toward Taiwan—favoring political and economic "carrots," while still sharpening the military "stick"—would be preferred to any dramatic shifts of course, either more coercive or more conciliatory. If anything, Chinese leaders may be increasingly willing over the next 2 years to exercise economic and political levers—without abandoning the steady military buildup—to entice and co-opt different Taiwan-based constituencies into sharing a vision of cross-Strait relations that is closer to Beijing.

Recommendations for U.S. China Policy

Having reviewed some of the likely future leaders of China and considered the issues that will occupy their attention over the course of 2002–2003, we can turn to some thoughts of how American policy can best take advantage of the situation to achieve outcomes favorable to U.S. interests.

Connections to the leadership. Given the nature of Chinese leadership transitions, Washington should keep channels open to the retiring elders of Chinese politics, as they will retain considerable authority in the years ahead, especially in the early years of the fourth generation. Jiang Zemin and Zhu Rongji will remain influential, and other third-generation leaders of experience, such as Li Ruihuan and Li Lanqing, may retain their posts on the Political Bureau Standing Committee and exercise important advisory functions.

But further efforts should be made to expand contacts with fourth-generation leaders who are likely to take up key posts. Following the 16th Party Congress in 2002 and the 10th National People's Congress in March 2003, envoys should be dispatched to meet with some of the new leaders. The management of relations with the United States will likely stay in Jiang Zemin's portfolio, so his equities will need to be acknowledged, but he will want to have his protégés gain the experience and favor of increased interaction with American leaders.

China's strategic concern of internal stability. Over 2002–2003, Chinese leaders will be consumed with issues of internal concern: undergoing the political transition, facilitating economic growth and restructuring, dealing with the many socioeconomic downsides of rapid modernization, controlling social and political disgruntlement, including separatist and terrorist activity, and remodeling the party. All of these issues are of fundamental importance not only for the stability of China but also for the legitimacy, viability, and even survival of the party itself. In this sense, China's domestic problems are of a strategic nature to its leaders and are taken very seriously in Beijing.

Washington should more creatively integrate this understanding into the policy calculus toward China. First, a clearer understanding of the enormous domestic challenges that China faces would bring some nuance to the concern with a rising China. U.S. security policy toward China, which focuses primarily on the Taiwan question and Chinese power projection capabilities, needs to be rebalanced in a way that takes greater account of China's domestic challenges and the security implications that may arise from them for the United States.

Second, the U.S. approach toward China should take into account the sense of domestic fragility that will pervade Beijing's thinking over 2002–2003. On the one hand, that should give the United States a good deal of leverage since Chinese leaders will recognize the criticality of a stable relationship with Washington. On the other hand, if Washington is perceived as taking advantage of Beijing's internal difficulties or probing into areas of vulnerability, Chinese leaders would have little choice but to react harshly.

Much could be gained from a policy that openly acknowledges the strategic nature of China's internal challenges and offers various forms of assistance to the Chinese government to help deal with them. These programs will need to be carefully designed to foster the kind of evolutionary change the United States would like to see in China without appearing to target party rule itself. Such assistance could promote:

- proper WTO implementation, adherence, and adjudication
- expanded opportunities for entrepreneurialism, venture capitalism, and innovative business management practices
- support for law schools, lawyer training, and rule of law initiatives
- corporate good governance, transparency, and accountability
- professional, accountable law enforcement and judiciary practices
- development of community-based, quasi- or nongovernmental social and civic service organizations
- improved customs and export control practices.

Engaging China in a new security era. The counterterror framework guiding U.S. security policy may offer new opportunities to draw China into a more cooperative and constructive international outlook more consistent with American interests. U.S. policy toward China can link numerous problematic bilateral issues to the broader framework of counterterrorism. The trick will be to convey the counterterrorism message in a way that gains greater Chinese support across a range of other issues that bedevil a productive U.S.-China relationship. For example, China's proliferation practices remain a difficult problem for U.S.-China relations. The message from Washington should be that if Beijing wishes to make an even stronger contribution to the fight against international terrorism and to improve its ties with the United States at the same time, it should proactively stem its proliferation practices with Iran, Iraq, North Korea, and Pakistan, given these government's known relationships with terrorist movements in Central, South, and Southwest Asia.

Similarly, the United States should seek even stronger acknowledgment from China of the value of the U.S.-led alliance system as an instrument for regional stability. In the current context, the alliance's ability to respond to threats emanating from Central and Southwest Asia provides an international public good from which Beijing clearly benefits. The new security paradigm also offers Washington a chance to promote more supportive policies from China on questions of sovereignty, intervention, peacekeeping, peace enforcement, and the role of great powers in rebuilding more stable regimes from failed states.

It is also an opportunity to engage Chinese leaders more vigorously on questions of human and political rights in China, especially in developing common understandings to distinguish clearly between a terrorist and those individuals and entities that are peacefully seeking more latitude and flexibility in their political relationship with Beijing, including Taiwan. On the Taiwan question, Beijing should be reminded that the U.S. commitment to a peaceful resolution is stronger than ever, as is its commitment to supporting the growth of democracies and markets, the most potent long-term tools to counter the terrorist threat to Western political systems and economies. Beijing should be strongly encouraged to open a political dialogue with the leadership of Taiwan and continue to place emphasis on economic and political means to resolve cross-Straits differences.

Chapter 3

China's New High Command

David Shambaugh

T he 16th Congress of the Chinese Communist Party (CCP) ushered in a new "high command" in the People's Liberation Army (PLA). A significant turnover of personnel occurred before, at, and after the Congress. This included retiring six and adding three new members of the CCP Central Military Commission (CMC); replacing the directors of the four general departments (General Staff, Logistics, Political, and Armaments), as well as many deputy directors in these departments; and appointing new commandants of the Academy of Military Sciences (AMS) and National Defense University (NDU). Over the year prior to the Congress, a wholesale rotation of commanders, deputy commanders, and political commissars of China's seven military regions also took place. While Jiang Zemin remained as chairman of the CMC at the Congress and Hu Jintao stayed on as vice chair, there was much more change than continuity in the military leadership as a result of the Congress. All other CMC members over the age of 70 retired.

Taken together, these personnel changes constitute the most thorough shakeup and turnover of leading PLA officers ever. Even in the aftermath of the purges of the Yang brothers (1992) or the Lin Biao clique (1971), such an extensive turnover did not occur. The fact that such a thorough vetting *could* occur absent a purge or crisis is testimony to how regularized and professional personnel procedures have become in the PLA. Unlike in the party, where the top posts were filled as a result of considerable nepotism and after lengthy political jockeying, high-level changes in the military were the result of standardized procedures, meritocratic criteria, a well-defined candidate pool, and relative transparency. To be sure, those who would occupy the top jobs were not publicly known until they were appointed—but the candidate pool from which they were drawn was well defined and well known. That is, the new CMC vice chairmen were chosen from the previous members under the age of 70, the new CMC members were drawn from the ranks of military region (MR) commanders (in two cases) and existing deputy directors of the general departments, and some interesting patterns of promotion occurred at the MR level. No dark horses, or "helicopters," were propelled from obscurity to the top ranks.

More importantly, as is described below, the prior career paths of the new military leadership reveal a number of commonalities that illustrate how regularized and institutionalized the tracks of upward mobility in the armed forces have become. Unlike the party, where one can reach the top through a variety of paths (although provincial service seems to be increasingly *de rigueur*), upward mobility in the military is progressively becoming more defined, predictable, and professional. This is not to say that personal ties and loyalties no longer operate at the top of the PLA—they do, as is evidenced by those promoted officers (Guo Boxiong, Liang Guanglie, and Liao Xilong) with ties to retiring generals Zhang Wannian and Fu Quanyou. But we should not assume that these officers were promoted *because* of their career ties to the retiring elders—rather, their career paths intersected with Generals Zhang and Fu, although they had established their own credentials for promotion.

Let us consider the collective backgrounds of the CMC members as a means to identify a typology of the new PLA high command. Some interesting patterns emerge that confirm the increasingly professional nature of the military leadership. Unfortunately, there is not yet enough biographical data available on the new crop of MR commanders or general department deputy directors to provide a sufficient profile of the new PLA leadership at these levels—although it is possible to track the channels of promotion.

Characteristics of the New High Command

The military leadership in China is comprised essentially of three levels: the CMC and associated organs; the four general departments; and the MR commands. Let us examine each in turn.

The New Central Military Commission

The new CMC is somewhat smaller than the outgoing CMC, with only eight total members.

None of the CMC members (other than Hu Jintao) attained a position on the Politburo Standing Committee (PBSC), although Guo Boxiong and Cao Gangchuan became members of the Politburo—replacing Zhang Wannian and Chi Haotian respectively. Interestingly, General Xu Caihou was appointed to the Central Committee Secretariat, although he

Table 3–1. **The Central Military Commission**

Member	Age	Previous Position(s)	New Position
Jiang Zemin	76	CCP General Secretary; PRC President; CMC Chairman	CMC Chairman
Hu Jintao	59	PBSC member; PRC Vice President; CMC Vice Chairman	CCP General Secretary; President; CMC Vice Chairman
General Guo Boxiong	60	CMC member	CMC Vice Chairman; Politburo member
General Cao Gangchuan	67	CMC Member; Director, General Armaments Department	CMC Vice Chairman; Politburo member
General Xu Caihou	59	CMC member; Executive Deputy Director, General Political Department; Secretary, PLA Discipline Inspection Committee	CMC member; CCP Secretariat member
General Liang Guanglie	62	Commander, Nanjing Military Region	CMC member; Chief of General Staff
General Liao Xilong	62	Commander, Chengdu Military Region	CMC member; Director, General Logistics Department
General Li Jinai	60	Political Commissar, General Armaments Department	CMC member; Director, General Armaments Department

is not a CMC vice chair (this puts Xu in a key position of interface between the civilian and military leadership). The failure to appoint a military man to the PBSC is not, in fact, unusual—nor does it really reveal any lack of PLA "influence" in high party councils. Historically, it has much more often been the case that leading PLA officers did *not* make the PBSC; in fact, over the past 20 years, only one uniformed officer (Liu Huaqing) was elected to the PBSC.

More broadly, it is interesting to note that PLA representation on the CCP Central Committee has fallen to nearly an all-time low. At the 8th Congress in 1956, it was 35 percent, rose to 45 percent at the 9th Congress in 1969, fell to 26 percent at the 10th Congress in 1973, rose again to 30 percent at the 11th Congress in 1977, declined to 22 percent at the 12th Congress in 1982, fell further to an all-time low of 19 percent at the 13th Congress in 1987, rose again (in the aftermath of Tiananmen) to 26 percent at the 14th Congress in 1992, declined to 23 percent at the 15th Congress in 1997, and fell further to 21 percent of total Central Committee members (full and alternate combined) at the 16th Congress. Unless a new CMC member (who can remain until age 70), most officers near the age of 65 were not reelected to the Central Committee. Examples include Deputy Chief of General Staff Kui Fulin, Beijing MR Political Commissar Du Tiehuan, Second Artillery Commander Yang Guoliang, and NDU Commandant Xing Shizhong. Fully 60 percent of the PLA representatives on the Central Committee are new members, and the number from the Lanzhou and Nanjing MRs is increasing. Of those elected to the Central Committee, it appears to have been entirely a function of protocol rank. That is, the commanders and political commissars of all military regions, directors and "executive" (first-ranking) deputy directors of all general departments, commanders and political commissars of all services and the People's Armed Police, and the political commissars of the three PLA educational institutions (NDU, AMS, and the National Defense Science and Technology University [NDSTU]) were all elected to the Central Committee. Alternate members included other deputy directors of the General Staff Department and General Armaments Department (GAD), the commandant of NDSTU, the commanders of the Xinjiang Military District, North Sea Fleet, and Macao Garrison, the chief of staff of the Shenyang and Nanjing MRs, and the commander of the 63d Group Army.

One well-known officer who was not elected to full membership on the Central Committee is the flamboyant and egotistical Deputy Chief of Staff General Xiong Guangkai. Xiong did eke out a position as an alternate but ranked 148 out of 158 alternate members. This is interesting not only because Xiong is the best-known PLA officer abroad (insofar as he is in charge of all PLA foreign exchanges and intelligence), but also because prior to the Congress he had audaciously bragged to a number of visiting foreign delegations that he would be promoted high up the hierarchy—possibly to become the Minister of Defense. Xiong's braggadocio resulted in a distinct rebuff at the "polls"—what one Hong Kong newspaper pointedly referred to as a case of "burning down the stove due to overheating."[1]

Also interesting is that the CMC was trimmed from 11 to 8 members. The net decline can be attributed to a couple of factors. First is the fact that, in recent years, the CMC has become increasingly an *ex officio* body—that is, with the directors of the four general departments represented along with two uniformed vice chairs (with a functional division of labor among them and one simultaneously serving as Minister of Defense). This is what can be considered a streamlined model for the CMC. The previous CMC included three individuals who did not have these portfolios (Wang Ruilin, Guo Boxiong, Xu Caihou). It is also interesting that the position of CMC secretary-general was not resurrected or filled. This slot has remained dormant and unfilled (although never formally abolished) since the purge of Yang Baibing in 1992. What this means in practice is that the director of the General Office of the CMC (currently Lieutenant General Tan Yuexin) administratively directs the CMC on a day-to-day basis, without a CMC member having this authority. Yang Baibing had used (and abused) this position to manipulate meetings, paper flow, and personnel assignments during his tenure.

The continuation of Jiang Zemin as CMC chairman, of course, is significant. There had been widespread speculation prior to the Congress (including by this observer) that he would step down from this post, but it was not to be. There was also speculation that Jiang would stay in the job until the March 2003 10th National People's Congress, when he would hand over the chairmanship of both the party and the state CMC to Hu Jintao.[2] This also was not to be, as Jiang was elected to a new 5-year term as chairman of the state CMC.[3] While Jiang's continuation in these twin posts brings continuity to command of the military and civil-military relations, it creates at the same time two procedural anomalies—with someone other than the CCP general secretary heading the party CMC and someone other than the state president heading the state CMC. Traditionally, the head of the party (either chairman or general secretary) has served as chairman of the party CMC, so as to illustrate the principle that the "party commands the gun." Also, according to National Defense Law of 1997, only the president of the PRC (along with the Standing Committee of the National People's Congress) can mobilize the nation for war or order the military forces into combat. Jiang's continuation as CMC chair while Hu Jintao has become state president violates these principles and law and obscures the chain of command. Indeed, Jiang's clinging to power has clouded an otherwise smooth succession. Many in China, including in the CCP, recognize this fact and grouse about it. Perhaps as a sign of this discontent, the vote of the National People's Congress to renew Jiang's position as chair of the state was not unanimous. Almost 10 percent of NPC deputies did not vote in favor of Jiang's reappointment (of the 2,951 delegates, there were 98 votes against him with 122 abstentions). Just as pointedly, the official Xinhua News Agency report that announced his reelection stated that the 16th CCP Central Committee "let Jiang stay on as Chairman of the CMC," while also noting that he had been "relieved of his official duty" as CCP general secretary but that he "relinquished willingly his state presidency."[4]

The reasons for Jiang's continuation as CMC chair, and the maneuvering he undertook to accomplish this continuation, have been the source of much speculation in and outside China.[5] Maintaining the positions will certainly continue to provide an institutional platform for him domestically and internationally. It will also, of course, give him some influence over military affairs. To be sure, the military has been comfortable with Jiang as their leader, and he has been good to the PLA.[6] In the run-up to the Congress, the PLA media engaged in a sycophantic propaganda campaign—presumably to bolster his position and to signal an institutional desire that he remain as chairman.[7] This media blitz followed the apparent decision taken at the summer 2002 leadership retreat at Beidaihe to allow Jiang to stay on in the CMC posts.[8]

So Jiang steps down from all other official positions (although it is still unclear if he will relinquish his positions on the Foreign Affairs, Taiwan, and National Security Leading Small Groups) but retains his military portfolio. How long he will do so remains in doubt. There is no statutory term for the party post, but there is a 5-year mandate for state positions. Whether Jiang remains for the entirety of this tenure, when he would be 81 years old, or hands the positions over to Hu Jintao before then remains to be seen. Jiang seems to fancy himself as a paramount leader qua Deng Xiaoping, and he is clearly trying to establish himself in such a role as a semiretired elder. Recall that Deng also held on to the CMC chairmanship while giving up his party and state positions at the 13th Party Congress in 1987. Jiang is cognizant of this precedent. While Jiang is no Deng, he does possess stature internationally, domestically within the party and nation, as well as within the military. Given the far-reaching leadership transition that took place at the 16th Party Congress and 10th National People's Congress, the military (and perhaps the party and government, too) are somewhat comforted by Jiang's continuation as the CMC chairs. But eventually, he will have to hand over to Hu Jintao (presuming Hu does not encounter difficulties as party and state leader).

Would the military be comfortable with Hu Jintao as their commander-in-chief? Yes and no. Although Hu has been a vice chair of the CMC since 1999, and the military has had 3 years to get used to him (and, more importantly, vice versa), he has no previous military credentials of his own and has not been engaged in military affairs. The only active role Hu has shown concerning the military in recent years was his high-profile involvement in the December 1998 order that required PLA units to divest themselves of their financial assets and to transfer them to the State Council. Hu's other involvement came when he was (briefly) party secretary in Tibet in the late 1980s, and particularly during the crackdown in March 1989. According to a recent Hong Kong press report, Hu was intimately involved in the military planning at the time—particularly with General Liao Xilong, then deputy commander of the Chengdu MR.[9] Liao was promoted to the CMC and position of director of the General Logistics Department at the Congress, and he is the *only* senior officer who evinces ties to Hu Jintao.

Until Hu proves his mettle to the military, he is likely to be viewed only with respect for his position as party and state leader—which *does* confer and convey authority to him—although he has not established a track record on military affairs. What he needs to do is exactly what Jiang did in the 1990–1991 period, after he was catapulted to the CMC chair in November 1989. Jiang very assiduously and carefully visited every military region, all of the general departments, and a large number of units. These visits, his speeches, and personal meetings with key PLA officers all addressed the various institutional and subinstitutional needs of the PLA—thus astutely building an inner-PLA bureaucratic coalition of support.[10] Within a short period of time (by 1993), Jiang's influence with the military had grown, and he had won the support of various PLA constituencies. Many of the regional commanders whom he had met on his tours were transferred to Beijing. Hu Jintao needs to take a leaf out of Jiang Zemin's book in order to cultivate and build his own independent base of support in the military. Jiang's continuation as CMC chair could work both ways: it could help or hinder Hu's ability to build this base.

As a group, the PLA officers of the new CMC display several notable characteristics:

- Their average age is 61. Only Cao Gangchuan is 67. This means that all the others will be members for the remainder of this decade.

- Their career paths are collectively diverse, but each has worked an entire career in different functional systems in the PLA. This provides a kind of division of labor among them. Three have commanded military regions (Guo Boxiong, Liang Guanglie, Liao Xilong), two come from GPD backgrounds (Xu Caihou and Li Jinai), and one (Cao Gangchuan) is a veteran of the military-industrial establishment. None have "helicoptered" to the top, and all have meticulously climbed the career ladder in their respective service or department.

- Several have commanded particularly important military regions and have overseen particularly sensitive operations, during which they have proved their political loyalty to their military superiors and the party: Guo Boxiong was commander of the 47th Group Army during the antiseparatist operations in Xinjiang between 1990 and 1992; Liao Xilong commanded the forces that quelled the rebellion in Lhasa, Tibet, in 1989; Liang Guanglie reportedly commanded the 54th Group Army to suppress the uprising in Beijing in 1989; and all three (particularly Liang Guanglie) have served as commander or deputy commander of military exercises directed against Taiwan.[11]

- CMC membership continues to be dominated by the ground forces, although arguably the air, naval, and missile forces are now more important in PLA orientation and potential missions. Li Jinai does have a background in the strategic and tactical missile forces (Second Artillery) but as a political commissar rather than as a technician or base commander.

- These are professional military men, with proven careers and a clear sense of mission. In addition to lengthy experience at the command level, they have all had some advanced professional military education.

Let us now briefly consider the backgrounds of each uniformed member of the new CMC.[12]

Guo Boxiong. General Guo was first appointed to the CMC in September 1999. It was clear at the time that he and Xu Caihou were to form the core of the "fourth-generation" officers on the post-Congress CMC; the only questions were whether Guo would become chief of logistics or chief of staff and whether he would rise to become a vice chairman or simply remain a member of the CMC. The answers became clear with his elevation to one of the three vice-chair positions. He inherits Zhang Wannian's portfolio, becoming the leading PLA officer with principal authority over doctrine, force structure, and training issues. Although General Guo has been rumored to be suffering some serious health problems since 2000 (reportedly stomach cancer), he is clearly the most important uniformed officer in the PLA today.

General Guo, a native of Shaanxi, has spent the majority of his military career in his home province. He joined the PLA in 1961 and did a 2-year course at the Military Academy in Nanjing (the forerunner to the National Defense University) during 1981–1983. Guo rose through the ranks of the Lanzhou MR, serving successively as a squad leader, platoon leader, regimental propaganda cadre, headquarters staff officer, and eventually MR Deputy Chief of Staff. He spent a total of 24 years (1961–1985) in these positions with a single unit: the 55th Division of the 19th Army Corps. From 1985 to 1990, he served as deputy chief of staff of the Lanzhou MR. From 1990 to 1993, he was commander of the 47th Group Army, directly under Fu Quanyou's command authority. In 1993, he was transferred to the Beijing MR and served as deputy MR commander until 1997, when he was transferred back to take over the Lanzhou MR command—capping his career in the region. He served in this capacity until 1999, when he was tapped for promotion to the CMC and returned to Beijing. Guo is considered a specialist in ground force operations and training; he was one of the first to experiment with large-scale force-on-force mechanized infantry exercises.

Cao Gangchuan. General Cao is now the second-highest-ranking officer in the PLA, with a portfolio covering both equipment and foreign military relations. He was appointed minister of defense at the National People's Congress in March 2003, succeeding Chi Haotian. Cao is a native of Henan and joined the PLA in 1954.

Two characteristics distinguish Cao Gangchuan's career path: expertise in conventional land armaments and ties to Russia. He began studying artillery in the PLA new Third Artillery Ordnance Technical School in Zhengzhou and graduated 2 years later. He was then sent to Dalian for a year of Russian language training before being sent to the Soviet Union for 6 years of study at the Artillery Engineering Academy of the Artillery Corps of the Soviet Armed Forces. He stayed through the Sino-Soviet split and returned to China in 1963. Cao's subsequent career track was entirely concerned with ordnance and military equipment in the General Logistics

Department (1963–1982). There are unconfirmed reports that he was sent to the frontlines on the Vietnamese border in 1979 to coordinate artillery fire. In 1982, he was assigned to the General Staff Department Headquarters, where he worked in the Military Equipment Department until 1989. He then began a 2-year stint as director of the Military Affairs of the General Staff. Following his appointment as director of the Military Trade Office of the CMC in 1990, Cao subsequently became the PLA point man for negotiating weapons purchases and military cooperation with Russia. In this capacity, he has played a key and instrumental role in the modernization of PLA weaponry and equipment. This lasted for 2 years, until he was promoted to be a deputy chief of General Staff from 1992 to 1996 (in charge of weaponry and equipment). In 1996, Cao succeeded Ding Henggao as director of the Commission on Science, Technology, and Industry for National Defense (COSTIND), and then presided over its reorganization and move under the administrative control of the State Council in a 1998 shakeup of the military-industrial complex. He had been known to express great frustration with COSTIND and its many failings to produce high-quality weaponry. General Cao was therefore the logical choice to be appointed as the inaugural GAD director when it was created in 1998. He became a CMC member at the same time.

With his promotion to become a CMC vice chair at the 16th Party Congress, Cao will be even more instrumental in guiding the modernization of PLA weaponry. As the new defense minister, however, his time will be increasingly shared with foreign travel and diplomatic duties. But given the importance of Russia to PLA modernization, there probably was not a better choice for minister of defense than Cao Gangchuan.

Xu Caihou. General Xu has had a career in PLA political and personnel work. Geographically, he has spent most of his career in Jilin Military District of the Shenyang MR—although at the time of his promotion to the CMC in 1999, he worked in the Jinan MR. In Jilin, Xu held a succession of propaganda and General Political Department (GPD) jobs. In November 1992, he was transferred to Beijing where he became assistant to GPD chief Yu Yongbo, but he also worked closely with Wang Ruilin. With this backing, Xu was destined to head the GPD following their retirements. In mid-1993, Xu also assumed co-editorship of the *Liberation Army Daily.* This was a sensitive time following the purge of Yang Baibing, when control needed to be garnered over the GPD apparatus. Xu performed well and was promoted to deputy director of the GPD in July 1994. From 1996 to 1999, he served as political commissar of the Jinan MR.

Xu is a native of Liaoning and joined the army in 1963. He obtained undergraduate and graduate degrees in electronic engineering from the Harbin Institute of Military Engineering in 1968 and was immediately sent to the countryside for manual labor, where he spent 2 years. He joined the party under the worker-peasant-soldier affirmative action program in 1971. From 1971 to 1992, he worked in various personnel management and political work positions in the GPD of the Jilin Military District of the Shenyang MR.

Xu will play a critical role in all personnel decisions in the PLA, including all senior-level promotions. In this regard, he will be an indispensable asset to Hu Jintao, if Hu decides to build his own network of loyal officers across military regions. Xu also has the distinction of being the only PLA officer serving on the Central Committee Secretariat—the body charged with running the day-to-day affairs of the party. This places Xu as a key interface with civilian party leaders, as well as *the* key individual for managing party-army relations and party influence in the military. This responsibility is buttressed not only by Xu's directorship of the GPD, but also the fact that he is the secretary of the CCP Discipline Inspection Commission in the PLA. If the party is to continue to command the gun, Xu Caihou will play an important role.

Liang Guanglie. A new CMC member and the new chief of General Staff is General Liang Guanglie. General Liang's 3 years of service as commander of the Nanjing MR has prompted a great deal of speculation in foreign media that the PLA will cast a more aggressive stance toward Taiwan.[13] It is true that Liang had an instrumental role in planning and executing the exercises that simulated scenarios for attacking Taiwan and that these exercises have increased in scope, pace, and intensity during his tenure, but he did not initiate this trend (it started post-1996), and it is very likely to continue well into the future.

A native of Sichuan, after joining the PLA in 1958 most of General Liang's early career was in the former Wuhan MR (which was divided between the Guangdong and Chengdu MRs in 1985). From 1958 to 1970, he served in a variety of engineering and infantry units (including a 14-month stint in an infantry academy) and then served in the Operations Department of the Wuhan MR from 1970 to 1979. From 1979 to 1990, he served in a succession of positions in the 20th Army Corps, based in Kaifeng, Henan, rising to become the commander from 1985 to 1990. During this time, Liang was twice sent for midcareer training: for a year (March 1982–January 1983) at the Military Academy in Nanjing, and for

4 months (August 1987–December 1987) at the National Defense University in Beijing. He also completed a continuing education correspondence degree in political theory from Henan University from 1984 to 1986. He became commander of the 20th Corps in 1985 and, according to his official biography, served in this position until 1990, when he was appointed commander of the 54th Group Army based in Xinxiang, Henan, where he served until 1993. However, a Hong Kong source indicates that Liang took command in September 1988 and that the 54th Group Army "enforced martial law in Beijing during June 1989."[14] It is unclear if this unit participated in the June massacre or entered the city later in the month; nor is it clear when the unit returned to base in Xinxiang.

Liang continued as commander of the 54th Group Army until 1993, although in 1991 he was once again selected for a 4-month specialized course at NDU in Beijing. After 8 years as a group army commander, Liang was tapped for promotion and assignment to the Beijing MR—where he served as chief of staff (1993–1995) and deputy MR commander (1995–1997). He was then assigned as commander of the Shenyang MR (1997–1999) and was shifted to command the Nanjing MR from 1999 to 2002. Thus, General Liang brings many years of experience commanding ground force units, including serving at the pinnacle of command in three different military regions. He is a logical and qualified choice to replace Fu Quanyou as PLA chief of staff.

Liao Xilong. General Liao is another example of an officer who has risen methodically through the ranks. Born into a poor farming family in a mountain village in poverty-stricken Guizhou Province, Liao joined the army at age 19. He has spent his entire career in the southwestern Kunming and (after 1987) Chengdu MR. He held command at the platoon, regiment, division, group army, and MR levels.

During the border war with Vietnam in 1979, Liao commanded a regiment that captured the border village of Phong To—for which he received a commendation from the CMC.[15] As a result, he was also promoted to division commander (31st) and again engaged Vietnamese forces at Lao Shan and Zheying Shan in 1984. The overall commander of PLA forces in this engagement was none other than Fu Quanyou. For his actions, Liao is said to have been personally decorated by Deng Xiaoping and was promoted to deputy army corps commander. Six months later, at the age of 44, Liao became the youngest group army commander in the PLA. Six months after that he was tapped to become deputy MR commander under Fu Quanyou (again the youngest in the country). He served in this position for 10 years, although General Fu was transferred to command the Lanzhou MR and eventually was promoted to the CMC. After Fu left, Liao continued to serve as deputy MR commander to Generals Zhang Taiheng, Liu Jiulong, and Kui Fulin. As noted above, he played an instrumental role in coordinating the 1989 crackdown in Tibet. Thereafter, he befriended Hu Jintao, who came to Chengdu due to his altitude sickness in Lhasa. In 1995, Liao was finally rewarded with the appointment as Chendu MR commander—a position that he served in for 7 years until he was brought to Beijing in 2002 and appointed director of the General Logistics Department and a CMC member. General Liao has very strong military credentials, but he also possesses important ties to a variety of other senior PLA officers with whom he has served. Being decorated by Deng Xiaoping and being close to Hu Jintao further burnishes his standing. At 62, Liao Xilong and Liang Guanglie will have the predominant impact on shaping PLA force modernization.

Li Jinai. The final member and new appointment to the CMC is General Li Jinai, who succeeds Cao Gangchuan as director of the General Armament Department. Unlike the other newcomers, Li moves up within the same organization—as he has served as GAD political commissar since 1998.

Li's prior career track has been a mixture of working at a series of missile bases and in the defense industrial and science and technology establishment—but, in both cases, it has been entirely on the political side. Although he has a degree in mechanical engineering from Harbin Institute of Military Engineering, he is not a "techie." His entire career since 1970 has been spent in PLA political and propaganda work. After joining the military in 1967, he did serve in an engineering corps construction regiment and as a regimental deputy platoon leader of the 807th Launch Brigade at Base No. 51 of the Second Artillery (1969–1970). From 1970 to 1971, he worked in the GPD propaganda section at Base No. 52 at Huangshan (Tunxi), Anhui Province. From 1971 to 1977, he held a similar position in the 811th Launch Brigade at Qimen, Jiangxi (part of the No. 52 base complex). From 1977 to 1983, Li was transferred to Beijing to head the youth section of the Second Artillery's Organization Department. From 1983 to 1985, he was transferred to the Luoyang strategic nuclear weapons base in Henan Province (Base No. 54), where he was deputy political commissar. In 1985, Li was tapped to return to Beijing as director of the GPD Cadres Department (one of seven departments), where he stayed until 1990. He was then promoted to be one of several GPD deputy directors for 2 years. In 1992, he was transferred to be deputy political commissar of COSTIND, where he served until 1998 when he was appointed as the political commissar of the newly created GAD. In this capacity, he worked closely with Cao Gangchuan, and he succeeded General Cao after the 16th Party Congress when Cao was promoted to be CMC vice chairman.

Thus, while General Li now heads up the key organ responsible for coordinating all defense industrial production and research and development, his career background is not, in fact, on the technical side. His background in the strategic rocket forces is an interesting fact, but it is not clear how much technical knowledge he gained during those assignments. His career has rather been on the political side, and he could be in line to succeed Xu Caihou as GPD director should Xu move up.

The Second Echelon

While we do not possess extensive biographical data on those officers beneath the CMC, it is also important to note that a number of changes in leading PLA personnel took place in the military regions, general departments, and services in the year prior to the Congress. While some of these personnel changes were precipitated by the promotion of other military officers or illness (Air Force Commander Liu Shunyao), leaving vacancies, others were the result of regular rotations. In these appointments, a relatively consistent pattern of promotion emerges, whereby officers are elevated progressively to the next level of command—from Group Army commander to MR deputy chief of staff to MR chief of staff to MR deputy commander to MR commander. In a few cases, officers leapfrogged two positions up the hierarchy,[16] but for the most part the promotion pattern was incremental. This was evident in the following appointments:

- Li Wenhua moved from Beijing Garrison Command political commissar to become Beijing MR deputy political commissar.
- Li Zhenwu went from deputy commander to commander of the Guangzhou MR.
- Song Wenhan went from Guangzhou MR chief of staff to MR deputy commander.
- Ye Aiqun went from commanding the 42d Group Army to replace Song Wenhan as Guangzhou MR chief of staff.
- Wu Shengli went from deputy commander of PLA Navy South Sea Fleet to become commander of the East Sea Fleet.
- Gui Quanzhi went from Chengdu MR chief of staff to become MR deputy commander.

- Liu Yahong went from commander of the 14th Group Army to replace Gui Quanzhi as Chengdu MR chief of staff.
- Qu Fanghuan went from Lanzhou MR chief of staff to MR deputy commander.
- Chang Wanhan went from commander of the 47th Group Army to replace Qu Fanghuan as Lanzhou MR chief of staff.
- Zhong Shengqin moved from Jinan MR chief of staff to deputy MR commander.

Thus, in the Beijing, Chengdu, Lanzhou, Guangzhou, and Jinan MRs there was a very clear pattern of officers moving directly up into the next billet (or two in the case of Zhu Qi).[17] It is also clear that, more than ever before, commands of divisions and group armies are a prerequisite for higher military region assignments. A similar pattern of incremental promotion is seen in the services and general departments (particularly the GAD).

The second echelon military leadership is indicated in tables 3–2 through 3–5. We see similar incremental promotion patterns in these institutions, although in PLA academies and universities some interesting precedents were set. The new NDU president, Lieutenant General Pei Hualiang, was transferred from his post as deputy commander of the Jinan MR. Given the importance of NDU in training group army commanders, it is appropriate that someone of Pei's service background head up NDU. Another precedent was set with the appointment of Vice Admiral Zhang Dingfa as president of the Academy of Military Sciences (the top PLA research organ). This is the first time that someone of a naval background

Table 3–2. **Military Regions**

Military Region	Commander	Political Commissar
Bejing	Zhu Qi	Li Wenhua
Chengdu	Wang Jianmin	Yang Deqing
Guangzhou	Li Zhenwu	Liu Shutian
Jinan	Chen Bingde	Liu Dongdong
Lanzhou	Liu Quanyuan	Liu Yongzhi
Nanjing	Zhu Wenquan	Lei Mingqiu
Shenyang	Qian Guoliang	Jiang Futang

Table 3–3. **The General Departments**

Department	Director	Deputy Directors
General Staff	Lian Guanglie	Ge Zhenfeng, Wu Xuanxu, Qian Shugen, Xiong Guangkai, Zhang Li
General Political	Xu Caihou	Tang Tianbao, Yuan Shoufang, Zhang Shutian
General Logistics	Liao Xilong	Zhan Wentai, Sun Zhiqing Wang Qian
General Armaments	Li Jinai	Li Andong, Zhu Fazhong

Table 3–4. **CMC Affiliated Educational Institutions**

Institution	Commandant
National Defense University	Pei Hualiang
Academy of Military Sciences	Zhang Dingfa
Science and Technology University for National Defense	Wen Xisen

Table 3–5. **Service Commands**

Service	Commander	Commissar
PLA Navy	Shi Yunsheng	Yang Huaiqing
PLA Air Force	Qiao Qingchen	Deng Changyou
PLA Second Artillery	Jing Zhiyuan	Jia Wenxian
People's Armed Police	Wu Shuangzhan	Zhang Yuzhong

(or nonground force) has served in this AMS capacity, or any leading PLA institution for that matter, as the ground forces have had a stranglehold over senior appointments to date. This still remains the case, despite Admiral Zhang's appointment. Prior to the 16th Congress, there had been some rumors that the three other service chiefs (air force, navy, missile forces) would earn seats on the Central Military Commission, but it was not to be.

Implications for Civil-Military Relations

Taken together, the personnel changes in the PLA high command have been sweeping. The Congress triggered some of the changes, but most were mandated by new standards and regulations that have been promulgated in recent years. This cohort represents not only the fourth generation of PLA leaders but also the fifth. It is from this pool of officers that the senior military leadership will be drawn in the years ahead.

They are individuals who continue to come predominantly from the ground forces, have had substantial field command experience at the group army level and below, possess university-level educations and have attended at least one military educational academy, and have methodically climbed the career ladder. However, they are not as well traveled abroad, cannot be considered as cosmopolitan, nor have they had actual combat experience (other than limited action along the Vietnam border). While the failure to promote naval or air force officers to senior levels outside of their own services follows traditional patterns, it is also odd considering the increased importance attached to these services for potential peripheral conflicts and "limited wars under high technology conditions."

Collectively, their policy proclivities can be expected to push ahead fully with the comprehensive modernization of the PLA—hardware, software, command and control, force structure, finance, logistics, science and technology, military education, reconnaissance and intelligence, among others.[18] Above all, they are professional soldiers who are steadily professionalizing the PLA with every passing day. They are not likely to intervene in high-level politics, nor do they wish to be pulled into performing internal security functions (which are to be left to the People's Armed Police). They have a singular, focused mission of comprehensive military modernization, and the PLA is being given the necessary resources to fulfill that mission. A quarter century from now, when the fourth- and fifth-generation officers again change the guard and retire, the PLA will be a far more modern and capable force for their efforts.

In terms of the evolving nature of civil-military relations, the turnover in the military leadership described above reflects several trends that have been noticeable in recent years.

First and most important, we are witnessing the further institutional bifurcation of party and army. This can be seen in a number of ways. The military played no apparent role in the civilian leadership succession before or at the 16th Congress and vice versa—that is, the civilian party leaders played no apparent role in the selection of the new military leadership (and that includes, in my view, Jiang Zemin). There was no praetorian impulse to intervene in politics, and the military was left to make its own succession choices. Furthermore, not a single senior party leader has one day of military experience—while none of the new military leaders have any experience in high-level politics. This is a trend that was noticeable for the past decade during the third generation of leaders but is a marked departure from the former "interlocking directorate" that symbiotically fused together the civilian and military leaderships. The continuing decline of military representation in the CCP Central Committee is yet further evidence of the bifurcation.

Second, this tendency toward bifurcation reinforces the ongoing trend toward corporatism and professionalism in the PLA. This is to say that the PLA as an institution is now exclusively, and more than ever before, concerned with purely military affairs. It is not involved in domestic politics, has withdrawn from its former internal security functions in favor of an exclusively externally oriented mission, has largely divested itself of its commercial assets and role in the civilian economy, and does not play a role or have much of a voice in foreign policy, and even its influence on Taiwan policy has become very circumscribed. To put it simply, the military in China today is concerned with military affairs. Just as importantly, the PLA is being permitted to look after its own affairs by the party—and it is being given the resources to pursue its program of comprehensive modernization.[19]

Third, and related to the above trends, we see few signs of politicization in the military. Except for the "Three Represents" campaign (which in the military is really more about increasing Jiang Zemin's stature than educating the military about recruiting entrepreneurs into the party), we see few indications of political indoctrination in the ranks of the PLA. The General Political Department today is far more concerned with improving the living standards of officers and their dependents than in indoctrinating the rank and file with ideological dogma. This is yet another signal of increased military professionalization. Along with the divestiture of commercial assets and involvement, the military is now exclusively focused on training and other professional activities.

Accordingly, for these reasons, it is now more analytically appropriate to consider *civil-military* rather than *party-army* relations in the PRC. The driving catalyst for all of these changes has been the professionalization of the armed forces.[20] To be sure, as is argued below, this evolution is ongoing and incomplete. The former model has not (and is not likely to) replaced the latter model completely. Yet along a number of criteria, it does seem clear that the PLA is moving away from its traditional communist institutional ethos into a new stage of *limited autonomy* from the ruling party.

Theoretically, in terms of the comparative study of civil-military systems, this new stage may also be viewed as the intermediate stage in a transition from a party-army to a national army. China and the PLA are clearly not there yet, and it is questionable whether a national army can exist within the context of a political system dominated by a single, ruling communist party. Yet there have been, and continue to be, subterranean discussions in China and the PLA about greater state control of the military, a military that serves the nation and not just the ruling party, and a military controlled by civilian rule and governed by legislative oversight. As if to put a fine point on the sensitivity of such considerations, there have been a series of ongoing condemnations of such "bourgeois" concepts in the party and military media from time to time. It is clearly a sensitive issue that cuts right to the core of PLA identity and CCP legitimacy, if not the efficacy of the PRC itself.

Is it feasible to have a national army in a Leninist system? Or can such a military only exist in a democratic system? Given the evidence of economic and educational reforms in China, to take but two issue areas, it is not inconceivable that a hybrid relationship of a professional national military could coexist with a ruling communist party, but within a framework of state and legislative control. Yet, on the other hand, many of the elements necessary to proclaim the PLA a national army seem anathema to the CCP and its rule. For example, it would require at least the following:

- a *real* Ministry of National Defense (not the hollow shell of the current ministry)
- a civilian minister of defense
- presidential chairmanship of the Central Military Commission
- thorough control of the military by the state president, National People's Congress, and State Council

- a series of established laws and procedures governing the use of force and mobilization of the military
- strong legislative oversight of the armed forces
- complete budgetary control over the military by the legislature and no extrabudgetary revenue
- no political content in professional military education.

By these criteria it is clear that the PLA remains a long way from becoming a national army—yet there are discussions and tendencies in this direction taking place in China and the PLA today.

While it must still be considered a party-army, as long as the CCP rules China and the institutional mechanisms of party penetration of the armed forces exist,[21] the PLA as an institution is clearly carving out its own corporate domain and is redefining its professional identity. At the same time, the government (the State Council and National People's Congress) has also attempted, in recent years, to gain greater authority over the military. This has been particularly evident in the fiscal and legal realms. Former Premier Zhu Rongji instituted a variety of important fiscal reforms that have deeply affected the military, including:

- divestiture of commercial assets
- an increased role for the Ministry of Finance in determining the annual military budget
- increased and strengthened auditing of PLA accounts
- zero-based budgeting (where unexpended funds cannot be rolled over to the next fiscal year and must be returned to the State Council).

In legal terms, the National People's Congress has enacted a range of laws—but particularly the 1997 National Defense Law—that stipulates greater authority and responsibilities for the state (as distinct from the party) over the military.

Changes in the interrelationship of party, army, and state in contemporary China must also be viewed in the context of emerging patterns of civil-military relations across Asia. With few exceptions (for example, North Korea and Vietnam), civil-military relations in East, Southeast, and South Asia have been fundamentally redefined in recent years in the process of democratization. In a number of countries that have known harsh authoritarian and military rule (South Korea, Taiwan, the Philippines, Indonesia, Thailand, Bangladesh, and Pakistan), the armed forces have been removed from political power and influence, made accountable to sovereign legislatures, and returned to the barracks. Militaries in mufti have been replaced by democratically elected civilians. In all of these countries, the emasculation of political power and praetorian tendencies of militaries has been a crucial element in establishing democratic institutions and rule. The trend in Asia follows that of Latin America and Africa.

The experiences of these countries, particularly Taiwan, are suggestive for future civil-military relations in China. So far, the emerging literature on the process of democratic transition in Asia has paid relatively little attention to the civil-military dimension,[22] although it is viewed as an important variable in the comparative literature.[23] More comparative research needs to be done on Asian militaries and civil-military relations.[24] Scholars of the PLA and Chinese politics need to place the recent changes in civil-military relations in the PRC outlined above in this broader regional context, while comparativists need to look more closely at the Chinese case. The current state of politics in the PRC certainly does not suggest that a creeping transition to democracy is silently taking place,[25] as the CCP retains its grip on power. But, at the same time, we must not mistake the potential significance of the legislative efforts to subordinate the PLA to state control.

The Chinese case must also be placed in the comparative context of former socialist states led by communist parties. Broadly speaking, the experiences of the former Soviet and East European militaries suggest that professionalization and party control are by no means mutually exclusive, but in not a single case were these militaries consciously placed under state control via legislative means. Indeed, in some cases, they fought (unsuccessfully) to save their ruling communist parties.[26] The problem for the Chinese military has never been to subordinate itself to civilian authority (as it has done so to the CCP) but rather to state control.

The PLA is moving—or rather is being moved—into an entirely new era of civil-military relations and corporate professionalism. As such, we would surmise that the PLA will not shirk from the task of defending national security against external enemies—but will it do so again against internal enemies who may threaten the rule of the Communist Party? This will be the ultimate test of the redefined relationship of the army to the party and state in China.

Notes

[1] N.A., "Military Representatives to the CCP Central Committee are 60% New Faces—Cao Gangchuan, Guo Boxiong, and Xu Caihou Step Up to the Plate," *Ming Bao* (Hong Kong), November 15, 2002, in *Foreign Broadcast Information Service–China* (henceforth *FBIS–China*), November 15, 2002.

[2] See, for example, Andrew Nathan and Bruce Gilley, *China's New Rulers* (New York: New York Review of Books, 2002).

[3] "Profile of Central Military Commission Chairman Jiang Zemin," *Xinhua News Agency,* March 15, 2003, in *FBIS–China,* March 15, 2003.

[4] Ibid.

[5] For one Hong Kong media account of how Jiang maneuvered and managed to keep the CMC portfolio, see Lo Ping, "Jiang Zemin Maneuvers to Hold on as Central Military Commission Chairman," *Zhengming* (Hong Kong), December 1, 2002, in *FBIS–China*, December 31, 2002.

[6] For studies of how Jiang has interacted with the PLA, see You Ji, "Jiang Zemin's Command of the Military," *The China Journal,* no. 45 (January 2001), 131–138; Tai Ming Cheung, "Jiang Zemin at the Helm: His Quest for Power and Paramount Leader Status," *China Strategic Review* 3, no. 1 (Spring 1996), 167–191; and David Shambaugh, "China's Commander-in-Chief: Jiang Zemin and the PLA," in *Chinese Military Modernization,* ed. C. Dennison Lane et al. (London: Kegan Paul International and AEI Press, 1996).

[7] For an excellent and careful analysis of this propaganda campaign, see James C. Mulvenon, "The PLA and the 'Three Represents': Jiang's Bodyguards or Party-Army?" *China Leadership Monitor,* no. 4 (Fall 2002), accessed at <www.chinaleadershipmonitor.org>.

[8] N.A., "Jiang Zemin to Stay on as Chairman of Central Military Commission for Another Five Years," *Kaifang* (Hong Kong), February 1, 2003, in *FBIS–China,* February 5, 2003.

[9] See Lin Jie, "Liao Xilong's Accession to the Central Military Commission Will Help Hu Assume the Reins of Military Power," *Xin Bao* (Hong Kong), November 21, 2002, in *FBIS–China*, November 21, 2002.

[10] This process is detailed in Shambaugh, "China's Commander-in-Chief."

[11] The author is indebted to James C. Mulvenon on this point. See Mulvenon, "The PLA and the 16th Party Congress: Jiang Controls the Gun?" *China Leadership Monitor,* no. 5 (Winter 2003), accessed at <www.chinaleadershipmonitor.org>.

[12] The biographical data used below are drawn from four principal sources: the official New China News Agency biographies issued on November 15, 2002; Zong Hairen, *Di Si Dai* (Hong Kong: Mirror Books, 2002); Ling Haijian, *Zhonggong Jundui Xin Zhangxing* (Hong Kong: Mirror Books, 1999); Zonghe, "Zhonggong Zhongyang Junwei de Xin Fangxiang," *Xin Bao* (December 2002), 28–30.

[13] See, for example, "Promotion of Liang Guanglie Indicates Military Pressure on Taiwan," *Ming Bao* (Hong Kong), November 16, 2002, in *FBIS–China,* November 18, 2002.

[14] Ling Haijin, *Zhonggong Jundui Xin Zhangxing,* 211.

[15] Lin Jie, "Liao Xilong's Accession." Liao's regiment was the 91st Regiment of the 31st Division of the 11th Army Corps.

[16] Zhu Qi moved up from Beijing MR Chief of Staff to Beijing MR Commander; and Zhu Wenquan did the same in the Nanjing MR.

[17] See "PRC Makes Pre-CCP Congress' Military Region Personnel Changes," *Ming Bao* (Hong Kong), February 9, 2002, in *FBIS–China,* February 9, 2002.

[18] These and other aspects are all discussed in David Shambaugh, *Modernizing China's Military* (Berkeley: University of California Press, 2002).

[19] The one (important) qualification to this trend is the increased role by the government (State Council) in monitoring and auditing PLA financial affairs.

[20] This is also recognized by You Ji in his "China: From Revolutionary Tool to Professional Military," in *Military Professionalism in Asia: Conceptual and Empirical Perspectives,* ed. Muthiah Alagappa (Honolulu: East-West Center, 2001), 111–136.

[21] These include the General Political Department, the CCP Discipline Inspection Commission, Party committees and branches down to the company level within the military, and the fact that all PLA officers above the rank of colonel are party members.

[22] See Larry Diamond and Marc F. Plattner, eds., *Democracy in East Asia* (Baltimore: Johns Hopkins University Press, 1998); and Larry Diamond, Marc F. Plattner, Yun-han Chu, and Hung-mao Tien, eds., *Consolidating the Third Wave Democracies* (Baltimore: Johns Hopkins University Press, 1997).

[23] See Larry Diamond and Marc F. Plattner, eds., *Civil-Military Relations and Democracy* (Baltimore: Johns Hopkins University Press, 1996).

[24] For a significant effort in this direction, see Muthiah Alagappa, ed., *Coercion and Governance: The Declining Role of the Military in Asia* (Stanford, CA: Stanford University Press, 2001).

[25] For one view to the contrary, see Minxin Pei, " 'Creeping Democratization' in China," in *Consolidating the Third Wave Democracies,* 213–227.

[26] See Gerald Segal and John Phipps, "Why Communist Armies Defend Their Parties," in *China's Military: The PLA in 1990/91,* ed. Richard H. Yang (Kaohsiung: National Sun Yat-sen University, 1991), 133–144.

˙ A similar version of this paper was presented at the Stanford University conference "New Leadership, New China" in January 2003. It will appear in a volume on the post-16th Party Congress edited by Ramon Myers, Chu Yun-han, and Lo Chi-cheng.

Part II

The Impact of Growing Nationalism

Chapter 4

PLA Conservative Nationalism

Nan Li

Because the People's Liberation Army (PLA) has withdrawn from the class-based politics of the Cultural Revolution and more recently from its extensive commercial activities, its policy attention should focus more on two new dimensions: first, irredentist claims-based and geostrategic concerns-driven nationalist agendas that stress security issues on the peripheries of China; and second, technology-driven force modernization to resolve these issues. This essay examines the first dimension, with particular emphasis on its conceptual basis: PLA conservative nationalism and its implications for Chinese politics and society. Specifically, it addresses the following questions: What is PLA conservative nationalism? How does such an ideology influence Chinese politics and society as the fourth-generation leaders take power? What major factors may aggravate or constrain the impact of PLA nationalism on Chinese politics and policy?

Several caveats are in order. First, this chapter is not intended to develop a theoretical argument about China's civil-military relations but rather to delineate the basic influential patterns of the new PLA ideology on politics and society. Because exploring the specific ways and areas in which the new ideology influences politics and society may contribute to the general goal of theory building, this is a worthwhile effort. Second, this is not a study of the origins of PLA conservative nationalism, but rather an analysis of the implications of the new ideology for politics and society. To the extent that examination of the origins has been done elsewhere,[1] and analyzing implications is more pertinent to designing policy to mitigate the new ideology, this study is justified. Finally, this study focuses on the dominant ideology but not alternative voices. Such a focus is reasonable largely because dominant ideology has more influence on policy, which may have more important implications for formulating coping strategies.

The essay is divided into four sections. The first section defines the concept of PLA conservative nationalism. The second and third address the major influence of this new PLA ideology on politics and society. The final section examines the major factors that may mitigate the impact of PLA nationalism on policy.

What Is PLA Conservative Nationalism?

As I have argued elsewhere,[2] conservative nationalism has become the dominant cognitive paradigm defining the thinking of China's security and military planners in the post-Mao era. PLA conservative nationalism has two major components: nationalism and conservatism. The central premise of nationalism is that in the post-ideology, post-Cold War era, the *nation-state* has become the central category that defines internal organization and hierarchy and external uncertainty and vulnerability. To the extent China exists in a competitive international environment where uncertainty and fluidity reign and relative gains matter, the survival and security of the Chinese nation have become of paramount importance. To achieve the goals of survival and security, it is first necessary to build up the Chinese economy and technology to reduce China's disadvantages relative to advanced countries. But for the development of economy and technology to proceed smoothly, it is also necessary for China to become externally secure. The external security of China defines the central role of the PLA.

To enhance China's external security, the PLA is supposed to fulfill several specific missions. First, it is to make significant contributions to China's territorial consolidation through reunification of the mainland and Taiwan. This reunification allegedly is essential to the survival of the Chinese nation because without such consolidation, China would remain divided and face the possible prospect of further fragmentation. Second, the PLA is to strive to preserve the integrity of the territories and security of the borders that are currently under Chinese control. Finally, the PLA is to enhance the security of economic resources, such as raw materials supplies, manufacturing platforms, infrastructure, and trading routes, to ensure the sustained development of the economy and technology.

For the last two missions, it is not sufficient to maintain the status quo but rather necessary to create a buffer zone through expanding a depth of defense moderately beyond the status quo. This expanded security zone is both desirable and necessary largely because, without it, China would become much more vulnerable and insecure under the condition of modern military technology, which allows longer range, more precise, and therefore more lethal military strikes. While diplomatic negotiations and promoting economic and cultural interactions may all serve to enhance China's security goal, the role of military force is indispensable and central. To the extent major challenges to China's territorial consolidation, border security, and economic resources security are military in nature, it is imperative for the PLA to develop the sufficient and appropriate military capabilities to deter such challenges and to fight and win wars if deterrence fails.

Besides nationalism, conservatism is another central feature that defines the role and missions of the PLA. Conservatism concerns the scope of the nationalist agendas. China's security goal through the prism of the PLA, for instance, stays relatively local and limited and, therefore, manageable. Such a goal deals mainly with the territorial and geostrategic issues on the margins of China, such as Taiwan, the dispute over the Spratly Islands in the South China Sea, the border dispute with India, the Korean Peninsula, and the ethnic and religious tension in western China, but not with ambitious superpower competition in places far away from China. Moreover, with the exception of Taiwan, the PLA has largely taken a conservative and defensive posture in handling these issues, with strong emphasis on conserving and consolidating what it has under its control rather than on acquiring what it has claimed. Even on the issue of Taiwan, arms buildup and military maneuvers seemingly are designed to achieve the immediate goal of deterring Taiwan from declaring independence, a rather limited and conservative step in the pursuit of the more ambitious goal of achieving the complete reunification.

Moreover, conservatism imbues the ways of realizing the nationalist agendas. Rather than overstretching resources stemming from revolutionary, radical changes, for instance, the PLA favors the gradual buildup of the national economy and technology, which should contribute significantly to national consolidation based on the enhanced comprehensive national power. It also favors national unity and internal social stability, the prerequisites for steady economic growth and technological development and for more effective competition in the highly vulnerable environment of external uncertainty. Finally, the PLA is highly skeptical of formal, tight alliances with foreign countries, largely because large partners in the alliance may engage in "buck passing" behavior (such as the Soviet Union with regard to the Korean War) and small partners in "free-riding" behavior (such as North Vietnam and North Korea), thus depleting Chinese resources.

One way to illustrate PLA conservative nationalism is to show what it is not. First of all, the new PLA ideology represents a significant departure from Maoism. The central premise of Maoism is that socioeconomic class, not the nation-state, defines internal organization and solidarity and external uncertainty and antagonism. Based on such a premise, the Maoist domestic policy would stress the formulation of rigid class categories and a class struggle-based "continuous revolution" to weed out "hidden class enemies" in the party and state bureaucracy, the PLA, and throughout Chinese society. Because Maoism assumes that socioeconomic classes and class struggle transcend national boundaries, it also justifies a proactive foreign policy of "world revolution" by providing doctrinal, manpower, and material support to the class-based radical, revolutionary movements in foreign countries. To the extent the PLA had withdrawn from its extensive involvement in the fierce domestic class struggle of the Cultural Revolution (because such struggle undermines national unity) and terminated its active support of the radical revolutionary movements in foreign countries (because such an endeavor would overstretch resources and undermine national economic development), it is apparent that Maoism is no longer the guiding ideology dictating PLA policy.

Another alternative voice in the current PLA discourse is the quasi-liberal one, which places emphasis on international institutions, diplomatic negotiations, and multilateral confidence-building measures for managing and alleviating interstate disputes. Such a voice, however, has not become the dominant PLA ideology for two major reasons. The first is that the quasi-liberal voice represents a minority among PLA thinkers and tends to be marginalized. Second, even among those who argue for policy along the quasi-liberal line, some are apparently under the influence of the conservative-nationalist voice. Some quasi-liberals treat participation in international institutions and diplomatic negotiations, for instance, as opportunities to enhance the relative gains of nation-states. Such involvement is regarded either as delaying tactics to gain preparation time for war, as a way to evade responsibility and to enjoy benefits, or as a stratagem to acquire technology and intelligence. This shows that conservative nationalism, but not quasi-liberalism, is the dominant ideology that shapes current PLA thought and practice.

Conservative Nationalism and Chinese Politics

PLA conservative nationalism influences Chinese politics in three major areas: ideology, personnel, and policy.

Ideology. In party-state ideology, the most dramatic change is the recent official endorsement of CCP General Secretary Jiang Zemin's theory of "three representations" (the CCP representing the advanced productive forces, the advanced culture, and the fundamental interests of China's broad masses), and his July 1, 2001, declaration that private businessmen would be allowed to join the CCP. Some sketchy evidence exists to show that the PLA has had input into the processes leading to such change. First of all, Jiang's theory is consistent with the PLA nationalist agenda of promoting national strength and unity in that it opens up the powerful domestic institutions to the highly productive segment of Chinese society, which contributes significantly to the tax revenue, the material basis of comprehensive national power. Such a measure also means that the CCP, by becoming more representative of increasingly diverse interests, would gain a new lease on life, which is good for stability. Without such an opening, the newly gained energy and resources released by decades of economic reforms within this segment would be channeled to other organizations, which may create new class struggle, undermine the party-state rule, and fragment the nation.

Second, Jiang's theory is the result of years of discussion on political reform, which began as early as before the 15th CCP Congress of 1997. Such a discussion has been primarily sponsored and coordinated by the CCP Central Policy Research Office and has involved major bureaucracies and think tanks at the central level, including PLA institutions, such as the Academy of Military Science. The discussion explored various options of political reform, including genuine democratization such as introducing multiparty competition for political offices. The multiparty competition option, however, was considered too radical and costly and was abandoned for two major reasons: it may trigger ethnic, religious, and provincial separatism, leading to China's disintegration (largely based on a reading of the collapse of the Soviet Union due to democratization); and it may cause the collapse of the family planning policy, which would abort the central objective of increasing per capita income by controlling population growth on the one hand and promoting economic growth on the other.

While the second reason reflects the view of the State Family Planning Commission, the first reason clearly represents the perspective of the PLA.[3] Rather than the radically liberal direction of multiparty competition at the expense of current political institutions, which may allegedly cause national disintegration, it now seems political reform has moved toward a more conservative and nationalist direction: opening up current political institutions to accommodate and alleviate the pent-up aspirations and frustrations associated with the rapid economic changes, which may avoid a new class struggle and enhance national unity and cohesiveness. To the extent Jiang's theory reportedly was extensively discussed by the CCP Politburo before its release, and the idea originated from two well known reform scholars from the CCP Central Policy Research Office, Teng Wensheng (office director) and Wang Hu'ning (deputy director and a professor from the Shanghai Fudan University), it is logical to assume that the theory is a collective product based on the aggregated input from major central bureaucracies, including the PLA.

Finally, the extensive interpretation of Jiang's theory in the *Liberation Army Daily*, not just in terms of its narrower implications for defense modernization[4] but also its implications for the broader nationalist agenda of national integration and unity,[5] shows a strong association between the PLA and Jiang's theory. Such association implies that the PLA is an active participant in formulating the theory as much as it is a subordinate institution in operationalizing and implementing the theory in its narrower functional specialties, or it just attempts to convert the skeptics in the PLA into true believers.

Personnel. Like ideology, PLA conservative nationalism had a role to play in personnel changes of the top party-state leadership during 2002–2003. On the one hand, such a role may remain moderate for several major reasons. First, there is no imminent CCP leadership crisis on the scale of the Cultural Revolution (causing collapse of the party-state bureaucracy) or the 1989 Tiananmen crisis (causing severe division among the CCP leadership on how to handle student demonstrations, which made it difficult to take preemptive measures). Unless a crisis of similar scale occurs and creates a political vacuum for PLA leaders to exploit, it is not likely that the PLA will play the blatant kingmaking role in party-state politics.[6] Some may argue that accelerated PLA professionalization may lead to a sharp divergence in values and interests between the PLA and CCP, to the point that the PLA may develop the incentive to advance its own values and interests by launching a coup against party-state rule.

But military professionalization may also mean that the PLA is gradually losing skills and interests in party-state politics, to the point it would rather concentrate on the narrower pursuit of functional and technical skills of the military profession than on civilian politics.[7] This does not suggest that the PLA would be totally detached from civilian politics, but its involvement in them may be narrowly focused on PLA institutional issues such as the defense budget, manpower policy, and so forth rather than the broader and more ambitious issue of seizing state power. In this sense, a more professionalized PLA may increasingly resemble a lobbying group engaging in mundane bureaucratic politics in the arena of party-state, not the palace guard unit that is more interested in usurping the supreme power. As the senior uniformed CMC members retire, for instance, those who are promoted to fill their positions may remain politically weak and less capable of influencing the party-state leadership politics because their positions and influence have yet to be consolidated. Finally, the 70-year retirement age rule for both the Politburo and CMC members, if followed, may reduce the incentive for individuals to exert influence over personnel changes through irregular, abnormal channels.[8]

On the other hand, it is just as wrong to argue that PLA leadership has an insignificant role to play in the party-state leadership transition. This role has been subtle and implicit and has been influenced by PLA conservative nationalism. The PLA leadership, for instance, has a profile of its preferred new party-state leadership. Such a profile connotes conservative nationalism and has three major components that the PLA leadership hopes the new party-state leadership would be well prepared to strengthen: national economic and technological development to enhance comprehensive national power; internal stability and national unity; and national defense-based PLA institutional interests.

In regard to economic and technological development, it is likely that PLA leadership prefers the new party-state leadership to be dominated by technocrats (for example, engineers and science and technology specialists) who have gained administrative experience by spending a number of years of their career managing a major bureaucracy, a major enterprise, or a province; technocrats understand the nuts and bolts of economics, technology, and management. They also tend to be pragmatists who prefer the incremental, cautious, and technical approaches to solving problems and, therefore, are more likely to produce concrete results in economic and technological development. On the other hand, PLA leadership may be highly skeptical and critical if the new leadership is dominated by the ideologues or the idealists of either the neoleftist (Maoist) or the neorightist (liberal) persuasion, or those who advocate radical, revolutionary changes through mobilizational methods or inciting propaganda. To the PLA, such leadership would do more harm than good to national economic and technological development.

PLA leadership wants the new party-state leadership to be capable of promoting leadership unity, a prerequisite for national stability and unity. This means that the new leadership should possess the skills in building consensus on major policy issues by regularly consulting major bureaucracies, by negotiations, and by sharing power. This also means the new party-state leadership should apply the established rules and norms and follow a policy of promoting to important positions people from the "five lakes and four seas" (all corners of the country) based on merits, but not engage too much in factional politics based on highly parochial, personalized ties; unmitigated factional politics would trigger intensive intraleadership rivalry, cause policy paralysis, and undermine leadership unity.

Finally, on national defense-based institutional interests, PLA leadership apparently would like to see that the military is well taken care of. This means that the new party-state leadership should place equal emphasis on both economic development and national defense but should not stress the former while neglecting the latter. It is also desirable that this leadership make an effort to:

- increase the defense budget
- improve the living conditions of the military personnel (by raising wages, improving housing conditions, and creating employment opportunities for military dependents and the discharged)
- consult the PLA on major national defense and foreign policy issues
- take a hands-on approach to PLA high-level personnel changes (by reviewing the list of candidates for high-level positions, soliciting opinion from the units of the candidates, and conducting interviews).

For the PLA, a good party-state leadership is one that is benevolent, considerate, and prudent—one that makes good judgments on taking care of the PLA. This, however, does not mean that the PLA leadership would like the new party-state leadership to micromanage the PLA. On the contrary, for the most part, it prefers that the new civilian leadership provides the general policy guidelines but leaves the PLA to flesh out the details, which also means more flexibility and space for the PLA to advance its own interests. By similar logic, the PLA clearly favors the collective and technocratic style of the current party-state leadership but not the charismatic and one-person dominance style of Mao and Deng; the relatively diffused nature of power in collective leadership means more leeway for the PLA to exploit the promotion of its institutional interests. This also translates into a higher level of institutional cohesiveness. In contrast, the highly interventionist "divide and rule" tactic employed by Mao and Deng from a strong center tended to divide the PLA leadership.

The consultation between the CCP Politburo and PLA leadership concerning the leadership transition focused largely on these three issues. How well or how poorly the party-state leadership matches this PLA profile may provide a clue why some party-state leaders fared better politically than others. One of the central reasons why Deng never had the confidence to relinquish the CMC chair position to Hu Yaobang and Zhao Ziyang, for instance, is that both were quite controversial among PLA leaders. Hu historically was a propagandist who had a flamboyant style. Both Hu and Zhao also mobilized political support from outside the party (among the liberal intellectuals and students) in the intraparty power struggle, rendering them politically vulnerable to violating the newly restored party rules and norms, as well as undermining leadership unity. Both also were considered too liberal. Most importantly, both (particularly Zhao) paid too much attention to economic issues but too little to the national defense-related PLA institutional interests.

In contrast, Jiang matches this profile much better than Hu and Zhao and, therefore, has been able to consolidate his influence in the PLA. On the other hand, some PLA leaders may feel quite uneasy that Jiang has retained his CMC chair position after giving up his CCP general secretary position at the 16th Congress; holding the CMC chair position without being the CCP general secretary is generally perceived as abnormal and irregular, except in extreme circumstances. Since there is no imminent political crisis in sight, this practice could undermine party norms (such as the mandatory retirement age), revive the personality-driven politics of "attending to state affairs behind the curtain," weaken the legitimacy of the CMC, and trigger intraleadership rivalry.

Hu Jintao fits the profile fairly well. Compared to peer competitors such as Zeng Qinghong, Hu has a few other comparative advantages. Hu has served as the CMC vice chair since 1999 and can use the opportunity to cultivate relationships and authority among PLA leaders. PLA leaders also appreciate Hu's service as the first party secretary of Tibet, a frontier province, and his credential of cracking down on the religious and ethnic separatism there. Zeng, on the other hand, has not had the opportunity or the credentials to cultivate more specific political favors from the PLA. Hu's responsibilities in handling PLA divestiture from businesses and managing the popular demonstrations against the U.S. bombing of the Chinese embassy in Belgrade, however, may displease some PLA officers, particularly at the lower levels. But to the extent most PLA high-level leaders agree that the divestiture from businesses would enhance PLA combat effectiveness and that popular demonstrations need to be managed so that they do not run out of hand and undermine social stability, such credentials should work favorably for Hu but should not undermine his chances in the upcoming succession.

What can PLA leaders do if the new party-state leadership does not meet the desires and needs of PLA leaders? First, the third and fourth generations of party-state leaders seemingly fit the profile well and operate within the broad, centrist paradigm of conservative nationalism. This should reduce the probability of a major political-military crisis. Also, the new party-state leadership does not have to cater to all the needs of the PLA but instead can take care of the more immediate issues, such as PLA institutional interests, to consolidate influence in the PLA. Moreover, if the PLA is unhappy with the new civilian leadership, it may send subtle messages through passive and tacit obstruction of the policy programs handed down from CCP Central, which should allow for the party-state leadership to respond and adjust. Finally, to the extent the current PRC leadership has a much higher level of political flexibility and sophistication than the dying old guard generation, both civilian and PLA leaders have ample time and opportunities to learn about each other's needs and to make necessary accommodations. Indeed, unless the top party-state position were hijacked by a hidden Maoist radical or a Chinese Gorbachev, routinized bureaucratic consultation and mediation among people who share a similar mindset should lower the odds of an imminent, major political-military crisis.

Policy. The influence of PLA conservative nationalism on policy has become narrowly confined to the national defense and security component of both foreign and domestic policy. In foreign policy, the PLA largely takes a more hawkish position than the civilian bureaucracies, whether the policy is about Taiwan, the South China Sea, proliferation issues, U.S. missile defense, or the current American fight against terrorism. Such a position usually reflects a paranoid mentality of a zero-sum game associated with an obsessive concern about relative gains. In early 2001, for instance, PLA leaders were able to persuade successfully the skeptical and reluctant Jiang and Zhu Rongji that a large-scale, months-long military exercise at Dongshan Island was necessary to prevent Taiwan independence. Without military deterrence, they argued, Chen Suibian's pro-independence Democratic Progressive Party would gain more legislative seats in the fall election in Taiwan. Taiwan independence thus would gain new grounds, particularly at a time when Sino-American relations had deteriorated due to the plane collision incident and as the U.S. Government had increased arms sales to Taiwan and allowed Chen to make a transit in the United States in his Latin America trip. Similarly, the constraints attached to the current cautious Chinese support for the American fight against terrorism, such as providing concrete proof, acting within the United Nations framework, and avoiding civilian casualties, also reflect PLA concern. The concern is that prolonged and expansive U.S. military operations in central Asia, if not constrained, would undermine Chinese influence in the region, which in the long run would render China's western frontier unstable and vulnerable.

In domestic policy, evidence of influence of PLA nationalism is also apparent and abundant. The PLA endorses any policy program that would enhance national integration and unity. The plan to shift capital investment to western provinces gained full PLA support because it would reduce wealth disparity between regions, thus enhancing national integration. An element of this plan is to build a railway line from Qinghai to Tibet. This project was proven to be too costly and unfeasible in engineering terms. But because the PLA insisted that the proposed line would achieve the strategic goal of integrating and consolidating Tibet, it was endorsed by the CCP Central and the State Council and would proceed.

One key policy area in which PLA influence is getting stronger is mobilizing civilian resources for national defense purposes, or integrating national defense into the national economic and social development plans under the new rubric of stressing both the marketplace and the battlefield. The recent decision jointly endorsed by the State Council and the CMC to train PLA officers in civilian schools, for instance, led to the development of a contractual system where PLA scholarship-supported students from China's key universities, upon graduation, would be directly recruited as active service officers by major PLA institutions. As a result, reserve officer training programs also have been established in China's major universities and selected high schools. Furthermore, the PLA has been developing systematic programs in mobilizing the civilian infrastructure for military purposes. These programs include integrating military design and requirements into construction or modification of highways, airports, seaports, railroads, and telecommunications; modifying commercial planes and merchant ships for military purposes; and exploring the organization, methods, management, and logistics of utilizing these resources through mobilizational exercises. The PLA has also been dispatching teams of technical specialists to identify and acquire dual-use technologies in the fast-growing technology-intensive joint ventures. Finally, the PLA has been developing technology-intensive reserve units in cities and regions where technology-intensive firms concentrate, and it has been recruiting technical experts in science, technology, and engineering to fill positions in these units.

Through what channels and institutions does the PLA exercise influence over civilian policy? At the very top on the party side, two uniformed PLA members (who are also the only two uniformed CMC vice chairs) serve in the 21-member CCP Politburo, but neither sits at its powerful 7-member Standing Committee. One of the two is also a member of the CCP Secretariat, which supervises the CCP central bureaucracies and operationalizes the Politburo decisions. Moreover, about 18 percent of the CCP Central Committee members are from the PLA. One uniformed CMC vice chair is also a member of the Foreign Affairs Leadership Small Group, an informal party grouping, which includes the heads of all party and state bureaucracies involved in foreign affairs. This group discusses foreign affairs, formulates foreign policy guidelines, and coordinates policy implementation. One PLA deputy chief of staff also serves as a member of the Taiwan Affairs Leadership Small Group, which fulfills similar functions on Taiwan affairs.

On the government side, a substantial number of PLA personnel serve as delegates to the National People's Congress (NPC), China's legislature. One uniformed CMC vice chair also serves as the defense minister of the State Council, China's cabinet. This person is also a state councilor and the highest PLA representative at the regular State Council-CMC coordination conference, which mediates between the two institutions and coordinates policy. Finally, this CMC vice chair, together with a vice premier of the State Council, heads the State National Defense Mobilization Commission (NDMC), a joint State Council-CMC policy discussion and coordination institution established in 1994. The NDMC has four major offices (people's arms mobilization, economic mobilization, people's air defense, and transportation and war preparation) under it, all of which are staffed by personnel from both the related State Council ministries and commissions and the PLA four general (staff, political, logistics, and armament) departments. A PLA deputy chief of staff serves as the secretary general of the NDMC.

Some reports suggest that the number of PLA members in the CCP Politburo and Central Committee would be substantially increased at the 16th Congress because the PLA leaders demand more seats to have more say on policy. Such a forecast may be premature for several reasons. First, the current level of PLA membership in the Politburo (9 percent) and the Central Committee (18 percent) has stayed constant and stable since the early 1990s. Unless there is a major political crisis, drastic changes to this level may cause questions and criticism from the civilian side, trigger intraparty rivalry, and undermine unity. Moreover, having more military members in these institutions does not necessarily translate into more effective PLA influence on policy. During the Cultural Revolution, PLA membership in the Politburo and Central Committee reached as high as 50 percent. This led only to the expanded participation of PLA leaders in the fierce intraparty leadership factional struggle, which blew back into the PLA and caused severe division among PLA leaders. This in turn translated into policy stalemate and paralysis, not policy effectiveness. Finally, these Party Central institutions, together with the CCP Secretariat, the leadership small groups, and the NPC, focus mainly on formulating general policy guidelines rather than on day-to-day operations. Some do not even meet regularly, and others serve merely as forums for discussion or as mechanisms of automatic approval of decisions made elsewhere. In comparison, the regular State Council-CMC coordinating conference and the NDMC are becoming substantial and meaningful institutions in expanding PLA influence on policy. To the extent the NDMC has been replicated at the provincial, prefecture, and county levels—and with the mandate of both the State Council and CMC, it goes out to commandeer civilian manpower, infrastructure, technology, and properties in the name of national security—it definitely deserves more careful analysis.

Conservative Nationalism and Chinese Society

Like politics, the influence of PLA conservative nationalism on society has become narrowly focused on propagating and socializing the nationalism-based security and military values associated with national defense. For the past few years, for instance, there has been a steady increase of security and military literature in the popular media. Articles address issues ranging from China's territorial and geostrategic vulnerability to its economic, energy, ecological, and information insecurity to ways to reduce such vulnerability and insecurity. There has also been a remarkable increase in technical literature that concentrates on military strategies and tactics, expenditures, technology, and organization. Chinese military history, both premodern and modern, is another literary area that has grown substantially. Such literature involves the interpretation of major historical military campaigns and battles; the strategies, tactics, organization, and technology employed; the performance of major military units and personalities involved; and the implications for China's historical destiny. Another area that attracts extensive attention of and interpretation by media pundits concerns major current foreign security and military events and issues and their security implications for China.

The substantial political and propaganda apparatus of the PLA has also been systematically explicating the instruments and means of propagating nationalist values. For example, *Liberation Army Daily*, the mouthpiece of the PLA, created *China National Defense Daily* to facilitate the social diffusion of national defense values. This can be seen clearly in the September 25, 2001, edition, which states that access to "literary products such as novels and reportage, movies and TV shows, and operas and plays, that feature war themes" is important. "Organizing the public to visit war memorials and museums, and 'holy places,' and observing memorial days and military holidays" can also inculcate national defense values. Another way is to propagate war heroes: "The names of war heroes and those who have made outstanding contributions to national defense construction can be used to entitle cities and towns, streets, city squares, and working units, as well as planes, military vehicles, and warships that are in active service." National defense model personalities can also "be organized for speech tours throughout the country, and enjoy generous government allowances and benefits." Organizing military sporting events such as "the cross-country and armed marathon competitions, and shooting competitions" should contribute to the cultivation of national defense values as well. During the conscription seasons, "regularly and repeatedly distributing the printed, audio and video materials that feature the historical evolution of military units, major military campaigns and victories, the lives of famous commanders and war heroes" should also achieve the effect. Finally, "funds can be raised either through the government's yearly allocation or society contribution" to construct "national defense education bases, and to improve the facilities, content, and means of such education." *China National Defense Daily* has gained wide circulation.

The PLA propaganda apparatus also has been producing a daily half-hour military news program, aired by China Central Television (CCTV). This program serves primarily the civilian audience, not the PLA. Moreover, this apparatus has been producing television movies and plays featuring military themes for CCTV. One report claims that in the current year, military theme-based television movies and plays have occupied more than 50 percent of CCTV prime time.[9] Finally, with the increasing popularity of personal computers, the Internet, and the World Wide Web, the number of cyber forums and chat rooms devoted to military subjects has been growing, and many are sponsored by PLA institutions.

Furthermore, the PLA has been providing regular military commentators for television news programs and forums on the Internet, which has created a few PLA celebrities. One of them is Zhang Zhaozhong, a navy captain who heads the science and technology teaching and research section of the National Defense University. For the past few years, Zhang has published a few nonfiction bestsellers, with titles such as *Who Can Fight and Win the Next War? How Far Is the War from Us?* and *Who Is the Next Target?*, creating a sensation known as the "Zhang Zhaozhong phenomenon" among China's book readers. The topics that Zhang comments on range from Taiwan, war in Kosovo and U.S. bombing of the Chinese embassy, information warfare, naval modernization, to U.S. missile defense.[10] Other PLA media celebrities include two air force senior colonels, Qiao Liang and Wang Xiangsui, who published the bestseller *Unrestricted Warfare*. Qiao and Wang are particularly fond of opining on asymmetrical warfare and its implications for a hypothetical Taiwan conquest scenario, as well as the recent terrorist attacks on the United States.

What conceptual rationale does the PLA provide to justify the socialization of national security and military values? This rationale has largely been driven by the new notion of propaganda warfare. Besides a propaganda offense such as media disinformation to mislead or demoralize the adversary, the PLA theorists particularly stress the importance of propaganda defense. The general goal of propaganda defense is to "enhance national cohesiveness . . . and defeat the infiltration of the adversary's ideological and cultural values through patriotism education." Under this general goal, there are three specific objectives to accomplish. The first is to "arouse and foster the consciousness of the broad masses to love the nation and the army; and to construct the spiritual great wall through cultivating the national spirit of self-respect, self-confidence, and self-strengthening." The second is to "enhance the psychological quality of the Chinese nationals, particularly in developing the psychological ability to adapt to the high-tech war, which tends to be unprecedentedly brutal and may generate tremendous psychological pressure." The psychological preparation through patriotism education in turn can translate into "the confident, optimistic, unifying and stable state of mind among citizens and soldiers in face of powerful enemy psychological deterrence." Finally, propaganda warfare not only should be treated as a component of the political and diplomatic struggles but also integrated into specific military operations, which means "more systematic analysis should be done regarding the methods of propaganda warfare at the campaign and battle levels, with an eye toward the primary operational adversary."[11]

How effective are the PLA programs in socializing national defense and military values? While there is no systematic public opinion survey on the effectiveness of these programs, there are a few reasons to believe that they may achieve some level of success. The first reason is the difference in the popular appeal between the old Maoist subnational and transnational values of class struggle and world revolution and the current nationalist values. The Maoist values have been discredited largely because class struggle is too narrow, and it excludes many people (those with "bad" class backgrounds) from identifying with the Chinese nation. Similarly, world revolution is too broad and elusive for an average person to grasp. In comparison, the nationalist values, with the goal of defending and securing the land and nation where one's ancestors lived for centuries, can be much more appealing to an ordinary Chinese. Moreover, the government-imposed restrictions on the diffusion of liberal values in the mass media may also have helped to channel public consciousness toward the nationalist direction. Finally, security and military values-based propaganda may be attractive because it may help to ease a prevailing sense of insecurity and vulnerability among the populace, a sense somewhat associated with rapid socioeconomic changes.

What Aggravates and Constrains PLA Nationalism?

Several major internal and external factors may aggravate PLA nationalism. Internally, continued economic growth, coupled with an effective mechanism to transfer more money from that growth to defense modernization, should contribute to heightened PLA nationalism. The absence of a major domestic socioeconomic crisis that would fully absorb the energy and resources of the PLA can lend it a freer hand in pursuing its nationalist goal. The near absence of routine legislative oversight and executive control of the PLA,[12] together with the marginalization of liberal voices and challenges, may also expand PLA influence on policy. But one major factor that has not been carefully explored before has to do with the style of PLA strategic analyses. Over the decades, the PLA has developed a highly positivist strategic style that strongly emphasizes a sharp dichotomy between friends and enemies and the identity of the positive and strong points of the PLA, as well as the vulnerabilities and weaknesses of the enemy.[13] Such a style has the potential to aggravate PLA nationalism, leading to reckless policy choices based on gross miscalculations, which may in turn cause major policy blunders.[14]

What then accounts for such a strategic style? Among other things, two cultural-psychological variables may be central to understanding it. The first is the Chinese concern about "face," which relates to traditional Chinese culture and originates from the Confucian teaching on the need to maintain "ritual" (the appearance of righteousness) to sustain moral authority. To save face, or not to lose it, for instance, the incentive is not only to show self-righteousness or all the good, positive, and strong points of the self but also to show the evil, negative, and weak points of the other, to the point that such a dichotomy no longer reflects the more complex reality because it is based on an exaggeration of the strength of the self and the weakness of the enemy. The second is the residual of Maoism. Even though the PLA is moving away from Maoism in policy substance, the Maoist influence on PLA style is still apparent and cannot be quickly eradicated. A central element of Maoism, for instance, is voluntarism, which stresses the power of the mind and consciousness that can overcome obstacles of material conditions. Such an ideology would continue to influence the thinking of PLA strategists to the point that some PLA strategic analyses may reflect not the balance of forces in the real world but rather an overestimation of PLA strength and an underestimation of the adversary's abilities.

Externally, to the extent PLA nationalism has largely focused on the issue of Taiwan and the U.S. commitment to its defense (such as arms sales), what the United States does about Taiwan may either aggravate or constrain PLA nationalism. The immediate PLA goal is to deter Taiwan from going independent, to the point that it would accept China's principle of one country, two systems. PLA strategists are confident that if the United States is not committed to the defense of Taiwan, the PLA can accomplish this goal, which also means that the PLA has a low regard for Taiwan and a much higher regard for the American commitment. Therefore, any sign of U.S. weakness in its commitment to the defense of Taiwan (not necessarily in terms of scaling down arms sales but just of being distracted by other issues) means an opportunity for the PLA to exploit. In this sense, the tragedy of September 11, 2001, may both constrain and aggravate PLA nationalism. In terms of constraint from the PLA perspective, the need declines to use military means, such as conducting highly visible military maneuvers to deter U.S. intervention and to intimidate Taiwan voters from voting for the Democratic Progressive Party candidates in the fall legislative election. American distraction from the Taiwan issue and its need for China's cooperation in fighting terrorism, together with China's imminent membership in the World Trade Organization and Taiwan's economic difficulties, may reduce Taiwan's leverage and produce the subtle deterrence effect on Taiwan independence, particularly with regard to whom the people in Taiwan would vote for in the upcoming election. On the other hand, the September 11 attacks may also aggravate the substance but not the means of PLA nationalism because, from the PLA perspective, the PLA nationalist goal of preventing Taiwan independence is more likely to be realized now by the "continuation of war by other means," such as the enhanced Chinese political, diplomatic, and economic leverages.

Besides factors that may aggravate PLA nationalism, a few major internal and external factors also exist that may constrain or weaken PLA nationalism. Internally, an economic recession or a weak mechanism incapable of transferring the necessary portion of the new civilian wealth to military modernization would constrain PLA nationalism. Moreover, democratization may constrain PLA nationalism in two major ways. First, if it goes badly, China may fragment, which means the PLA would either fragment along the liberal and hard lines, or along provincial, local, and ethnic lines (as happened to the Soviet Army during Russian democratization). Or the PLA may choose to stay together and launch a coup to take over the weakened national government to prevent disintegration. Either way, the PLA would be fully absorbed into an acute domestic crisis, which should weaken PLA nationalism. Second, if democratization goes well to the point at which genuine liberal and democratic institutions—such as the rule of law, a system of multiparty competition, and a free press—take hold, PLA nationalism should also be substantially constrained. The PLA, for instance, would switch its allegiance from a communist party to the constitution and become nonpartisan. With the removal of the CCP from the PLA, NPC, and State Council, more effective legislative oversight and executive control of the PLA would be established, thus curtailing the policy influence of the PLA. Similarly, the debate on security and military policy would become more civilianized and less dominated by the PLA, which should translate into reduced PLA influence. This means that it would be much easier for the liberal voices and values to challenge and contain the nationalist values of the PLA to the point at which the PLA would gradually withdraw from the policy arena into the narrower domain of the functional and technical specialties of the military profession. All these would substantially constrain PLA nationalism.

Externally, an American policy that combines a balance-of-threat strategy and an engagement strategy should constrain PLA nationalism. Currently, the PLA pursues a deterrence strategy of arms buildup and military exercises with regard to Taiwan. The most potent and threatening weapons in the PLA arsenal are the theater ballistic missiles. Therefore, a balance-of-threat strategy may focus on how to defuse this missile threat, for instance, by developing a missile defense system. Some may argue that such a strategy may play into the hands of China's hard-liners (such as the PLA) by militarizing the Taiwan issue and exacerbating an arms race, thus aggravating PLA nationalism. Such an argument is flawed for several reasons. First, it is the PLA that has militarized the Taiwan issue through its arms buildup and exercises. Second, to the extent the goal of the PLA deterrence strategy is to force the adversary to yield without the actual use of force, not doing anything to defend oneself amounts to yielding, which clearly plays into the hands of China's hard-liners such as the PLA. Third, a balance-of-threat strategy may actually strengthen the hands of China's moderates and quasi-liberals but not its hard-liners because this strategy may enable the moderates and the quasi-liberals to argue that PLA deterrence strategy is too costly and traps China into an arms race and therefore does not work. This may constrain PLA nationalism by causing the Chinese to switch from militarized means to political and diplomatic ones in handling the Taiwan issue.

The balance-of-threat strategy should also be accompanied by an engagement strategy. It does not have to be a policy of appeasement as long as it is backed by a balance-of-threat strategy that can incur high cost for cheating behavior; and it is designed in a way in which it does not provide an easy conduit for the PLA to acquire technology and intelligence. The second track diplomacy-based engagement strategy may serve to increase the transparency of each other's military intentions and capabilities and to work out ways to prevent accidents. Equally important, such a strategy may include educational programs that aim to modify Chinese domestic norms by inculcating the liberal values among China's policy elite, including values concerning the role and functions of the military in a rule-of-law-based environment. To the extent a small but expanding group of moderates and quasi-liberals does exist in China's policy circle (including the PLA) who are more receptive to new ideas and norms, an engagement strategy apparently can work to constrain and undermine PLA nationalism.

Notes

[1] See Nan Li, *From Revolutionary Internationalism to Conservative Nationalism: The Chinese Military's Discourse on National Security and Identity in the Post-Mao Era*, Peaceworks No. 39 (Washington, DC: U.S. Institute of Peace, May 2001).

[2] Ibid.

[3] A PLA interlocutor, who serves on the editorial board of *China Military Science* (a journal published by the Academy of Military Science), provided this information. This person also holds a position at the National Defense Mobilization Commission, a State Council-Central Military Commission coordinating mechanism for mobilizational matters. For the most recent PLA commentary on ways to prevent ethnic separatism, see Tang Min, "Minzhu tuanjie, shanhe yonggu" ("Once Unity among Nationalities Is Achieved, the Land Becomes Forever Secure"), *Liberation Army Daily*, October 12, 2001, 3.

[4] For discussion of the theory's implications for PLA modernization in general, and for PLA joint training and exercises, knowledge-intensive personnel development, technology, and arms development, doctrinal development, and organizational development in particular, see Guo Anhua, "Bawo qiangda zhandouli de shidai yaoqiu" ("Call of the Time to Gain Mastery of the Powerful Fighting Capabilities"); Zhang Zengshun, "Hongyang kexue jingshen, hangshi 'da'ying' genji" ("Promote Scientific Spirit, Solidify the Foundation of 'Fight and Win'"); Wei Jianzhong, "Zuohao 'jiefang sixiang' da wenzhang" ("Do Well the Great Work of 'Emancipating Thought'"); Chen Yilai et al., "Tongguo lianhe xunlian juji 'da'ying' nengli" ("Build up the Ability to 'Fight and Win' through Joint Training"); Zhou Shihua, "Rencai peiyang gengyao qianghua 'shijie yan'guang'" ("More Emphasis Should be Placed on the 'World Outlook' in Cultivating and Training Personnel"); Zhang Bibo et al., "Jianshe zhuangbei fazhan xin zuobiao" ("Construct the New Coordinate for Armament Development"); Huang Youfu et al., "Zhuigan shidai chaoliu, chuangxin junshi lilun" ("Catch up with the Trend of the Time, Innovate Military Doctrine"); and Wang Wei et al., "Kao kexue de tizhi bianzhi shifang zhangdouli" ("Rely on Scientific Organizational System and Scale to Discharge Fighting Capabilities"). All articles appear in *Liberation Army Daily*, July 24, 2001, 6.

[5] One commentary, for instance, argues that the theory implies the Chinese Communist Party should be the vanguard of not just the working class but also of the Chinese citizens' nation. See Wu Qiliang, "Zenyang lijie dang yao 'tongshi chengwei zhongguo renmin he zhonghua minzhu de xianfengdui'?" ("How to Comprehend that the Party Should 'at the Same Time Become the Vanguard of the Chinese People and the Chinese Nation'?"), *Liberation Army Daily*, August 22, 2001, 6.

[6] This is not to suggest that an acute crisis of a massive scale is totally inconceivable, particularly if one is keenly aware of the serious challenges that the current Chinese leadership faces, such as rampant bureaucratic corruption, the mass army of unemployed due to privatization of agriculture, the state-owned enterprises reforms, and the rapidly widening gap in wealth between the coast and the hinterland, and between cities and countryside. On the other hand, the recent massive crackdown on official corruption, the attempt to develop a social security system to provide unemployment and other welfare benefits, the plan to eliminate the rigid residential registration system, the program to shift capital investment from the coast to the inner provinces, and the crackdown and, therefore, lack of political opposition may somewhat reduce the probability of an imminent crisis.

[7] As the PLA continues to downsize and modernize its weaponry, it may have increasing difficulty in the future dealing even with the kind of mass demonstrations that took place in the summer of 1989; the PLA may lose the necessary manpower and low-tech arms to handle such a massive domestic unrest.

[8] If this rule is strictly followed, six of the nine uniformed CMC members, including Zhang Wannian, Chi Haotian, Fu Quanyou, Yu Yongbo, Wang Ke, and Wang Reilin, should retire at the 16th Party Congress.

[9] See *Liberation Army Daily*, September 8, 2001, 1.

[10] Zhang is also the translator and publisher of Tom Clancy's *Hunt for Red October* in China.

[11] Li Feng et al., "Jujiao xuanchuan duikang" ("Focus on Propaganda Warfare"), *China National Defense Daily*, June 4, 2001, 3.

[12] The CMC, for instance, does not answer to the National People's Congress and the premier of the State Council but rather to the CCP Politburo and its Central Committee, which do not meet regularly to manage daily government affairs.

[13] PLA strategists acknowledge that, unlike Western analysts who try to learn lessons about one's own vulnerabilities and the strength of the enemy in analyzing past military campaign cases, PLA analysts would skip PLA mistakes and enemy strong points and concentrate on learning the positive lessons about the PLA and the negative lessons about the enemy in such analyses. Such an open acknowledgment, however, may mean that the PLA is beginning to see this as a problem and is taking steps to change it.

[14] The EP–3 incident, for instance, illustrates this potential. Before any joint investigation into the causes of the incident, the U.S. side was immediately held responsible and therefore became the imagined enemy. As a result, all Chinese leaders, including those from the PLA, refused to answer phone calls from the U.S. side. While the Americans believe that establishing bilateral channels of communication at all levels through track-two diplomacy would be beneficial to mediating differences and conflicts, particularly in a crisis, the closure of these channels by the Chinese side in a crisis shows that the latter has a very different understanding about the purpose of these channels.

Chapter 5

Chinese Nationalism: Challenge to U.S. Interests

Edward Friedman

T his chapter establishes two seemingly contradictory propositions. First, from the point of view of international relations, contemporary Chinese nationalism is usefully understood as a political project whose goal is Chinese hegemony in Asia. This Beijing project compels America and its friends and allies in the Asia-Pacific region to act vigilantly.

Second, despite the apparent fundamental conflict of this project with the interests of America and its friends and allies in the region, neither the government in Beijing nor Chinese foreign policy need be considered by the U.S. Government as an enemy. That is, the rhetoric of Chinese chauvinism is not the actual source of Chinese foreign policy.

What follows is a brief sketch to establish the validity of these two propositions and, more importantly, to explain why these two apparently incompatible claims need not be considered as such. America must respond to both sides of Chinese foreign policy, both the expansive chauvinism and the need of ruling groups in Beijing to grapple with serious domestic challenges by utilizing the advantages gained in peaceful international exchanges. The alleged incoherence that many critics claim to find in American policy toward China is actually a natural and necessary response to schizophrenic policy at the core of Chinese politics.

Let us first explore current Chinese chauvinism. While chosen starting points are inevitably self-serving and arbitrary, many analysts accept the end of the Cold War as a turning point in Chinese-American relations. When President Richard Nixon moved toward normalizing relations with the People's Republic of China (PRC), the government in Beijing was actually or potentially part of the effort to contain Brezhnev-era militarism, an effort that endured, as in the 1979–1989 resistance to the Soviet invasion of Afghanistan. China provided weapons to Afghanistan. China was an ally of the late Cold War era.

By the Gorbachev era, however, the number of American critics of allying with China to contain Soviet Russia grew. These analysts found either that China was too weak to be helpful in the Cold War against Soviet-backed anti-American efforts or that China's interests were incompatible with America's or that Gorbachev's Soviet Union, in contrast to Brezhnev's, did not need containing, or that Washington, in the post-Brezhnev era, could cooperate with Moscow. In sum, it was not in America's interest to make major political concessions to woo China to be an ally since China increasingly seemed unwilling to or incapable of contributing to American purposes in Asia, except in Korea, where Beijing and Washington had major overlapping interests in avoiding war.

In a similar manner, by 1981, China's post-Mao paramount leader, Deng Xiaoping, moved away from Mao's tacit Cold War alliance with America against the Soviet Union. Instead, Deng moved toward an independent policy including normal relations with Soviet Russia, a policy that was pursued even during the war to resist the Soviet invasion of Afghanistan. Deng wooed Moscow to serve, first, the needs of an economically rising China, and, second the goal of incorporating Taiwan under Beijing's sovereignty.

In other words, even before the Cold War imploded in 1989–1991, both the United States and China had already begun to abandon the deepest premises of the policy that had facilitated U.S.-Chinese detente starting with the Nixon administration. The end of the Cold War sped up dynamics that had already been unleashed in both nations. Consequently, U.S.-Chinese relations would no longer be premised on a basic, shared common interest, checking Brezhnev-era militarism. Naturally, in the absence of a shared and central adversary, the amoral and self-interested nature of ordinary international relations virtually guaranteed a more adversarial quality to Sino-American relations. The new challenges are not the consequences of malign intent. Yet America was reinterpreted in China as that nation's enemy number one. Why?

The killer poison in the new relationship resulted from a number of negative factors. First, the 1989–1991 end of the Cold War coincided with a major contingent political factor that turned the inevitable end of U.S.-Chinese detente into a situation where each side became an adversary for the other. Deng Xiaoping's decision to crush China's great 1989 nationwide democratic mobilization led to sanctions of China by all the Group of 7 democracies. The American support for the Chinese democracy movement led to the rise of a feeling within China that the regime's stability was at stake; in fact, nothing seemed more important than regime survival. America, therefore, was redefined by ruling groups in Beijing as China's most immediate and pressing political enemy. The United States was reimagined as on the side of forces and policies, the democratic movement and economic sanctions, which threatened to destabilize China by subverting control by the ruling Chinese Communist Party (CCP). Of course, the top priority of CCP leaders was maintaining the system that kept them in power. The narrow self-interests of the Chinese ruling group in Beijing consequently redefined America as an ultimate enemy.

Other factors and forces made this elite interest in China harmonize with popular concerns. When the Soviet Union fell apart in 1991, yet another contingent factor, the conjuncture in timing with post-June 4, 1989, anxieties intensified China's anti-American nationalism. Russia seemed a negative example. Politically conscientious Chinese tended to experience China's primary objective as not ending up weak, vulnerable, and humiliated, as a diminished Russia seemed to be. Chinese patriots wanted China to rise. If Russia, a negative example, were democratic and pro-Western, then China had to be the opposite. China's traumatized people wanted national glory and social stability, not international decline and division as in Russia. Consequently, for both elites and the general public in China, unity and stability became primary goals. This reorientation suddenly made projects such as democratization seem an alien language of another age, a naive project of people mesmerized by foreign lures and evils. America consequently was demonized.

The new nationalism of Deng's regime also raised the prominence of Taiwan on China's political agenda. Beijing's new antidemocratic, unity-driven nationalism rose at a time when Taiwan was democratizing and its nationalism was surging. In the context of 1990s Chinese hopes and anxieties, peaceful developments on Taiwan led to a super-patriotic logic and language in Beijing demanding action against enemies of the Chinese nation, the democratic people of Taiwan, whom the Chinese perceive as a separatist entity threatening the very unity of a fragile, sacred, and economically hopeful China. That is, if Taiwan splits from China so could Tibetans and Uighurs and others. The Chinese saw themselves as defenders responding to unprovoked life and death challenges.

After Deng's January 1992 southern tour reignited economic reform in the PRC, a surge of confidence spread throughout the nation. China was not Russia. The popular experience became that China could succeed and rise where Russia failed and fell. A feeling grew among patriots that a restrengthened but still threatened China should strike back at all obstacles and indignities. Again, at both elite and popular levels, it seemed indubitable that an ill-intended America was supposedly hurting China not only by backing democrats (disorder) and imposing economic sanctions but also by acting as the provider of weapons and military guarantees to democratic Taiwan. It seemed obvious that America was on the side of forces that would hold China down and prevent it from a return to greatness, as had long and painfully been the sad reality of the premodern era, the Opium War era, as Chinese patriots imagined history. America seemed to have malignly chosen the role of the villainous imperialist enemy of China.

In 1991, China worried that American boasting of winning the Cold War, defeating the Soviet Union, and making a new world order meant that Washington would target Beijing next. Chinese rulers imagined America as continuing the Cold War in Asia, not just to contain China but actually and aggressively to subvert its Communist Party dictatorship. Nationalistic understandings spread widely in China, which defined the United States as the enemy of Chinese stability, unity, and a Chinese return to greatness. In short, contingencies, conjunctures, history, and narrowly self-serving leadership choices in Beijing conspired to unleash an extraordinary surge of anti-American nationalism in China.

This buildup of factors and forces making for a reinterpretation of America as a dangerous anti-China force was palpably manifest in 1993 when the new anti-American brand of Chinese patriotism exploded. China expected to be rewarded with the 2000 Olympic games for its recent economic rise, an extraordinary feat that won global plaudits. After all, Japan had been rewarded with the Olympics in the 1960s and South Korea in the 1980s when they both rose economically.

However, China learned, as the decision neared, that the U.S. Congress voted against awarding the Olympics to the regime and city responsible for the June 4, 1989, massacre. It was a nonbinding resolution. When Sydney won the 2000 Olympics bid and Beijing barely lost the vote, China raged at America. The United States was held responsible for a humiliation of the Chinese nation, making China less than Korea or Japan. It seemed palpable proof that American hegemony in Asia took China as its enemy. An immoral America was understood as practicing Cold War containment in an effort to suffocate and humiliate China, preventing its rise, denying it living space, using all means to maintain American predominance in the Asia-Pacific region. In China, Beijing-Washington relations had come to be framed in a way that—almost whatever the facts, even in spite of the facts—America would have to be portrayed and experienced as an evil villain and China an innocent victim.

Actually, as everyone knows, the nonbinding resolution on the Olympics by the U.S. Congress did not even decide the vote of the independent U.S. representatives on the International Olympic Committee (IOC). In fact, Sydney won the 2000 Olympics by successfully bribing (that is, by playing by the same rules as Atlanta, Nagano, and Salt Lake City) the IOC. Beijing was not as effective a briber in 1993. But it was America that was scapegoated.

In reality, pre-1993 forces of an overwhelming nature had preshaped Chinese nationalistic consciousness such that America was already considered China's number one enemy. The 1993 Olympic decision was a mere spark that ignited anti-U.S. tinder that had long since piled up. Alleged American misdeeds did not cause a Chinese backlash. Something had profoundly changed Chinese political consciousness in ways that targeted and vilified America. Chinese patriots interpreted events by way of a paradigm that framed American policies and intentions such that America was imagined and reimagined as an evil party continuing a Cold War against an innocent and fragile China. Chinese patriots regarded China as passive and defensive, while they regarded America as active and aggressive.

With such innate presuppositions, the Chinese worldview must cast America as the immoral leader of an imperialist West pursuing an anti-China crusade against the will and interests of the innocent people of China and even against the interests both of world peace and all the people of the world. This framing of the issue is decisive in interpreting events such as the Yin He incident and the war in Kosovo and in reinterpreting the 1991 Gulf War, the last moment in the 1990s when many confused Chinese could still respect American power and even seek to enroll in the U.S.-led force dislodging the expansionist Iraqi military from extinguishing an independent nation, Kuwait, a member of the United Nations.

Given this anti-American framing of U.S.-Chinese relations, patriotic Chinese tend to interpret events so they fit a particular paradigm. In China's nationalistic consciousness, the Chinese are portrayed as martyrs and Americans as murderers. In summer 2001, for instance, I learned that the nationalistic Chinese tended to "know" and confidently assert that the American military had invaded Chinese airspace over Hainan Island and intentionally hit a defending Chinese Air Force plane, wantonly murdering the pilot. In both popular and elite consciousness, it did not matter that Beijing never claimed that the U.S. surveillance flight was *not* over international waters.

The manifest passion since 1993 that infuses this anti-American attitude in China as well as its assertive political project of reestablishing Chinese predominance in the Asia-Pacific region to replace a presumed American hegemony still needs clarifying to illuminate its political project. This can be done by looking at the emotional popular response in China to the rise of Lee Teng-hui as president of a democratic, autonomous Taiwan. The key is that President Lee was seen in China as a continuation and proof of the resurgence of brutal, militaristic Japanese imperialism.

With anti-Japanese nationalism as the stomach-turning passion of Chinese patriots, the revenge-filled emotion stoked by Beijing policies since 1982 teaches the Chinese people that the only way to preclude a repeat of the pre-PRC tragedy of hideously brutal and murderous Japanese aggression is to have China rise to dominance in the Asia-Pacific. The pro-Japan performance of President Lee in Taiwan became tangible proof to anxious patriots in China that Beijing had to be willing to act militarily to preclude a repetition of the horror of horrors: militaristic Japan on the move again in Asia. Obviously, as with the irrelevance of actual American policy, the reality of Japan's quite constrained foreign policy actions has no impact on the surging Chinese chauvinism. It is important to remember how ungrounded in international reality China's domestically-driven expansive chauvinism is. That passion, however irrational, is war-prone.

Given Beijing's framing of the world, Taiwan also is understood in a way that distorts history. President Lee grew up when Taiwan was a colony of Japan. He went to college in Japan, and he spoke Japanese far better than he spoke Mandarin Chinese. His generation was appalled at the brutality and corruption of the Taiwan takeover by the mainland Chinese Kuomintang (KMT) after Hirohito's imperial Japan surrendered in 1945. With a post-war and newly democratized Japan home to anti-KMT Taiwanese forces in the 1950s, Lee Teng-hui devoured the works of Japanese intellectuals. On Taiwan, anti-KMT, prodemocratic political forces naturally had a strong pro-Japanese content, with post-World War II democratic Japan acting as the major haven for anti-KMT dissidents escaping a murderous white terror by recent arrivals on Taiwan from China. As Taiwan modernized in the 1960s and 1970s, politically conscious Taiwanese utilized Japanese-type policies of state-promoted development, as China began to do in the post-Mao era of reform and openness. With these Taiwanese looking at stagnant, miserable Mao-era China, they, of course, imagined their great fortune as having enjoyed the benefits of Japanese culture—health, education, and modernization—while a chaotic and stagnant China was at war with itself and its people suffered. Chinese in the 1990s had no empathetic understanding of the impact of Taiwanese history on Taiwanese consciousness and politics. What ruling groups in China instead saw on Taiwan was race traitors opposed to the return of Han China to glory and greatness.

Consequently, the president of a democratic Taiwan entering the 1990s, Lee Teng-hui was interpreted in super-patriotic China as the carrier, if not the embodiment, of pro-Japanese tendencies (an immorality akin to being pro-Nazi), which in the PRC felt like treason, insanity, or worse. President Lee gave an interview to a Japanese reporter in Japanese, noting his long-time embrace of and admiration for Japanese culture. To patriotic Chinese, totally ignorant of the pacifist and antinuclear strains in Japan's postwar political culture or of Taiwanese political development, it seemed as if Japan's East Asian coprosperity sphere was reviving. The vile language aimed at President Lee and his successor President Chen from Beijing is understandable only in terms of the ill-informed yet palpable political will in China to avoid the worst evil, a return of brutal Japanese hegemony in Asia, as in the imperial era of Hirohito.

In China, Japan is still represented by the image of Showa-era wartime General Tojo. One cannot overstate the surge of nationalistic fire in Chinese bellies crying out for action against a possible return of the Japanese evils of old. Chinese patriots will even dismiss President Jiang Zemin's embrace of Wang Wei, the pilot who went down after he collided in April 2001 with a routine U.S. reconnaissance flight over international waters, demanding to know why President Jiang silenced the commemoration of the Hong Kong Chinese martyr who earlier died in protesting the alleged imperialist expansionism of Japanese chauvinistic rightists at China's Diaoyutai Islands (actually Japan's Senkaku islets).

Few Chinese patriots praise their president as a proper nationalist. Instead, he is seen as weak, a virtual American toady, the leader of the pro-American faction. Nationalists demand military action against the enemies of China, supposedly as Mao would have done earlier. Given Jiang's actual promotion of military modernization combined with both Mao's and Deng's orders after 1953 to avoid military conflict with America, this patriotic demand for a Chinese leader tougher on Americans than Jiang cannot help but be worrisome. Many informed Chinese insist that after President Jiang is gone, real patriots will finally come to power in China. Jiang, in power, to obtain what he wants in other realms, keeps conceding to hawks on the other Taiwan issue.

Something very worrisome is happening in China. The Chinese government, by stoking hate-filled anti-Americanism, is riding on the back of a tiger. As with Islamicist regimes in Pakistan and Saudi Arabia, which try to buy legitimation by supporting fundamentalist, anti-Western education of the young, a chauvinistic force also is being created in China that could one day attack the rulers for being insufficiently patriotic. The political atmosphere in this China precludes accurate descriptions of Japan, America, or Taiwan and makes self-interested, common-sense compromises by the Chinese government seem, to many Chinese, to be virtual treason. Therefore, the Chinese do not readily appreciate how others see their foreign policies.

The Chinese do not believe that their missile threat to Taiwan is offensive intimidation that undermines peace in the region, which it is, but instead merely a deterrent preventing Taiwanese independence. Patriots in China demand more. They insist on action against an allegedly new separatist threat. In Beijing, the rise of Taiwanese presidents, first Lee Teng-hui and then Chen Shui-bien, is seen as but the tip of a surging Taiwan independence movement. The Chinese are never told that President Chen has always wrapped himself in the symbolism of the Republic of China, not an independent Taiwan.

This Chinese understanding of Taiwan separatism as a growing threat is pure militaristic chauvinism. It does not relate to any reality in Taiwan. There is no independence movement on Taiwan. The one pro-independence party never gets more than a couple of percent of the popular vote. The three main parties on Taiwan are all moderate status quo parties. They contend that the Republic of China, which was born in 1911 under Sun Yat-sen's aegis, continues on Taiwan as a sovereign entity. Therefore, a declaration of independence would be redundant and unnecessary. Independence would only be triggered by a Chinese military offensive against Taiwan. The government on Taiwan seeks peace and mutually beneficial cooperation.

In short, the Chinese missile threat to Taiwan is the opposite of what it claims to be. It alienates Taiwan from China. It is not a deterrent precluding Taiwan independence, since independence is not on the mainstream political agenda in Taiwan.

Chinese nationalism is worrisome because its blinding passion can keep rulers in Beijing from acting as their interests would otherwise dictate. This super-patriotism has an irrational and dangerous quality to it. Chinese chauvinism consequently has to make others in the Asia-Pacific region anxious and vigilant.

The dynamic of the new Chinese nationalism aimed at Chinese hegemony in the Asia-Pacific region is deep and angry. It assumes America will grow tired with the cost of its efforts in Asia and therefore is plotting one day to leave Japan in its place. Since Japanese predominance in Asia, understood as a return of Japanese militarism, is immoral and unacceptable for historically victimized Chinese nationalists, the only moral alternative is Chinese hegemony in that Asia-Pacific region. This goal is beyond debate, and to challenge it is to reveal oneself a traitor to China.

The imagined future for Chinese nationalists thinking of a glorious hegemonic 21st century includes enrichment facilitated by the incorporation of a wealthy Taiwan and the resource-rich South China Seas into the PRC such that a subordinated Japan and a respectful set of lesser nations in Asia will do nothing to challenge China's interests and predominance in the Asia-Pacific region. Ruling groups in Asia instead will submit, as a South Korean journalist did at the October 2001 Asia Pacific Economic Cooperation (APEC) summit in Shanghai, polite, prearranged questions so that China's political leadership can present its view of Asia's future as unchallenged, at least in Asia.

Such an accomplishment would undermine basic American interests in the region, but not because of any American interest in hegemonic domination. Rather, the United States seeks a balance of power in which democracies can flourish without fear of being rolled back by an antidemocratic, anti-human rights, hegemonic China. America, therefore, hopes to preclude a region subordinated to an anti-American and antidemocratic China.

Despite Beijing's singular anti-American nationalistic project, the government in China is not and should not be considered as the implacable expansionist foe of vital American interests in the Asia-Pacific region. Indeed, China should be treated as a potential partner. But why? How could that be, given the pervasiveness of a threatening Chinese chauvinism?

First, there is no public opinion in China, only public sentiment. The kind of ill-informed feelings sketched in this essay are highly volatile. They have no solid formation in informed debate. They can change overnight. One day, the Cultural Revolution will save the world; the next day, it is a disaster. The same holds with the character of Lin Biao. Sentiment lacks substance. The chauvinistic passion in no way captures some Chinese essence, not even the essence of Chinese nationalism.

The Chinese do not even know that America defeated Japan in World War II. Annually, at the end of the summer, as China commemorates the defeat of Japan in World War II, I read the Chinese press essays celebrating that event year after year. The Chinese people have yet to be properly informed as to why it was the American General Douglas MacArthur who received the Japanese surrender on the USS *Missouri*. They are taught that Mao and the CCP freed China from Japanese aggressors or that socialist allies in the north helped them defeat Japan.

In a free and open political atmosphere, Chinese opinion could change hugely and rapidly. The world is replete with instances of such seemingly impossible transformations. In Ukraine, just before the Soviet Union split up, a survey of public sentiment showed almost 90 percent in favor of staying in the Soviet Union. The next year, in a free vote, 90 percent voted the other way.

A similar change could occur in the content of Chinese nationalism. The myths informing patriotism are ambiguous and contestable. Despite surging Chinese chauvinistic sentiment and anti-Americanism since 1989, there is no reason to believe that that is what would win out in a democratizing China. Instead, the very act of democratization would highlight cooperation rather than opposition. Suddenly, it would be both obvious and important that China and America were allies in the war against fascist racism, allies in World War II.

If a political opening were to occur in China, it is almost inconceivable that it would not have a transforming impact on Chinese foreign policy, larger even than the death of Mao and the rise of Deng had in terms of rapprochement with Russia and openness to the world economy. This yet larger change is likely because the Chinese would suddenly learn, among many other paradigm-shattering things, that Mao was complicit with Stalin in the aggression that launched the Korean War and led to almost one million Chinese casualties, that Beijing has long propped up a uniquely brutal regime in Pyongyang, that China was the major military backer of the Khmer Rouge, the cruelest regime in modern Asian history, that Beijing in 1979 launched an unprovoked war against Vietnam, and that China has long remained the major military backer of the thieving tyranny in Burma.

In short, the People's Republic of China has actually been a victimizer of Asian peoples. The CCP record can compare with the inhumanities perpetrated on Asian peoples by the Showa-era imperial Japanese armies of Hirohito. A fall of the dictatorship could discredit the chauvinistic mythos of the CCP. The Maoist framing of Chinese consciousness in which the Chinese people are singular innocent victims of evil foreigners could implode. A new world of possibilities would open up.

Issues would be reframed as well. Sino-Japanese conciliation would become possible. China would then not threaten its neighbors. Trust and cooperation would grow all over Asia. The APEC and Association of Southeast Asian Nations (ASEAN) and ASEAN/ARF (ASEAN Regional Forum) could fulfill their promise for peace, prosperity, and pluralism in Asia, much as the North Atlantic Treaty Organization and the European Union have done for Europe. In short, there is good reason for America promoting a long-term policy of full engagement with China, whatever the painful challenges and short-term setbacks that flow from Chinese chauvinism.

Second, the opposites of what prevails today are also in China but repressed. The voices of win/win liberal internationalism could emerge victorious in an open debate. Culture should never be essentialized. It is not this *or* that but this *and* that. No matter how loud and strong militaristic sentiment is today, there is, after all, a good case that it is in China's interest to maximize economic benefit from Taiwan and to bet on long-term peaceful evolutionary forces to resolve the cross-Strait issue. It is inconceivable that Taiwan could resist the attraction of a federalized, democratic, common-market-oriented and prospering China.

Similarly, an energy-importing China would benefit from peace in the South China Seas that would allow all sides to pump the oil freely and securely. Peace and cooperative development are in China's most basic interests. It is important not to be mesmerized by today's seemingly homogeneous super-patriotic consensus. There are major structured economic interests that keep restoring both normal Beijing-Washington relations and regional stability after what seem to be, time after time, relationship-breaking crises. So far, these strong forces have been denied a voice reflective of their actual weightiness.

Some Chinese insist that the revanchist nationalism described in this essay is actually more worrisome to the regime than it need be to America; ruling groups in Beijing understand well that the real target of the chauvinists is China's corrupt rulers, seen as serving only themselves. Ruling groups are not actually caught up in this chauvinist sentiment. It is not a basis for making Chinese foreign policy. Many among ruling groups would like a safe way to get off the back of the tiger that they have been riding because the chauvinism actually threatens China's rulers.

Even in the military, many of whose officers come from central China, that is, neither the rich coastal regions nor the peripheral non-Han regions, people from central places whose suffering by Han Chinese leads the military to have reservations about reform openness and globalization, seen as not benefitting their people, their anti-foreign chauvinism is actually mainly a complaint about domestic Chinese priorities and policies. The military is looking for a better deal for its support base. It uses nationalism to convince the party not to favor coastal regions tied to the global economy, claimed to be causes of societal polarization in China. But, as the party leadership, the military also is not looking for war with America.

Despite economic openness, China remains a monist state. The leadership and line at any one moment make other possibilities invisible. When Mao died in 1976 at a time when Jiang Qing's ultras dominated the propaganda apparatus, the reform possibility was hidden. Yet reform won out. So it is today that chauvinistic anti-American sentiment obscures much that is also there. One does not hear of the students who did not join the May 1999 anti-American riots because they opposed anything associated with the corrupt and brutal CCP dictatorship. One does not hear southern voices who have faith that, in the long run, an economically successful, democratized, and federalized China is an irresistible magnet to the Taiwanese. Such people believe that the war-mongering chauvinists who would use military power against Taiwan are actually narrow patriots who would sacrifice the long-term economic rise of China on a selfish altar of careerism. In short, at both elite and mass levels, there are strong forces that would resist and defeat the aggressive nationalists.

The change of certain popular doggerel hints that Beijing chauvinists may be more isolated than they seem at first glance. In the 1980s, when the southern city of Canton seemed the core of a new and burgeoning economy integrated through Hong Kong to America, it was rhymed, "*Beijing aiguo, Shanghai chu guo, Guangzhou maiguo*" (Beijing people love the country [are patriots], Shanghai-ese leave the country, Cantonese betray the country). By the end of the 1990s, when trade flourished between Taiwan, the new leader in investment in China, especially with Xiamen across the Taiwan Strait in China's south, a Taiwan portrayed in Beijing as the separatist threat to stability, it was then said, "Beijing wants war, Shanghai seeks peace, Xiamen would surrender." The expansive chauvinism of China may be, first and foremost, a Beijing phenomenon. There is good reason to think of the south, whose population has increased recently by 50 million as northerners flee there for work, as China's better future. The south is not just a region. It is a consciousness, a project of peaceful coop-eration whose voice is drowned out by the propaganda of chauvinism, a project that can be embraced in Beijing, too, a politics that could yet win out in China.

In addition, new interests are being created by the economic rise of China which can learn, in contrast to the chauvinists whose framing of in-ternational relations precludes such learning, that China can benefit from win/win multilateralism. Some people believe that China's positive re-sponse to the American effort against the perpetrators of the September 11 mass murders has again opened space for such win/win people to woo other Chinese to their side.

The reason for supporting an American engagement policy accom-panied by quiet vigilance, therefore, is not naivete and ignorance about today's Chinese chauvinism and its war-prone hegemonic project. There are indeed dangerous forces within Chinese politics. But analysts must heed other forces, better prospects, which are rendered misleadingly invis-ible by the propaganda monism of the authoritarian state. America should both prepare for the worst and build on the better forces.

It certainly would be naive to support engagement with the as-sumption that freedom will naturally and necessarily evolve from wealth expansion. This faith is based on a misreading of the histories of Taiwan and China. In fact, peace, multilateralism, and democracy are all political projects that have to be won by political struggles in a semiautonomous political arena. They will not evolve automatically or swiftly. They also will not be overly helped by the aid, intervention, or good wishes of for-eigners. These are internal Chinese matters. China is a great nation, not a banana republic subject to foreign manipulation. China's political fate will be decided by the Chinese in China. Politics is a politically contingent matter involving struggles in China. The single nasty voice of anti-Amer-ican chauvinism is not the only dog hunting in Chinese politics. One should not confuse propaganda with deeper political dynamics.

All American engagement can do for the potential win/win forces that already exist in Chinese politics is not to make political success more difficult than it already is for these peace-prone, cooperative political forces. The most important achievements of an American engagement policy with China would flow from the success of America's global poli-cies. America can strive to make possible an international world where the Chinese, as others who choose to do so, can, in fact, play win/win games. Given the challenges of the new moment in globalization, with its volatility and out-of-control financial forces, success for such a global policy is in no way guaranteed. But it may be crucial for the success of engagement in the Asia-Pacific region. That is, building a new international financial architecture facilitating growth with equity can have a major impact on peace in the Taiwan region.

Consequently, given how little America can do to impact Chinese politics directly, the fate of engagement rests mainly with forces in China. There is a tense and angry domestic world in China that makes the chauvinists strong and popular. It is those internal political dynamics that are most decisive for the political fate and economic future of China, and, therefore, for the American policy of engagement. Moreover, one cannot be sanguine about China's domestic dynamics.

Today's Chinese super-patriots do not see the world in ways that would lead them to embrace win/win policies. Indonesia's 1997 financial crisis and the subsequent fall of dictator Suharto show the dangers of corrupt Asian authoritarianism. For stability and a continuing economic rise, to avoid Suharto-era-type ills, China should democratize so that crooks can be held accountable and be peacefully removed from office. But rulers in Beijing interpreted those Indonesian events in a way that denied the importance of political reform. Instead, they took the Indonesian crisis as proof that a centralized authoritarianism in Indonesia, as already had been the case in Russia and Yugoslavia, could fall apart if it did not maintain a strong, centralized, successful, and unchallengeable center. Authoritarianism interprets matters to relegitimatize its own power premises. The result has been an increase of repression in China, not an opening to democracy.

But if China begins a democratic transition, Indonesia would be seen differently, seen in a way more in harmony with American interests and values. It is crucial to remember that, in nation after nation, political reform, once seen as the enemy of real power groups, nevertheless was embraced as the only way to make more stable progress likely. The same possibility exists for China. The future is wide open. Best and worst possibilities are in conflict. As a result, America needs a foreign policy as nuanced as Chinese uncertainties and complexities.

The chauvinistic and military realities of China dictate for America not a mere policy of engagement but one of engagement with vigilance. But this is not because dangerous forces in China must win out. China can be analogized to late 19th-century Germany and Japan. There was no inevitability in the 1890s that the expansionist regimes of the 1930s would rise and emerge triumphant. Many observers thought that both

Taisho and Weimar democracy would emerge victorious. That they did not, most historians agree, has a lot to do with out-of-control global forces, contingent events such as the Great Depression, the end of win/win international trade, and the lack of an international financial architecture capable of blocking these worst-case economic events, thereby making a win/win international economy virtually impossible.

The better forces can be weakened or defeated by international factors that shape domestic possibilities. That is why a good China policy for America is mainly the offshoot of enlightened international policies in general. The better Chinese leaders actually understand this deep and long-term logic.

America should be presenting itself and acting in the world to build the international architecture that would once again, as in the Bretton Woods era, facilitate growth with equity. It does not help America's goals for itself to act as the supposed sole superpower, the supposed indispensable nation needed to solve all global issues. America too must abjure self-serving unilateralism for win/win multilateralism.

Consequently, America should acknowledge that globalization weakens all states and makes ever more important the building of broad international cooperation to grapple with vital issues that are beyond the reach of any single state, even the strongest, both China and America. Such a cooperative project seemingly takes us far from the challenge of Chinese nationalism to American security interests. Yet it may be the heart of the military issue. It reminds us that the worst-case scenarios inherent in the Chinese challenges to a peaceful, prosperous Asia of open, pluralist societies, prospects that obviously require continuing American vigilance, including military vigilance, are best dealt with in a framework much larger than U.S. policy with China, no matter how crucial that matter is to America's most vital interests.

Part III

Military Trends

Chapter 6

The PLA Army's Struggle for Identity

James C. Mulvenon

Before the atrocities of September 11, 2001, ground forces appeared to be the big loser in the current evolutionary phase of modern warfare. The clean, precise style of airpower, combined with the decline of conflicts calling for large land battles, had increased the institutional momentum for air and naval forces at the expense of their ground force counterparts. Similar trends had upended the historic dominance of ground forces in the Chinese military, which had moved over the last 20 years from a focus on massive land battles with the former Soviet Union to littoral defense and power projection from its eastern coast against the dominant planning scenario, Taiwan. While the necessity for homeland defense has possibly generated an additional, powerful institutional rationale for the U.S. Army, Chinese ground forces continue to struggle with issues of identity and mission. Once the unchallenged heart and soul of the People's Liberation Army (PLA), Chinese ground forces remain the dominant service in the military in terms of manpower, resources, doctrine, and prestige. The other services, however, are clearly in the ascendance, while the ground forces have been in a long, slow decline.[1]

This chapter examines the evolution of Chinese ground forces from their guerrilla origins through their period of preeminence to the difficult challenges of the current era. Current trends are examined, including changes in the roles and missions of the force, as well as its strategy and doctrine, organizational structure, equipment, and training. The essay concludes with some speculation about future trajectories for the ground forces.[2]

Evolution of China's Ground Forces

Long before the People's Republic of China (PRC) fielded significant numbers of naval, air, or strategic rocket forces, there was the Red Army, a ragtag collection of foot soldiers schooled in the tenets of Maoist guerrilla struggle. Only after this revolutionary vanguard defeated the modern militaries of the Empire of Japan and the Kuomintang did the Chinese Communist Party (CCP) leadership seriously consider forming the other elements of a modern military. Even so, the wars of the first 30 years of the PRC were predominantly land wars, fought by foot soldiers in Korea, India, and Vietnam.

Among the many continuities of the era stretching from the 1920s to the late 1970s was the doctrine of People's War, which was centered on the ground forces and their continental orientation. The strategy implicitly assumed that China's nascent power projection forces, including littoral naval and frontline air assets, would act as little more than a speed bump for an invading high-tech enemy, which was defined as the United States from 1949 to the mid-1960s and the Soviet Union from the mid-1960s to the mid-1980s. The real battle would be fought from an inner defense line, staffed with a mixture of main-line ground forces and local militia. The ground forces themselves were organized by infantry corps, called field armies, which generally had three infantry divisions and smaller support units. These units were attributed with a light infantry operations capability, along with some combined arms assistance, with militia units providing combat and logistical support for "luring deep."[3]

The late 1970s and early 1980s were a transitional period for the ground forces, defined by the seemingly contradictory slogan of "People's War Under Modern Conditions."[4] This strategy called for the armed forces to defend China closer to its borders, fighting the Soviets "in a more mobile style of war with combined arms and joint force."[5] As Dennis Blasko has outlined, the emphasis in the ground forces shifted to "more tanks, self-propelled artillery, and armored personnel carriers, which added mobility and also offered the possibility of protection from Soviet NBC (nuclear, biological, chemical) attacks."[6] The majority of group armies were deployed in garrison locations along expected avenues of attack from the former Soviet Union and Mongolia. Nearly one-half of the group armies were located to protect Beijing and Manchuria from a Soviet attack, while two group armies in the Lanzhou military region were tasked with fighting the Soviet Red Army as it crossed the desert. The necessary modernization to achieve these goals was never completed during this short-lived period because the costs were judged to be prohibitive.

In the mid-1980s, Deng Xiaoping began to redefine PLA orientation radically, beginning with a reassessment in 1985 of the overall international security environment that lowered the probability of a major or nuclear war. Instead, Deng asserted that China would be confronted with limited, local wars on its periphery. The natural consequence of this sweeping reassessment was an equally comprehensive reorientation of the Chinese military. The number of military regions was reduced from 11 to 7, and the 37 field armies were restructured to bring "tank, artillery, anti-aircraft artillery, engineer, and NBC defense units under a combined arms, corps-level headquarters called the Group Army."[7] Between 1985 and 1988, the 37 field armies were reduced to 24 group armies, and thousands of units at the regimental level and above were disbanded.[8] Overall, the PLA was reported to have cut more than one million personnel from the ranks, though Yitzhak Shichor has thoroughly dissected the many empirical problems associated with these announcements.[9]

The period between 1985 and the present has been marked by restructuring, reform, doctrinal experimentation, and implementation. The ground forces have witnessed few real tests since these changes took effect, with the exception of operations in 1987 on the Vietnam border. Ironically, the largest mobilization of ground forces took place during the 1989 Tiananmen crisis, when the combat skills of the troops were practiced on lightly armed or unarmed civilians in the streets of the capital. Since then, however, the focus of the entire military has shifted to a single, dominant planning scenario: Taiwan. While many elements of the PLA welcomed the emergence of the Taiwan scenario as a tangible justification for increased budgets and procurement, the ground forces likely view this situation with mixed emotions, since the 100 miles of water separating Taiwan from the mainland offer little direct role for the Army. Instead, the scenario is dominated by the newly ascendant naval and air forces, with the ground forces pushed to the rear in support. The next section explores the contours of this new reality for the army.

Current Trends in the Ground Forces

Roles and Missions

In outlining the roles and missions of the Chinese ground forces, official sources provide general, aggregated, and thus ultimately unsatisfying definitions. According to the 1997 National Defense Law:

> The active units of the Chinese People's Liberation Army are a standing army, which is mainly charged with the defensive fighting mission. The standing army, when necessary, may assist in maintaining public order in accordance with the law. Reserve units shall

take training according to regulations in peacetime, may assist in maintaining public order according to the law when necessary, and shall change to active units in wartime according to mobilization orders issued by the state. Under the leadership and command of the State Council and the Central Military Commission, the Chinese People's Armed Police force is charged by the state with the mission of safeguarding security and maintaining public order. Under the command of military organs, militia units shall perform combat-readiness duty, carry out defensive fighting tasks, and assist in maintaining the public order.[10]

To understand the true role of the ground forces at a higher level of detail, it is necessary to step back from discussions of particular scenarios and instead derive the missions from China's national military objectives. David Finkelstein has done the work for us, identifying China's three national military objectives:

- protect the party and safeguard stability
- defend sovereignty and defeat aggression
- modernize the military and build the nation.[11]

The ground forces have a role to play in each of these objectives. More than any other service, the ground forces and related paramilitary units (such as the People's Armed Police [PAP]) are the front line in defending the party from both internal and external enemies, and thus safeguarding stability. As for the second objective, sovereignty and aggression are complicated concepts for the Chinese, as they can be both offensive and defensive in nature. For example, the ground forces clearly have a central role in defending the sovereignty of the continental landmass from external aggression, though active defense demands that naval and air forces initiate contact with the aggressor away from China's shores. At the same time, however, the Chinese definition of defending sovereignty also includes assertion of sovereignty over Taiwan, which falls disproportionately on the backs of China's power projection forces in the People's Liberation Army-Navy (PLAN) and the People's Liberation Army Air Force (PLAAF). Given that Taiwan is the core-planning scenario for a military operating with growing but still finite resources, the bulk of funds for modernization is therefore allocated to non-ground force units in the navy, air force, and strategic rocket forces.

Within these guidelines, the main roles and missions of the ground forces primarily involve *continental defense* and *internal security*. As for continental defense, Blasko et al., capture the current dynamic succinctly:

The PLA faces no immediate land threat to the integrity of the Chinese landmass. Even if such a threat existed, the PLA's current size, structure, deployment, level of training, equipment and doctrine of a "people's war" is probably sufficient to deter an attacker from an invasion because of the casualties the existing force could inflict on the invader.[12]

Moreover, as the PLA shifts its doctrine to deal with local wars on the periphery of China, the navy and air force have risen in importance, receiving priority in PLA modernization efforts and naturally growing larger in proportion to the total force. In terms of internal security, Blasko writes, "the primary mission of the active duty force is external defense, while the PAP is tasked with internal or domestic security. As a secondary mission, the active duty and reserve PLA forces and militia may assist the PAP in maintaining domestic security."[13]

Doctrine

China's primary military doctrine is defined by the phrase active defense (*jijifangyu*).[14] While this forward-leaning doctrine relies heavily on littoral naval and air assets, the ground forces still have important roles to play. Specifically, they are expected to "conduct joint and combined arms operations of a limited duration along the periphery of China using existing weapons."[15] These forces are expected to suffer attrition from enemy air forces and other long-range strike assets and then wage mobile, positional warfare against invading forces. In this scenario, rapid reaction forces would serve as the core of the ground forces response, with mobile units likely flowing into the theater of operations from adjacent military regions. Given the low probability that an enemy would make the same mistake as the Japanese in the 1930s and deploy ground troops to the Chinese landmass, however, the ground force role in active defense has been limited to exercises with existing equipment and has not enjoyed the same high procurement priority as advanced fighter aircraft or submarines. Moreover, ground forces do not play a large role in the active revolution in military affairs debate within the PLA, further sidelining the army's influence over the future trajectory of PLA concept development and doctrinal evolution.

Organizational Structure

The traditional structure was divided into three rough categories: main force units, local or regional forces, and militia units. Prior to 1985, the main force units were corps, also known as field armies. After 1985, the main force unit was the group army, composed of approximately 60,000 troops divided into 3 infantry divisions, a tank division or brigade, an artillery division or brigade, an antiaircraft artillery division or brigade, a communications regiment, an engineer regiment, and a reconnaissance battalion. Beneath the group army, the ground forces are further divided into several levels of deployment:

- division/brigade (*shi/lu*)
- regiment (*tuan*)
- battalion (*guan*)
- company (*lian*)
- platoon (*pai*)
- squad (*ban*).

The specific configuration of individual group armies is often dictated by geographic location. Different military regions (MRs) face strikingly different scenarios, and thus group armies display combinations of units and equipment appropriate to their unique area of responsibility. Among the ground force-heavy regions, the Lanzhou, Beijing, and Shenyang MRs are configured for land threats from the north, while the Lanzhou MR is also equipped for suppression of separatist activity in Tibet and Xinjiang. Similarly, the Shenyang MR is prepared for Korea contingencies. The Chengdu and Lanzhou MRs are also for Indian scenarios, and the Chengdu and Guangzhou MRs are arrayed for Southeast Asian threats. Among the least ground force-oriented are the Jinan MR, which is directed toward blunting maritime threats from the Sea of Japan and the Nanjing MR, which is focused on Taiwan.

Other important organizational trends include significant downsizing, the emergence of brigades and rapid reaction units, modernization of the command, control, communications, computers, and intelligence (C⁴I) infrastructure, the rise of a noncommissioned officer corps, and the divestiture of ground force unit business enterprises.

Downsizing

In 1978, Deng Xiaoping and the reformers inherited a military ill suited to the needs of modern warfare. In a 1975 speech, Deng summed up his feelings about the state of the PLA, describing the army as suffering from "bloating, listlessness, arrogance, extravagance, and laziness [*zhong, san, jiao, she, duo*]."[16] One of the first items on the agenda was a reduction in personnel. From 1985 to 1988, more than one million personnel were reportedly trimmed from the ranks, though Shichor's analysis brings into question many of the numerical assertions by official Chinese sources. In particular, he points out that "it is unclear whether the cut of one million military personnel announced in 1985 includes or excludes the more than half a million troops collectively demobilized since 1982."[17]

At the 15th Party Congress meeting in September 1997, Jiang Zemin announced an additional cut of 500,000 personnel over 3 years. Among the service branches, the ground forces suffered disproportionately, reflecting the ascendancy of the air and naval branches. Blasko writes:

> According to the July 1998 Defense White Paper, ground forces will be reduced by 19%, naval forces by 11.6%, and air force personnel by 11%.[18] These percentages amount to a reduction of about 418,000 ground forces, 31,000 naval personnel, and 52,000 air force personnel.[19] Of the 500,000 personnel to be reduced, the ground forces will account for nearly 84% of the total. An important implication of the 500,000 man reduction under way is that the percentage of PLA ground forces within the total force structure will decrease as the percentages of naval and air forces increase.[20]

At the same time, however, the ground forces after the cuts still comprised 73 percent of the total force structure, with the navy and air force only about 10 percent and 17 percent, respectively. Thus, it is important to contextualize the downsizing trends by noting that the PLA is likely to remain dominated by ground forces for several more decades.[21]

The downsizing in the ground forces had direct consequences for the organization of units. Three group armies (the 28th in Beijing MR, 67th in Jinan MR, and 64th in Shenyang MR) were reportedly disbanded, and many if not all of the remaining group armies were slated to lose a full division through "deactivation, resubordination, or downsizing."[22] Several divisions were demobilized, 14 were reassigned to the People's Armed Police, a few were transferred from one group army to another, one was transformed into the second PLAN marine unit, and several were downsized to brigade level.[23] Subordinate elements of demobilized headquarters and units were transferred to other ground forces headquarters.

Some of the PLA units in the 1997–2000 downsizing were transferred to the People's Armed Police.[24] Currently, PAP strength is approximately 800,000[25] but is probably on its way to about one million as the PLA continues its reduction through the year 2000.[26] In addition, the PLA created a system of reserves.[27] An April 1998 expanded meeting of the Central Military Commission emphasized the need to expand the reserve forces. After the meeting, the military districts were ordered to step up the implementation of plans to build reserve units.[28] Equipment not needed in the PAP could be retired, put in storage, or transferred to the reserves or militia.

Rapid Reaction Units

From the mid-1980s to the mid-1990s, the most important organizational reform for the ground forces was the creation of rapid reaction units (RRUs). Their mission is to be "the first PLA forces to respond in time of crisis," ready to mobilize in 24 to 48 hours.[29] In addition to the 15th airborne group army, which is an air force unit, the PLA has designated four group armies (the 38th, 39th, 54th, and 23rd) as RRUs.[30] Within each military region, one or more divisions has been designated as an RRU and equipped partially with new equipment. These units were expected to deploy either within their military regions or nationwide.[31] They received priority in training and participated in doctrinal experiments.[32] Eventually, RRUs were projected to include 10 to 25 percent of the entire force. In June 2000, the Department of Defense (DOD) reported that "approximately 14 of [PLA ground force] divisions are designated 'rapid reaction' units: combined arms units capable of deploying by road or rail within China without significant train-up or reserve augmentation."[33] At the same time, RRUs have reportedly created new sets of problems related to force coordination, logistics support, and command, control, communications, and intelligence (C³I).[34]

Brigades

With the relative decline of interest in rapid reaction units, attention has shifted to the development of brigades (*lu*). Commanded by a senior colonel, these units are composed of several battalions, but with significantly smaller combat service support units than divisions.[35] Overall, brigades are manned with approximately one-third to one-half the strength of a division of the same arm. Regiments will serve as intermediate headquarters between brigade and battalion level for independent brigades. Brigades are intended to make PLA combat units "more rapidly deployable and flexible."[36] According to a 2000 DOD report, "China's ground forces are comprised of 40 maneuver divisions and approximately 40 maneuver brigades."[37]

C⁴I Modernization

PLA ground forces have long suffered from an inadequate communications infrastructure, characterized by outdated technology, limited capacity, and lack of secure communications. In the past, these weaknesses have severely limited the army's ability to transmit and process large amounts of information or coordinate activities between regions or units, thereby reducing military effectiveness. To overcome these deficits, the PLA has embarked on a well-financed effort to modernize its C⁴I infrastructure, resulting in a dramatic improvement of transmission capacity, as well as communications and operational security. For their part, the ground forces have contributed significant labor to the construction of this infrastructure, and many ground forces units serve as key nodes of the networks.

Open sources also reveal information about specific pieces of C⁴I infrastructure, most if not all of which would directly benefit the ground forces. A vague article from *Xinhua* describes the PLA communications system as comprising underground networks of fiber optic cables, communications satellites, microwave links, shortwave radio stations, and automated command and control networks.[38] A series of articles in *Liberation Army Daily* between 1995 and 1997 is more specific, describing the C⁴I system as being composed of at least four major networks: a military telephone network, a confidential telephone network (alternatively described as "encrypted"[39]), an all-army data communications network (also known as the all-army data exchange network or all-army public exchange network[40]), and a "comprehensive communication system for field operations."[41] A third account merges the two accounts, arguing that the PLA underground networks of optical fiber cables, communications satellites in the sky, and microwave and shortwave communications facilities in between form the infrastructure for a military telephone network, a secure telephone network, an all-army data communications network, and the integrated field communications network. Specific details about three of the four networks are scarce. A 1995 article in *Liberation Army Daily* asserts that the army data network, which was begun in 1987, "is responsible for the all-army automatic transmission and exchange of military information in data, pictures, charts, and writing."[42] The PLA signal corps has trained over 1,000 technicians so far, it is claimed, to operate and maintain this system, which covers "all units stationed in medium and large cities across China and along the coast."[43]

One important development for the PLA communications infrastructure has been the laying of fiber optic lines. From an information security perspective, the advantages of fiber optic cables are that they can carry considerably more communications traffic than older technologies, transmit it faster (rates of 565 megabytes per second and higher), are less prone to corrosion and electromagnetic interference, and are lightweight and small enough for mobile battlefield command as well as fixed military headquarters, while at the same time offering much higher levels of operational security. A recent article in the *Wall Street Journal* highlights many of the difficulties that fiber cables pose for the National Security Agency global signals intelligence effort. Indeed, in the 1980s, some U.S. Government agencies were opposed to the sale of fiber optic technologies to the Soviet Union and other countries, including China, for this very reason.

PLA interest in fiber optic cables began in 1993, when the former Ministry of Posts and Telecommunications and the General Staff Department Communications Department agreed to cooperate in constructing 100,000 kilometers of fiber optic cable to form the core of China's long-distance, fiber optic transmission networks and trunk lines.[44] By 1995, the two organizations had jointly constructed 15,000 kilometers of fiber, spanning 19 provinces and municipalities. From 1993 to 1998, more than 1 million officers and men, mainly from the ground forces, worked on these key national optical fiber telecommunications lines. In 1999, an official source asserted that the PLA and PAP participated in the construction of more than 10 large optical fiber communication projects.[45] The military reportedly receives a percentage of the fibers in any given trunk for its own use, making disaggregation of military and civilian communications much more difficult, and the army units stationed along the lines have connected themselves to the backbone.

In terms of specific civilian backbone networks, table 6–1 is a partial list of PLA participation in military-civilian fiber optic cable construction.

In addition, the PLA is building its own set of dedicated fiber optic lines, under a program known as the 975 Communications Trunk Line Project.[46] These networks reportedly connect the central military leadership in Beijing with ground force units down to the garrison level.[47]

As a result of the efforts outlined above, PLA C[4]I capabilities have reportedly increased substantially. According to a 1997 article, more than 85 percent of key armed force units and more than 65 percent of coastal and border units had upgraded their communications equipment. The same article also offered an early assessment of the operational consequences of these changes:

> The use of advanced optical fiber communications facilities, satellites, long-distance automated switches, and computer-controlled telephone systems has significantly accelerated the Chinese armed forces' digitization process and the rapid transmission and processing of military information. The speedy development of strategic

Table 6–1. **Ground Force Unit Participation in Fiber Optic Construction**

Line	Date	Participating Units and Comments
Lhasa to Xigaze	Sept 1995	In September 1995, an optical fiber telecommunications line between formally went into operation. The Tibet Military District built 250 km of the 300-km long cable line, dispatching more than 60,000 man-hours of officers and soldiers in 8 months.[1]
Hangzhou-Fuzhou-Guiyang-Chengdu	June 1995	"After receiving a flood-fighting order, officers and men of a certain PLA unit who had just completed the "Hangzhou-Fuzhou-Guiyang-Chengdu" optical fiber communication project plunged into a new battle without taking a break."[2]
SDH optical fiber line	Dec 1995	A key project under the Eighth Five-Year Plan, the 840-mile SDH optical fiber line cost RMB 220 million.[3] It involved more than 15,000 soldiers stationed in Changchun and was completed in December 1995 after only 80 days.[4]
Lanzhou-Xining-Lhasa		Units of the Lanzhou Military Region and Chengdu Military Region by 1997 had completed the Lanzhou-Xining-Lhasa cable, spanning 2,754 km of some of China's most inhospitable terrain.[5]
Beijing-Wuhan-Guangzhou	1998	Identified in military newspaper.[6]
Lanzhou-Urumqi-Yili	Sept 1999	The Xinjiang Production and Construction Corps built the communications fiber-optic cable.[7]
Qomolangma area		In May 2000, almost 1,000 officers and soldiers of the Chinese PLA are participating in building the first fiber optical cable project at the Qomolangma area.[8] The 300-km-long cable is being built at a height 5,000 meters above the sea level, winding through numerous mountains and rivers.
N/A	Dec 1999	A certain base is lauded for "taking advantage of the state's long-distance optical fiber cable laying project to 'opportunistically' build the military optical fiber communications network," saving 8 million yuan of funds.[9]

Table 6–1. Ground Force Unit Participation in Fiber Optic Construction
—continued

Line	Date	Participating Units and Comments
Hohhot-Beihai	April 1998	On April 11, a brigade of the infantry of the Inner Mongolia military district, totaling 1,200 officers and men, began the construction of the Inner Mongolia section of the optical fiber communication line.[10]

[1] "Troops Participate in Tibet Telecom Project," *Central Television Program One Network*, September 16, 1995; and Lan Peng, "Lhasa-Xigaze Optical Fiber Cable Project Is Underway in Joint Efforts of Army and Locality," *Jiefangjun bao*, May 7, 1995, 1.

[2] "Troops, Militias Fight Floods in Various Provinces," *Xinhua Domestic Service*, June 29, 1995.

[3] "Changchun Troops Help Build Jilin's Communication Line," *Jilin ribao*, December 16, 1995, 1.

[4] Ibid.

[5] The plan was first mentioned in Xie Liangjun, "Cable Crosses to 'Roof of World'," *China Daily*, June 26, 1997, 1. The completion of the cable was heralded in Ding Daoquan and Fan Qing, "Lanzhou Military Congratulated on Laying Optical Cable," *Xinhua*, October 9, 1997, in *FBIS*, October 11, 1997.

[6] Liu Huadi, "Army and People Join Hands in Developing Telecommunications—Interview with Wu Jichuan, Newly Appointed Minister of Information Industry," *Jiefangjun bao*, April 9, 1998, 5, in *FBIS*, April 29, 1998.

[7] Xu Jinzhang, "Xinjiang MD Force Building Defends the Border with Outstanding Merit," *Xinhua Domestic Service*, September 9, 1999.

[8] "PLA Troops Work on Fiber-Optic Cable Project in Tibet," *Xinhua*, May 11, 2000.

[9] Zhang Jiajun and Wu Xudong, "Experts of the Second Artillery Corps Enjoy four 'Prerogatives'," *Jiefangjun Bao*, December 29, 1999.

[10] Ma Yuning, Zhang Zhedong, Xu Guozhao, "Construction of Hohhot-Beihai Optical Fiber Line Starts," *Neimenggu Ribao*, April 13, 1998, 1. "The Hohhot-Beihai communication line is one of the important long-distance optical fiber line project of the Ninth Five-Year Plan of the Postal and Telecommunication Ministry. The optical fiber cable ran from north to south through Inner Mongolia, Shansi, Henan, Hubei, Hunan, and Guangxi. It started from Hohhot to the Beihai city of the Guangxi Zhuang Autonomous Region. The total length amounts to 4,054 km, and the section in Inner Mongolia amounts to 170 km. When the project is finished, its northern end will link with the Beijing-Hohhot-Yinchuan-Lanzhou optical fiber cable and with the Hohhot-Xian optical fiber cable, and its southern end will connect with Guangzhou-Kunming-Chengdu and Beihai-Haikou-Sanya optical fiber cables. Besides, the line has some more connection points with other optical fiber cables, thus becoming the core of south-north communication line through China."

communications networks has shortened the distance between command headquarters and grass-roots units, and between inland areas and border and coastal areas. Currently the armed forces' networks for data exchange have already linked up units garrisoned in all medium-sized and large cities in the country as well as in border and coastal areas. As a result of the automated exchange and transmission of data, graphics and pictures within the armed forces, military information can now be shared by all military units.[48]

The available open sources consistently forecast continuity in PLA C⁴I modernization. In other words, the PLA will continue to build an infrastructure that is increasingly digitized, automated, encrypted, faster, more secure, and broadband.

Personnel Changes: Noncommissioned Officer Corps

Historically, the ground forces lacked a dedicated noncommissioned officer (NCO) corps. In the 1990s, the PLA began experimenting with the creation of NCOs. According to Blasko, the stated purpose of this move was "to attract higher quality soldiers and to increase the proportion of NCOs to conscripts by making voluntary extensions more attractive."[49] Specifically, the PLA sought to cut the number of conscripts from 82 percent of its total force to less than 65 percent by 2000.[50] Since then, a system of ranks has been developed for these volunteers who remain in service beyond their period of obligatory service. Training courses for NCOs at military academies have been established. However, most NCOs in the system by 1995 were still not in leadership positions, but instead were specialists and technicians.[51] In early 1999, however, the terms of service for conscripts was cut from 3 years (army) and 4 years (PLAN and PLAAF) to 2 years for all services. This placed additional burdens on the NCO corps, which must now shoulder a greater leadership burden in teaching basic soldiering skills and leading recruits through the training cycle.

Equipment

In 1982, Harlan Jencks asserted, "it seems clear that Beijing does not intend to refit the entire PLA with modern weapons and equipment. The majority of the PLA's 100-plus ground force divisions will remain low- to medium-tech forces."[52] Throughout the 1980s and 1990s, Beijing selectively equipped only a portion of the ground forces with new weapons, while leaving the remainder to make do with existing equipment. By contrast, the air force, navy, and strategic rocket forces during this period were clearly singled out for priority in equipment modernization. Given the failures of the defense-industrial base to produce indigenously the necessary advanced systems, these services were even permitted to procure small quantities of platforms from foreign suppliers, in particular the Russians. For the ground forces, however, only limited amounts of foreign weapons and equipment (for example, BMP–3s and helicopters) have been introduced into the forces, and the indigenous Chinese defense industry, despite its many failings, continues to be designated as the source of the majority of modern ground force weapons.[53]

The lack of new equipment has forced the ground forces to modify operations and tactics, especially against a high-tech opponent. In the absence of new systems, the ground forces were instead instructed to "look for ways in which existing equipment can defeat high-technology weapons, while providing advanced weapons to select units."[54] Also, ground force units were told to hide existing inventory with better camouflage, concealment, and deception. Despite these efforts, however, Blasko is correct when he argues that

> the vast majority of existing weapons in the PLA inventory, even when their capabilities are maximized by equipment modification or employment techniques, simply do not have the range to be used in an offensive manner against many modern high technology weapons systems with long-range target acquisition, stand-off, and precision strike capabilities.[55]

In spite of these problems, however, the strategy of gradually equipping the ground forces continues to make sense. There will never be enough budgetary largesse to equip such a large army fully, nor does the leadership desire to elevate even the majority of the ground forces to advanced status. The current military environment, which is focused on littoral warfare, does not justify such a huge expense. Moreover, the bulk of ground forces personnel are not prepared for the introduction of modern equipment, either in terms of education level or comfort with advanced technology. Jiang Zemin directly addressed this point when he said, "we should let qualified personnel wait for the arrival of equipment rather than let equipment wait for qualified personnel to operate it."[56] For the foreseeable future, therefore, the ground forces will modernize at a slow pace, equipping select units with new systems while allowing the bulk of the force to fade into obsolescence.

Training

The ground forces currently train at three levels: individual skills, basic units, and combined arms regiments and divisions. RRUs receive priority in training.[57] The PLA has increased the number of joint and combined arms exercises (by definition large-scale exercises conducted at division or higher levels) since 1990,[58] as well as night operations, opposing forces training, and live fire exercises.[59] Many of these exercises could be described as deliberately "experimental."[60] After a specific unit conducts an exercise, the lessons learned are analyzed, codified, and eventually promulgated.[61]

Changes in conscription have affected training. Until the late 1990s, the ground forces were hampered by the limitations of the conscription. Blasko et al., outline the problem:

> Because of its annual conscription and demobilization cycle (both of which take place in the late autumn) and method of providing basic training at the unit level (division or below during December and the

first months of the calendar year), the PLA is confronted with a situation in which one-quarter to one-third of the troops in its units are always first-year soldiers. As such, small unit leaders must spend large blocks of a training year on basic, individual soldier tasks. Until they master these tasks, soldiers can only partially contribute to and learn from larger collective or unit training. Although officers remain in their basic units for many years, the turbulence resulting from enlisted rotations implies that every time a unit completes it training cycle it does so with a significantly different mix of enlisted personnel. This puts a heavier weight on the officer corps and probably limits the level at which tactical and operation proficiency can be achieved.[62]

When ground forces conscription was reduced to a 2-year commitment in early 1999, this situation became even more serious, as up to one-half of all recruits would be first-year soldiers.

Future Trajectories

The Chinese ground forces have undergone a tumultuous two decades, marked by significant personnel cuts and organizational restructuring. The army also has suffered an important diminution in institutional reputation, thanks to its disastrous performance in Vietnam in 1979 and its brutality in Tiananmen Square in 1989, as well as shrinking institutional equity at the hands of ascendant air, naval, and missile service branches. Despite these upheavals, however, the army appears to have established the parameters for the type of force it would like to become: a smaller, more rapidly deployable, combined arms force equipped with weapons that increase the range from which it can strike the enemy.

To achieve this goal, many of the organizational changes outlined above will need to be continued and even expanded. In particular, the downsizing of the ground forces remains the necessary precondition for modernization since a smaller force frees up budget monies for the essential equipment and training goals of the army. Following the conclusion of a reportedly successful effort from 1996 to reduce the PLA by 500,000 personnel, Jiang Zemin in 1998 asserted that "further troop reduction may be required to ensure that the troops are well-equipped and highly-mobile."[63] Outside observers believe that the PLA, through a mix of genuine cuts, transfers, and needed recategorization of personnel, could cut a surprisingly large number of troops with little tangible impact on PLA capabilities. Blasko opines that "*a reduction of one million* from the 2.2 million-strong ground forces [note: this project was made in 1996, prior to the current round of reductions] conducted over the next 12 years *would have no adverse impact on the PLA's ability to project force* beyond their borders."[64]

Much of this cut could be achieved simply by disaggregating civilian defense employees (*wenzhi ganbu*) from active-duty military personnel. Additional transfers will likely increase the size of the reserves and the People's Armed Police. Augmentation of the PAP would potentially free the PLA from the specter of the internal security mission. As Blasko writes:

> Strengthening the PAP will make intervention by the active duty PLA less necessary, and therefore less likely, in a future domestic crisis (though always an alternative). Both the PAP and PLA will also be able to focus on and train more to perform their respective primary missions, rather than spending undue amounts of time on secondary missions. As the PLA becomes more technically advanced and complex, it will become less suitable for domestic security missions and will require more specific, intensive training to maintain its proficiency in its mission to defend China from external foes.[65]

Similarly, Blasko believes the downsizing of the PLA will have a direct impact upon the reserves:

> Much of the equipment and many of the personnel affected by reductions in the ground forces (who do not go to the PAP) in the next decade can be expected to find their way into the reserves. Eventually, the reserves could outnumber the total of PLA active duty forces, perhaps up to a total of 2 million if the PLA undergoes another 500,000-man reduction. A larger number of reserves than active duty forces would not be unique to the PLA. A larger reserve force also would be able to assist many of the disaster relief and community service missions that the PLA, PAP, and militia are often called to perform.[66]

The future therefore could witness the emergence of a much more variegated force, with sharper definitions of division of labor among mainline, paramilitary, reserve, militia, and civilian defense personnel.

For the mainline units, downsizing also makes possible many other necessary element of future progress. At a fundamental level, the reductions in force will save money that can be spent on other priorities. As the force becomes smaller, for example, it becomes easier to outfit the remaining troops with advanced weapons and equipment. Moreover, the remaining troops will be able to undergo more training using these new weapons. This will undoubtedly be a slow process. If pursued with deliberate commitment, however, the result could be dramatically reformed Chinese ground forces, focused on the missions of the 21st century.

Notes

[1] David Shambaugh, unpublished manuscript.

[2] Acknowledgments for this essay must first begin with a heavy dose of modesty, humility, and proper attribution. The topic of Chinese ground forces is not my area of expertise, and this essay has drawn from the excellent opus of work on the subject. In particular, I must mention the contributions of Dennis J. Blasko, a former ground-pounder who has spent a career tracking the activities of the men in green. The proliferation of footnotes from his works are a testament to his contribution, which has frankly left few if any stones unturned.

[3] Dennis J. Blasko, "PLA Force Structure: A 20-Year Retrospective," in *Seeking Truth from Facts*, ed. James C. Mulvenon and Andrew N.D. Yang (Santa Monica, CA: RAND, 2001).

[4] For the best explication of PMOC, see Harlan W. Jencks, "People's War Under Modern Conditions: Wishful Thinking, National Suicide, or Effective Deterrent?" *China Quarterly* 98 (June 1984), 305–319.

[5] Blasko, "PLA Force Structure: A 20-Year Retrospective."

[6] Ibid.

[7] Ibid.

[8] The precise structure of the group army is discussed in the later organization section of this essay.

[9] Yitzhak Shichor, "Demobilization: The Dialectics of PLA Troop Reductions," *China Quarterly* 146 (June 1996), 336–359.

[10] "'Law of the People's Republic of China on National Defense,' Adopted at the Fifth Session of the Eight National People's Congress on March 14, 1997," *Xinhua Domestic Service*, in *Foreign Broadcast Information Service—China* (henceforth *FBIS–China*), March 14, 1997.

[11] David Finkelstein, "China's National Military Strategy," *The PLA in the Information Age*, ed. James C. Mulvenon and Andrew N.D. Yang (Santa Monica, CA: RAND, 1999).

[12] Dennis J. Blasko, Philip T. Klapakis, and John F. Corbett, Jr., "Training Tomorrow's PLA: A Mixed Bag of Tricks," *China Quarterly* 146 (June 1996), 522.

[13] Dennis J. Blasko, "A New PLA Force Structure," *The PLA in the Information Age*, ed. James C. Mulvenon and Andrew N.D. Yang (Santa Monica, CA: RAND, 1999).

[14] Contrary to popular opinion, the phrase *limited, local war under high-tech conditions* is not a doctrine but a description of the universe of conflict scenarios deemed most likely in the short to medium term by the leadership.

[15] Blasko, Klapakis, and Corbett, 489.

[16] Shichor.

[17] Ibid., 346.

[18] Information Office of the State Council of the People's Republic of China, *China's National Defense*, July 1998.

[19] These specific numbers are derived by multiplying white paper percentages by figures of 2.2 million, 265,000, and 470,000, found in International Institute for Strategic Studies, *The Military Balance, 1996/97* (London: Oxford University Press, 1996), 179–181.

[20] Blasko, "A New PLA Force Structure."

[21] Ibid.

[22] Dennis J. Blasko, "PLA Ground Forces: Moving towards a Smaller, More Rapidly Deployable, Modern Combined Arms Force," *The PLA as Organization*, ed. James C. Mulvenon and Andrew N.D. Yang (Santa Monica, CA: RAND, 2002).

[23] Blasko, "PLA Ground Forces."

[24] The best study of the PAP is Murray Scot Tanner, "The Institutional Lessons of Disaster: Reorganizing the People's Armed Police after Tiananmen," in *The PLA as Organization*.

[25] International Institute for Strategic Studies, *The Military Balance, 1997/98*, 179; and Liu Hsiao-hua, "Armed Police Force: China's 1 Million Special Armed Troops."

[26] Blasko, "A New PLA Force Structure."

[27] Blasko, "PLA Ground Forces."

[28] Liu Hsiao-hua, "Jiang Zemin Convenes Enlarged Meeting of Central Military Commission."

[29] International Institute for Strategic Studies, *The Military Balance, 1996/97*, 186.

[30] Tai Ming Cheung, "Reforming the Dragon's Tail: Chinese Military Logistics in the Era of High-Technology Warfare and Market Economics," in *China's Military Faces the Future*, ed. James R. Lilley and David Shambaugh (Armonk, NY: M.E. Sharpe, 1999), 236.

[31] Blasko, Klapakis, and Corbett, 517.

[32] Blasko, "PLA Force Structure: A 20-Year Retrospective."

[33] U.S. DOD Report to Congress Pursuant to FY00 National Defense Authorization Act, June 2000.

[34] Andrew N.D. Yang and Milton Wen-Chung Liao, "PLA Rapid Reaction Force: Concept, Training and Preliminary Assessment," in *The PLA in the Information Age*.

[35] Blasko, "PLA Ground Forces."

[36] Ibid.

[37] U.S. DOD Report to Congress.

[38] Li Xuanqing (*Jiefangjun Bao*) and Ma Xiaochun (*Xinhua*), "Armed Forces Communications Become Multidimensional," *Xinhua, FBIS–China*, July 16, 1997.

[39] Liu Dongsheng, "Telecommunications: Greater Sensitivity Achieved—Second of Series of Reports on Accomplishments of Economic Construction and Defense Modernization," *Jiefangjun Bao*, September 8, 1997, 5, in *FBIS–China*, October 14, 1997.

[40] See Tang Shuhai, "All-Army Public Data Exchange Network Takes Initial Shape," *Jiefangjun Bao*, September 18, 1995, in *FBIS–China*.

[41] Cheng Gang and Li Xuanqing, "Military Telecommunications Building Advances Toward Modernization With Giant Strides," *Jiefangjun Bao*, July 17, 1997, in *FBIS–China*.

[42] Tang Shuhai, "All-Army Public Data Exchange Network Takes Initial Shape."

[43] Ibid.

[44] "PLA Helps With Fiber-Optic Cable Production," *Xinhua*, November 13, 1995, in *FBIS–China*, November 13, 1995.

[45] Luo Yuwen, "PLA Stresses Military-Civilian Unity," *Xinhua Domestic Service*, March 5, 1999.

[46] "Domestic Fiber-Optic Cable Maker Unveils New Civilian, Military Products," October 6, 1997, in *FBIS–China*, October 6, 1997.

[47] Cheng Gang and Li Xuanqing, "Giant Strides."

[48] Li Xuanqing and Ma Xiaochun, "Armed Forces' Communications Become 'Multidimensional,'" *Xinhua Domestic Service*, July 16, 1997.

[49] Blasko, "PLA Force Structure: 20-Year Retrospective."

[50] "Army Seeks Mobility in Force Cuts," *Jane's Defense Weekly*, December 16, 1998, 24.

[51] Blasko, Klapakis, and Corbett, 494.

[52] Harlan W. Jencks, *From Muskets to Missiles: Politics and Professionalism in the Chinese Army 1945–1981* (Boulder, CO: Westview Press, 1982), 47–48.

[53] Blasko, "A New PLA Force Structure."

[54] Blasko, Klapakis, and Corbett, 491.

[55] Blasko, "A New PLA Force Structure."

[56] Kuan Cha-chia, "Military Authorities Define Reform Plan; Military Academies to Be Reduced by 30 Percent," *Kuang chiao ching*, no. 306, March 16, 1998, 8–9, in *FBIS–China*, March 25, 1998.

[57] Blasko, Klapakis, and Corbett, 517.

[58] Ibid., 499.

[59] Ibid., 491.

[60] Ibid., 490.

[61] Ibid.

[62] Ibid., 493.

[63] Liu Hsiao-hua, "Jiang Zemin Convenes Enlarged Meeting of Central Military Commission, Policy of Fewer but Better Troops Aims at Strengthening Reserve Service Units," *Kuang chiao ching*, no. 308, May 16, 1998, 50–53, in *FBIS–China*, June 10, 1998.

[64] Blasko, "A New PLA Force Structure."

[65] Ibid.

[66] Ibid.

Chapter 7

The PLA Navy and "Active Defense"

Bernard D. Cole

This chapter addresses Beijing's view of the People's Liberation Army Navy (PLAN), focusing on Chinese concepts of how the navy may be employed. These concepts are active defense, offshore, the use of island chains as strategic delineators, and blue water navy as a force describer. The PLAN ability to fulfill the missions implied by these terms is then evaluated.

China is obviously expanding and modernizing its naval capabilities. This is unsurprising in terms of classic maritime strategy, given the nation's offshore territorial disputes, concentration of economic growth in its coastal regions, and increasing dependence on extended sea lines of communication (SLOCs).

Chinese Maritime Strategy

PLAN officers have studied classic maritime strategists since the 1950s, including Alfred Thayer Mahan, but current Chinese maritime strategy is usually credited directly or indirectly to General Liu Huaqing, PLAN head from 1982 to 1987 and Central Military Commission vice chairman from 1988 to 1997. Most notably, he called for expanding the navy's operations from coastal defense to offshore active defense.

Liu reportedly expressed this concept in terms of a three-stage naval development process, applied to two strategic maritime areas of vital concern to the nation. The *first island chain* encompasses the first of these, usually described as a line through the Kurile Islands, Japan and the Ryukyu Islands, Taiwan, the Philippines, and Indonesia (Borneo to Natuna Besar).[1]

No national security goal is more important to China than the reunification of Taiwan, however, and a more reasonable definition of the first island chain would extend it well east of that island, perhaps to a point 200 nautical miles (nm) from the mainland.[2] This first island chain area encompasses the Yellow Sea, facing Korea and Japan; the western East China Sea; and the South China Sea, extending deep into Southeast Asia. It addresses many of China's maritime national interests: the concentration of economic investment along the coast, offshore territorial claims, oceanic resources, and coastal defense. It is ambitious in scope, extending from approximately 200 to 700 nm from the mainland, to include Taiwan and the South China Sea land features claimed by Beijing as sovereign territory.

The *second island chain* bounds Liu's second strategic maritime area: a north-south line from the Kuriles through Japan, the Bonins, the Marianas, the Carolines, and Indonesia. This is a much more ambitious goal than that implied by the first island chain, since it encompasses maritime areas out to approximately 1,800 nm from China's coast, including most of the East China Sea and East Asian SLOCs.

The third stage of Liu's putative maritime strategy poses the PLAN as a global force built around aircraft carriers, deployed by the middle of the 21st century. This goal would imply a PLAN many times larger and more air-capable than China's current force. Alternately, however, global naval force might be deployed in a fleet of ballistic missile submarines (FBMs) capable of launching intercontinental ballistic missiles (ICBMs) and long-range land-attack cruise missiles.

China currently has just one FBM, the *Xia*, which may not be operable. Its successor class, the Type-094, is probably under design with Russian assistance, but its completion date and class size are not known. The eventual size of the China FBM force will be determined in large part by Beijing's perception of how many ICBMs have to be deployed to form an effective nuclear deterrent against possible enemies, including the United States.[3]

Beijing's current naval modernization is almost always discussed in the context of Liu's theory. But what if Liu Huaqing's maritime strategy is not operative? What if "China's Mahan" is more like "China's Tirpitz," theorizing more for the purpose of domestic and service politics than for future fleet operations?[4] We return to this question below, along with the significance of Taiwan as the target for Beijing's maritime strategy: Would the island's reunification be the end or the beginning of Chinese naval expansion?[5]

Active Defense

Liu also offered doctrinal direction, proposing:

- stubborn defense near the shore
- mobile warfare
- surprise guerrilla-like attacks at sea.[6]

This paradigm appears to have been taken directly from Mao Zedong's writings, which may well indicate Liu was most concerned with convincing a domestic audience—perhaps the Chinese Communist Party and PLA leadership—of the need for a maritime strategy.

In fact, Mao Zedong's strictures seem to influence current PLAN operational thinking. *Active defense*, for instance, is a concept Mao discussed in the mid-1930s, when his army was fighting a superior enemy in relatively unconstrained geography. At the level of operational art, Mao described the advantages of operating on interior lines, which allowed him "to choose favorable terrain [and] force the [enemy] to fight on our terms." Chinese forces must "pick out the enemy's weaker units for attack," he argued, and "always concentrate a big force to strike at one part of the enemy forces." He insisted on a "war of movement" to achieve victory on the battlefield.[7]

Mao emphasized mobility, surprise, dispersion, flexibility, concentration, "the alert shifting of forces," and retaining the initiative: "the attack must be made on [our] initiative. . . . it is only by attack that we can [win]." He did not view "defense" as a passive concept.[8] Mao's principles still appeal to PLAN strategists: the Chinese navy holds the maritime equivalent of "interior lines" with respect to naval conflict in East Asia, would almost certainly face superior maritime and air forces in relatively unconstrained geography, and would have to depend on mobility, initiative, and surprise to achieve its objectives.

Offshore

The meaning of *offshore* is less obvious. First, Alexander Huang has done the most complete job of analyzing the concept, noting the distances that might be involved. These range from strictly coastal operations within 100 nm of the shoreline, to the 700 nm required to patrol the South China Sea's Spratly Islands.[9] PLA officers and civilian commentators also have discussed the distances involved if the PLAN is no longer constrained by old-fashioned concepts of coastal defense, and their estimates fall within the band of ranges discussed by Huang.

Second, the concept of offshore may be linked to the ranges of PLA weapons systems. China's longest-range, shore-based systems include three surface-to-surface missiles: the HY–2, with a 52-nm range; the HY–4, with an 84-nm range; and possibly the C–601, which has a 54.5-nm range.[10] Increased overwater experience and expertise for the People's Liberation Army Naval Air Force (PLANAF) and the People's Liberation Army Air Force is another relevant factor. The newest Chinese aircraft, the Su-27 and Su-30, have combat radii of 800 and 1,600 nm, respectively, although these allow very little time "on station."[11] The PLANAF B–6 bombers have a combat radius of 1,700 nm. FBMs, of course, imply global coverage.

Third, offshore may be defined by Beijing's insular territorial claims. The most distant of these is the Spratly Island group in the southern South China Sea, about 700 nm from the PLAN South Sea Fleet bases on Hainan Island.

Fourth, possible opponents also may bound China's naval ambitions. South Korea is just across the Bohai, Japan is almost as close, and Taiwan is within 100 nm; these fall within the first island chain. India and the United States pose geographic issues of a different magnitude since China does not have the traditional naval or air capability to threaten them credibly, except with missiles, although the American bases in Japan and South Korea fall within the first island chain. However, Beijing might consider the continental United States to be fair game in an all-out maritime campaign, employing information warfare, special operations forces, and biological-chemical attacks.

To sum up, *offshore* may be defined by:

- various Chinese strategists
- PLA capabilities
- territorial claims
- potential maritime opponents
- or some combination of these factors.

None of these lead to a conclusive definition of offshore; it is likely that a doctrinal definition of offshore is not tied to specific distances but is derived from the operational objective at hand. For instance, the current PLAN commander, Admiral Shi Yunsheng, has been quoted as describing offshore as "not a concept of distance, denoting 'how far it is from the coast,' but covers a vast maritime space within the second island chain of the Pacific ocean, including Taiwan."[12]

Blue Water

Naval operations may be framed in terms of maritime geography, usually under four categories:

- riverine
- brown water
- green water
- blue water.

These categories designate operations ranging from inland waters to global deployments by large, relatively self-sufficient fleets. The latter three are not neatly, consistently delineated areas, but in China's case, *brown water* may be defined as reaching from the coast to about 200 nm to seaward. *Green water* refers to the ocean areas from the seaward end of brown water to a point, marked by the Caroline and other islands, about 1,800 nm from the coast. *Blue water* refers to the remaining global ocean areas.

Brown water is the most important maritime arena for China, as it is for any nation, since it includes coastal traffic, territorial waters, the contiguous zone, and the claimed exclusive economic zone.[13] In these areas occur the great majority of a nation's maritime police, customs, environmental, and economic concerns. China's territorial claims heighten the importance of its brown water as a naval arena; Taiwan is the most important of these, of course, but maritime disputes also exist with Korea, Japan, and most of the Southeast Asian nations.

Beijing's most important maritime strategic concern in the green water arena is probably homeland defense against sea-based, long-range missiles. Other concerns include regional sea lines of communication, and economic resources both in the continental shelf area and even further afield, especially fisheries.

As far as the blue water realm is concerned, the PLAN is already active in terms of the naval mission of *presence*—that is, of sending naval units on long voyages to extend diplomatic reach and spread the nation's influence. Another blue water capability is represented in China's sea-based ICBM force, limited though it is.

Force Structure

The PLAN, like all the world's significant navies, may be viewed as composed of three forces: surface, aviation, and subsurface. China's maritime force is augmented by one of the world's largest merchant marines, an organization that is the world's largest if coastal and riverine craft are included in the count.[14]

The PLAN surface force is modernizing at a measured pace, in line with overall naval improvements. The force is led by two *Sovremenny*-class guided-missile destroyers purchased from Russia. These ships were laid down by the Soviet Union approximately 15 years ago and lay idle until completed for China in 1999 and 2000. Hence, they may suffer long-term lack of hull maintenance; this class, equipped with steam-driven turbines, is also reported typically to suffer significant engineering problems.

The ship's single meaningful strength is the *Moskit* (SS–N–22 Sunburn, in North Atlantic Treaty Organization parlance) antisurface ship cruise missile with which they are armed. Eight of these large, supersonic missiles are carried on board. Because of their speed, ability to fly close to the ocean's surface, and especially the terminal flight maneuvers they are capable of executing, the *Moskits* are difficult weapons to counter. The *Sovremenny* also is armed with two twin-100 millimeter gun mounts, antisubmarine torpedo tubes and mortars, four rapid-fire gatling gun weapons for short-range air defense, a relatively short-range (25-kilometer) antiaircraft missile system, and supporting sensor and fire-control systems. The ships also are capable of embarking helicopters. China has apparently agreed to purchase two additional *Sovremennys* from Russia, but the status of this agreement is in question. The most significant aspect of this new acquisition is that the ships would be built from the keel up, which would give China the opportunity to modernize and improve their capabilities.

The PLAN also deploys one *Luhai*-class and two *Luhu*-class guided-missile destroyers, all built in China. The *Luhai* is much larger than the *Luhus*, displacing 6,600 to their 4,800 tons, but all three are armed with similar sensor and weapons suites. These include antisurface ship, subsonic cruise missiles, a single twin-100 millimeter gun mount, antisubmarine torpedo tubes and mortars, eight rapid-fire gatling guns, and the same 25-kilometer-capable antiaircraft missile system. They also have flight decks and hangars for embarking helicopters. These three ships are all powered by gas turbine engines, U.S.-built units in the two *Luhus* and Ukranian-built engines in the *Luhai*. Additional *Luhais* are under construction in Dalian-area shipyards.

The only other modern surface ship in the PLAN inventory is the *Jiangwei*-class frigate, of which eight have been deployed, with additional units under construction. Displacing just 2,100 tons, these ships are equipped with the same antisurface ship cruise missiles short-range antiaircraft missile system and gun mount as the *Luhus*; have antisubmarine mortars and four gatling guns; and are able to embark a single helicopter. They are powered by German-designed diesel engines.

The other surface ships in the PLAN are essentially of 1950s vintage: some of the 17 *Luda*-class guided-missile destroyers have been modernized and should not be discounted because of their capable antisurface ship cruise missile systems. The 21 *Jianghu*-class frigates are not modern combatants, lacking centralized control stations, but they are equipped with cruise missiles, albeit much older models, and cannot be completely discounted. China still deploys a large number of small combatants, missile and torpedo-armed patrol boats, as well as minesweepers and fleet support ships.

The PLANAF flies older models and has far fewer aircraft than does China's air force. The most modern aircraft are the navy's 28 helicopters, primarily French- and Russian-designed craft that are very capable. The PLANAF also flies fighter, attack, and surveillance aircraft as part of its approximately 500-unit strength.

The most formidable PLAN force is its submarine arm, led by four *Kilo*-class, conventionally powered attack submarines purchased from Russia. The *Kilo* is a circa 1980 design but remains a very capable ship, armed with wire-guided torpedoes. The Chinese are also building the *Ming*- and *Song*-class conventionally powered classes of submarine, with 17 to 20 of the former and 3 of the latter currently deployed. These are not as capable as the *Kilos*—the *Ming* is an improved version of the circa 1950s Soviet-designed *Romeo*-class boat—but add measurably to the PLAN capability as a naval fighting force. China's inventory of nuclear-powered submarines, composed of the one fleet ballistic missile boat and five attack boats, is obsolete, and the PLAN is working to replace them, with Russian assistance, with the new Type-093 attack and Type-094 ballistic missile boats.

The PLAN still maintains an unknown number of the old *Romeo*-class submarines, probably 35 to 40. These too are obsolete, but if the navy has sufficient personnel to man them, they will present a threat at sea to any opposing fleet.

In sum, the PLAN is the largest navy in East Asia—and one of the largest in the world. It includes a wide variety of surface, aviation, and subsurface units, none of them state of the art in comparison to many U.S. weapons systems. Almost all of them are capable, however, and the PLAN is a force to be reckoned with, especially in any scenario in which the United States is not directly involved.

Capabilities

The PLAN will have to rely on speed, mobility, flexibility, and surprise/preemption in a contest with a strong opponent, especially the United States. The goal will be to deploy enough naval strength to tip the balance in a limited, regional scenario.

This raises the issue of the revolution in military affairs, widely written about by PLA authors.[15] Effectively managing information flow and the electronic spectrum will be key to PLAN operations. This does not mean information warfare as such, but does refer to a historical constant in naval warfare: *situational awareness*—that is, knowing the location of one's own and one's opposing forces.[16] Achieving full situational awareness requires the "effective fusion of reconnaissance, surveillance, and intelligence information."[17] The PLAN is not capable of accomplishing this.

Sea denial is a particularly attractive option for even a small naval power in littoral waters, if it has access to mines, missiles, small surface ships and submarines, and shore-based aircraft—as the PLAN does. An effective submarine force is key.[18] The most practicable way for China to pursue a sea-denial strategy is to employ the PLAN against specific naval threats, integral to a PLA campaign plan with land-, air-, and space-based assets. This strategy would have to be strictly limited in its objectives and fully acknowledge potential opposing forces and possible negative outcomes of both success and failure—including political, economic, social, and even environmental consequences.

China has more than 50 active, medium sized or larger surface warships, but only very few of these possess modern capabilities. The two *Sovremenny*-, one *Luhai*-, and two *Luhu*-class guided-missile destroyers and the eight *Jiangwei*-class frigates are the most capable of China's ships because of their potent antisurface-ship cruise-missile batteries. Yet not a single one of these ships is armed with a capable area air-defense missile system, and their antisubmarine systems are almost as limited. Furthermore, PLAN ships might be viewed as relatively expendable in a Taiwan scenario since the nearby mainland provides ample air and missile power.

Conclusion

Is China's maritime doctrine indeed based on active offshore defense embodied in a blue water navy? Dramatic naval expansion toward a PLAN with global reach is doubtful, given current modernization priorities and the low level of threats to China's national security.

Beijing is being very selective in pursuing even a restricted slice of sea power. For instance, it does not have and is not building a significant amphibious assault capability, either in the PLAN or in its merchant fleet.[19] China also is not moving rapidly to acquire the systems and conduct the training in aerial refueling crucial to extending airpower to seaward. The PLAN is a large, growing, modernizing force, but one that will have to isolate its objectives and narrow the ocean area in which it wishes to prevail.

Is the three-stage navy-building plan attributed to Liu Huaqing moving toward the development of an expansionist Chinese naval strategy? PLAN modernization during the past decade has been steady but quite slow; obviously, China is making no attempt to meet Liu's strategic deadlines. Hence, the effect of Liu's tenure is probably as much domestic as international. He should be considered more as an effective bureaucrat than an enduring maritime strategist.

Taiwan has been the predominant issue during the past 15 years of PLAN modernization. Historic instances of Chinese naval building would indicate that the PLA will continue as an army-dominant military, with just enough naval strength maintained for coastal defense—and the first island chain is a convenient way to describe *coastal* in this construct—and enough blue water capability to continue executing the naval mission of presence. Some form of seaborne nuclear deterrence is also likely, although the size of this force will depend on the progress of the Type-094 currently in the design/early construction stage.

The PLAN is positioned to play an increasing role in China's national security process, but one that does not require a blue water navy. Doctrinal development to support active, offshore defense appears to be occurring, evidenced in PLAN single-ship, multi-unit, and fleet-level exercises.[20] China wants a PLAN able to oppose successfully any East Asian force that stands in the way of achieving China's objectives in the region.[21] The PLAN almost certainly intends concentrating its operational capabilities in waters within a couple of hundred miles of its coast: it is not in China's interest to expand the geographic scope of a naval contest.

Notes

[1] See Alexander Huang, "The Chinese Navy's Offshore Active Defense Strategy: Conceptualization and Implications," *Naval War College Review* 47, no. 3 (Summer 1994), 16ff, for a good discussion of the *first* and *second island chains.*

[2] One nautical mile equals approximately 1.2 statute miles.

[3] Alistair Iain Johnston, "Prospects for Chinese Nuclear Force Modernization: Limited Deterrence versus Multilateral Arms Control," *The China Quarterly* (June 1996), 548–576. This article remains key to gaining an understanding of Chinese thinking about nuclear deterrence.

[4] See, for instance, Jeffrey Goldberg, "China's Mahan," United States Naval Institute *Proceedings* 122, no. 3 (March 1996), 44–47. Cynthia A. Watson suggested this question.

[5] One might argue that historically Chinese governments, whether the Song or the Ming, have deployed large navies to achieve relatively limited goals, and once those have been achieved, the navy has been again relegated to secondary status.

[6] Discussed in Alexander Huang, "Chinese Maritime Modernization and Its Security Implications: The Deng Xiaoping Era and Beyond" (Ph.D. diss., The George Washington University, 1994), 225ff.

[7] See Mao Zedong, *On the Protracted War* (Beijing: Foreign Languages Press, 1954), 83, 88, 101; Mao Zedong, *On Guerrilla Warfare*, 2ᵈ ed., trans. Samuel B. Griffith (Baltimore: Nautical and Aviation

Publishing, 1992), 81, 119; Mao Zedong, *Selected Military Writings of Mao Zedong* (Beijing: Foreign Languages Press, 1967), 97, 105, 160, 233.

[8] Paul H.B. Godwin, "China's Defense Modernization: Aspirations and Capabilities," paper prepared for the Asia-Pacific Symposium, *Asian Perspectives on the Challenges of China*, at the National Defense University, Washington, DC, March 7–8, 2000.

[9] Huang, Ph.D. diss., table 5–1, 231, lists distances from "coastal" and "inshore," to "EEZ [exclusive economic zone] + Continental shelf," which would equate to 350 nm, out to "600+ nm."

[10] Norman Friedman, ed., *The Naval Institute Guide to World Naval Weapons Systems, 1997–1998* (Annapolis, MD: Naval Institute Press, 1998), 321. *C–601* designates a system designed for foreign sales.

[11] "If War Starts in the Taiwan Seas, Where Will the U.S. Carriers Assemble?" accessed at <http://military.china.com/zh_cn/critical3/27/20010823/10087071.html>, states that the Su–27 "would be able to extend the Chinese front lines 900 km out to sea."

[12] "Jiang made the Final Decision on Adopting Offshore Defense Strategy," *Hung Fang Jih Pao*, August 24, 2001, in *Foreign Broadcast Information Service–China (henceforth FBIS–China)*.

[13] The United Nations Convention on the Law of the Sea defines four areas of national concern: a nation's *sovereign waters* is the maritime area from a nation's coastline to a point 12 nm to seaward; the *contiguous zone* extends to a point 24 nm from a nation's coastline; the *exclusive economic zone* out to 200 nm, and a nation's *continental shelf* may reach to a maximum distance of 350 nm from its coastline.

[14] The best work in English on China's merchant marine remains Wayne S. Hugar, "The Sea Dragon Network: Implications of the International Expansion of China's Maritime Shipping Industry," (Master's thesis, Naval Postgraduate School, 1998).

[15] See Michael Pillsbury, *Chinese Views of Future Warfare* (Washington, DC: National Defense University Press, 1997), and *China Debates the Future Security Environment* (Washington, DC: National Defense University Press, 2000), for a unique and valuable sampling of these writings. A third volume is forthcoming.

[16] The March 1996 arrival of two U.S. aircraft carrier battle groups, which reportedly became known to China through the Cable News Network, showed severe PLA limitations in this vital area.

[17] Wayne P. Hughes, Jr., *Fleet Tactics: Theory and Practice* (Annapolis, MD: Naval Institute Press, 1986), 44.

[18] Ibid., 138.

[19] This may be wise on Beijing's part, since only one successful amphibious landing under active opposition has occurred since 1950—the British assault on the Falklands.

[20] See Bernard D. Cole, *The Great Wall at Sea: China's Navy Enters the 21st Century* (Annapolis: Naval Institute Press, 2001), chapter 7.

[21] China's leaders might decide to engage in naval warfare despite likely third-party intervention if they believe that they have been backed into a corner—that their political position as national leaders is so threatened by a national security situation that likely war with the United States would be a justified risk. Any such belief would be intensified by the extremely defensive view—approaching paranoia—so often apparent in China's press. See, for instance, Yi Jun, Hua Shan, and Xu Shujun, "Behind the U.S.-South Korea 'RS012001' Exercise," *Jiefangjun Bao*, April 30, 2001, 12, in *FBIS–China*, for the claim that "the United States is seeking to restore the arc of blockade against socialist countries in Asia in the 1950s."

Chapter 8

PLA Air Force Equipment Trends

Richard D. Fisher, Jr.

T he People's Liberation Army Air Force (PLAAF) is pursuing its first large-scale overall modernization to enable the conduct of all-weather offensive and defensive operations in a modern high-technology environment. This endeavor is consistent with the general doctrinal goal to build a People's Liberation Army (PLA) capable of waging "local war under high-tech conditions." Expansion of all-weather offensive capabilities, a relatively recent and ominous trend in the PLAAF, could include offensive naval strike missions for the PLAAF and greater consideration of using airborne forces in a strategic strike capacity.

Perhaps the most important driver of current trends in PLAAF equipment modernization is the evolution of doctrine that stresses high-tech, multirole platforms capable of offensive and defensive operations. This process began to gather steam under the leadership of former PLAAF commander Wang Hai.[1] Relatively recent statements by current PLAAF Commander Liu Shunyao and even President Jiang Zemin indicate that the PLAAF is seeking a greater offensive capability.[2]

Critical to the PLAAF goal of being able to implement offensive operations within a joint warfare environment, as is the case with all PLA services, is access to modern information resources. For the PLAAF and missile services, an important information source critical for targeting will be a constellation of new imaging and radar satellites. Recent reports indicate that the PLA may be planning to field 16 new reconnaissance (8 imaging and 8 radar) satellites.[3] The new radar satellites, which are not inhibited by cloud cover, appear to feature synthetic aperture radars marketed by Russian NPO Machinostroyenia[4] that can detect objects less than one meter in length.[5] The planned constellation would allow for four daily revisits by each satellite type.

There is also a sense that the PLAAF is being built up to take a leading role in strategic offensive operations at a time when the PLA is placing great stress on building the capacity for joint operations. As You Ji has observed, "Hardware modernization will bridge the gap between the doctrinal design and application."[6] However, training and upgrading training technology are also critical. As such, PLAAF equipment modernization is showing the following trends:

- a new interest in modern training aircraft and simulators
- great emphasis on obtaining large numbers of multirole combat aircraft
- acquisition of new types of antiair and ground attack munitions
- greater emphasis on support platforms: tankers, electronic warfare (EW), and electronic intelligence (ELINT)
- indications of an interest in increasing air transport assets
- indications that airborne troops are to be increased and given strategic offensive missions
- a buildup in air defense forces to provide greater support for offensive operations.

Training Systems

The PLAAF will need to invest far more in training to transform itself into a modern air force capable of a range of offensive and defensive missions. The force currently relies on a very large fleet of obsolete training aircraft, but this situation could change if the PLA decides to spend money. A modest effort to incorporate modern simulators appears to be gaining momentum. In addition, the PLA may be building its own air combat maneuvering instrumentation (ACMI) system.

Training aircraft. The current training fleet comprises about 340 jet trainers (40 Su-27UBKs, 50 JJ–7s, 150 JJ–6s, and 100 JJ–5s) and 1,000 CJ–5/CJ–6 piston engine primary trainers.[7] While this fleet may be adequate to teach basic maneuvering and air combat skills, it is insufficient to teach combined air and ground attack maneuvers in a joint service environment. Even the Su-27UBKs lack the modern cockpit, datalink, and ground attack technologies associated with modern air combat. Throughout the 1990s, the Hongdu Company tried to sell the PLAAF its K–8 primary jet-powered trainer, which has the potential to be equipped with modern cockpit and communication systems. However, the PLAAF has been reluctant to purchase the K–8 because the trainer was inappropriate for PLAAF needs, and it relies on foreign engines.

At the September 2001 Beijing Airshow, Hongdu revealed a model of its L–15 concept trainer. Similar in size and shape to the Yak-130 or the Japanese T–4, it is a twin-turbofan dedicated trainer that boasts supersonic speed, modern cockpit systems, and the ability to train in counterair and ground attack missions.[8] The L–15 would seem to be an ideal modern trainer to allow PLAAF pilots to transition to the Su-30 MKK (*Mnogafunk-tuanli Kommertsial Kitayski,* or Multifunctional Commercial for China) as well as the J–10. However, like the K–8, the L–15's future depends on whether it has the PLAAF's blessing and whether funding is available.[9]

Competition for the L–15 could come from Guizhou's FTC–2000 trainer, revealed in model form at the November 2000 Zhuhai Airshow. The FTC–2000 is based on the JJ–7 but has side intakes and a larger front fuse-lage able to house modern radar and a refueling probe. It boasts a supersonic speed and likely will have an advanced cockpit to facilitate practice of air-to-air and ground attack missions. Should the PLAAF prefer a trainer that can utilize an existing logistics train and possibly require a shorter development period, the FTC–2000 may be a better candidate than the L–15.

Simulators. The PLAAF appears to have increased its previously low level of investment in advanced simulators. The speed with which the PLAAF integrates simulators into actual units will suggest the priority that it places on building a modern force. For multirole combat, aircraft simu-lators are essential for training and mission rehearsal.

At the 1998 Zhuhai Airshow, a promotional video was played in which an undetermined number of large domed air-combat simulators was visible. Other sources note that Sukhoi has sold one or two Su-27 simula-tors to the PLAAF. Also, various Chinese Web sites show pictures of new simulators that appear intended for new Su-30MKKs and of PLAAF pilots making use of personal computer (PC)-based simulators. The 2000 Zhuhai show featured a new PC-based virtual-reality simulator by the Beijing Uni-versity of Aeronautics and Astronautics, which it claimed was being used by J–8 fighter units. The same show also revealed new full-motion simulators, but they were configured for arcade rides, and their manufacturers seemed disappointed at the lack of PLAAF orders.

Another potentially important training aid revealed at the 2000 Zhuhai show was the FC–03 flight data recording and processing system of the China Jinan Aviation Central Factory. Intended as a tool to diagnose crashes, it can also record and depict the progress of a flight in terms of the instrument panel or in a 3–D picture of the track of the flight.[10] An un-known number of systems has been installed in J–7, J–8, and JH–7 aircraft.

While it is not clear whether the data can also be transmitted and presented in real time, which is the case in modern ACMI systems, it can at least be viewed and assessed after a flight. The PLAAF has long sought a modern air ACMI and reportedly tried to purchase one from Israel. If the flight paths of multiple aircraft could be collated, then the PLAAF could use the FC–03 as a cheap ACMI.

Combat Aircraft

A clear shift is under way in the PLAAF toward multirole combat platforms and more support platforms. Multirole combat aircraft are intended to fulfill doctrinal requirements for more offensive-capable aircraft to complement a buildup in ballistic and cruise missile forces. In some respects, a buildup of attack-capable aircraft is more important since aircraft, not missiles, carry the most ordnance to the target. Aircraft also can fly multiple sorties, whereas missiles cannot.

Older platforms such as the Chengdu Aircraft Factory J–6 (MiG–19) and Chengdu J–7II/III/E (MiG–21C+) copied Soviet designs, and the indigenous twin-engine Shenyang Aircraft Factory J–8I and early J–8II fighter interceptors are being succeeded by such new or modified multirole aircraft as the Russian Sukhoi Su–30MKK fighter bomber, the Chengdu J–10 multirole fighter, the J–8IIC multirole fighter, and the Xian Aircraft Corporation JH–7. It is possible that even the highly capable Su–27SK is being deemphasized in favor of multirole platforms. It is not yet clear that the PLAAF will retire all of its over 1,000 J–6s or its hundreds of J–7s. But as an elite force within the PLAAF, the number of modern multirole fighters can be expected to increase substantially.

If current reporting on purchase or production numbers holds true, 300 to 400 new or modified multirole combat aircraft could enter the PLAAF inventory by about 2005.[11] Such a number of attack-capable combat aircraft would pose a formidable threat to a Taiwan Air Force, especially one that may suffer substantial attrition from initial PLA missile and special forces attack. The PLAAF could also pose a substantial threat to U.S. air forces in the region, on Okinawa, or to a sole carrier assigned to the 7th Fleet.

After 2005, further increases can be expected, as the PLAAF may purchase more Su–30MKKs or switch the Shenyang Su–27 coproduction line to Su–30s, and J–10 production may ramp up. By 2010, it is also possible that a new indigenous fighter, the J–12 or XXJ, may appear. To be sure, such estimates about future numbers are only that and are made with the assumption that the PLAAF continues to receive the finances to purchase such expensive aircraft, their related munitions, and the necessary training and logistical support.

Multirole Combat Aircraft Programs

Sukhoi Su-30MKK. The purchase of the Sukhoi Su-30MKK marks perhaps the single most important increase in PLAAF combat capability since PLAAF modernization began in earnest in the 1990s. When outfitted with its new Phazotron Zhuk M–E radar, the Su-30MKK will be the most potent multirole fighter in the PLAAF or, for that matter, in the Taiwan Strait. In the Su-30MKK, the PLAAF will have a platform that will be better equipped for air superiority missions than its Su-27SK fighters. But more important, the Su-30MKK will be the first PLAAF combat aircraft able to deliver precision guided bombs and missiles, plus antiradar and antiship missiles, in all weather conditions.

A development of the Su-27UBK twin-seat trainer, the Sukhoi Su-30MK twin-seat strike fighter debuted in 1993.[12] The Su-30MK contains two sets of weapon and flight controls that allow either crewmember to fly or guide weapons, though the rear position is designed for a weapons systems officer. Both cockpits are dominated by two large multifunction displays, and the pilot can also utilize a helmet-mounted sight.

This type became the basis for an Indian purchase of 40 Su-30K/MK/MKI fighters in 1996. The Su-30MKK prototype first flew on March 9, 1999. Through 1999 and 2000, Russian data sources indicated that the PLAAF Su-30s would differ from the Su-30MKIs being ordered by India in several respects. First, the PLAAF fighters would not be as sophisticated as their Indian counterparts, lacking such super-maneuverable additions as thrust-vectored engines and forward canards. In addition, the PLAAF fighters would incorporate neither the advanced phased-array radar that Russia was developing nor the Western avionics that the Indians were requesting.

The initial 20 Su-30MKKs to be delivered will have the NIIP N001VE pulse-Doppler radar with an 80- to 100-kilometer (km) range that can track up to 10 targets.[13] However, PLA Su-30MKKs will then be equipped with the much-improved Phazotron Zhuk–M–S.[14] The Zhuk–M–S has a 150-km range in the air-to-air mode and can track 20 targets while attacking up to 4. But its real improvement is in the air-to-ground mode, in which it can detect a destroyer at 300 km, a railway bridge at 150 km, and a group of moving tanks at 25 km.[15] The Su-30MKK already has an integral infrared scan

Table 8–1. **Estimates for Known PLAAF Multirole Combat Aircraft**

	2002	2005	2010–2020
Sukhoi Su-30MKK	38	80+	200
Chengdu J–10	6	30	500
Xian JH–7	15	40	200
Shenyang J–8IIC/H		50–70	100
Sukhoi Su-27/ J–11	80–90	158	100
XXJ or J–12			50
Estimated Totals	139–149	358–378	1,150

Notes: 2002 and 2005 Su-30MKK, J–10, and Su-27/J–11 figures based on published estimates; J–8IIC/H numbers estimated based on number of Russian radars to be purchased. Post-2005 numbers based on published estimates and author estimates.

Sources: "Fighter Figures point to Chinese air supremacy," *Flight International,* September 26, 2000, 22; John A. Tirpak, "Foreign Fighters Get Better," *Air Force Magazine,* October 2001; Jon Lake, "Sukhoi's Super Flankers," *Air Combat,* March-April 2001, 242; and Douglas Barrie and Jason Sherman, "China Seeks British Engine," *Defense News,* July 2, 2001, 1.

and track system designed for air-to-air engagements and would likely use instrument pods for low-light and laser designation for laser-guided bombs.

The Su-30MKK has 12 weapons pylons, 10 of which can carry guided missiles including the 1-mile-range Kh-59M television (TV)-guided missile; the 125-mile-range Kh-31P antiradar missile; the Kh-29T TV-guided missile; and a range of laser and TV-guided bombs. It can also carry the existing range of Russian antiaircraft missiles (AAMs) to include the helmet-sighted Vympel R–73, the medium-range semiactive-radar-guided R–27, and the medium-range active-radar-guided Vympel R–77. At the 2001 Moscow Airshow, the Raduga bureau revealed its Kh-59MK radar-guided antiship missile (ASM). Its 285-km range correlates with the search range of the Zhuk–M–S radar and opens the possibility that PLAAF Su-30MKKs may in the future have a significant antinaval mission.

While not as important as its systems and munitions, the respectable aerial performance of the Su-30MKK should not be forgotten. At low fuel states, it should have the formidable maneuverability of the Su-27, the effect of which will be enhanced by its helmet-sighted short-range AAMs. In close-in combat, the Su-30MKK should be able to dominate older Northrop F–5Es and Lockheed-Martin F–16s not equipped with helmet-sighted missiles—almost all the inventories for these types in Taiwan and in Southeast

Asia.[16] As a strike fighter, the Su-30MKK will also have an impressive reach due to its aerial refueling capability. Its advertised unrefueled radius of 1,600 km extends to 2,600 km with 1 aerial refueling and to 3,495 km with another.[17] Such reach will become possible when the PLAAF receives Ilyushin Il-78 MIDAS tankers expected to be delivered in 2002.[18]

Reporting about the PLA purchase of the Su-30 first surfaced in 1997 in conjunction with the purchase of *Sovremenny* destroyers. By August 1999, agreement had been reached that China would purchase its first batch.[19] At China's request, the Russians agreed to produce the Su-30MKK in the Komsomolsk na Amur Aircraft Production Organization (KnAAPO) plant in western Russia, instead of the Irkutsk Aircraft Production Organization (IAPO). This was a considerable blow to IAPO, which previously had an arrangement with KnAAPO. The latter would fill Su-27 orders, while IAPO would fill Su-30 orders. China did not want Indians near their aircraft, and KnAAPO had already established a deep relationship with the PLAAF over production of Su-27SKs and their components. In mid-1999, one Hong Kong report noted that coproduction of 250 Su-30MKKs could follow the purchase of Russian-built aircraft.[20] A more recent source report notes that Shenyang coproduction may switch to Su-30MKKs after about 80 Su-27SKs are completed.[21] So far, between 10 and 20 Su-27s have been built in Shenyang.

In December 2000, the first 10 Su-30MKKs were delivered to the PLAAF. It is possible that this first batch was stationed at Wuhu Air Base, which also hosts a Su-27SK unit. A second batch of about 10 were delivered in August 2001. The remaining 18 of the first Su-30MKK order reportedly will be delivered by the end of 2001. The PLA apparently was so pleased with the Su-30MKK that in conjunction with the Jiang-Putin summit in July 2001, it ordered 38 to 40 more. These are to be delivered by the end of 2003. Given the PLAAF doctrinal emphasis on obtaining multirole fighters, plus the difficulties that have plagued the Shenyang coproduction efforts and the superior performance of the Su-30MKK, the PLA quite possibly will order more Su-30MKKs from KnAAPO.

Chengdu J–10. The J–10 is shaping up to be the second most important multirole PLAAF fighter in terms of performance, but apparently it may become the most important in terms of numbers. Long the object of Western derision as well as intense speculation because of its over 20-year development program, 5 or more J–10s may now be flying in a test and evaluation program. The J–10 is expected to enter production, and up to 30 could be built by 2005.[22] Another estimate puts eventual production at 500.[23] Some compare the performance of the J–10 to the F–16 Block 30,[24] which was the first F–16 to incorporate AIM–120 active-radar-guided AAMs.

The origins of the J–10 are in the J–9 program that began at Shenyang in the early 1960s. Intended to respond to the new threat of the U.S. Mc-Donnell-Douglas F–4 PHANTOM, the J–9 was first proposed as a tailless delta wing design. The program was shifted to the Chengdu Aircraft Factory, and by the early 1970s, the J–9 was redesigned as a 13-ton mach 2.5, canard-delta design, very similar to the Swedish Saab J–37 VIGGEN. The J–9 program was discontinued in 1980, but its basic canard configuration persisted in the later J–10 proposal.[25] The J–10 was by this time the PLA response to emerging Soviet fourth-generation fighter threats.

Having been denied U.S. funding for its LAVI fighter program, Israel exported that technology to the People's Republic of China (PRC) by the end of the 1980s. Unconfirmed information suggests that Israel even sold a complete LAVI prototype, with its U.S. F–100 turbofan engine, to the PRC. According to an unsubstantiated report, a J–10 prototype completed in 1993 was practically a copy of the LAVI, including the F–100 engine.[26] This would conform to the famous model of the J–10 with Li Peng. At any rate, the J–10 is widely reported to have benefited from both Israeli and Russian design input, with Israel providing critical fly-by-wire technology and advanced cockpit instrumentation.

The J–10 could have benefited from U.S. technology in two ways. First, the Israeli LAVI was greatly influenced by access to General Dynamics F–16 technology. Israel passed on the knowledge of some of this technology, which may have included avionics, advanced composite materials, and flight control specification,[27] to Chengdu. Fly-by-wire technology may have been shared as well. Also, Taiwanese sources say the J–10 benefited from PLA access to Pakistan's F–16 fighters. Such access presumably would include inspection of the aircraft as well as flight evaluation against PLAAF fighters.

If the "Li Peng" model does represent an early design configuration (or even the first prototype), then the J–10 was severely redesigned by the late 1990s. This redesign reflected the requirement to use a 27,500-pound-thrust Russian Saturn-Aluyka AL–31 engine and the doctrinal requirements to have an attack capability. Another report notes that the PLA is developing a 26,700-pound-thrust engine but has experienced difficulties in completing it.[28] The availability of a suitable domestic engine will likely be critical to the success of the J–10 in export markets.

The long-awaited revelation of the J–10 occurred not in an official sense but rather through leaks of pictures over the Internet in early 2001. These pictures show a side view of the J–10 on the ground, and several pictures show the J–10 in flight.[29] They reveal an F–16-size canard fighter with a square engine inlet rather than the round inlet on the Li Peng model/LAVI/F–16. Compared to the Li Peng model, the true J–10's vertical stabilizer and main wing are also larger.

The canard configuration confers good short takeoff capability and maneuverability, which are useful in interception and air combat missions. The J–10 is also expected to benefit from an indigenous helmet-sighting system, perhaps similar to that revealed at the 2000 Zhuhai Airshow. Such a sight will likely be able to guide Russian Vympel R–73, Israeli Python-4, or perhaps an indigenous HMS-guided AAM like the PL–9. Long-range missile options might include the Russian R–27 and R–77 or a new indigenous active-guided medium-range AAM derived from the AMR–1 program. For longer-range engagements, the J–10 will be equipped with a multimode radar of unknown origin. Reported possibilities include the Russian Phazotron Zhuk PD, Zhuk ZEMCHOUG, Phazotron SOKOL phased array radar, and the Israeli Elta EL–2032. These radars would have the capability for multiple track and attack and for ground attack.

Other reports point to the possibility that the J–10 could have up to 11 hardpoints for carrying ordnance.[30] Each wing is thought to have three hardpoints, one of which is for a fuel tank, and the fuselage has five hardpoints. This configuration would allow the J–10 to carry a low light/laser designator pod on a forward fuselage hardpoint, indicating that the J–10 could have a precision guided munition (PGM) capability. Attack missiles might eventually include the C–801/802/701 or their variants. Supersonic attack missiles might include the Russian Kh–31 or a new ramjet-powered Chinese attack missile revealed at the 2001 Zhuhai show.

Despite its long development period, the J–10's future in the PLAAF apparently is becoming more secure. At the 2001 Paris Airshow, it was revealed that China might purchase up to 300 more AL–31 engines especially modified for the J–10.[31] This would indicate that the PLA has lost its patience in waiting for a suitable domestic engine and that a high priority has been placed on moving the J–10 into production. Future versions could feature thrust-vectoring and stealth enhancements.

Shenyang J–11 Multirole. In mid-2002, both Russian and Chinese Internet sources revealed that Shenyang intended to build a new multirole variant of the J–11 coproduced version of the Su–27SK. The Russian sources indicated that Shenyang intended to fit the new J–11 version with an indigenous radar, most likely a multimode radar, so that the J–11 could fire the new Project 129 active-guided AAM.[32] Then at an exhibition, Shenyang displayed a model of its J–11 armed with Kh-31 ground attack missiles and an active-radar-guided AAM, offering confirmation of its J–11 multirole variant. It likely also would be able to carry other PGMs, such as laser-guided bombs. This new J–11 would serve to correct the deficiencies of the Su-27SK/J–11 family of which the PLAAF learned from its expensive experience. It would also allow the J–11 to conform with new PLAAF doctrinal goals. Moreover, there would be the added advantage for Shenyang of being able to offer the PLAAF another competitor to the Chengdu J–10.

Shenyang J–8II. The new PLAAF zeal for multirole aircraft is also extending to the venerable Shenyang J–8II. Though it is an obsolete fighter that would be better replaced with Sukhois or the J–10, the one major advantage of the J–8II (availability) probably has made it worthy of a multirole upgrade. The PLAAF may acquire up to 100 multirole-capable J–8IIs. That the PLA is again investing its scarce resources in the J–8II indicates that increasing the numbers of multirole fighters may be as important to it as introducing more modern systems.

Shenyang J–8IIs have been improved incrementally since their introduction. The first major effort to improve the fighter was the "Peace Pearl" program led by Grumman in the late 1980s, which sought to outfit the fighter with a variant of the APG–66 radar used in the F–16. When this program ended as part of U.S. sanctions after the Tiananmen massacre, the PLA turned to Russia. In 1996, the J–8IIM emerged, modified to carry the Phazotron Zhuk-8II multimode radar and Russian R–27 semiactive medium-range AAMs. Pitched as an export-only program, the J–8IIM had no takers.

However, reports surfaced by early 2001 that the PLAAF was indeed proceeding with a multirole capable version of the J–8II, variously referred to as the J–8IIC or the J–8IIH.[33] It will carry a Russian radar and a more powerful Wopen WP–14 engine. The PLA will purchase up to 100 new Phazotron Zhuk radars to modify the J–8II. The radar will be the same Zhuk-8II developed for the J–8IIM and will be able to cue R–27 class AAMs and direct ASMs such as the C–801/802. The J–8IIC/H also might carry the new Chinese supersonic ASM.

Other sources note that the J–8IIC/H will be a development of the J–8IID, which carries a fixed aerial refueling probe.[34] At the 1998 Zhuhai

Airshow, a prominent picture showed a J–8II with a low-light/laser targeting pod similar in configuration to the Israeli LITENING laser/low-light pod. This could indicate that the J–8IIC/H may be able to carry laser-guided bombs. At the 2000 Zhuhai Airshow, officials from the China Jinan Aviation Central Factory noted that J–8IIs were also being equipped with their new FK–2 datalink system to improve communication. It is likely the FK–2 datalink would be used on the J–8IIC/H.

While the J–8IIC/H may always be less capable than such U.S. fighters as the F–16 and F/A–18, it is being turned into a formidable weapon system when armed with stand-off missiles and employed for offensive attack missions. In an air-to-air role, the J–8IIC/H might also be valuable as a long-range escort for attack-dedicated Su-30MKKs or JH–7s. The J–8IIC/Hs might draw off the combat air patrol for a U.S. carrier that would allow a strike force to get close enough for an attack.

Xian JH–7. Another subject of a prolonged development program, the Xian JH–7 fighter-bomber has also emerged in recent years as a viable program intended to add numbers to the complement of PLAAF multirole fighters. As with the J–10, an urgency to advance production has prompted a return to Britain for the Rolls Royce Spey Mk202 engine, about 20 years after the failure of the first Rolls Royce Spey venture. China has just acquired 80 to 90 old Spey Mk202 engines and intends to revive its coproduction,[35] meaning that at least 25 more JH–7s can now be produced[36] beyond the 15 to 20 completed thus far. If Spey coproduction is successful, one estimate holds that more than 150 more JH–7s could be built.[37] However, the future of the JH–7 is unclear given the possibility that U.S. opposition could prevent eventual Spey coproduction.

Development of the JH–7 (also known as the H–7 and B–7) is thought to have started in 1975 at about the same time Rolls Royce entered into its first coproduction venture with the PRC.[38] Although it first flew in 1988, the JH–7 was not revealed to the public until the 1998 Zhuhai Airshow, where it was pitched as the FBC–1 Flying Leopard for export. It was also intended to showcase the ability of China's aerospace industry to produce the range of systems needed to assemble a modern fighter.[39]

The JH–7 looks like a fat British/French JAGUAR but is about the same size as an F–4 PHANTOM. Its high-wing configuration is ideal for its primary mission of low-level attack. While the exact radar used by the JH–7 is not known, it has been shown as a testbed for the CLETRI JL–10A multimode radar, which has an 80-km search range and a 40-km tracking range. The JH–7 has also been linked to the CLETRI "Blue Sky" low-altitude radar/forward-looking infrared pod, to assist low-level navigation and targeting.[40] This pod is similar to the U.S. LANTIRN low-level navigation pod. Its advertised maximum payload is 14,330 pounds, which can consist of up to 3 external fuel tanks, up to 4 C–801/802ASMs, freefall bombs, and 2 wing-tip-mounted AAMs. At the 2000 Zhuhai show, a model of the JH–7 was prominently displayed with a new type of indigenous ramjet-powered supersonic cruise missile, similar in shape to the French ASMP tactical nuclear armed ramjet-powered cruise missile. Also, at the September 2001 Beijing Airshow, a JH–7 model was shown armed with a jet-powered version of the FL–2 ASM. The JH–7 has also been pictured armed with a Russian Kh-31 ramjet-powered attack missile.

The JH–7 probably would be hard pressed to hold its own against current U.S. combat aircraft. However, it is also likely that it will be employed mainly for ground attack and will avoid air combat. It can more than adequately fly low and fast to deliver its weapons. The prospect that the JH–7 will in the future be armed with longer-range supersonic attack and stand-off attack missiles makes this weapon system even more formidable.

Multiroles for export. The new emphasis on building multirole fighters extends to designated PLA export offerings, Chengdu's FC–1 and J–7MF. Both are considered export programs because the PLAAF ability to purchase the FC–1 is in question. Chengdu sources interviewed at the 2000 Zhuhai show did not indicate that the PLA would purchase their new J–7MF.

The FC–1 emerged from the 1980s Grumman-Chengdu program to modify the J–7 into a more capable fighter, the "Super-7." When this foundered after Tiananmen, Russia's MiG bureau was invited to continue the program, which then developed into a nominal codevelopment program with Pakistan. While Pakistani officials have often expressed their support for the FC–1, the PLAAF has been less enthusiastic. This reluctance likely is due to the FC–1's high dependence on foreign components, such as its Russian Klimov RD–93 engine, and a range of Russian and European offerings for its main radar and attack systems. The recent reluctance of the Europeans to supply radar and other key components,[41] and the prospect of intense Indian opposition to the sale of Russian components to Pakistan, has cast even more doubt on the program. However, the recent ending of the U.S. arms embargo on Pakistan and the new U.S. willingness to give Pakistan embargoed F–16s[42] could result in Europe again approving component sales that would revive FC–1 prospects.

As a consequence of the FC–1 troubles, Chengdu began several years ago to design an alternative, which emerged as the F–7MF at the 2000

Zhuhai show. It is essentially a J–7E with a larger forward fuselage, small fixed canards, and an underslung engine intake—like the J–10. There is also the expectation that it will carry modern Chinese, Russian, or European radar, designator pods, and precision guided munitions. The first prototype was due to fly in 2000, but that has yet to be reported.[43] Not to be outdone, the FC–1 team stepped up its marketing in 2001. In April of that year, it revealed a full-sized mockup of the FC–1 shown armed with what may be a new type of Chinese medium-range AAM.[44] New promotional literature also shows the FC–1 equipped to carry Western and Chinese weapons, to include laser-guided bombs.

While it is not yet clear that either Chengdu program will succeed in foreign markets, let alone with the PLAAF, the latter should not be discounted. The example of the J–8IIM export-oriented program turning into the J–8IIC/H modernization program could possibly apply to the successful Chengdu program. If the FC–1 or the J–7MF prove successful, there is at least a chance that the PLAAF will acquire the fighter as well. Such a prospect, however, would most likely depend on an intense requirement for more half-modern multirole fighters and the failure of other programs, such as the J–10.

Future combat aircraft. Since the late 1990s, there has been speculation about the PLA's next-generation combat aircraft, called the XXJ by the U.S. Office of Naval Intelligence (ONI) in 1997. ONI estimated an initial operational capability of 2015 for the XXJ, which would be "a large multirole fighter with an emphasis on air combat and a reduced radar signature design."[45] The design projected by ONI resembled a U.S. Boeing F–15 EAGLE fighter.

Recently, however, a number of alleged future PLAAF fighter designs have appeared on Chinese Web sites that show more designs may also be considered. What appears to be a wind tunnel test model of one design closely resembles the U.S. F–22. Another design also resembles the F–22 but uses canards in addition to horizontal stabilizers, like the Su-37.[46] One source calls this configuration the "New 93" and notes that it is a 15-ton fighter with a warload of 4,860 kilograms and a performance that exceeds the Su-27 in many respects except range.[47] Both designs make healthy use of stealth shaping and, very likely, thrust-vectored engines.

The canard design could indicate that the Russians already have had a hand in the XXJ. Russia, however, is seeking the partnership investments of India and China for its next-generation fighter, slated to compete with the Lockheed-Martin F–35 Joint Strike Fighter. However, it is unclear that

Russia will succeed in organizing an effective fifth-generation fighter program among its many competing aircraft factions, much less pay for it.

Unmanned combat platforms. The PLA has a strong interest in unmanned air and sea platforms for military missions. It has long used unmanned reconnaissance drones. Its CHANG HONG series is based on U.S. FIREBEE drones captured during the Vietnam War. The latest CHANG HONG revealed at the 2000 Zhuhai show was modified with global positioning system (GPS) guidance. Officials noted that the CHANG HONG was back in production after a long period. It is possible that the CHANG HONG could be developed for ELINT in addition to reconnaissance missions. Also revealed at Zhuhai was the ASN–206 small battlefield reconnaissance drone that may incorporate some Israeli technology. In all, about 11 new unmanned aerial vehicles (UAVs) were introduced at the 2000 Zhuhai Air Show.

The most interesting UAV at the show was the stealthy twin-engine Guizhou WZ–2000. This UAV could form the basis for the PRC's first bomb-dropping unmanned combat aerial vehicle (UCAV). Guizhou officials noted that the WZ–2000 could be built in multiple sizes to fit customer needs. Also at the show, the Beijing University Institute for Aeronautics and Astronautics demonstrated a virtual-reality control system, which it says is already in use for fighter training and could be applied to UCAVs.

Single Role Combat Aircraft

Sukhoi Su-27SK/UBK. The PLAAF is working on acquiring about 78 Russian-made Su-27SK and Su-27UBK twin-seat training fighters. About 50 were acquired in 2 batches in 1991 and 1996, and about 28 more Su-27UBKs were ordered in 2000. There could also be an additional 20 or so Su-27SKs assembled from KnAAPO-built knockdown kits in Shenyang, the result of a 1996 agreement giving Shenyang a license to build up to 200 of these fighters. At the 2000 Zhuhai show, a high Shenyang Aircraft Corporation official indicated that Shenyang might not build all 200 Su-27s allowed for in the agreement.[48] This statement would lend credibility to previously cited reports that Shenyang coproduction might switch to Su-30MKKs after the completion of 80 Su-27SKs. It would be logical for the PLAAF to prefer the Su-30MKK over the Su-27SK for reasons of doctrine and utility: the Su-27SK only has a secondary ground attack capability, and the PLAAF likely understands the better performance of a twin-crewed attack fighter.

Nevertheless, the Su-27SK has provided the PLAAF with a robust introduction to the complexity, expense, and improved combat potential of modern fourth-generation fighters. The PLAAF has had some highly publicized challenges and problems in incorporating the Su-27SK into its force. It is still not clear that the fighters are being utilized to the extent of their potential. Russia likely has tried to market radar and weapons upgrade kits to China to enable the Su-27SK to become a true multirole fighter. But it is not clear that the PLAAF is going to favor this investment while it is concentrating on the Su-30MKK.

Close air support. Beyond the long-serving Nanchang Q–5 ground-attack fighter, the PLAAF has not acquired a modern close-air support fighter like the U.S. Fairchild A–10 THUNDERBOLT II or the Sukhoi Su-25 FROGFOOT. The A–10 and Su-25 can fire a variety of PGMs and carry heavy-armor-busting machineguns. They are also equipped with heavy armor protection to allow the fighter to dwell over the battlefield to provide continuous protection. Unconfirmed reports indicate that some Q–5s are being modified to carry laser-guided bombs. Recent reports discussed an abortive program for a Q–6 fighter, which resembled the swing-wing Mikoyan MiG–27 FLOGGER ground-attack fighter.[49] It is also possible that the Hongdu L–15 trainer could be developed into a ground-attack variant, as have many other trainers in its class. The L–15 high-wing configuration makes possible a useful weapons load, and its twin engines enhance survivability over the battlefield.

For near-term PLA close air-support needs, however, a large number of dumb-bomb-carrying Q–5 and J–6 fighters may be sufficient. In addition, the army's Z–10 attack helicopter may be produced in sufficient numbers to provide a necessary level of close air support.

Bombers. The PLAAF is credited with about 100 H–6 (Tu-6) medium bombers, a type that first entered PLAAF service in 1959. With a 1,800-km combat radius, the H–6 is obsolete in most combat roles. Beginning with the PLA Navy (PLAN) H–6D version, this bomber was modified to carry standoff attack missiles. However, early missiles such as the C–601/C–611 derivatives of the Silkworm cruise missile had a short range and thus exposed the H–6 to most U.S. and Taiwanese defensive fighters. But a 2000 report suggested that up to 25 H–6s would be modified to carry 4 new TV-guided YJ–63 land-attack cruise missiles, also a derivative of the C–601/C–611 series.[50] It is also conceivable that the H–6 could carry the new jet-powered version of the FL–2 revealed at the 2001 Beijing Airshow. This suggests that the H–6 may be given new offensive roles that give this old aircraft a new lease on life. Equipped with a land-attack cruise missile (LACM)-armed H–6, the PLAAF could join an initial assault on Taiwan that would otherwise be led by the short-range ballistic missiles of the Second Artillery and the Army.

There is relatively little open information on PLA attempts to develop a successor to the H–6. Internet sources have offered pictures of what is referred to as the H–8, which is an H–6 with 4 wing-mounted turbofan engines. Such an idea likely suffered a quick death. Occasional references are made to an H–9 project, said to be a new stealthy bomber being developed in cooperation with Russia.

The PLA might prefer Russian assistance in developing a new modern long-range bomber. But one might surmise that the PLAAF would prefer to have a near-term replacement for the H–6, such as an available Russian alternative. One recently noted possible PLA bomber purchase from Russia was for the Sukhoi Su-32, also called the Su-34,[51] which would provide the PLAAF with a more capable multirole strike platform than the Su-30MKK. Its main difference is a redesigned front fuselage that provides much more space for electronic systems, fuel, and the crew—a rare commodity in Russian combat aircraft. It has galley and toilet facilities, which would allow the crew to perform 10-hour missions. Unlike the Su-30MKK, the Su-32 can carry 2 Raduga MOSKIT (SS–N–22 SUNBURN) supersonic ASMs or 3 NPO Machinostroyenia YAKHONT supersonic ASMs. Also, in addition to the usual range of Russian AAMs and PGMs, the Su-32 can also be outfitted for antisubmarine warfare.[52]

Despite much reporting in the early 1990s that the PLA would purchase the Tupolev Tu-22M3 BACKFIRE bomber, it has yet to do so. At the time Russian reluctance nixed the sale. But before the 2000 summit of Russian President Vladimir Putin and Chinese President Jiang Zemin, a Russian arms export official noted that Russia might permit the sale of strategic systems such as the BACKFIRE to China after the signing of a new friendship treaty.[53] Following Russia's leasing of four BACKFIRES to India, a sale or lease to China becomes increasingly possible.

For the PLAAF, a small number of BACKFIRES, perhaps 6 to 12, would add a new capability as well as enhance the prestige of the service and the PLA. Its usefulness to the PLA, however, would depend much on Russia's willingness to sell long-range supersonic attack missiles like the 300-mile-range Kh-22, designed to attack U.S. carrier battlegroups. The BACKFIRE can carry up to 3 Kh-22s. It can also carry 3 of the newer stealthy Kh-101 3,000-km-range cruise missiles. It can also carry a bomb load of 22 tons. Because of the Strategic Arms Limitation Talks and

Strategic Arms Reduction Treaty, Russian BACKFIRES do not have aerial refueling probes, which limits their combat radius to about 1,300 miles. Not encumbered by such agreements, the PLA would be free to modify its BACKFIRES for aerial refueling to extend their range.

Hypersonics. As in the United States, Russia, and elsewhere, the PLA probably is researching the possibility of building future ultra-long-range hypersonic strike vehicles. The United States is giving serious consideration to such vehicles as a successor to the strategic bomber and intercontinental ballistic missile (ICBM).[54] Built on technology developed for the space shuttle and the now aborted X–33 single-stage-to-orbit test vehicle, a hypersonic strike vehicle could be as fast as an ICBM but could also be recalled if necessary—and could strike again. It could deliver highly accurate nonnuclear warheads, the destructive impact of which are compounded by their hypersonic speed.

At the 2000 Hannover Exposition in Germany, China revealed a model of a future small manned space plane comparable in size to the Japanese Hope shuttle concept and to several Soviet-era small space plane concepts. While such a space plane is initially intended to support its manned space program, this program has the potential to support a strike vehicle program. At the 1998 Zhuhai show, an apparent unmanned space shuttle shape was also revealed, indicating another possible design for a space strike vehicle.

These vehicles are encumbered by the need for an unwieldy rocket booster. China probably is turning to Russia to explore novel single-stage-to-orbit concepts that are less reliant on land-based rocket boost. In early 2001, a Russian report noted that China was negotiating to contribute to a novel hypersonic suborbital program of the Leninets Holding Company called AYAKS.[55] Leninets officials at the 2001 Moscow Airshow confirmed China's interests. AYAKS proposes a novel kerosene-fueled magnetoplasmochemical engine that would allow the vehicle to go from Russia to the United States in 1.6 hours.[56] NASA and some U.S. companies are familiar with this work but have chosen not to invest in it. In addition, at the 2001 Moscow Airshow, officials from the Molniya Company noted Chinese interest in their air-launched MAKS concept space plane. The MAKS manned space plane weighs 27 tons with a crew of 2 and has a payload of 8.3 tons.[57] It is about the same size as the Chinese concept space plane revealed in Hannover.

Advanced Munitions

A key element of PLAAF modernization, consistent with trends toward higher technology and higher reliance on information, is the development or acquisition of advanced aerial munitions. The PLAAF has made strides in this area over the last decade mainly due to the purchase of advanced Russian missiles and guided bombs. However, great effort is being devoted toward the indigenous development of new antiair and ground attack munitions.

AAMs. Access to advanced Russian air-to-air missiles has resulted in significant advances for Chinese air-to-air missiles. At the 1996 Zhuhai show, China revealed its helmet-sighted PL–9 short-range infrared-guided AAM. The PL–9 is a Chinese copy of the Israeli PYTHON–3 (PL–8) slaved to the Ukrainian Arsenel helmet-sighting mechanism of the Vympel R–73 (AA–11 ALAMO). However, after all this effort, it is still not clear that the PLAAF has adopted the PL–9 and seems instead to rely on the R–73 for its Sukhoi fighters.

The real advance for PLAAF AAMs will come when the Vympel R–77 (AA–12) becomes operational. In mid-2002, U.S. intelligence sources revealed that the R–77 had begun operational testing from PLAAF Su-30MKK fighters. [58] These missiles feature an active-guided radar system that allows the missile to find the target without being "painted" by the aircraft radar, in the same fashion as the U.S. AIM–120 advanced medium-range air-to-air missile.

The PLA also has its own active-radar-guided AAM program. At the 1996 Zhuhai show, it revealed its AMR–1 active seeker for a medium-range AAM. According to one source, the AMR–1 forms the basis for the PL–12 medium-range AAM.[59] In mid-2001, a new medium-range AAM recently was revealed in conjunction with the mockup of the Chengdu FC–1. In mid-2002, Russian sources noted that this missile was called the Project 129 and combined the Russian AGAT radar, guidance and datalink from the R–77 with a Chinese missile motor. As such, it would likely have better range than the R–77, which has suffered from an insufficient engine.[60] The export designation for this AAM is SD–10.

Antiradar Missiles. The Raduga Kh-31P was the first advanced antiradar missile (ARM) acquired by the PLAAF. It is a longer-range variant of the Kh-31 (AS–17) ramjet-powered attack missile. The Kh-31P has a range of about 125 miles, which confers a comfortable standoff attack capability on the Taiwan Strait. The Kh-31P will arm PLAAF Su-30MKKs and has been seen on at least one JH–7, indicating this attack fighter may also be so armed. Another possible ARM is the new ramjet-powered air-to-surface missile revealed at the 2000 Zhuhai show. About the size of a C–802, this missile also resembles the French ASMP tactical nuclear delivery missile. This missile would also be useful for land attack or antiship missions as well.

Land-Attack Cruise Missiles. The PLAAF may already have fielded several new LACMs. The reported YJ–63, a TV terminal-guided variant of the C–601/C–611 series, may already be in service. While such a missile may not have a great range, it would certainly give PLA commanders more flexibility in targeting key command, communications, or political nodes. Such a missile's utility, however, may be limited by the weather.

A more interesting possible LACM is the turbofan-powered FL–2 variant revealed at the 2001 Beijing Airshow. The presence of a new laser-guided bomb on the same JH–7 model points to the new FL–2 variant having a land-attack mission. The rocket-powered FL–2 weighs 1,300 kg, has a 365-kg warhead, and a range of 50 km.[61] A turbofan variant could increase the range from 100 to 200 km. It is also likely to be equipped with GPS/global navigation satellite system (GLONASS) precision guidance for land-attack missions.

Most Russian illustrations of the Su-30MKK, as well as models of the same, show the aircraft armed with the turbojet-powered Raduga Kh-59M (AS–18 KAZOO) land-attack missile. It has a 200-km range and is guided by a TV seeker that relays its images via datalink to a weapons systems officer. At the 2001 Moscow Airshow, Raduga revealed its Kh-59MK ASM. Based on the Kh-59M, the Kh-59MK features a more powerful engine and a longer 285-km range. The Kh-59MK also has an active guidance radar designed for antiship missions.[62] The degree to which Raduga is linking the Kh-59MK to the Su-30MKK in its promotional literature indicates this missile is intended for the PLAAF.

Guided bombs. Internet-related sources have revealed that the PLAAF likely has had a laser-guided bomb (LGB) for some time. It is a gimballed laser-seeker similar to the U.S. PAVEWAY series of LGBs. A new PLAAF LGB, very likely in the 250-kg range, was revealed at the 2001 Beijing Airshow on a model of a JH–7. At the 1998 Zhuhai show, a poster showed a laser and low-light designating pod being used by a J–8II fighter. The Chinese pod bore a close resemblance to the Israeli LITENING targeting pod that the U.S. Air Force recently purchased.

The Su-30MKK could also be armed with other Russian guided munitions. In promotional illustrations, the Su-30MKK is shown firing the

Kh-29 (AS–14 KEDGE) ASM. This missile is similar to the U.S. MAVER-ICK system. The Kh-29 can be laser- or TV-guided and comes in versions with ranges from 10 km to 30 km. Russia also markets a range of laser and TV-guided bombs, which are also compatible with the Su-30MKK.

Another alternative would be GPS/GLONASS-guided bombs. The reported Chinese capture of an unexploded U.S. GPS-guided bomb following the mistaken attack on the PRC embassy in Yugoslavia may have given the PLA a template to make its own version. However, the technology for GPS-guided bombs is not very complex and is within China's capability to build. However, no reports indicate that the PLAAF currently possess GPS/GLONASS-guided bombs.

Information and Electronic Support

The PLAAF investment in information and electronic support aircraft is growing. The most obvious example is the airborne warning and control system (AWACS) program, which has acquired the Russian Beriev A–50E. Recent reports note that the PLAAF will initially purchase four of this aircraft.[63] The A–50E, however, is the PLAAF's second choice, having been denied its first choice, the Israeli Elta PHALCON phased-array radar equipped A–50, because of intense U.S. pressure to cancel this sale in 1999 and 2000. The Israeli radar would have offered advantages in stealth and flexibility, with the potential to be modified for EW/ELINT missions. This capability may explain why China persists in trying to get Washington to reverse its decision.[64]

The A–50E is the most advanced version of this Russian AWACS aircraft. Its AK RLDN radar system can detect a bomber-size target at 650 km and a fighter at 300 km and can track up to 300 targets and command 12 fighters.[65] Systems operators also benefit from modern flat-panel display stations, which are probably more reliable than early A–50 radar systems. At the 2000 Zhuhai show, officials from the China Jinan Aviation Central Factory noted that they would build the datalink for the PLAAF A–50s, which was not disputed by Russian officials from the MNIIP bureau that makes the A–50 radar. Russian officials did note that if the PLAAF followed Russian training procedures, it would take 1.5 years to train a crew to operate the A–50E.

Inasmuch as India may acquire A–50s with the more powerful PS–90A turbofan[66] (35,000 pounds of thrust versus 26,000 for the D–30KP), PLAAF A–50Es could be similarly outfitted. The PS–90A would confer greater speed and range. On internal fuel, the A–50 with D–30KP engines can remain on station for 4 hours at a point over 500 miles from its base. However, both modified H–6 bombers plus expected Il-78 refueling aircraft, can be used to extend the A–50 time on station. Two A–50Es flying continuously over the Taiwan Strait probably would be sufficient to facilitate offensive and defensive operations.

A second AWACS aircraft is already entering PLAN service: the Y–8 transport equipped with the British Racal (now Thales) SKYMASTER aerial early warning (AEW) radar. The SKYMASTER is a version of the Racal SEARCHWATER radar used by British NIMROD patrol aircraft. The PLA purchased 6 to 8 SKYMASTER radars in 1996. The British government justified this sale by saying that China wanted these aircraft to crack down on smuggling. However, reports emerged in early 2000 that the PLA was using its SKYMASTER-equipped Y–8s to vector LUDA-class destroyers in naval exercises.[67] At altitude, the Y–8/SKYMASTER could be used to support naval battles, especially with long-range targeting, or by vectoring offensive or defensive aircraft.

In spring 2001, Internet sources revealed that the PLA has also pursued a domestic AWACS program to succeed its old Tu-4-based AWACS. Pictures of a Y–8 with a radar dome over the fuselage and an aerodynamic test model of the same could be seen on Chinese military-oriented Web pages. It is not clear whether the Y–8-based AWACS represents an active development program or one that has been superceded by the A–50E. Internet sources also revealed that a model of the Y–10, China's attempt to copy the Boeing 707, has also been considered with a radar dome in a configuration just like the U.S. E–2 AWACS.[68] This program apparently was not pursued beyond the test model stage.

Yet another indigenous AWACS program was revealed by Chinese Internet sources in mid-2002. This system used a Y–8 to carry a thin lengthy antenna mounted above the fuselage in a manner similar to the Swedish ERIEYE radar. This radar uses a steerable phased-array radar beam and offers aerodynamic and weight advantages over a rotating saucer array. It is possible that the PLAAF is developing this system in lieu of Y–8 with the rotating array.

Electronic intelligence. For ELINT support, the PLAAF reportedly has modified four Russian Tu-154M airliners with ELINT systems.[69] At the 1998 Zhuhai show, the Southwest Institute of Electrical Engineering revealed its large KZ800 Airborne ELINT system, which the PLAAF probably uses in its modified Tu-154Ms. In late 2000, a photograph of a China United Airlines Tu-154M showed what appeared to be a synthetic aperture radar (SAR) structure under the fuselage.[70] The configuration is similar to that on the U.S. E–8 JSTARS. The PLA has been developing ground-mapping SAR systems, some based on technology from the U.S. Loral Corporation, though the PLA has likely also had access to Russian airborne SAR technology. China United Airlines has 16 Tu-154Ms that would be likely candidates for conversion to EW/ELINT/SAR platforms.

Electronic warfare. The PLAAF is also developing an active EW capability. In the early 1980s, it modified some old H–5 (Il-28) light bombers for EW missions, calling them the HD–5.[71] Though an early 1950s design, the H–5 has a top speed of 540 miles per hour and a range of 1,400 miles. Its capabilities would be sufficient to accompany strike packages going to Taiwan.

The Su-30MKK armed with the Raduga Kh-31P antiradar missile will present a potent electronic attack capability. With a 125-mile range and supersonic speed, the Kh-31P will pose a real threat to hostile electronic emitters such as radar. The second batch of Su-27SKs delivered in 1996 featured the KNIRTI SORBTSIYA active jamming pods. This system is able to detect and classify radar signal threats, prioritize the threats, copy and rebroadcast threat signals with jamming modulations, or cause intercepting missiles to deviate from their intercepting path. It can undertake multiple simultaneous jamming operations and is designed to counter fire-control, missile guidance, and AWACS radar.[72] The SORBTSIYA pod is also configured so that it can continue jamming while maneuvering, something that is difficult for the U.S. EA–6B PROWLER, which has a more restrictive antenna configuration.[73]

At the 1998 Zhuhai show, Xian officials noted that an EW variant of the JH–7 was under development.[74] At the same show, the Southwest Institute of Electronic Engineering revealed its KG300G jamming pod and its KZ900 tactical ELINT pods. These could be carried two each by a JH–7 in a manner similar to the U.S. EA–6B PROWLER. If armed with the Kh-31P, the EW version of the JH–7 could also attack enemy emitters.

Tankers

The PLAAF operates one type of aerial refueling tanker and may soon obtain another. It clearly needs to extend the range or endurance of its combat aircraft, for which aerial refueling is necessary. With the refueling capability, the PLAAF can extend the range of its Su-30MKKs to reach Guam or undertake long-range patrols over the disputed Spratly Islands in the South China Sea.

The PLAAF has converted more than 10 of its H–6 bombers[75] to refuelers, known as the H–6U or HU–6.[76] They differ from standard H–6s in that they have two wing-mounted refueling drogues, most likely of Israeli origin, and the nose area glass for the bombardier is faired over. There appears to be a PLAN version that does not have fairing over the nose.[77] If the H–6U/HU–6 compares to the Russian tanker version of the Tu-16N, it may be able to carry about 42,000 pounds of fuel[78]—a light load compared to U.S. tankers. However, it is useful in extending the range of a few fighters like the J–8IID or the Su-30MKK. In addition, it provides the PLAAF with a system for establishing and practicing the complex methods and procedures for aerial refueling.

The PLAAF was expecting to take delivery of the first of four Ilyushin Il-78M MIDAS dedicated tanker versions of the Il-76 transport in 2002.[79] Ilyushin has spent many years promoting the Il-78M in China, beginning with its appearance at the 1996 Zhuhai Airshow. Should it enter service, the Il-78M will be a far more capable tanker than the H–6U/HU–6. The Il-78M can carry a maximum load of 304,233 pounds of fuel, of which 233,068 pounds is transferable.[80] The Il-78M can transfer 60 to 65 tons of fuel out to 1,800 km and 32 to 34 tons out to 4,000 km.[81] The PLAAF is purchasing its Il-78Ms conjunction with its A–50E AWACS, so the tankers can be expected to support the AWACS aircraft.

Transport Aircraft

The PLAAF dedicated aerial transport fleet has been very small relative to the size of the PLA and the country. The largest aircraft in this fleet now comprises about 20 Ilyushin Il-76MDs, about 25 Y–8/An-12s, and about 42 Y–7/An-28s. There are even two C–130L–100–30 transports acquired in 1987 but operated by a civilian company.[82] A transport fleet of this size would be hard pressed to handle PLAAF unit rapid deployment requirements for Taiwan operations, let alone undertake simultaneous airborne projection missions. However, there are some indications that this small fleet could soon grow. The PLAAF also must account for the ability to assemble an irregular transport fleet from PLAAF-owned airlines and the much larger non-PLA civil transport sector.

Of particular importance to the PLAAF transport fleet will be the future of its medium transports. These aircraft, such as the long-serving Xian Y–8, a copy of the Ukrainian Antonov An-12 CUB, have a better short field capability. It can carry a maximum load of 20 tons. Despite its obsolescence and the availability of better aircraft, the Y–8 is being improved. The latest

Y–8–400 features more high-powered Pratt-Whitney Canada engines and improved payload capability. This version might offer the PLAAF a less expensive choice to build up the transport fleet, but it is not clear that the PLAAF is interested. According to Xian officials at the 2000 Zhuhai Airshow, Antonov has been approached to help improve the Y–8.

But a more interesting alternative being promoted heavily in China by Antonov is its advanced An-70.[83] The An-70 can carry 35 tons, approaching the capacity of the Il-76, and it uses turboprop engines that consume nearly half the fuel of the turbofans of the Il-76.[84] Its use of advanced materials and advanced cockpit technology makes the An-70 among the most modern medium transports available. Coproduction of the An-70 would constitute a significant air transport technology upgrade for China. However, at the Zhuhai show, Xian officials downplayed their coproducing the An-70, citing its expense. More recent reporting notes that China may be invited in as a significant investment partner for the An-70, with no coproduction in China.[85]

Another Antonov offering being promoted for China is the An-74TK–300, a new development of the An-74 turbofan-powered short-takeoff-and-landing (STOL) cargo transport. An August 2001 report noted that China might purchase up to 30 of these smaller jet transports.[86] With a 10-ton payload, this ramp-loaded transport would be ideal for supporting rapid deployment for PLAAF units.

In 1991, the PLAAF began acquiring the Ilyushin Il-76MD, its first modern strategic military transport. Its 40-ton payload is sufficient to carry light airborne tanks such as the Russian BMD airborne tracked armored personnel carrier (APC) and a number of light gun- or missile-armed APCs or wheeled vehicles very likely intended for PLA airborne units. With a lighter load, about 30 tons, the Il-76 can land on unprepared strips. The PLAAF is variously reported to have acquired 12 to 20 Il-76s so far.[87] The Il-76 fleet is thought be attached to the PLAAF 13th Division, and much of its work is dedicated to the 15th Airborne Army, whose troops are often seen in its exercises. Some Il-76s are seen in the markings of the PLAAF-owned China United Airlines, and one has been pictured in the markings of the state-owned China Ocean Shipping Company.[88]

In 2000 and 2001, uncollaborated Russian reports noted that the PLA might purchase between 10 and 40 more Il-76s.[89] If the aircraft are to be new production, they could also be the new Il-76MF version, with better engines that can lift up to 54 tons. The PLA would acquire a greater strategic projection capability with the purchase of more Il-76s, whatever the version.

Irregular transports. If airborne projection operations were to be a large part of a future Taiwan operation, the PLA may intend to use civilian airliners for the bulk of its trooplift and some cargolift as well. For example, Hong Kong-owned airliners could be used to ferry surprise shock troops to begin operations to capture an airfield, to be followed up by PLAAF transports, assault helicopters, and civilian cargo jets. Civilian airliners could then ferry the bulk of troops necessary to secure and build on a bridgehead.

China United Airlines is used to transport troops, as it did for PLA peacekeeping troops sent to Cambodia in 1993. The PLA theoretically could have access to the 23 cargo versions of the Boeing 747 operated by Mainland and Hong Kong airlines. These aircraft can carry up to 122 tons of cargo,[90] though they require special offloaders as they do not have loading ramps. In addition, the PLA could have access to about 600 Western- and Russian-built jet transports in about 26 mainland, Hong Kong, and Macau-based airlines.[91] Recall that when the U.S. 82^d Airborne Division made its emergency deployment to Saudi Arabia in 1991, the troops flew mainly on chartered jumbo airliners.

Airborne Forces

The PLA 15th Airborne Corps, said to be largest unit that could come under the direct control of the Central Military Commission in an emergency,[92] is normally under the control of the PLAAF. A recent article from Taiwan's *Defense International* presents the PLA airborne forces as beginning to achieve a stature and size that is allowing them to move beyond an auxiliary, supporting arm to that of a decisive arm, especially in a Taiwan invasion.[93] In a Taiwan campaign, airborne forces alone would capture key targets in Taipei and cut off the capital city. Some in the PLA view such an attack, when combined with massive electronic, missile, and air attack, as sufficient to force Taiwan's capitulation.[94]

But for the PLA, such an operation would require intense preparation for its airborne forces that have had no modern combat experience. Nevertheless, PLA airborne exercises appear to be growing in size and complexity. The Soviet use of airborne forces in Hungary and the U.S. airborne deployment to the Gulf are models of intense study by PLA airborne forces.[95] In early December 2000, the commander of Russian airborne forces visited China to meet with PLA airborne leaders and to visit their units. He praised the training of PLA airborne troops and called for closer Russian-PLA cooperation in airborne unit training.[96]

PLA airborne forces are said to number about 30,000. The *Defense International* article notes the secret formation of a new brigade and the pending formation of 2 new airborne divisions (16th and 17th), for a total of 5 divisions. The article's author projects that PLA airborne forces could grow to 70,000 men. Chinese General Li Yuliang reportedly proposed that the PLA have the ability to paradrop 100,000 troops at a time by early in this century.[97]

New airborne weapons. Airborne forces and special forces are receiving new weapons. The PLA recently revealed a new 1,950-kg light buggy for airborne troops.[98] Airborne forces could also have access to 5 new types of large-gun-armed APCs, to include two 122-millimeter (mm) guns,[99] a 120-mm gun,[100] a 105-mm gun, and a 120-mm mortar.[101] The mortar-armed APC appears to be a copy of the Russian NONA–SVK mortar-armed APC designed to use laser-guided shells. Although the degree of PLA use of these new APCs is unknown, such vehicles could be carried by Il-76 or An-70 size transports and would provide airborne troops with mobile heavy guns needed to secure an airfield. For air dropping, PLA airborne forces also have an unknown number of Russian BMDs. The PLA also has a purpose-designed small truck armed with an HJ–8 antitank missile, which most likely also can be airdropped.[102]

Perhaps taking its cue from the U.S. LAND WARRIOR program, the PLA also is seeking to add digital connectivity to select ground units, most likely starting with special forces. At the October 13, 2000, PLA exercise/firepower display outside Beijing, the PLA revealed special forces equipped with a helmet-mounted TV camera and view screen.[103] The apparatus is quite unwieldy but perhaps represents an early attempt to digitize ground units. Nevertheless, the equipment would be useful for sensitive missions of high political impact, such as the capture of Taiwan's political leadership.

Integrated Air Defenses

The PLA is building perhaps one of the most formidable air defense networks in the world. Especially since the Gulf War and Kosovo, the creation of an integrated air defense network has become a high PLAAF priority. One recent report notes the PLA Air Force is building 68 new radar sites near Taiwan.[104] A robust air defense is viewed as a critical component for supporting offensive forces.[105] There is a heavy emphasis on defeating U.S. PGMs and stealth platforms. The last decade has also seen a heavy investment in a range of new radar systems, including counterstealth radar. New surface-to-air missiles (SAMs) from Russia are

being integrated into PLAAF and Army air defense units while new indigenous SAMs are appearing. A likely hallmark of this investment is to
integrate space, airborne, and radar sensors to defend the sensor network
while directing missiles and guns. The PLAAF may press to control
China's space defense and missile defense forces in the future.

New radar. The PLA has been developing over-the-horizon (OTH)
radar since 1967, but whether this technology has been developed for extensive use is unclear. Early efforts focused on groundwave OTH with a
range of 250 km. Such radar would be most useful for tracking ships. In
the 1980s, the PLA revealed efforts to build skywave OTH, which bounces
radar waves off the upper atmosphere and has the potential to detect targets out to 3,500 km.

The PLA has developed many long-range surveillance and tactical
radars. For long-range surveillance the PLA has developed the YLC–4, a
410-km-range 2-dimensional (2–D) radar, meaning it can only find the
height and range of a target. This radar is advertised as having a potential
antistealth capability. The JY–14 is a 320-km-range 3-dimensional (3–D)
radar that is resistant to clutter and jamming. The YLC–2 is a more trans-
portable 300-km-range 3–D radar that employs a variety of electronic
counter-countermeasures to survive enemy jamming. The JY–11 is a new
180-km-range 3–D radar that is accurate enough to supplant weapon
guidance radar, allowing it to turn off, thus decreasing its vulnerability to
attack by antiradar missiles.[106]

The PLA knowledge of phased array radar was likely increased when
it acquired the Russian Almaz S–300PMU long-range antiaircraft missile
system in the early 1990s. The phased array 76N6 CLAM SHELL radar is
able to detect targets out to 90 km and down to 500-meter altitude. It can
track up to 180 targets. Its phased array configuration means that it can
focus periodic points of radar energy on a target instead of bathing the sky
in radar waves. This allows the radar to avoid triggering aircraft radar-
warning devices that might result in ARM attacks.[107] The PLA also has purchased the S–300PMU1, which employs the more powerful 96L6 3–D
phased array radar that can track 100 targets simultaneously out to 300 km.

The PLA is also developing a new phased array radar that allows for
electronic beam steering and allows the radar beam to be focused to achieve
longer ranges. Such a radar was revealed at the 2000 China International
Defense Electronics Exhibition. It is possible that this same phased array
radar is also being developed for naval air defense.

The PLA Army is also introducing new radar systems. The YLC–6 is a 180-km-range low-altitude surveillance radar that is said in tests to have detected a U.S. AH–64 APACHE attack helicopter out to 30 km. The CLC–3 is a new mast-mounted radar that is useful for detecting low-flying objects such as helicopters and cruise missiles. Also known as the AS901, this is a solid-state L-band radar that can track up to 10 targets at a 3,500-meter altitude, up to 25 km, and out to 15 km at 100 meters.[108] The CLC–2 is a new tactical air defense radar mounted on a tank chassis to provide cueing for the new PZG–95 self-propelled missile/gun antiaircraft tank, which itself carries the short-range CLC–1 defense radar. A new army phased array radar is the SLC–2, which can detect incoming artillery out to 50 km to direct counterbattery fire.

Counterstealth radar. To counter the growing U.S. reliance on radar-evading stealth in its platforms and weapons, the PLA is devoting considerable effort to develop counterstealth radar. One area of particular PLA effort is in the area of metric-wave radar, of which the PLA uses several. At the 1998 Zhuhai Airshow, the Institute No. 23 of the China Aerospace Corporation marketed its J–231 radar, which is advertised as having "high capability of detecting antiradiation missile, high antistealth capability."[109] The PLA also operates other metric-wave radars, such as the 2–D YLC–14 and the larger 3–D YLC–9. Many PLAN warships, including the newest *Luhai* class, use the Type 636 metric-wave radar. Russia now markets several new and upgraded metric-wave radars that incorporate solid-state electronics, countermeasures, automatic processing features, and modern displays. Russians complain that the PRC has stolen their technology to upgrade metric-wave radar.[110]

The PLA may also be exploiting a U.S. technology called passive-coherent detection, reported to have been purchased from a U.S. company. This technology, developed by Lockheed-Martin, is able to detect disturbances in television broadcast signals caused by aircraft. When this data is combined with normal radar data, detection of stealth aircraft is possible. The PLA may also be exploring bistatic radar, in which the transmitter and receiver are separated by some distance to overcome stealth shaping.[111]

Obscurants and decoys. Smoke, chaff, lasers, and decoys figure heavily in PLA defensive operations, especially to counter the U.S. advantage in laser- and radar-guided PGMs. To defend against PGMs, the PLA uses BODYGUARD, which consists of a wheeled chassis that contains a smoke and chaff launcher, very likely combined with a laser sensor and dazzler system.[112] When a threat is near, BODYGUARD automatically fires smoke and chaff and its laser to confuse the aim of PGMs. The PLA also uses a range of decoys. Full-scale representations could include missiles, ships, aircraft, tanks, command vehicles, and other vehicles.[113] Replicas are said to include full-scale representations of a tank type first seen in the 1999 military parade, to include simulating the tank's radar and infrared profile.[114] The PLA has also used radar reflectors, inflatable structures with metallic sides that reflect and obscure radar returns, in exercises.

Antiaircraft systems. PLAAF air defense units were gradually upgraded in the 1990s, but this could change. In the early 1990s, the PLA received Russian S–300 and S–300PMU (SA–10) SAMs. These are still among the most effective antiaircraft missiles in the world, and their guidance system is very difficult to jam.[115] Unconfirmed reports note that the PLA may already have the Russian S–400 SAM, which boasts a 250-mile range. PLA units probably have the TOR–M1 (SA–15) SAMs that have a shorter range but are fast enough to intercept PGMs such as laser-guided bombs. The TOR was designed to defend S–300s and other high-value targets. In 1998, the PLA revealed its FT–2000 SAM, which uses a unique passive guidance system targeted against such U.S. EW aircraft as the EA–6B PROWLER. The FT–2000, which draws from Russian SAM technology and likely the U.S. PATRIOT as well, is expected to form the basis for an active-guided SAM. In the near term, this new SAM—and other SAMs developed, most likely with Russian assistance—can be expected. In the meantime, PLAAF missile units continue to use new variations of the HQ–2 (SA–2). It is an old system, but little is known about its more recent variants.

The PLA has also continued to develop antiaircraft guns, unlike the United States. Its copy of the Swiss SKYGUARD 35-mm radar/camera directed gun system is now in production. It fires shells that fragment in unison so as to create a hail of shrapnel that can destroy incoming missiles or bombs. The PLA is also building the PGZ–95 tracked quad-25-mm gun system for army air defense units.

Space defense. It is not clear which PLA service will take the lead in future space and missile defense missions. However, given its investments in air defense, the PLAAF may press for leadership in space defense missions. In 2000, the PRC revealed its large SL–4 mobile phased array radar designed to support the manned space program. This radar is intended to track satellites and could also be used to provide early warning for incoming ballistic missiles. However, it is not known whether this radar is being developed as part of an early warning network. It is also possible that Russia and China will collaborate on developing new missile defenses. Russia is marketing its new MARS decimeter-band mobile missile defense radar that can detect hyperspeed and space-based targets out to 2,000 km and also guide interceptors.[116]

China likely has had a long interest in missile defenses. A mid-2001 report in the PRC magazine *Hang Tien* noted that the PLA ABM program included the construction of two antimissile systems: the FAN JI 1 (Counterattack 1) and the FAN JI 2. The latter was tested five times. A FAN JI 3 was also designed, but the FAN JI program reportedly did not survive the chaos of the Cultural Revolution.[117] At the 1998 Zhuhai show, officials connected to the FT–2000 SAM stated that this missile would be developed into an active-guided missile that eventually would have an antitactical ballistic missile capability. There are likely laser antisatellite (ASAT) and micro- or nanosat ASAT programs under way. The latter may be based on microsatellite bus technology obtained from Britain's Surrey Space Systems and a new solid-fueled mobile space launcher revealed at the 2000 Zhuhai show. This new mobile space launch vehicle, called the KT–1, may be based on the DF–21 intermediate range ballistic missile.

Implications for the United States

At a time when the United States is increasingly preoccupied by its war on terrorism, it must also confront a growing challenge from the accumulating air power of the PLAAF. Despite the myriad challenges of assembling, training, maintaining, and paying for an air force to succeed in a high-tech, joint doctrine environment, the PLA is continuing to make significant strides to those ends. It is clearly making the necessary investments. As such, it would be foolish for Washington to proceed with business as usual. In just a few years, should the PLA conclude that it has achieved a necessary level of military superiority over Taiwan and Washington remains distracted by the current crisis or even greater crises, Beijing may yield to a real temptation to strike.

As has been noted by the annual Department of Defense reports to the Congress on PLA modernization, the airpower balance on the Taiwan Strait could favor the PLAAF after 2005.[118] By that time, it would have 80 or more Su-30MKKs, over 100 Su-27SKs, plus the A–50E AWACSs and Il-78M tankers needed to support distant and Taiwan theater strike operations. Su-30MKKs, JH–7s and H–6 bombers will also be able to deliver several new ARMs and LACMs to complement initial SRBM strikes. Initial and follow-on PLAAF strikes could be cued by a network of space-based and airborne reconnaissance systems. What remains of Taiwan's air force could be quickly dispatched by R–77-armed Sukhois, J–10s, and J–8IIC/H fighters. With air superiority established, the PLA could then proceed with airborne or amphibious assaults designed to force a final political capitulation in Taipei.

This trend in PLAAF modernization also places greater pressure on U.S. forces in the region. Should the war on terrorism drag on for many years, it may not be possible to maintain a constant carrier battlegroup presence in Northeast Asia. But even if one carrier could be maintained, it might be alone in responding to what would most likely be a surprise attack on Taiwan. After 2005, the PLAAF assets that could be concentrated on a single carrier battlegroup would be formidable. The PLAAF would have enough fighters to attack the carrier's combat air patrol, while strike aircraft could launch scores of standoff missiles that could saturate closer defenses. If airstrikes could be coordinated with submarine missile strikes and land-based missile strikes, the result could be devastating for the United States.[119]

Addressing the air component of deterrence is but one element in a complex military and political matrix necessary to deter a Chinese attack on Taiwan. This should include a robust effort to increase Taiwan's active and passive missile and air defenses. First, Taiwan also would require a massive effort to place critical aircraft and command assets underground and to make communication grids redundant and secure. Taiwan would need PATRIOT PAC–3, AEGIS, and even laser-based missile defense systems to be able to deal with the volume of incoming missiles and cruise missiles. In addition, Taiwan would require aircraft such as the Boeing A/V–8B+ HARRIER vertical/short takeoff and landing (V/STOL) fighter to be able to disburse its air defense forces. Taiwan also should be encouraged eventually to consolidate its aircraft types around the V/STOL version of the Lockheed F–35 Joint Strike Fighter. Taiwan needs the means to be able to attack and disrupt a gathering PLAAF/PLA airborne strike. If the United States cannot sell Taiwan long-range standoff attack missiles or systems like the Army Tactical Missile Systems missile, then it should provide Taiwan with technology to make its own.

For its part, more U.S. military should be closer to the Taiwan theater, a requirement recognized by the September 2001 Quadrennial Defense Review.[120] Part of the solution would be to revive substantial military cooperation with the Philippines, which would allow the United States to open a southern defensive front in the event of a PLA attack. The United States also needs assets that can survive PLAAF attack and enable an immediate retaliation. Theater missile defense for U.S. forces in the western Pacific is essential as soon as possible. Plans to convert two to four TRIDENT nuclear-powered ballistic missile submarines to carry cruise missiles should be accelerated as quickly as possible. In addition to LACMs, the United States should develop new heavy nonnuclear attack loads that can be placed on the first stage of an unused submarine-launched ballistic missile. These are needed to be able to attack concentrations of PLA air and naval forces within hours, not the days or weeks needed to deploy conventional forces.

In addition, the United States must also accelerate the introduction of advanced combat aircraft and longer-range AAMs to defeat the growing numbers of PLAAF Su-30MKKs and J–10 fighters. To give U.S. pilots a better edge, U.S. Pacific Command (PACOM)-based F–15, F–16, and F–18 fighters should be given priority for the new helmet-sighted AIM–9X missile, and development of longer-range versions of the AIM–120 should be accelerated. Navy F/A–18E/F fighter-bombers should receive more powerful engines with new active array radar planned for the Block 2 configuration. PACOM should also receive new F–22 fighters as soon as possible. In addition, PACOM should have priority to receive the F–35 joint strike fighter and new unmanned reconnaissance and combat aircraft.

It is also clear that as the PLAAF intends to benefit from space-based information sources, it may also play a role in denying space to its enemies. This means that the PLA intends to target Taiwanese and U.S. space-based reconnaissance and communication satellites in the event of a Taiwan conflict. As such, it is critical that the United States increase the survivability of planned new satellite constellations and give organic antisatellite capabilities to U.S. air and naval forces that would operate in a Taiwan conflict.

Conclusion

Viewed from the perspective of the mid-1990s, the PLA Air Force has made great strides toward fulfilling the objective to build a force capable of offensive as well as defensive operations. This essay has not focused extensively on the necessary developments in doctrine, training, maintenance, and funding that are critical to ensure the success of PLAAF modernization. But from the narrow perspective of equipment, it appears that the PLAAF is receiving the resources to create a competent core capability of multirole offensive-capable platforms that will be supported by necessary tanker, AWACS, and ELINT platforms. As official U.S. assessments have stated, absent compensating measures by Taiwan and the United States, the PLAAF could gain a measure of superiority on the Taiwan Strait after 2005. Also by this time, a single U.S. aircraft carrier sent to support Taiwan could face overwhelming danger, largely from a more capable PLAAF. As such, it is critical that Taiwan and the United States undertake actions necessary to preserve an adequate military balance to support continued deterrence.

Notes

[1] You Ji, *The Armed Forces of China* (London: I.B. Tauris, 1999), 125.

[2] Remarks noted in Ken Allen, "PLA Air Force Modernization and Operations," in *People's Liberation Army After Next*, ed. Susan M. Puska (Carlisle, PA: U.S. Army War College and the American Enterprise Institute, 2000), 189–190.

[3] Reports in 2001 noted that the PRC would eventually launch four imaging and four radar satellites, but a new report says eight more will be launched, indicating a similar division of four more imaging and four more radar satellites. See Craig Covault, "Chinese Plan Aggressive Satellite Development," *Aviation Week and Space Technology*, November 12, 2001, 56.

[4] Ibid. China may also be developing radar satellites that use a planar antenna similar to that used by Canada's RADARSAT.

[5] Interview with NPO Machinostroyenia officials, Moscow Airshow, 2001.

[6] Ji, 128.

[7] David Donald, "China, People's Liberation Army Air Force," *International Air Power Review*, Summer 2001, 87.

[8] Brochure, "L–15," Hongdu Aircraft Company.

[9] The author thanks Ken Allen for this observation.

[10] Brochure, "Flight Data Recording and Processing System," China Jinan Aviation Central Factory, obtained at the 2000 Zhuhai Airshow.

[11] "Fighter Figures Point to Chinese Air Supremacy," *Flight International*, October 26, 2000, 22.

[12] Development of the Su-30MK is covered in some detail by Yefim Gordon in *Sukhoi Su-27 Air Superiority Fighter* (Shrewsbury, Great Britain: Airlife Publishing, 1999), 58–60; and *Flankers: The New Generation* (Hinckley, Great Britain: Aerofax Midland Publishers, 2001), 29–64.

[13] "Su-30MK Twin-Seat Mulitrole Fighter," *Air Fleet,* June 2000, 10.

[14] "China's Su-30MKKs Will Have Multi-Mode Radar," *Flight International*, August 21, 2001, 27.

[15] Brochure, "Zhuk-M-S," Phazotron Company, obtained at the 2001 Moscow Airshow.

[16] Singapore may have Israel's helmet-sighted Python-4 AAM for its F–16s. Malaysia also has the Vympel R–73 for its MiG–29s.

[17] Gordon, *Sukhoi Su-27*, 148.

[18] "China-Russia 'Mainstay' Deal is Revitalized," *Jane's Defence Weekly*, October 5, 2001.

[19] "Overview of Russia-PRC Military-Technical Cooperation," *ITAR–TASS*, January 16, 2000.

[20] Cary Huang, "Beijing to Buy 72 Russian Jet Fighter-Bombers," *Hong Kong Standard*, June 21, 1999, 1.

[21] Jon Lake, "Sukhoi's Super Flankers," *Combat Aircraft*, March/April, 2001, 242.

[22] "Fighter figures point to Chinese air supremacy," *Flight International*, September 26, 2000, 22; "Chinese J10A To Be Mass Produced Next Year," *Kanwa News*, September 10, 2001, accessed at <www.kanwa.com/free/2001/11/e1103a.htm>.

[23] John A. Tirpak, "Foreign Fighters Get Better," *Air Force Magazine*, October 2001.

[24] Ibid.

[25] Jake Collins, "Chinese Fighter Evolution," *Air Forces Monthly*, October 2001, 54–55; see also "The Mist of PROC's J–9 Fighter," in *Defense Technology Monthly*'s *PROC's PLA Power* (Taipei, 1997), 30–33.

[26] Collins, 56.

[27] Larry Wortzel, "U.S. Commits to Security of Its Allies," *Taipei Times*, March 15, 2001.

[28] "China's fighter skips generation," *Flight International*, March 27, 2001, 22.

[29] Many of these pictures are in the excellent collection of Hui Tong, who maintains a useful Web site entitled Chinese Military Aviation, accessed at <www.concentric.net/jetfight>.

[30] "China's fighter skips," op. cit.; Hui Tong, op. cit.

[31] Nikolai Novichkov, "China to buy Russian engines for F–10 fighters," *ITAR–Tass*, June 15, 2001; Yihong Chang, "Beijing Engine Deal With Russia Heralds Up To 300 F–10s," *Jane's Defence Review*, July 4, 2001.

[32] Douglas Barrie, "China Builds on Russian Adder To Develop Active Radar Missile," *Aviation Week and Space Technology,* June 3, 2002, 26.

[33] "USA rethinks view of China's next generation XXJ fighter," *Flight International*, April 3, 2001, 21; Hui Tong, "J–8IIM."

[34] "USA rethinks," op. cit.

[35] Reporting on the possible PLA purchase of more Speys emerged in early 1999. By late 2000, a deal was concluded and the engines apparently were delivered during summer 2001. Douglas Barrie and Jason Sherman, "China Seeks British Engine," *Defense News*, July 2–8, 2001, 1; "Chinese Speys Being Delivered," *Air Forces Monthly*, August 2001, 4.

[36] "FBC–1 with Chinese ramjet missile," *Air Forces Monthly*, January 2001, 24.

[37] Barrie and Sherman, op. cit.

[38] Jon Lake, "Xian JH–7," *Air Forces Monthly*, December 2000, 38.

[39] Richard Fisher, "Xian JH–7/FBC–1, The nine lives of the Flying Leopard," *World Airpower Journal*, Summer 1999, 23.

[40] Ibid.

[41] Paul Lewis, "European hesitation holds up Sino-Pakistani Super 7 fighter," *Flight International*, January 18, 2000, 20.

[42] Paul Lewis, "USA lifts arms embargo to Pakistan and offers to supply more F–16s," *Flight International*, October 16, 2001, 11. At the time this essay was written, the Bush administration had so far refused to allow Pakistan to obtain the 28 F–16s that had been embargoed in the early 1990s.

[43] "Chengdu reveals details of F–7MF," *Flight International*, November 21, 2000, 18.

[44] The FC–1 mock-up and new AAM appeared in a substantially detailed article, "'Advanced' Launch of Chinese Super Seven," *World Flight (from PRC)*, May 2001, 14.

[45] Office of Naval Intelligence, *Worldwide Challenges to Naval Strike Warfare* (Washington, DC: Government Printing Office, 1997), 19.

[46] "USA rethinks view," op. cit.

[47] Collins, 56.

[48] Interview, Zhuhai Airshow, November 2000.

[49] Described in an article on ground-attack aircraft in the Mainland magazine *Weapon*, July 2001, 22.

[50] "China's new cruise nears service," *Flight International*, August 22, 2000, 26.

[51] Piotr Butowski, "Su-32 could hit market by 2002," *Jane's Defence Weekly*, August 9, 2000, 12.

[52] Yefim Gordon, "Flankers," op. cit., chapter 3.

[53] "China to Remain Largest Russian Arms Importer in Coming Years," *Interfax*, July 17, 2000.

[54] For a useful overview of U.S. efforts, see David Baker, "Global Hyperstrike," *Air International*, October 2001, 208–212.

[55] "Leninets Company and Chinese Government Delegation Sign Agreement to Participate in Creation of Hypersonic Flying Apparatus," *Vedmosti*, April 23, 2001, in *Roy's Russian Aviation Resource*, accessed at <www.royfc.com/news/apr/2301apr02.html>.

[56] Nikolai Novichkov, "Russia in the Forefront of Aerospace Technology," *Military Parade*, (May/June 1994), 68–71.

[57] Brochure, "MAKS, Multipurpose Aerospace System," Molniya Joint Stock Company, obtained at the 2001 Moscow Airshow.

[58] Bill Gertz, "China test-fires new air-to-air missile," *The Washington Times,* July 1, 2002, p. 1.

[59] Hui Tong, "PL–12?," *Chinese Military Aviation*, accessed at <www.concentric.net/~Jetfight/missile.htm>.

[60] Douglas Barrie, "China Builds on Russian Adder To Develop Active Radar Missile," *Aviation Week and Space Technology,* June 3, 2002, p. 26.

[61] Brochure, "FL–2," China Nanchang Aircraft Manufacturing Company, obtained at the 1998 Zhuhai Airshow.

[62] Brochure, "Kh-59MK," Raduga Bureau, obtained at the 2001 Moscow Airshow.

[63] "China-Russia Mainstay deal," op. cit.

[64] "China seeks U.S. reversal," *Flight International*, October 30, 2001, 21.

[65] Brochure, "A–50E," Moscow Scientific and Research Institute of Instrument Engineering (MNIIP), obtained at the 2001 Moscow Airshow.

[66] "A–50 Airplanes Planned for Delivery to India May be Equipped with PS–90A–76 Engines," *Interfax-AVN*, October 24, 2001.

[67] "China converts Y–8s for AEW role," *Flight International*, March 14, 2000, 15.

[68] These pictures appeared on the now defunct <www.star.net> Chinese language military Web site.

[69] Hui Tong, "Tu-154M/D *Careless*," *Chinese Military Aviation*, accessed at <www.jetfight.1avenue.com/y-8x_sh-5_a-50I.htm>.

[70] "Chinese Airborne Command Post," *Air Forces Monthly*, January 2001, 16.

[71] Hui Tong, "HD–5 Beagle," *Chinese Military Aviation*, op. cit.

[72] "KS–418E Jammer Pod," KNIRTI brochure, obtained at the 2001 Moscow Airshow.

[73] At the 2001 Moscow Airshow, KNIRTI revealed the configuration for its SORBITSYA antenna, which shows an omini-directional broadcast capability that would less likely be blocked by the airframe, whereas the jamming pods on the PROWLER can be blocked if the airframe is at the right angle to the pod.

[74] Ibid.

[75] Robert Sae-Liu, "Chinese expand aerial refueling capability to navy," *Jane's Defence Weekly*, June 21, 2000, 14.

[76] Hui Tong, "H–6U/HU–6," *Chinese Military Aviation*, accessed at <www.jetfight.com/ft-7_k-8_il-76.htm>.

[77] Ibid.

[78] Jon Lake, "Tupolev's Badger Family," *World Airpower Journal*, Winter 1992, 125.

[79] "China-Russia Mainstay deal," op. cit.

[80] Yefim Gordon and Dimitri Kommisarov, "The Red Starlifter," *World Airpower Journal*, Winter 1998, 123.

[81] "Delivery of Il-78MK Refueling Airplanes to India Will Begin in 2003," *Interfax-AVN*, October 24, 2001, in *Roy's Russian Aviation Resource*, accessed at <www.royfc.com/news>.

[82] As of 1993, these 2 C–130s were operated by Air China Cargo. Colin Ballantine and Pamela Tang, *Chinese Airlines* (Shrewsbury, Great Britain: Airlife Publishing, 1995), 42.

[83] "An-70 Will Be Built in China," *Segodnya*, June 20, 2000, in *Roy's Russian Aircraft Resource*, accessed at <www.royfc.com/news/jun/2000jun03.html>; "Antonov ANTK and Chinese AVIC II Company Collaboration," *Foreign Media Reports*, November 10, 2000, in *Roy's Russian Aircraft Resource*, accessed at <www.royfc.com/news/nov/1000nov01.html>.

[84] Vladimir Karnozov, "Future Imperfect," *Flight International*, November 6, 2001, 47.

[85] "Negotiations Under Way Regarding China's Participation in Creation and Production of An-70 Airplane," *Interfax-AVN*, October 24, 2001, in *Roy's Russian Aviation Resource*, accessed at <www.royfc.com/news/>.

[86] "Possibility of Purchase by China of 30 An74TK–300 Airplanes Not Ruled Out in Ukranian Government Apparatus," *Finmarket Agency*, August 23, 2001, in *Roy's Russian Aircraft Resource*, accessed at <www.royfc.com/news/aug/2301aug01.html>.

[87] The larger number is noted by Yefim Gordon, who supplies the aircraft registration numbers in Dimitry Komissarov and Yefim Gordon, *Ilyushin Il-76, Russia's Versatile Airlifter* (Hinckley, Great Britain: Aerofax Midland Publishing, 2001), 109.

[88] The COSCO Il-76 was viewed by the author on the COSCO Web site.

[89] *Nezavisimoye Voennoye Obozreniye No. 45*, May 12, 2000, in *Roy's Russian Aircraft Resource*, accessed at <www.royfc.com/news>; "Il-76 Sale to China will Permit Assigning Russian VPK Enterprises Manufacturing Parts for this Airplane with Orders," *Finmarket Agency*, July 5, 2001, in *Roy's Russian Aircraft Resource*, accessed at <www.royfc.com/news/may/0701may03.html>; Komissarov and Gordon, op. cit., 109.

[90] Bruce A. Smith, "Boeing Broadens Product Line for Cargo Transport Aircraft," *Aviation Week and Space Technology*, August 27, 2001, 54.

[91] Numbers of Chinese civil cargo and passenger airliners from "World Airlines, Parts 1, 2 and 3," in *Flight International*, March 20, March 27, and April 3, 2001. For a cross-reference by airliner type, see "World Airliner Census, Over the Precipice," *Flight International*, October 16, 2001, 40–69.

[92] Ibid.

[93] Lin Chu-chin, "PLA Special Operations Exclusive—PLA Airborne Operations," *Chun Shih Chia (Defense International)*, May 2001, 24–39, in *Foreign Broadcast Information Service*, May 1, 2001.

[94] Ibid.

[95] Ibid.

[96] Andrei Kirillov, "Georgy Shpak Supports Sharing Experience Between Russian, Chinese Paratroopers," *ITAR–TASS*, December 8, 2000.

[97] Ji, 145.

[98] *Bingqi Zhishi*, March 2001; Christopher Foss, "China fields fast-attack vehicle," *Jane's Defence Weekly*, June 13, 2001, 13.

[99] *Bingqi Zhishi*, August 2001.

[100] *Bingqi Zhishi*, June 2001; Yihong Chang, "China unveils 120mm 8x8 tank destroyer," *Jane's Defence Weekly*, June 30, 2001, 32.

[101] *Bingqi Zhishi*, May 2001; Yihong Chang, "China reveals SP mortar," *Jane's Defence Weekly*, June 6, 2001, 9.

[102] *Bingqi Zhishi*, December 2000.

[103] Ibid.; many pictures of the new digital communications gear can also be viewed on the PLA pictoral Web page.

[104] Al Santoli, report for the American Foreign Policy Council.

[105] Ji, 139–140.

[106] Radar data in this paragraph from brochures of the China National Electronics Import and Export Company.

[107] Steven Zaloga, "Airpower's Future Nemesis," *Air Forces Monthly*, January 2001, 35.

[108] Yihong Zhang, "China Launches New AS901 Radar," *Jane's Defence Weekly*, July 4, 2001.

[109] Brochure, "J–231 Mid-Range Surveillance Radar," Institute No. 23 of China Aerospace Corporation.

[110] Interview, Moscow Airshow, August 2001.

[111] L. Neng-Jing, "Radar ECCMs New Area:Anti-Stealth and Anti-ARM," *IEEE Transactions on Aerospace and Electronic Systems*, 31 (July 1995), 1120–1127; W. Xu, "The Challenges and the Ways to Deal With—Where is Airborne Fire Control Radar Going," *Proceedings of the National Aerospace and Electronics Conference*, NAECON 1993, 1, 303–309.

[112] Brochure, "China National Electronics Import and Export Corporation."

[113] PLA skill at building exact decoy replicas was displayed at a Guangzhou region military exhibition in early 2001, covered in *Bingqi Zhishi*, May 2001, and in *Defense Technology Monthly (Taiwan)*, March 2001.

[114] "Magicians on the Battleground: Experiencing China's Camouflage Units," *Jeifang Rabao*, May 31, 2001, in *Foreign Broadcast Information Service*, May 31, 2000.

[115] Zaloga, op. cit.

[116] Sergei Boyev, "Shrewd Eyes and Mind of the Missile and Space Defense High-Potential Radars; Past Present and Future," *Military Parade*, September 2001, accessed at <www.milparade.com/2001/47/02_01.shtml>.

[117] "China Steps Up ABM Technology Research," *Kanwa News*, accessed at <www.kanwa.com/free/2001/06/e0613b%20df31.htm>.

[118] U.S. Department of Defense, "Annual Report on the Military Power of the People's Republic of China," Report to Congress Pursuant to the FY 2000 National Defense Authorization Act, June 2000, 21.

[119] The PLA intention and capability to target U.S. carriers is further explored by the author in "To Take Taiwan, First Kill A Carrier," *China Brief,* July 8, 2002, accessed at <www.jamestown.org>.

[120] U.S. Department of Defense, *Quadrennial Defense Review Report* (Washington, DC: Department of Defense, 2001), 27.

Chapter 9

Analyzing Chinese Military Expenditures

Richard A. Bitzinger

Seek truth from facts.

—Deng Xiaopeng

Defense budgets can be a useful, even critical, indicator of national defense priorities, policies, strategies, and capabilities. The size of a country's defense budget, the rate of growth or decline in its military expenditures, and what it spends its defense dollars on can reveal much about a country's strategic intentions and future military plans. Defense budgets can also be a good indicator of a country's military modernization priorities and therefore its possible future military capabilities. Finally, military expenditures can serve as a gauge of a nation's defense commitment and resolve or its potential to threaten others.

Consequently, it is not surprising that China watchers in the West are keen to know more about Chinese defense spending. As China looms ever larger in the Western, and particularly U.S., security calculus, concerns over China as an actual or potential military challenge have grown correspondingly. One important piece of the China threat puzzle is understanding where current Chinese strategic and military priorities lay, and whether the Chinese are investing sufficient resources in these priorities to constitute a serious security concern for the West.[1]

So just how much is China spending on its military? The question is simple, perhaps, but it is one that has increasingly preoccupied and perplexed Western China watchers, not to mention their governments and militaries. Moreover, it is particularly prominent every March, when Beijing releases its defense budget for the next year. In early 2001, for example, China reported that it would spend 141 billion yuan ($17 billion) on the People's Liberation Army (PLA)—an increase of 17.7 percent over the previous year and continuing a 12-year trend of real growth in Chinese military expenditures. Likewise, given China's inflation rate of practically nil, this increase constituted its largest real rise in defense spending in more than a decade.

Not surprisingly, this announcement unleashed a flurry of speculation as to what the budget says about China's strategic intentions and its future military plans and whether its expanse translates into a growing Chinese threat to the West—particularly the United States and its friends and allies in East Asia. Beijing further fanned the flames by asserting that the increase in defense spending was necessary in order "to adapt to drastic changes in the military situation of the world and prepare for defense and combat given the conditions of modern technology, especially high technology."[2]

On top of this, analysts widely accept that the official budget released by the Chinese every year accounts for only a fraction of actual defense spending. In particular, whole categories of military expenditure are believed to be missing from official figures, seriously undervaluing real PLA spending and reinforcing beliefs that Beijing's lack of candor and transparency regarding its defense budget is yet another indicator of its aggressive and irredentist intents. At the same time, Western attempts to fill in the gaps in Chinese military expenditures—however much they are good-faith efforts to be scientific and "reasonable"—still largely consist of guesswork and hence contain a considerable margin of error. In addition, such estimates vary widely from each other, which have only further clouded the whole issue of analyzing and assessing Chinese defense spending.

Consequently, Western efforts at Chinese defense budget analysis have reached a methodological dead end. The salient issue now is, where do we go from here? In this regard, this essay has two purposes. First, by discussing what we do and do not know—and, more importantly, what we will probably *never* know—about Chinese military expenditures, it attempts to determine the limits to using defense budget analysis as a research tool for inferring and evaluating Chinese military priorities, policies, strategies, and capabilities. Second, it offers some suggestions and alternative approaches for improving and reinvigorating this line of research, including offering at least one approach for assessing likely future Chinese procurement costs and expenditures. In particular, this essay recommends that we get away from simply focusing on making bottom-line assessments and rather attempt to link military capabilities and requirements to budgetary demands to determine if there is a spending-capabilities mismatch.

What Do We Want Defense Budgets to Tell Us?

What insights do we hope to get from analyzing defense budgets and military expenditures? Ideally, such analysis should inform us better as to:

- intentions and resolve: As an indicator of the country's determination to modernize its armed forces over the long haul, what are China's long-term commitments to defense spending? Is Beijing willing to increase defense spending both in real terms and over a sustained period? How does this compare with neighboring states and potential rivals?

- the burden on the national economy: Is China spending an inordinate amount of money on defense, compared to other nations? How sustainable are current levels of spending?

- modernization priorities: Which defense technologies, military research and development (R&D), and arms procurement programs are receiving priority spending? How many of a particular type of weapon system are being produced and acquired? What does this say about current or emerging Chinese military doctrine or strategy? How much is being spent on personnel versus operations and maintenance (O&M) versus equipment, all of which indicate different priorities for force improvement and have different timelines for payoffs? Is one area of expenditure starving out the others?

- future military capabilities: How much funding is going to which branch or branches of the military? Is more money being spent on modernizing the navy and air force and hence on increasing power projection capabilities, or on ground forces and territorial defense (that is, the People's War)? Is the PLA putting more funding into technologies relating to the so-called revolution in military affairs (RMA), particularly information warfare and precision-strike, which could result in increased capabilities to fight an unconventional or asymmetric war?

Facts and Assumptions about Chinese Military Expenditures

We can utilize defense budgets to see if (and where) a country is putting its money where its mouth is concerning national security and defense. As such, the strength of defense budget analysis is its use of hard, empirical information—such as fiscal authorizations, appropriations, and outlays—that can be quantified and charted. This information, in turn, can be compared, tracked, and trend-lined over time and subjected to a variety of statistical analyses. Thus, it can reveal insights into a country's plans, priorities, and likely capabilities.

However, before we can use defense budgets and military expenditures to address such quantifiable issues, we must first have the budgetary figures to work with. More than almost any other field of inquiry, defense budget analysis is a highly data-dependent field of study; in other words, it involves a lot of number-crunching. Consequently, it demands having a lot of numbers to crunch, and the more numbers we have, the more detailed (and useful) will be our analysis. Despite the need for large amounts of data, few areas of Chinese military studies actually have access to *less* reliable data than defense budget analysis. The issue of data— or rather, the lack thereof—is therefore the greatest obstacle to constructing useful methodologies for studying and interpreting Chinese defense spending in-depth.

So what do we know? First of all, we possess a few firm facts when it comes to Chinese military expenditures and defense budgeting:

We know the official topline figure for Chinese military expenditures. Every March, as part of its annual state budget, the Chinese release a single overall figure for national military expenditures. In 2001, this figure was approximately 141 billion yuan ($17 billion) while in 2000 it was 121 billion yuan ($14.6 billion). We possess similar topline figures for Chinese defense spending going back to 1950. Consequently, we can argue fairly confidently that official Chinese military expenditures have increased significantly in real terms over the past decade. Armed with reasonably reliable data regarding China's inflation rate (that is, the national consumer price index), we can estimate that, after inflation, China's official defense budget has more than doubled between 1989 and 2000 and in particular has risen 58 percent just between 1995 and 2000 (figure 9–1). In addition, recent press reports indicate that China will continue to boost defense spending with double-digit annual increases for at least the next 5 years; this would double the defense budget to $30 billion by 2005.[3] From these efforts to increase military funding, we may deduce that Beijing is seriously committed to modernizing the PLA and to overcoming current personnel, equipment, and O&M-related impediments to fielding an advanced military force. We may also infer that the Chinese are using these budget increases to signal their intentions to potential adversaries—especially Taiwan and the United States—that it is serious about using military force, if necessary, to gain certain political-military objectives, such as the return of Taiwan.[4]

Figure 9–1. **Chinese Defense Budgets, 1989–2000** (in billions of yuan)

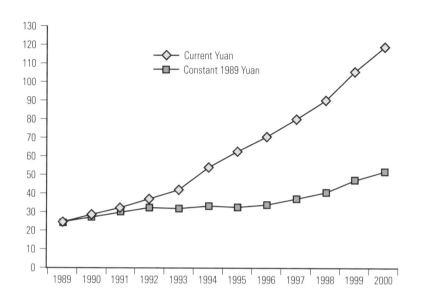

Source: China State Statistical Bureau.

We know the official defense budget as a percentage of government spending and of China's gross domestic product (GDP). Since we have the overall figure for the annual state budget and can roughly calculate China's GDP, we can determine that during the past decade, the defense budget comprised approximately 9 to 10 percent of central government expenditures and less than 2 percent of GDP. Both figures have fallen significantly from their levels during the 1970s and 1980s, indicating that even as defense budgets are increasing, military spending is actually a *declining* burden on the Chinese economy.

We possess a rough breakdown of official defense expenditures. According to Beijing's 1995, 1998, and 2000 defense white papers, the official defense budget is distributed almost equally among personnel, O&M, and equipment. In 2000, for example, the exact apportionment was 34 percent for personnel (40.6 billion yuan, or $4.9 billion), 35 percent for O&M (41.8 billion yuan, or $5 billion), and 32 percent for equipment (38.9 billion yuan, or $4.7 billion). In addition, Beijing has long maintained that the growth in defense spending goes mainly to raising soldiers' salaries and living conditions. In addition, we now possess data on the PLA budget for personnel, O&M, and equipment for 4 years (1997–2000). Even a cursory analysis of this data reveals some interesting facts:

- While all three areas of military spending have remained roughly equal to each other, spending on personnel grew only 39 percent between 1997 and 2000, compared to a 52 percent increase in the equipment budget and a 58 percent rise in the O&M account.
- During the same period, the personnel budget secured only 26 percent of all additional military spending. In comparison, 38 percent of these additional monies went to O&M spending, while the equipment budget received 36 percent.

Therefore, despite assertions by China that the lion's share of the recent growth in Chinese military expenditures has gone toward improving PLA soldiers' salaries and quality of life, it is clear—at least when looking only at the official defense spending figures—that procurement and O&M have benefited much more than personnel in recent budget increases.[5] This could mean that the PLA is placing a higher priority on hardware or on readiness than on personnel. Alternatively, it could mean that raising living standards in the PLA is less expensive than advancing other types of modernization goals.

In addition, most Western analysts of Chinese defense spending are reasonably certain that the official budget omits a number of critical expenditures, including:

- Research and development (R&D) costs. It is generally believed that military R&D is funded from other parts of China's state budget. Wang Shaoguang, in fact, argues that the Chinese freely acknowledge this fact and that defense R&D is specifically covered under the country's general R&D fund and from a special fund for "new product promotion."[6]
- Arms imports. Most arms imports are also believed to be extra-budgetary purchases, often covered under special or supplemental appropriations. During most of the 1990s, for instance, China imported an average of $775 million worth of arms every year.[7]
- Expenses for the People's Armed Police (PAP) and militia/reserve forces. Expenditures for the paramilitary PAP are paid out of a separate central government budget, while costs for PLA reserves and militia forces are partly borne by provincial budgets.[8]

- State support for China's military-industrial complex. Much of China's backward, bloated, and inefficient military-industrial complex operates at a loss.[9] Official defense budgets likely do not include the costs of direct subsidies to Chinese defense industries or (in more recent years) forced loans by state-owned banks to arms factories, many of which end up having to be written off as non-performing.[10]

- Earnings from PLA-run businesses. Until their forced divestiture in late 1998, the PLA operated thousands of commercial enterprises, including farms, factories, hotels, discotheques, arms exports, and other services. The profits or budgetary offsets from these activities could be counted as additional sources of revenue for the military.[11] It is still unclear how many PLA-owned businesses were actually sold off (most PLA-run farms were exempted, for example), how many are still secretly owned by the army (for example, through dummy partnerships), and how many divestiture orders were simply ignored.[12]

Second, we are reasonably certain that some kind of purchasing power parity (PPP) formula should be applied to Chinese defense expenditures to provide a more accurate reflection of their true value in terms of relative spending power. Many goods in the Chinese defense spending basket cost much less than they would in the West: conscription and lower living standards in the PLA save money on personnel, while lower wages at defense factories depress the cost of arms procurement. These disparities should be corrected by some kind of PPP multiplier, especially when attempting to compare Chinese defense spending to military expenditures in other countries.

Unfortunately, after these few facts and reasonable assumptions, reliable data regarding Chinese defense expenditures get much shakier. In fact, the unknowns and the unknowables concerning Chinese military expenditures greatly outnumber our known data. For example, beyond the highly aggregated spending figures for personnel, O&M, and equipment, we lack any further details as to how China's official defense budget is distributed. Specifically, we do not know how much funding goes to the army, air force, or navy; how much is spent on which particular R&D and procurement programs; the amounts and types of weapons (aircraft, ships, tanks, or missiles) being procured annually; or how much support is specifically accorded to categories such as training or logistics, or toward improving soldiers' living standards. In addition, we lack such detailed budgetary figures over time, which would permit trend and tradeoff analyses.

Compounding this lack of detail concerning the declared defense budget, we do not know the actual amount of China's extrabudgetary military expenditures. For example, while we are reasonably certain that defense R&D costs are not reflected in the official budget, we have no idea how much the Chinese really spend on R&D or on what particular programs and how much funding is allocated to each project (both annually and over time). Nor can we ever be certain how much the PLA nets from its commercial business activities or the percentage of these profits that actually ends up benefiting the military rather than being siphoned off into private overseas bank accounts or spent on new automobiles for senior officers.

Finally, while we are reasonably sure that some kind of PPP exists for Chinese defense spending, we have no clear idea what it actually is; PPPs for China vary widely. In addition, many PPPs do not account for the inferior quality of Chinese products (such as weapon systems) or services (such as the effectiveness of individual soldiers) relative to the West; therefore, they may actually overvalue Chinese expenditures. As one Western defense analyst has stated, "Unfortunately, purchasing-power parity measures are very difficult to compute and inherently imprecise. Among the chief challenges are uncertainty over which goods to place in the 'defense spending basket' and which goods to consider strictly comparable between one country and another."[13]

Given the absence of data regarding Chinese military expenditures, Western analysts have been forced to fall back upon extrapolation, inference, and conjecture to come up with reasonable guesses as how large extrabudgetary spending is, how it should be valued (that is, how large a PPP should be applied to the data), and how much is likely spent on defense R&D and procurement. This approach is fraught with many methodological pitfalls. For example, in attempting to calculate a reasonable procurement budget, analysts typically factor two "guesstimates" (how much a particular item might cost and how many might be purchased); basic probability theory should caution us that the resulting budget figure would be a highly unreliable number.

It should come as no surprise, therefore, that these efforts have resulted in a broad range of estimates of likely Chinese defense spending (figure 9–2) that—depending on one's assumptions regarding extrabudgetary inputs, their valuations, and PPPs—differ from each other by more

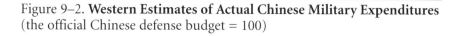

Figure 9–2. **Western Estimates of Actual Chinese Military Expenditures** (the official Chinese defense budget = 100)

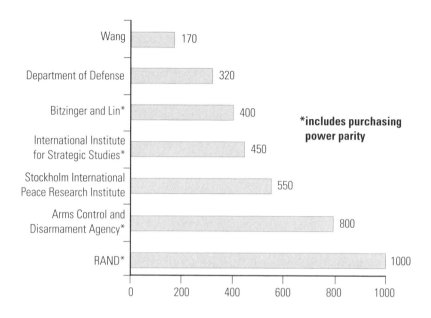

Sources: Wang Shaoguang, "The Military Expenditure of China, 1989–98," *SIPRI Yearbook 2000* (Oxford: Oxford University Press, 2000); Department of Defense, *Annual Report on the Military Power of the People's Republic of China* (Washington, DC: Department of Defense, July 2002), 2, accessed at <http://www.defenselink.mil/news/Jul2002/d20020712china.pdf>; Richard A. Bitzinger and Chong-Pin Lin, *The Defense Budget of the People's Republic of China* (Washington, DC: Defense Budget Project, 1994); International Institute for Strategic Studies (IISS), "China's Military Expenditures," *The Military Balance 1995/96* (London: IISS, 1995), 270–275; David Shambaugh, "World Military Expenditure," *SIPRI Yearbook 1994* (Oxford: Oxford University Press, 1994); Department of State, Bureau of Verification and Compliance, *World Military Expenditures and Arms Transfers 1998* (Washington, DC: Department of State, 2000); Charles Wolf, Jr., et al., *Long-Term Economic and Military Trends, 1994–2015: The United States and Asia* (Santa Monica, CA: RAND, 1995).

than a factor of 10. Even if one excludes the most extreme estimates, Western calculations of Chinese military expenditures still vary by around 300 percent. This bigger-than-a-breadbox/smaller-than-an-elephant type of analysis does little to help us understand the practical implications of actual Chinese defense spending.

Nor do we possess sufficient detail about Chinese military expenditures to make assertions about specific military priorities, intentions, plans, or procurement. In particular, we have no data as to how defense spending is directly affecting power projection capabilities, training, morale, living conditions, R&D, and high-tech weaponry. Consequently, defense budget analysis provides little help when it comes to assessing Chinese defense modernization efforts and likely future military capabilities. We may argue that higher or increasing defense spending is "threatening," but we cannot identify specifically where and to what extent.

Speculation about Chinese Procurement Spending

In the absence of additional budgetary data, analysts can do little more to advance the field of Chinese defense budget analysis. We might press the Chinese to be more forthcoming and transparent about military expenditures—to release more detailed defense budgets, along with additional (and more detailed) defense white papers—but we should not be too optimistic that this will garner significant results in terms of data. While Chinese-language sources probably exist that could provide additional insights into the defense budget, these are also unlikely to include the kind of detailed, over-time data conducive to more in-depth budgetary analysis.[14]

Therefore, more than searching for additional sources of data, we should attempt to use what is known about Chinese military expenditures to engage in innovative or alternative approaches to analysis and assessment. For example, we might attempt to assess how far likely spending levels could go in covering basic defense requirements for near-term procurement (2002–2006). Such an approach is based on several assumptions:

- The official Chinese defense budget will continue to grow at recent rates, approximately 10 percent annually, in real terms. As a result, the PLA would receive a total of $114.2 billion for the period 2002–2006 (table 9–1). Alternatively, expenditure growth could slow (to approximately 5 percent per annum) or increase (to approximately 15 percent per annum); in these cases, aggregated Chinese military spending for 2002–2006 would range from $98.8 billion to $149.1 billion.
- The equipment budget will continue to account for approximately one-third of the overall official PLA budget; consequently, total funding available for procurement for the period 2002–2006 would be $32.6 billion (at 5 percent annual real growth), $37.8 billion (10 percent), or $49.1 billion (15 percent) (table 9–1).
- Expenditures for defense R&D and for arms imports will each average approximately $1 billion to $2 billion annually.

Table 9–1. **Projected Increases in Chinese Defense Spending and Procurement, 2002–2006** (in billions of dollars)

	2002	2003	2004	2005	2006	Total
A. 5% Real Annual Growth	17.9	18.8	19.7	20.7	21.7	98.8
B. 10% Real Annual Growth	18.7	20.6	22.6	24.9	27.4	114.2
C. 15% Real Annual Growth	19.6	22.5	25.9	29.8	34.3	149.1
Procurement (A)	5.9	6.2	6.5	6.8	7.2	32.6
Procurement (B)	6.2	6.8	7.5	8.2	9.1	37.8
Procurement (C)	6.5	7.4	8.5	9.8	11.3	49.1

- We can make certain assumptions about procurement costs for major weapon systems for the period 2002–2006, based on educated guesses as to likely unit costs and the total number of such weapons (both low and high, to provide a range) likely to be procured (table 9–2). Such estimates, of course, have a wide margin for error and should be taken as rough guides only.
- Procurement for nonmajor weapon systems—such as ammunition and ordnance, communications systems, sensors, trucks, uniforms, and food—will absorb approximately 50 percent of all equipment funding (in keeping with rates usually found in other countries).

Armed with these assumptions, we simply total up likely procurement costs for this period (controlling for possible extrabudgetary items, such as defense R&D and arms imports) and compare this to likely procurement budgets (figures 9–3, 9–4, and 9–5). What we find is that, in most cases, projected expenditures fall below projected budgets. Therefore, it would appear that, at a 10 percent or even 5 percent annual growth rate, the Chinese could conceivably afford a modest arms buildup (including R&D and arms imports) over the next 5 years, based solely on official budgetary numbers. Naturally, if defense R&D and arms imports are truly extrabudgetary, or if defense spending grows at a higher rate, then the buildup could be even more substantial. If the Chinese are able to maintain 10 percent real annual average growth in

Table 9–2. **Estimated Procurement and Procurement Costs for Major Chinese Weapon Systems, 2002–2006**

	Unit Costs ($ millions)	Low Procurement (units)	High Procurement (units)	Costs (Low) ($ millions)	Costs (High) ($ millions)
F–7 fighters	5	120	240	600	1,200
F–8 fighters	15	60	120	900	1,800
Su-27 fighters	20	80	160	1,600	3,200
Misc. aircraft (trainers, transports, helicopters)	3	75	150	225	450
Major surface ships	320	8	16	2,560	5,120
Submarines	150	5	10	750	1,500
Main battle tanks	1	300	600	300	600
Other armored vehicles	0.5	300	600	150	300
Ballistic missiles	1.2	500	1,000	600	1,200
Cruise missiles	1	500	1,000	500	1,000
Totals				**8,185**	**16,370**

defense spending out to 2010, then by the end of the decade the PLA could conceivably possess:

- 200 Su-27 and Su-30 fighters
- 20 relatively new major surface combatants (*Luhu*-, *Luhai*-, and *Sovremenny*-class destroyers; *Jiangwei III*-class frigates)
- 12 relatively new diesel submarines (*Kilo*- and *Song*-class), one new nuclear-powered attack submarine, and one new nuclear-powered missile submarine
- 1,000 tactical ballistic missiles (DF–11 and DF–15)
- 1,000 cruise missiles (antiship and land-attack)
- Some F–10 fighters, DF–31 intercontinental ballistic missiles, and JL–2 submarine-launched ballistic missiles

At the same time, China's defense burden is likely to remain manageable, provided the economy continues to grow. At 7 percent annual

Figure 9–3. **Estimated Aggregated Procurement Costs, 2002–2006** (based on 5% real annual growth)

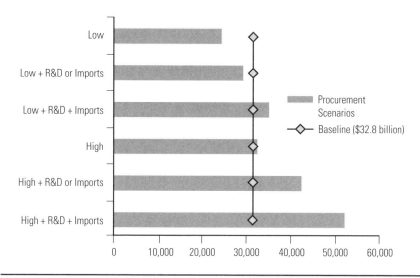

Figure 9–4. **Estimated Aggregated Procurement Costs, 2002–2006** (based on 10% real annual growth)

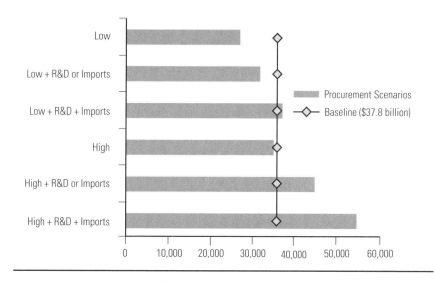

Figure 9–5. **Estimated Aggregated Procurement Costs, 2002–2006** (based on 15% real annual growth)

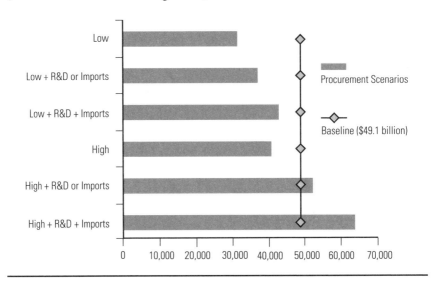

Table 9–3. **Official Chinese Defense Spending as Percentage of GDP** (based on 7% real annual growth in GDP)

	2001	2002	2003	2004	2005	2006
10% Real Annual Growth in Defense Expenditures	1.6	1.6	1.7	1.7	1.8	1.8
15% Real Annual Growth in Defense Expenditures	1.6	1.7	1.8	2.0	2.1	2.3

Note: Defense R&D and arms imports, if extrabudgetary, adds at most an additional 0.3% of GDP annually ($4 billion per year).

GDP growth, even a 15 percent annual increase in the defense budget would absorb less than 3 percent of China's GDP by the middle of the decade (see table 9–3).

Of course, all this speculation is fraught with caveats. Growth rates of 10 to 15 percent may ultimately be unrealistic or unsustainable, from either an economic or political standpoint. In addition, procurement costs could be much higher than estimated. Consequently, the PLA could be facing a considerable "procurement bow-wave" by the middle of the decade, as several new and expensive weapons programs come online after 2006 or so. Finally, personnel and O&M costs could rise significantly over the next several years, as Beijing attempts to compensate the PLA for business divestitures, as China attempts to meet growing quality-of-life needs for its soldiers, and as the PLA expands training, readiness, and logistics to meet the demands of a more high-tech force. Overall, therefore, while the PLA may be the beneficiary of an increasing defense budget, it may also be saddled with growing requirements that will strain its available financial resources.

Suggestions for Attempting Future Analysis

In thinking about ways to address the issue of Chinese defense budgets and military expenditures further, we can attempt to improve our methodologies and make our work more intellectually rigorous and honest. Specifically:

We should discount unsophisticated analytic approaches that simply fix military expenditures at a "reasonable" percentage of GDP. We should also discount analysis based on old, highly massaged data. (I specifically refer here to the U.S. Arms Control and Disarmament Agency [ACDA] approach to calculating Chinese military expenditures, which is based on a PPP conversion rate that is nearly 20 years old. In fact, ACDA admits that its estimations of Chinese military spending "should be treated as having a wide margin of error."[15])

We should avoid politicizing Chinese budgetary analysis. This includes both "kitchen-sinking" and "low-balling" extrabudgetary expenditures to produce a desired budgetary figure that either supports or undermines a "China threat" argument. At the same time, we should be careful not to get caught up in groupthink and purposely skew our data to fit the middle of the bell curve.

We should discount approaches that do not include some kind of PPP formula. Just because we do not know precisely what the PPP formula is for Chinese defense budgets does not mean that one does not exist. We should endeavor to come up with better and more reliable methodologies for calculating PPPs for Chinese military expenditures.

We should not let worst-case thinking dominate budget assessments. In particular, we need to address and argue specifically why extrabudgetary or increasing military expenditures should be considered threatening and not just take it as a self-evident fact. Likewise, we should be careful when stating that "Chinese defense expenditures could be as high as . . ." since one person's high-end estimates often become another's baseline arguments.

We should attempt to be more interdisciplinary and engage more outside functional experts—particularly genuine number-crunching budgetary analysts—in our research. We should also query Western Sovietologists as to how they came up with estimates of Russian defense spending during the Cold War. At the very least, these sources of expertise can validate our methodologies.

Above all, *we should resist the easy temptation to make the bottom line the crux of our analysis*—to give out a single figure of X billion yuan or dollars as the likely Chinese defense budget and simply leave it at that. In this regard, we are only perpetuating the same dilemma that we encounter with the official top-line figure for Chinese defense spending: we fail to provide any reliable indicators of *where* the money is going and *why*. In the absence of any further data—that is, what the Chinese are specifically spending their defense budget on and whether it is cost-effective, what their spending trade-offs are, how this spending compares to other countries' military expenditures—such an effort offers little useful information or analysis.

Finally, we need to be honest with ourselves: Given the current (and probably ongoing) paucity of data, we should acknowledge the severe limitations of any effort to analyze and assess Chinese military expenditures. Moreover, the consumer of our research deserves to know the considerable uncertainty and high probability of error present in our methodologies and outcomes. Until we have more data, defense budget analysis of Chinese military affairs will function best as an adjunct to or a check on other types of empirical research—areas where the arguments are likely to be more impressionistic and less quantitative.

Notes

[1] Recent Western literature on Chinese defense expenditures includes David Shambaugh, "Wealth in Search of Power: The Chinese Military Budget and Revenue Base," paper delivered to the Conference on Chinese Economic Reform and Defense Policy, Hong Kong, July 1994; Bates Gill, "Chinese Defense Procurement Spending: Determining Intentions and Capabilities," in *China's Military Faces the Future*, ed. James R. Lilley and David Shambaugh (Washington, DC: American Enterprise Institute, 1999); Arthur Ding, "China Defense Finance: Content, Process, and Administration," *China Quarterly*, June 1996; Wang Shaoguang, "Estimating China's Defense Expenditure: Some Evidence from Chinese Sources," *China Quarterly*, September 1996; Wang Shaoguang, "The Military Expenditure of China, 1989–98," *SIPRI Yearbook 2000* (Oxford: Oxford University Press, 2000); International Institute for Strategic Studies (IISS), "China's Military Expenditures," *The Military Balance 1995/96* (London: IISS, 1995), 270–275; and Richard A. Bitzinger and Chong-Pin Lin, *The Defense Budget of the People's Republic of China* (Washington, DC: Defense Budget Project, 1994).

[2] Robert Karniol, "PRC Spending Continues to Rise," *Jane's Defense Weekly*, March 14, 2001 (Internet version).

[3] Lester J. Gesteland, "China Defense Budget Up 15–19% This Year," *ChinaOnLine News*, January 31, 2000, accessed at <http://www.chinaonline.com>.

[4] Craig S. Smith, "China Sends Its Army Money, and a Signal to the U.S.," *The New York Times*, March 11, 2001 (Internet version).

[5] Si Liang, "Increase in China's Military Is Still at a Low Level," *Zhongguo Tongxun She* (Hong Kong), March 8, 2001, translated and reprinted by *Foreign Broadcast Information Service* (Internet version); Sun Shangwu, "China Daily Interviews PLA Logistics Deputy Director on Military Budget Increase," *China Daily*, March 12, 2001 (Internet version).

[6] Wang, "The Military Expenditure of China, 1989–98," 339.

[7] U.S. Department of State, Bureau of Verification and Compliance, *World Military Expenditures and Arms Transfers 1998* (Washington, DC: U.S. Department of State, 2000), 129.

[8] Wang, "The Military Expenditure of China, 1989-98," 338; David Shambaugh, "World Military Expenditure," *SIPRI Yearbook 1994* (Oxford: Oxford University Press, 1994), 447.

[9] John Frankenstein, "China's Defense Industries: A New Course?" in *The People's Liberation Army in the Information Age*, ed. James C. Mulvenon and Richard H. Yang (Santa Monica, CA: RAND, 1999),197–199; John Frankenstein and Bates Gill, "Current and Future Challenges Facing Chinese Defense Industries," *China Quarterly*, June 1996, 419–420; "Three Kings: Over Half of China's Industrial Profits in Jan.-Apr. Ruled by 3 Sectors," *ChinaOnline News*, June 28, 2000, accessed at <www.chinaonline.com>.

[10] Harlan Jencks, "COSTIND is Dead, Long Live COSTIND! Restructuring China's Defense Scientific, Technical, and Industrial Sector," in *The People's Liberation Army in the Information Age*, ed. James C. Mulvenon and Richard H. Yang (Santa Monica, CA: RAND, 1999), 61; "The Crisis of State-Owned Enterprises in Mainland China Worsens," *Cheng Ming* (Hong Kong), November 1, 1996, 54–57.

[11] Wang, "The Military Expenditure of China, 1989–98," 344–347; Shambaugh, "Wealth in Search of Power," 15–20; IISS, "China's Military Expenditures," 273.

[12] For more on PLA commercial business activities and subsequent divestiture, see James C. Mulvenon, *Soldiers of Fortune* (Armonk, NY: M.E. Sharpe, 2000).

[13] Michael E. O'Hanlon, "The U.S. Defense Spending Context," in *The Changing Dynamics of U.S. Defense Spending*, ed. Leon Sigal (Westport, CT: Praeger Press, 1999), 14.

[14] David Shambaugh and Bates Gill have identified a few Chinese sources on the defense budgeting process, but these appear to be overviews of the budgeting process and budget management, rather than detailed accountings of military expenditures. See *Zhongguo junshi jingfei guanli* (*Chinese Military Expenditure Management*), ed. Lu Zhuhao (Beijing: Jiefangjun Chubanshe, 1995); *Zhongguo junshi caiwu shiyong daquan* (*Complete Practical Guide to Chinese Military Finance*) (Beijing: Jiefangjun chubanshe, 1993); Liu Yichang and Wu Xizhi, *Guofang jingjixue jichu* (*Basics of Defense Economics*) (Beijing: Junshi Kexue Chubanshe, 1991).

[15] See *World Military Expenditures and Arms Transfers 1998*, 203–204.

Part IV

Key Policy Changes

Chapter 10

China's "New Concept of Security"

David M. Finkelstein

Many China watchers first came upon the "New Concept of Security" in the context of the July 1998 defense white paper, *China's National Defense*. The concept was featured in the important first section entitled "The International Security Situation."

This, however, was not the first time the concept was put forth. Indeed, the defense white paper merely capped off more than a year and a half of clarion calls throughout the Asia-Pacific region by high-level Chinese foreign policy and defense officials for such a new alternative concept:

- It was officially unveiled by the People's Republic of China (PRC) in March 1997 at a meeting of the Association of Southeast Asian Nations (ASEAN) Regional Forum.
- In their joint statement at the conclusion of their April 1997 summit, President Jiang Zemin and Russian President Boris Yelstin called for a "new and universally applicable security concept."
- In December 1997, Foreign Minister Qian Qichen outlined and explained the "New Concept of Security" during activities marking the 30th anniversary celebration of the ASEAN.
- In February 1998, Defense Minister Chi Haotian called for the establishment of a "New Concept of Security" in a speech in Tokyo to the National Institute of Defense Studies, and again in a talk presented to the Australian College of Defence and Strategic Studies during his visit to Canberra.

Nothing in the concept seemed very new or extraordinary. At the time of its release, it seemed to be merely a repackaging of China's time-honored "Five Principles of Peaceful Coexistence" and China's discovery of what most other developed nations already understood: to wit, that economic security is just as important as military security.[1]

What *was* compelling about the New Concept of Security at the time was the context in which it was trotted out. China was clearly leaning forward in the international community to offer an alternative vision, however vague, of how nations should pursue national security in the post-Cold War world order. This was clearly not in line with Deng Xiaoping's oft-quoted dictum that in international affairs, China should "keep a low profile and never take the lead." So my interest in the concept began with my own questions as to whether we were about to see a fundamental shift in Chinese foreign policy behavior since it was during this period that Jiang Zemin was globetrotting to create numerous "strategic partnerships."[2]

Conceptually, there was not, nor is there today, anything in the concept that one would feel compelled to take issue with. But from an American perspective, what has been troubling about the New Concept of Security has been the packaging used to promote it, especially when it was first brought out.

In the past, the Chinese repeatedly have referred to the New Concept of Security as an alternative to the "Cold War mentality" of "some nations" that continue to rely on military alliances and "military blocs" to secure or promote their interests. It does not take much of a stretch to fill in the blanks. Moreover, at the time the new concept was unveiled back in 1997 and 1998, one read much more about what China was against than about how China planned to operationalize this alternative international system.

China's New Security Concept

The relations among nations should be established on the basis of the Five Principles of Peaceful Coexistence:

- Mutual respect for territorial integrity and sovereignty
- Mutual non-aggression
- Non-interference in each other's internal affairs
- Equality and mutual benefit
- Peaceful coexistence

These are the political basis and premise of global and regional security. Each country has the right to choose its own social system, development strategy, and way of life, and no other country should interfere in the internal affairs of any other country in any way or under any pretext, much less resort to military threats or aggression.

In the economic field, all countries should strengthen mutually beneficial cooperation, open up to each other, eliminate inequalities and discriminatory policies in economic and trade relations, gradually reduce the development gaps between countries, and seek common prosperity.

This is still more or less the case. Clearly, the use of the concept as a rhetorical vehicle to castigate U.S. foreign and security policy reached fever pitch in Beijing's October 2000 defense white paper.

Overall, then, starting with the April 1997 Sino-Russian Joint statement and continuing through the defense white paper of October 2000, Beijing has in the past felt a need to argue the merits of the New Concept of Security by juxtaposing it against thinly veiled or openly direct criticisms of U.S. foreign policy mechanisms or specific U.S. security policies. In effect, Beijing accuses the United States of perpetuating a security system that will prove inherently dangerous and destabilizing, both regionally and globally. This tack may ultimately detract from serious consideration of the essence of the concept, especially in the United States, if it continues to be perceived as nothing more than another rhetorical device with which to attack U.S. policies.

Why the New Concept of Security?

Explaining why Beijing promulgated the New Concept of Security is very much tied to Chinese security concerns throughout the mid- to late 1990s, many of which persist today.

Beijing's call for a New Concept of Security is an indication of China's dissatisfaction and frustration with the unfolding international system. China's much-hoped-for multipolar world has not come about with the

Such steps can form the economic basis of global and regional security. Maintaining a normal and sound economic, trade, and financial order calls for not only a perfect macro-economic management system as well as a sound system of economic operations, it also calls for strengthening regional and international economic contacts and cooperation, so as to jointly create a stable and secure external economic environment.

All countries should promote mutual understanding and trust through dialogue and cooperation, and seek the settlement of divergences and disputes among nations through peaceful means.

These are the realistic ways to guarantee peace and security. Security is mutual, and security dialogues and cooperation should be aimed at promoting trust, not at creating confrontations, still less at directing the spearhead against a third country or infringing upon the security interests of any other nation.

Excerpted from Information Office of the State Council of the People's Republic of China, "China's National Defense," July 27, 1998, 6–7.

end of the Cold War, as Chinese international relations theorists had predicted. Instead, what they face is an increasingly globalized world with an increasingly strong and dominant power—the United States. In as much as China had declared in many foreign policy statements that it would work to create a multipolar world, the New Concept of Security provided a framework for political, economic, and security relations in a future multipolar world order. This framework had been missing from previous Chinese prognostications about the movement of the international order toward multipolarity. The concept, therefore, served as a theoretical device.

The New Concept of Security clearly was a direct Chinese reaction to policies and actions by the United States that Beijing perceived as threatening, especially Washington's strengthening of its military alliances. The concept continues to serve as a counterargument to the U.S. assertion that East Asia's economic prosperity—past, present, and future—is a direct result of the peace and stability that is underwritten by the forward presence of U.S. military forces and military alliances.

At the time, the concept was a clear reaction to the movement to expand the North Atlantic Treaty Organization (NATO) into Eastern Europe, which began in 1995, as well as to NATO interventions in the Balkans. It was also a reaction to Chinese concerns that the Partnership for Peace was encroaching into Central Asia—onto China's doorstep. The U.S. Atlantic Command's combined military exercise with Kazakhstan and Russia—CENTRAZBAT 97—evinced tremendous concern among Chinese security analysts at the time.

In addition, the New Concept of Security was a reaction to Beijing's assessment that in the long term, the United States would maintain its primacy as the sole military superpower by developing and fielding advanced defense technologies. Hence, many of Beijing's verbal attacks on the U.S. ballistic missile defense (BMD) programs have often couched in terms that argue that developing these systems "run counter" to the aspirations of many countries that want to see an end to the "Cold War mentality."

Also, the New Concept of Security was likely China's response to the Clinton-Hashimoto Joint Statement in April 1996 and the promulgation in 1997 of the U.S.-Japan Revised Guidelines for Defense Cooperation. This point, admittedly, is very tentative, but the timing between the two events does suggest the possibility of linkage.

When first issued, the New Concept of Security constituted a concerted attempt by Beijing to present a kinder and gentler face within the region, especially in Southeast Asia. Officials of the People's Republic of China (PRC)

Ministry of Foreign Affairs (MFA) generally agree that, at least from an MFA perspective, a critical target audience for the new concept was the nations of Southeast Asia. (Recall that the new concept was first formally enunciated at the 1997 ASEAN meeting.)

Beijing had good reason to be proactive in the region. Throughout the 1990s, some Asian nations began to view China's growing national power and Beijing's perceived regional aspirations with increasing suspicion and concern. These concerns arose from confrontations over the Spratly Islands, Chinese claims in the South China Sea, and China's apparent willingness to engage in demonstrations of force in the Taiwan Strait, especially in 1995 and 1996. All this was exacerbated in some regional quarters by Beijing's minimal defense transparency.

Moreover, Chinese officials were likely taken aback by the united front among ASEAN states when, at the Hangzhou Conference in 1995, Southeast Asian ministers protested China's actions at Mischief Reef in the Spratly Islands. As a result, the New Concept of Security was offered to the region as part of a larger diplomatic effort to debunk the "China threat theory," as it is referred to by the PRC. Other actions taken by the PRC to soften its image in Southeast Asia included:

- capitalizing on its favorable image as a "responsible actor" during the Asian financial crisis
- acting in concert with the "nuclear club" countries to condemn the South Asian nuclear detonations
- heralding its "strategic partnerships" around the globe
- grandstanding about its decision at the 15th Party Congress to demobilize another 500,000 troops from the PLA
- taking modest but welcome steps toward defense transparency as characterized by the publication of the July 1998 defense white paper and China's participation in multilateral Track I and Track II security forums
- agreeing in principle to take part in talks aimed at establishing a code of conduct in the South China Sea.

These, then, are the three main reasons I see as explaining why the new concept was offered in the first place. Let us turn now to military issues.

The Military Dimension

Conspicuously absent from the formal articulation of the New Concept of Security is a military dimension. At best, it only states that nations should not "resort to military threats or aggression."

This absence of a formally articulated military dimension likely led to some confusion within the PLA, especially given the fact that Defense Minister and Central Military Commission Vice Chairman General Chi Haotian was one of the most audible voices calling for a new international security order. General Chi still refers to it in his publicized comments to visiting foreign defense officials.

The first order of business for the PLA when the new concept was articulated was to show its political support for it publicly. Consequently, on December 23, 1997, the editorial department of *Zhongguo Guofang Bao* held a seminar to discuss and laud the New Concept of Security. As least as publicized, the seminar did little other than to applaud the new concept, declare it another indication of the correct leadership of Jiang Zemin and the third-generation leadership of the Chinese Communist Party, denounce Cold War security arrangements, and assert how proud the PLA was that "China is the first to advocate a new security concept and a new peacekeeping mode in the world."[3]

The next day, *Jiefangjun Bao* carried a lengthy signed article (with an editor's note to preface the importance of the new concept) based on the premise that the world must get out of the "shackles of Cold War mentality." At least half of the author's explanation of the new concept was devoted to its political and economic dimensions. But there also was an attempt (albeit an extremely weak and self-serving one) to define the role of national military establishments, aimed, obviously, at propagandizing the greater Chinese military readership:

> From the viewpoint of military security, the security concept requires: The military force shoulders the important mission of defending a state's territorial sovereignty and integrity, resisting foreign aggression, and safeguarding state unification. Therefore, it is necessary to strengthen army building, develop armaments, and reform military organizations. The defense policies and military strategies of all countries should be defensive, be based on avoiding conflicts and wars, preventing crises, and checking the escalation of conflicts. The military forces of all countries should play a role in the broader scope such as cracking down on terrorism and drug trafficking, rescue work, and humanitarian aid. All countries should not and are not allowed to pursue the doctrine of military interference and resort to military force at every turn. The military cooperation and munitions trade between countries should be based on the principle which is "not aimed at any third party."

The article later acknowledges the following types of activities for national military establishments:

- peacekeeping operations (which, it was argued, were in danger because certain countries were using them as the excuse to interfere in the internal affairs of other countries)
- security dialogues
- confidence-building measures
- security consultations
- security agreements based on mutual benefit.[4]

And that was about it. Although I cannot claim exhaustive knowledge of the military dimensions of the New Concept of Security as represented in the Chinese literature, I have seen nothing that gets any more granular than the points outlined above. In September 2001, Deputy Chief of the General Staff Lieutenant General Xiong Guangkai referred to the concept in a speech on China's national defense. His remarks are no more specific about the role of the military than the two articles already cited, which were written over three years earlier:

> ... China advocates a new security concept with mutual trust, mutual benefit, equality and coordination at the core, and stands for the promotion of multilateral security and security cooperation, including effective international arms control and disarmament on the principles of justice, reason, comprehensiveness and equilibrium through dialog and negotiations on the basis of the five principles of peaceful coexistence and the strengthening of economic cooperation.[5]

What all of this suggests is that the New Concept of Security is much more a political and economic construct than a military one. It indicates that, as usual, the role of the PLA will be to support foreign policy through all of the military diplomacy mechanisms that it usually employs. The New Concept of Security was not a PLA initiative. For the most part the Chinese armed forces have had to figure out where they fit into the greater scheme, if at all.

Various PLA articles and speeches by its leaders suggest that the PLA believes the role it had been playing in foreign military diplomacy and its limited participation in UN-sponsored observer efforts was already appropriate to the newly articulated security concept. Chinese foreign military diplomacy around the globe is quite extensive and far beyond the scope of this chapter.[6]

Is the New Concept of Security Viable?

Is Beijing's new concept going to gain enough traction to shape the greater international post-Cold War security system? The answer is simple: certainly not, for several reasons:

- Very little in the concept is actionable. The new concept is little more than a set of principles—admirable principles in the main, but ones bereft of a framework around which to build a serious alternative international security structure on a global scale.

- The packaging of the concept has in the past been too heavily laced with anti-U.S. rhetoric. While many countries will find the principles attractive in theory, many are not going to be disposed to sign on to a construct that often takes on an anti-U.S. flavor. The exception, of course, will be those nations that already oppose the United States.

- At least three of the five major poles in China's multipolar world order construct—namely Japan, Western Europe, and the United States—seem to have their own ideas about what the post-Cold War order should look like. And the fourth pole, Russia, is now straddling both sides of the fence, as a result of the terrorist events of September 11, 2001.

- Those nations in Asia that are convinced that the presence of the U.S. military in the region is a force for stability are not going to be talked out of it by Beijing. Indeed, U.S. defense relations with Australia and Japan have strengthened in the past few years, and some Southeast Asian nations, Singapore for one, are eager to be accommodating to that presence.

- NATO is not going to disband. If anything, it has been strengthened by the peacekeeping operations in the Balkans and the invocation of Article 5 pursuant to the attacks on the United States in September 2001. Moreover, NATO remains quite attractive to current non-members in Eastern Europe, some in Central Asia, and, potentially, Russia itself. Moreover, in spite of the ambivalence of some European nations over the U.S. national missile defense program and U.S.-European frictions over the Euro Corps, security relations on both sides of the Atlantic remain strong.

In retrospect, in the 4 years since I first encountered the New Concept of Security, it appears less and less to have been intended to replace the larger international order than to shape China's peripheral security environment.

Is the New Concept of Security an Empty Concept?

Although the New Concept of Security is not going to drive the international world order by any stretch of the imagination, it cannot be considered an entirely meaningless initiative. In an ironic twist of circumstance, there is one region of the world in which the concept is being given form, where it is in the process of being operationalized, and in which new security policy precedents are taking shape. That region is in Central Asia, where the Shanghai Cooperation Organization (SCO) is operating.

The SCO was formally established in June 2001; it was an outgrowth of the Shanghai Five group consisting of China, Russia, Kyrgyzstan, Kazakhstan, and Tajikistan. With the establishment of the SCO, a sixth member, Uzbekistan, joined the group. The original Shanghai Five was established in 1996 for the express purpose of:

- working out extant border disputes peacefully
- instituting military confidence-building measures among the respective armed forces in the border regions
- coordinating and cooperating about cross-border security due to the terrorist, separatist, and criminal activities that had been plaguing each in the border areas.[7]

With the creation of the SCO, the prospect of security cooperation among the members is growing. Decisions have been made to establish an antiterrorism center in Bishkek, and the possibility of combined military exercises to secure the border areas has been under consideration since at least June 2001.

This type of activity is unprecedented for China. This is the first time in the history of the PRC that Beijing is a formal signatory to a multinational convention, the primary purpose of which is security. Second, if the SCO countries actually do conduct a combined military exercise, it would be a first for the People's Liberation Army. But beyond these first two points, this is the first time that the PRC has taken the lead, an active role, in the creation of a multilateral security organization. Indeed, many Chinese observers consider China's leading role in the SCO a turning point in post-1949 PRC foreign policy.

The Shanghai Five and its successor, the SCO, have been and continue to be hailed by the Chinese as the epitome of what the New Concept of Security is supposed to be about. As they see it, the SCO is primarily concerned with security but has political and economic components as well. It is about mutual security and working out differences amicably. It is about enhancing collective security "without being aimed at a third

> ## Key Events for the Shanghai Five and the Shanghai Cooperation Organization
>
> **1996 (Shanghai):** Agreement on Confidence Building in the Military Sphere in Border Areas
>
> **1997 (Moscow):** Agreement on Mutual Reduction of Military Forces in the Border Areas
>
> **1998 (Astana):** Meetings to finalize 1996 and 1997 agreements on border issues
>
> **1999 (Bishkek):** Meetings to finalize 1996 and 1997 agreements on border issues
>
> **2000 (Dushanbe):** Meetings to finalize 1996 and 1997 agreements on border issues. Dushanbe Declaration promulgated
>
> **April 28, 2001 (Moscow):** Meeting of Shanghai Five Foreign Ministers
>
> **June 14, 2001 (Shanghai):** Meeting of Defense Ministers of Shanghai Five Plus Uzbekistan
>
> **June 15, 2001 (Shanghai):** Shanghai Treaty on Cracking Down on Terrorism, Separatism, and Extremism (also known as Shanghai Convention). Decision made to establish a counterterrorism center in Bishkek to combat "terrorism, separatism, and extremism." Looked at possibility of future combined military exercises among SCO members.
>
> **June 15, 2001 (Shanghai):** Declaration of the Formation of the Shanghai Cooperation Organization

party." In short, Beijing is pointing to at least one instance in which the New Concept of Security can arguably be said to have taken form.[8]

But even here, the PRC has not always been content to showcase the SCO and the "Shanghai Spirit" on its own merits. Beijing has borrowed some Shanghai Five joint statements to condemn various U.S. policies, such as the BMD program, and to rally support for the sanctity of the 1972 Anti-Ballistic Missile Treaty and all that it implies for the U.S. BMD program.[9] It is difficult to accept at face value that the governments in Bishkek, Dushanbe, or Astana feel that the theoretical prospect of the deployment of U.S. missile defense systems in the Pacific would pose a threat to their national security interests. This is unfortunate because if one stands back from the polemics, a case actually can be made that the SCO *is* a unique form of post-Cold War international security cooperation.

At the same time, consider what this particular "success" for the New Concept of Security in Central Asia says about the concept in a larger framework.

The concept has *not* taken hold in the primary region in Asia for which it was originally intended—Southeast Asia. This is probably because the U.S. presence (political, economic, military, and cultural) is too strong, and affinities in the region for many U.S. security policies are considerable. This also probably is the case because some nations in Southeast Asia view China as the potential cause of instability, not its potential solution. Moreover, the countries in this region have no common set of overarching security concerns that draw them together—and in some cases they have extant security differences, hence the utility of the United States as honest broker.

Assuming that the New Concept of Security *does* work in at least one region of the world, Central Asia, how is this explained? First, all of the countries in the region agree that they share a common security problem: vulnerable borders and what the Chinese and other SCO members term the "three evils" of "terrorism, splittism, and fanaticism." Second, Central Asia is a region where for the most part there was little U.S. political, economic, or military presence (at least before September 11). Third, and related to the previous point, it is a region where China and Russia have traditionally been the dominant powers. And fourth, it is one region where some countries see China as a potential solution to concerns about a lingering (pre-independence) Russian hegemony.

Ironies do abound, however. Whereas the New Concept of Security had found fertile ground in Central Asia via the SCO prior to September 11, one does wonder what the new U.S. presence in the region—especially its new and enhanced security relations with some SCO members—portends for the viability of the organization.

Conclusion

First, the New Concept of Security does not seem to have had much of an impact around the globe to date as an alternative international security architecture; it is a set of principles in search of actionable suggestions. The principles are fine, but how are the nations of the world expected to execute them?

Second, the New Concept of Security has not had the greatest impact where it was originally intended—among the countries of Southeast Asia. This is most evident by the recent (August 2002) repackaging and distribution of the concept as a position paper at the ARF.

Third, the anti-American packaging that the new concept has in the past often been wrapped in detracts from it. In theory, the principles should be appealing, especially in these troubled times. It is, however, ironic that the very concept that is supposed to replace the "Cold War mentality" has often been propagated in rhetoric that recalls Cold War wordsmanship between the United States and the Soviet Union.

Fourth, the New Concept of Security probably will have limited influence beyond the Chinese periphery. It may accrue supporters in principle in the greater developing world (for example, Africa, Latin America, perhaps the Middle East), but such support will more than likely go no further than lip service agreement to the principles in the concept. In regions where the United States or some of its key allies and supporters (NATO and beyond) have a presence and commitment (not merely military but political and economic), the concept will have difficulty accruing any gravitas.

Fifth, Chinese leaders will continue invoking the New Concept of Security in meetings with foreign officials and at international gatherings—it has become symbolic of China's desire to be viewed as a serious world player. And, even if only theoretical, the concept represents Beijing's need to attempt to shape the international security environment as it becomes more and more enmeshed in the global political economy.

The events of September 11 have underscored the key weakness of the New Concept of Security as originally formulated. The new concept is mainly a preventative formula. It offers ways in which nations should conduct their relations to avoid conflict or, in the worst case, to resolve security differences. It does not offer much in the way of what should happen when political relations and negotiation break down. The concept was not meant to address security threats from nonstate actors, although the entire Shanghai Five and SCO framework has evolved quickly to address such threats specifically.

It may turn out that the terrorist attacks, and especially the U.S. *and* the international community response to them, will define post-Cold War international security relations in ways no one, not even the Chinese, could have imagined. The wide-ranging international cooperation and support that the United States is enjoying from some quarters around the globe was hitherto difficult to imagine. It may just be that another new concept of security is de facto starting to unfold that is not necessarily at odds with the principles in the original Chinese version. But, ironically, if the international response and realignments due to the events of September 11 do in fact form the basis for a new concept of international security, then it will have occurred because of what the United States did, not because of China's enunciation of a need for new principles. There is every reason to hope that Washington and Beijing will want to cooperate in the post-Cold War international security environment that is unfolding, regardless of preferred frameworks and theories. The October 2001 and February 2002 meetings between Presidents Bush and Jiang in Shanghai and Beijing, and their stated desire to seek a cooperative relationship, are hopeful signs.

Notes

[1] The "Five Principles of Peaceful Coexistence" were originally articulated by Premier Zhou Enlai, first during the Geneva Conference on Indochina (1954–1955) and subsequently (and most well remembered) at the Bandung Conference of Afro-Asian Nations in April 1955.

[2] The question of whether Chinese foreign policy initiatives in the late 1990s were reaching too far from Beijing's traditional interests was one of the issues hotly contested in Chinese analytic circles during the great "peace and development debate" of 1999. See David M. Finkelstein, *China Reconsiders Its National Security: The Great 'Peace & Development Debate' of 1999* (Alexandria, VA: The CNA Corporation, 2000).

[3] Niu Junfeng, "Cultivate New National Security Concept, Advocate New Peacekeeping Mode; *Zhongguo Guofang Bao* Holds 'New Security Concept and 21st Century National Security Mode' Seminar," *Jiefangjun Bao*, December 26, 1997.

[4] Li Qinggong and Wei Wei, "The World Needs a New Security Concept," *Jiefangjun Bao*, December 24, 1997.

[5] Chen Jing: "Xiong Guangkai Elaborates on Two Characteristics of China's National Defense Policy," *Zhongguo Xinwen She*, September 11, 2000.

[6] For an overview of this subject, see Ken Allen and Eric McVadon, *China's Foreign Military Relations* (Washington, DC: Stimson Center, 1999) and David M. Finkelstein, *Engaging DoD: Chinese Perspectives on Military Relations with the United States* (Alexandria, VA: The CNA Corporation, 1999). On the topic of PLA participation in international peacekeeping operations, see Bates Gill and James Reilly, "Sovereignty, Intervention, and Peacekeeping: The View From Beijing," *Survival* (Autumn 2000). Readers may be surprised by the statistics in the Allen-McVadon and Gill-Reilly papers.

[7] Of course, the creation of the Shanghai Five offered the collateral benefit of countering what was perceived in both Beijing and Moscow to be tentative moves by the United States to achieve some degree of presence in Central Asia. For example, U.S. military engagement activities in the region were, from early on, focused on Kazakhstan due to concern over extent stockpiles of former Soviet nuclear fissile materials, and I have already made reference to the Central Command exercise CENTAZBAT 97. In the case of Tashkent, the U.S. Central Command had been building ties to the Uzbek military since at least 1995. See C.J. Chivers, "Long Before War, Green Berets Built Military Ties To Uzbekistan," *The New York Times*, October 25, 2001, 1.

[8] For articles by Chinese analysts that link the SCO with the New Concept of Security, see Xu Tao, "Promoting the 'Shanghai Five' Spirit for Regional Cooperation," *Contemporary International Relations* 11, no. 5 (May 2001), 14–24; and Xia Yishan, "The Shanghai Cooperation Organization As I See It," *Foreign Affairs Journal*, no. 61 (September 2001), 8–13.

[9] See the Dushanbe Statement of the Shanghai Five (July 2000) for statements opposing the spread of theater ballistic missile defense to the Pacific, the sanctity of the Anti-Ballistic Missile Treaty, opposition to so-called humanitarian interventions outside of United Nations Security Council auspices, and so on.

Chapter 11

The PLA and the Taiwan Issue

Cynthia A. Watson

The People's Republic of China (PRC) and the People's Liberation Army (PLA) both can expect wide-ranging changes under the 16th Party Congress ratification of the fourth-generation leadership. This chapter considers what role Taiwan might play as a strategic consideration within the PLA during this time of transition.

One crucial aspect of this analysis is that all concerned parties—the PLA, Chinese Communist Party (CCP), and decisionmakers in Taiwan and Washington—will be heavily affected by personal and corporate perceptions—their beliefs about a relationship, an issue, or an event. In each case, the perception may be skewed or imprecise.

Not only are those perceptions often unclear, but also, with the recent narrowing of military-to-military contacts with the United States, PLA leadership views on an array of issues are less obvious than would be desirable to answer the questions authoritatively about the future. Complicating the resolution of different views is the lack of direct links between Taiwan and the PLA and the limited number between the U.S. military and its Chinese counterparts. This leads to decisionmaking problems, some with potentially catastrophic effects. As Taiwanese officers noted in May 2001, no mechanisms currently exist between Beijing and Taipei to cope with a crisis similar to the EP–3 incident of April 1, 2001.

The PLA as Party-Army

The PLA role does not fit the traditional Western definition in which the civil-military relationship is expected to be nonpartisan. The PLA, with its unique responsibility to protect the party rather than the state per se, thus views threats to the party and its ability to maintain power as taking precedence over more traditional security threats. The PLA sees its mission as protecting not only the physical aspects of China's territory and people but also party legitimacy.

If CCP legitimacy requires a particular supporting action, then the PLA as a party-army would execute that action as part of its core values. Defense of the CCP is as much a part of PLA patriotic spirit as marching against an enemy or preparing a ship for extended deployment. Loyalty to the CCP does not mean the PLA is not thoroughly imbued with a sense of patriotism and nationalism; it is and will continue to reach the Chinese people through various methods.

Further complicating the party-army relationship are changes in the PLA resulting from its professionalization. A more professional PLA may in fact be more nationalistic than any predecessor party-army because professional militaries have a far more acute sense of need to defend the nation than a civilian political party.[1] A more professional military also might be less personality-based and more concerned with national values.

This phenomenon also might create difficulties as the party-army attempts to keep its roots with the people while reaching toward more grandiose national goals—including modernization of its organization and armaments, a process potentially at odds with other goals in the hierarchy of national modernization goals.

Crucial to the leadership transition is the continuity in China's governance that the PLA represents. The CCP is concerned that protecting its power will increase in importance as subsequent generations of civilians, with no PLA background (hence having less credibility on military matters, particular with an increasingly professional military), continue to lead the country. Jiang Zemin is the first of these purely civilian leaders, in contrast to leaders who were seasoned military veterans, such as Mao Zedong, Zhou Enlai, and Deng Xiaoping.

The issue of protecting party interests versus enforcing Chinese territorial integrity would almost certainly create rifts within the leadership, but CCP legitimacy demands sovereignty over claimed territory, especially Taiwan. Furthermore, as Ellis Joffe has pointed out, the PLA can be increasingly professional while still remaining loyal to the CCP. It may be that the PLA now sees its interests as sufficiently defined independently of the CCP as to merit actions when those military interests are under attack. Professionalism, in short, may have unexpected consequences.[2]

The CCP view of the party-army will be just as important as the latter's view of the CCP. The lack of military experience among top civilians is also likely to influence their feelings about the PLA role and national aspirations.

The Taiwan Reunification Issue

Many senior Chinese leaders view Taiwan's status as the final, unresolved issue of the Chinese civil war (1927–1949) or even of the Century of Humiliation (1842–1949, marked by Japan's colonization of Taiwan from 1895 through 1945). They are concerned that historic Chinese territory remains outside national control. Additionally, eventual reunification is further shadowed by the possibility that the United States will not accede to Taiwan rejoining the mainland.

As a party-army, however, the PLA undoubtedly shares the view with the Chinese public and the party that the reunification of Taiwan is more important than domestic economic growth and development. In the words of a senior Academy of Military Science officer who visited Washington in 2000, Beijing would sacrifice economic growth to make sure Taiwan remained part of China. He said that China knew it might experience economic sanctions and significant disruption to current economic growth if war broke out over Taiwan, but his assessment was blunt: China would sacrifice mightily to maintain its national sovereignty.[3]

To summarize, the CCP might have to make some hard choices about retaining power. The choice might come down to keeping Taiwan through forced reunification or pushing economic development to keep the population on the same trajectory toward an improved standard of living. In that event, the PLA appears willing to sacrifice the living standard for national integrity. This decision would be consistent with both the thought of other militaries around the world and the PLA commitment to defending the party, with the latter believing its continued rule is necessary to maintain Chinese national integrity.

Taiwan will remain the major territorial issue for Beijing in part because of its psychological impact on Chinese policymakers. The concern about reunifying China carries with it important psychological baggage that could drive Beijing to make strategic decisions in ways difficult for foreign observers to anticipate. If foreign observers believe that September 11, 2001, had unexpected consequences on the United States and its reactions to terrorism, various steps toward Taiwan's independence could provoke similar reactions that outsiders might not see in advance.

It bears noting as well that the PLA might react differently to various steps along the continuum toward complete Taiwanese independence. An outright, formal declaration of independence probably would be the threshold at which the PLA would find Taiwan's actions intolerable. More modest steps might also provoke a reaction, but that PLA response would be conditioned by a raft of domestic PRC conditions as well, including reactions to and comfort with the new CCP leadership.

Finally, the PLA might want to consider the international context, regardless of statements to the contrary, before responding to any Taiwanese moves toward independence. Issues that might raise caution within the PLA would include Washington's particular level of interest in other events in Pakistan, Central Asia, or the overall war on terrorism. While these issues would not necessarily stop the PLA from acting to defend its national interests, any one of them might give pause. The PLA may believe Washington's concerns currently are directed toward the war on terrorism, but its focus could shift back to Taiwan with enough PLA saber rattling or overt actions.

The Strategic Equation

Mainland observers increasingly seem to believe time is on Beijing's side—and that Taiwan is reaching the same conclusion. Several factors fuel this assumption, including the significant economic slump that hit Taiwan's economy in 2000–2001. Some are discussing this economic recession in exaggerated terms, as if it were a full-fledged depression. It is a reflection of the problems that East Asian systems have faced in meeting natural economic cycles and does not resemble the unrealistic growth patterns that characterized much of the period between 1975 and 1997. Some polls have indicated increased favorable views toward reunification among Taiwan citizens as a result of the island's economic problems.[4]

A second reason for Beijing's growing self-assurance is PLA confidence in its military modernization program. Some in the PRC who hear Bush administration concerns about U.S. ability to defend Taiwan in the face of a Chinese attack are bound to feel emboldened by knowledge that PLA capability is growing. This is where Chinese parochialism can play a dangerous role: PLA members who have not traveled widely may be unaware of the serious gaps still existing between U.S. and PLA forces. Without grasping these disparities, some PLA officers think their military capable of launching attacks that would achieve reunification with Taiwan—albeit with significant casualties. While PLA capabilities are improving, particularly relative to those elsewhere in East Asia, they are not on a par with the United States and would be stretched significantly to counter any likely U.S. reaction to a military attempt to reunify Taiwan with the PRC.

Another reason for growing PLA confidence about Taiwan may be the reality that faced the Bush administration in October 2001, as it chose a coalition-building approach to countering terrorism. As an important participant in coalition building, China has taken on a new, more positive role in the U.S. calculus and finds its position enhanced. The administration is gradually easing off the post-April 2001 restrictions on interaction with the PLA (although the relationship remains far more constrained than during the Clinton administration).[5]

The PLA and CCP are likely to interpret this loosening of restrictions as a return to more normal relations, highlighted by China's role in the coalition and its presumed global leadership. Beijing may view PLA leverage on U.S. actions as increasing, with reduced U.S. focus on Taiwan as a quid pro quo for support against terrorism.[6] President George W. Bush made clear during his visit to the Asia Pacific Economic Cooperation meeting in Shanghai in October 2001 that there was no quid pro quo for Taiwan, but perceptions to the contrary are likely to persist, both in Taipei and Beijing.

Additionally, the Bush administration, for all of its initial criticism of Beijing and support for Taiwan, is likely to adopt the same relatively benign policies with the PRC and PLA as have prior U.S. administrations.[7] The Bush administration chose not to sell Taiwan Aegis-equipped *Arleigh Burke* destroyers in April 2001, to Taiwan's chagrin and Beijing's approval. It did, however, agree to sell diesel submarines, even though no obvious source for constructing these submarines has emerged.

While the overall arms sales decision irritated both sides of the Taiwan Strait, the overarching impression may be that the Bush administration will not greatly up the ante in the arms that it offers Taiwan. The PLA certainly understands that the United States could have sold Taiwan more objectionable arms; the PLA must be pleased and may interpret this as a strengthening of its hand in the region. This turn of events may have been different from what Beijing anticipated, but the evidence indicates that Beijing is more important to the United States than is Taiwan.

Finally, the PLA may view its modernization as a direct threat to Washington, hence promoting an anti-China U.S. strategy. With this interpretation, the PLA could see the United States doing whatever it can to keep China in a subservient position. This might include encouraging Taiwan to seek formal independence as a manner of handicapping the PRC, instead of allowing the country to return to its natural boundaries and nationhood. If Taiwan took on that strategic a position for PLA strategists, the need to unify the country and follow a comprehensive path toward national modernization would be crucial.

Conclusions

Increasing PLA professionalism makes it less likely to swing violently among domestic factions but makes its desire to protect the Chinese national entity more likely. The lack of ties with the PLA by the new generation of leaders may be crucial. It could mean more leverage by the PLA, as well as much greater tension about its party-army character.

Taiwan is merely a portion of this story: equally important is the PLA role in responding to growing social tensions caused by World Trade Organization membership and attendant state-owned enterprise reform. The People's Armed Police should be expected to maintain civil order, but questions about their competency and attendant political nuances abound. Whether the PLA has to respond to a declaration of independence by Taiwan or a riot in the streets of Lanzhou, its ability to succeed is important to its prestige at home and abroad as well as to its internal prioritization of responsibilities. This emphasizes PLA importance in the domestic political environment and the cycle of questions about leadership, transition, loyalty, and professionalism that are tied to Taiwan and issues of social stability.

PLA links to the CCP are a crucial element in the Taiwan question. If the party finds it necessary to retake Taiwan through military means, the PLA will respond accordingly. If tensions develop over reunifying with Taiwan versus protecting economic achievements of the past two decades, the PLA will again likely choose the historical responsibility of keeping Taiwan part of China. The PLA is much more confident today of its abilities than in the past and may be more assertive in the forthcoming post-transition period, since it represents continuity as a major organ of state and party. Its perception of its abilities, rights, responsibilities, and challenges will play a significant part in future Chinese actions.

Notes

[1] There is a rich literature on civil-military relations and sovereignty/nationalism concepts that far outstretches the scope of this essay.

[2] Email discussion with Ellis Joffe, October 23, 2001.

[3] Academy of Military delegation member, August 25, 2000, Washington, DC.

[4] Based on May 2001 discussions in Taiwan.

[5] Secretary of Defense Donald H. Rumsfeld apparently personally made all decisions on the interactions between DOD personnel and the PLA in the aftermath of the EP–3 collision in April 2001, according to Michael Gordon of *The New York Times*. The Secretary has made no bones about his concerns regarding growing Chinese military threats; hence, the interactions were drastically curtailed. By fall 2001, the interactions appeared gradually to be resuming, coincident to the APEC summit in Shanghai,

if nothing else. One other anecdotal indication that things are easing was that students from the National Defense University, along with many other visitors, were prohibited from scheduled visits to China in spring 2001 but an active-duty naval officer was authorized to attend a course in Beijing by October.

[6] China, of course, has its own concerns about terrorism and is quite happy to see the United States adopt positions that validate Beijing's concerns about the Hui problem that periodically pops up across the country, but is a sustained separatist concern in Xinxiang.

[7] James Mann, *About Face* (New York: Knopf, 1999), and Patrick Tyler, *A Great Wall* (New York: Basic Books, 1999), both argue strongly that the desire to enhance U.S. business interests' entrance into the burgeoning Chinese market overwhelms campaign rhetoric and other concerns. The case for Bush being any different from predecessors is not as straightforward as originally thought. First, President Bush gave an impassioned interview in late April 2001 with the Cable News Network in which he seemed to go well beyond the legal requirements of the Taiwan Relations Act (1979), the only law actually on the books about U.S. defense commitments to the island. Having said that, however, recall that President George H.W. Bush took a fairly gentle approach to the PRC in the aftermath of Tiananmen. Further, to Taiwan's consternation, the younger Bush merely authorized the sale of *Kidd*-class destroyers, not the requested Aegis-equipped ships, in the April 2001 arms negotiations. In light of Secretary Rumsfeld's clear concerns about growing PLA capability and perceived weaker U.S. ability to defend Taiwan, this does not bode well for Taiwan. In sum, the record on how the administration will behave in relation to Beijing is far from obvious.

Chapter 12

Taiwan Politics and Leadership

John Tkacik

O ne of the main reasons that the United States is committed to aiding the defense of Taiwan, as a matter of both policy and law, is that Taiwan is truly one of the most dynamic and vibrant democracies in Asia. Of course, the United States also has extensive economic interests in Taiwan (where we exported 50 percent more in U.S. goods annually during the 1990s than we did to the People's Republic of China).[1] Moreover, the United States has a compelling strategic interest in denying control of the sea and air lines of communication around Taiwan to another major Eurasian power.[2] But the true American interest in Taiwan is to maintain the survival and success of Taiwan's democracy, which is one of the major accomplishments of America's postwar presence in Asia.

To understand the success of Taiwan's democracy, one must understand the nature of the dynamic political environment in which it thrives. Half of that dynamism is generated by four troubled decades of history from 1945 to 1988, during which deep interethnic antipathy festered and the native Taiwanese majority became increasingly insistent on self-determination and, indeed, independence from China and the transplanted mainland Chinese minority that ruled Taiwan during that period.[3] The fact that several top leaders of Taiwan's political opposition until 1986 were accomplished lawyers[4] who were trained to take advantage of constitutional processes gave the opposition movement a tradition of working within the electoral system and Taiwan's legislative structures. Another factor livening up Taiwan's politics emerged when Taiwan Independence advocates, formerly blacklisted and living overseas, were permitted to return to Taiwan and enter politics.[5] Steeped in American, Canadian, and European traditions of healthy partisan but highly confrontational political campaigning, these returning exiles brought to Taiwan's electioneering an edginess never before seen in Taiwan—or in China for that matter.

219

Throughout the long period of political repression in Taiwan (1945–1992), "Taiwan Independence" was the main rallying cry of the non-Kuomintang (KMT) underground opposition. Moreover, Taiwan independence was premised on the demand that Taiwan's ethnic majority, the nonmainlanders, should determine the future of their country.[6]

Another factor that exaggerates the dynamism of Taiwan's democracy is its complex legislative electoral system. A good case can be made that the electoral structure is conducive to competition among at least five separate political parties and that it rewards strong party organizations (as opposed to independent candidates).[7]

Another constitutional quirk of Taiwan's electoral system is that the president and the legislature are elected in different years and have different terms—a situation that both of the major political parties hope to resolve in the coming years.

As a result, the vibrancy and dynamism of Taiwan's democracy produced a minority president in March 2000, who had to struggle with a legislature dominated by the majority opposition. The result of that has been gridlock in policy, guerrilla warfare in government, and growing bitterness among the various ethnic groups that gravitate to one political party or the others.[8]

The Dirty Little Secret

Before getting into the complexities of Taiwan's electoral system, we must first admit a dirty little secret of Taiwan politics: Taiwan politics is *ethnic* politics. The major cleavages in Taiwan's political culture fall along ethnic lines, that is, mainlanders, Hoklo Taiwanese,[9] Hakka Taiwanese, and, to a smaller extent, Malayo-Polynesian aborigines. It was this reality that made the March 18, 2000, presidential election a turning point in Taiwan's political history. It was a classic realignment election that changed the entire complexion of Taiwan's political dynamics. This ethnic dynamic—which the Taiwanese call *Shengji Jingjie* or the "Provincial Complex"—was strengthened in the December 2001 electoral fight for control of Taiwan's Legislative Yuan.[10]

For a rough idea of how this ethnic dynamic plays out in elections, let us consider the apparent results of the March 2000 presidential election.[11]

The ethnic Hoklo Taiwanese in Southern Taiwan voted generally for Democratic Progressive Party (DPP) candidate Chen Shui-bian. The North Taiwan Hakkas and the entire mainlander population voted solidly for mainlander independent presidential candidate James Chu-yu Soong.

Kuomintang (Nationalist or KMT) candidate Lien Chan generally got the Hoklo Taiwanese vote that didn't go to the DPP candidate.

In the 1996 presidential election, the KMT party nominee, former Taiwan president Lee Teng-hui, won over 54 percent of the vote against 4 opponents, yet only 4 years later, despite an economy that was booming and a president who was still overwhelmingly popular, the KMT presidential candidate only managed to get 23 percent of the vote—a 31 percent drop from 1996.

In the 2000 election, former Taipei mayor Chen Shui-bian was the nominee of the pro-independence DPP candidate, and he received nearly 40 percent of the vote—19 percentage points above what the DPP candidate, Peng Ming-min, received in 1996.

Also in 2000, independent presidential candidate James Chu-yu Soong received 36 percent of the vote, 11 percentage points more than the combined vote in 1996 for the 2 mainlander-leaning candidates, Lin Yang-kang and Chen Lu-an, the ascetic and devoutly Buddhist mainlander who preached peace with mainland China.[12]

In 1996, Taiwan's incumbent president, the ethnic Taiwanese Lee Teng-hui, who had bemoaned the "tragedy of being Taiwanese" and called his own Kuomintang party "an alien regime" (*wailai zhengquan*), garnered most of the ethnic Taiwanese vote.[13] Together with the DPP candidate Peng Ming-min, the pro-independence advocate (in fact, the father of the Taiwan Independence Movement), they claimed over 75 percent of the vote in Taiwan.

The mainlander vote, about 15 percent of the electorate, which went to Lin Yang-kang and Chen Lu-an in 1996, went to James Soong in the March 2000 balloting. Soong also had strong support among both ethnic Hakka and "good government" Hoklo Taiwanese, giving him an additional 21 percent of the vote.

James Soong, with a 1974 doctorate in political science from Georgetown University, was probably Taiwan's most astute politician and a keen reader of opinion polls. Moreover, he knew how politics works in Taiwan, especially ethnic politics. Soong was a former Government Information Office chief and later became secretary general of the Kuomintang. He was reputed to have been the architect of Lee Teng-hui's consolidation of power in the 3 years after the death of Chiang Ching-kuo.[14] In 1994, when he ran for Taiwan provincial governor, his spoken Taiwanese was said to be so bad that President Lee Teng-hui himself campaigned on the stump with Soong smiling silently at his side. Soong won the gubernatorial election with nearly 56 percent of the vote[15] and spent the next 4 years lavishing provincial money on Hakka districts throughout Taiwan in a highly successful effort to ingratiate himself to the Hakka voters—and to Taiwan's aborigines. Soong learned to speak the Hoklos' "Minnan" dialect without an accent, and by the end of his term he could carry on a conversation in the Hakka dialect.

In the March 2000 presidential election, Soong handily carried virtually all of Taiwan's Hakka districts, and Hakkas count for about 15 to 20 percent of the vote. The same goes for the aborigine vote: all went to Soong, except for pockets of voters in Taitung to Lien Chan.

So Who Are These People?

Hoklo are the Taiwanese whose forebears came from China's Fujian province in the century before last, and 18,000 of whose forebears were arrested and executed by Chiang Kai-shek's mainlander soldiers in the aftermath of the February 28, 1947, rebellion.[16] The dead were 18,000 young Taiwanese men of the intelligentsia, Japanese-educated, who fought for the emperor in the war, whose families owned land and were merchants, and who rebelled against an unbelievably corrupt nationalist Chinese occupation of Taiwan from October 1945 to February 1947.

The Hakka are the same clannish and fiercely independent "Guest People" who migrated southward from ancient wars in North China during the Song Dynasty (960–1279 CE) and who suffered centuries of discrimination in imperial China's coastal Guangdong and Fujian provinces. In the 18th and 19th centuries, Hakka populations migrated to Taiwan, where their unusual clothes and language again made them objects of derision in the eyes of the majority Hoklo. The Hoklo pushed them off into the poorer, hilly lands where they were fated to become even more clannish and poor and generally came to look to the Japanese and later the KMT government to settle their disputes with Taiwanese.

Now numbering not quite a million, the aborigines are the Malayo-Polynesian peoples whom the vast migration of incoming Hoklo from the 17th to the 19th centuries pushed off the flatlands of Taiwan and into the mountains. The aborigines also looked to the Japanese and the KMT for protection against the Taiwanese.

The mainlanders were the remnants of Chiang Kai-shek's defeated army and the legendary 2 million boat people who fled China in 1949–1950 after the Communist victory. But the February 28 rebellion began before these hordes actually arrived. In 1947, an incident was sparked when ragtag Nationalist customs troops beat up an old woman selling contraband cigarettes at the Taipei train station. Local boys accosted the hated outlanders, killed them, and unleashed pent-up hatred against the mainlanders. For several days, marauding Taiwanese gangs hunted down every mainlander they could find. Chiang Kai-shek dispatched three divisions of garrison troops to Taiwan, put down the rebellion, and arrested or executed not only the troublemakers but also the intellectual elites who could potentially cause trouble in the future.

While the 1947 executions touched most Hoklo Taiwanese families, the Kuomintang's 1949 Land Reform program had the additional economic effect of confiscating larger Hoklo landholdings and transferring them to poorer farmers, of whom the Hakka were arguably the biggest winners.[17]

It is not difficult to understand the ethnic rivalries and cleavages that color Taiwan's current politics. There are many other issues as well, such as cross-Strait relations and Taiwan independence, but these are a byproduct of the ethnic identity issue. Among urban voters, even more important issues are economic policies, environmental concerns—and *staggering* corruption.

Taiwan's Political Leaders

The preeminent political icon in Taiwan is former president Lee Teng-hui. He towers above everyone else, both literally (he is over 6 feet tall) as well as figuratively. Lee's tepid support for his own chosen candidate, Vice President Lien Chan, is believed to be the cause of Lien's ignominious distant-third-place showing in the March 2000 elections.[18]

Lee's visible happiness at Chen Shui-bian's victory, his emergence in June 2001 on the stage with President Chen to inaugurate the new "Northern Association,"[19] a not-so-thinly veiled advocate of Taiwan independence, and the ensuing uproar in the press about Lee's strategy to split the KMT and form a new party to support President Chen's Democratic Progressive Party are all manifestations of Lee's unhappiness with the KMT. By August, the former president had presided over the assembly of the Taiwan Solidarity Union, which subsequently registered as a formal political party.[20] After an agonizing 2 months, the KMT disciplinary commission voted, on September 21, 2001, to revoke Lee's membership in the party.[21]

The KMT had hoped to sidestep this move, which they worried would only crystallize the KMT image among ethnic Taiwanese as a mainlander-dominated organization.[22] But, in the end, Lee's incessant haranguing of the KMT as the source of Taiwan's political gridlock, as well as his attacks on the party for abandoning his Taiwan First political agenda, proved more than the mainlander elders of the party could take. The KMT top Hakka, Vice Chairman Wu Po-hsiung, lined up with the mainlanders against Lee, giving further evidence of the Hakka-Mainlander alliance that is the backbone of KMT support.[23]

The other leader is James Soong. It was then-President Lee who managed to get James Soong—a mainlander—elected Taiwan provincial governor in 1994 in the island's first popular election. At the time, Soong was seen as Lee's acolyte. But by 1996, seeing that Soong was positioning himself for a run for the presidency, Lee took steps to weaken Soong's campaign by engineering the constitutional abolition of the Taiwan provincial government. Lee wanted to "Taiwanize" or "localize" (*ben tu hua*) Taiwan's political culture and rid it once and for all of its mainlander domination. This was a move that alarmed the old-guard mainlander factions in the KMT. In 1993, in fact, a sizeable chunk of the mainlanders left the party to establish the China New Party (CNP) dedicated to the proposition that Taiwan was part of China.

The move to abolish the Taiwan provincial government not only yanked the old rug out from under mainlander upstart James Soong but also was seen in mainlander circles as the thin end of the wedge for making Taiwan an independent state without even a figleaf of a connection to China.

Soong's exit from the political stage in late 1998 was not a pretty scene. Soong resigned and plotted his revenge. Soon after, Lee warned Soong in public not to "think only of himself"—it was a calculated insult. Lee froze Soong out of the contention for the KMT presidential nomination in 2000. Not surprisingly, Soong and like-minded mainlanders formed an independent presidential campaign that split the KMT. President Lee probably was happy to see the mainlanders go because the move would leave the KMT in his hands.

However, Lee had not considered Soong's popularity with the Hakkas and aborigines upon whom he had been lavishing public funds for 4 years. In the end, Soong was able to call in enough favors to attract away virtually the entire mainlander vote from KMT Lien Chan in the election, as well as most of the Hakkas and aborigines. He also attracted a good number of "good-government" voters in Taiwan's urban north.

Soong won 36 percent of the vote and after the election quickly formed his own political party, the People First Party (PFP). The PFP is made up of disaffected mainlanders in the Legislative Yuan, a number of top Hakka personalities, and a handful of prominent Taiwanese politicians who had suffered personal insults (some intentional, some not) arising from President Lee Teng-hui's imperious manner. A year and a half later, as the smoke cleared from the March 2000 presidential election, Soong remained the only real political leader in the PFP.

Unfortunately for the PFP, Soong seems to be all there is of the party. Pundits in Taipei say, "The PFP has no money, it has no candidates, it has no policies, all it has is Soong." Earlier, the PFP had hoped to be a refuge for ethnic Taiwanese and Hakkas from the Kuomintang who were fed up with KMT corruption and not likely to get renominated for legislative seats. KMT polls showed the party's share of the electorate shrinking. In the end, it was Lee's Taiwan Solidarity Union (TSU) that attracted the KMT castaways. This, apparently, was the ulterior TSU strategy all along. As one analyst in Taipei explained, the primary purpose of the TSU was to ensure that the PFP did not get any plausible legislative candidates, not that the TSU actually thought these candidates would win under the TSU banner.

The tactic worked. A much-ballyhooed KMT–PFP alliance that supposedly would pull together the so-called Pan Blue Army of the KMT and its splinter parties did not perform as well as some had hoped. Soong himself bemoaned the inability of the KMT to deal forthrightly with his party. Soong was desperate to claw votes away from the mainlander-heavy Taipei city, where on October 24, 2000, he slammed President Chen and former president Lee for "fomenting ethnic divisions." Still, Soong was wary of alienating his ethnic-Taiwanese constituency, and the next day he campaigned for PFP legislators in Eastern Taiwan by slamming President Chen and former President Lee, not for "ethnic divisions," but rather for "neglecting" the economic development of Eastern Taiwan.

What Is Left of the KMT

This leaves Lien and the Kuomintang. In March 2000, when all the votes were counted, Chen Shui-bian carried the ethnic Hoklo areas downisland (about 40 percent of the vote), while Soong got the mainlanders, Hakka, and aborigines (about 36 percent). Lien was left with the ethnic-Taiwanese votes controlled by the KMT party machine. In the end, it was only 23 percent.

Ironically, when Lien lost so badly, the mainlanders, who had not supported Lien in the first place, rioted for 2 days in Taipei. They demanded that President Lee resign as the party's chairman and turn the reins over to Lien Chan. Even the popular KMT mayor of Taipei, mainlander Ma Ying-jeou, joined the chorus calling for Lee's ouster, a move that did not endear Ma to Taiwanese. But it was a move that did make him popular with the mainlanders.

After several days, Lee finally resigned, leaving the shattered KMT—and its $3 billion (U.S.) war chest—in the hands of Lien Chan. In Lee's wake was left a KMT with a mostly Taiwanese rank-and-file, but a leader who was, and remains, desperate to bring back the schismatic mainlanders. Now, however, KMT chairman Lien Chan is surrounded by pretenders to the throne. The obvious successor, when Lien finally stumbles, is ethnic Taiwanese Vincent Siew, former premier and classic politician.

Siew will be challenged by the attractive, razor-sharp and self-confident Mayor Ma of Taipei, a former justice minister with a good reputation. But Ma was also the Brutus who thrust the unkindest cut of all into Lee Teng-hui in 2000. Aside from these two, there are no other potential leaders in the KMT hierarchy.[24]

The DPP—Not an Organized Political Party

Finally, there is the Democratic Progressive Party. When I think of the DPP, I am reminded of Will Rogers, who said, "I don't belong to any organized political party, I'm a Democrat." The same observation can be made about Taiwan's DPP. Or, perhaps, the DPP is *over*organized into at least five major factions and myriad smaller caucuses, forums, and mutual-admiration societies.[25] Two of the three living former DPP chairmen have already left the party; one wants to form an alliance with the PFP, and the other wants to reunify with the mainland. He is, of course, a Hakka.[26]

The current DPP leader is, of course, President Chen Shui-bian. Unfortunately, unless one is the leader of the majority party in the legislature, being Taiwan's president is a troublesome occupation. And President Chen has been berated by a particularly vicious legislature.

Fortunately for Chen, Taiwan's public appears disgusted with the legislature. In fact, former President Lee was quoted as blaming *all* of Taiwan's political woes—and economic ones for that matter—on the legislature, and Lee specified that he was talking about the *opposition* parties. Moreover, Lee went on record as "wanting to cry after seeing what's happened to 12 years' work" as chairman of the KMT. President Lee spent 2 months actively campaigning for TSU candidates who were likely to help Chen form a "stable majority."

Clearly, the KMT has been stung by this. Lien Chan continuously charges that Lee and Chen Shui-bian have "played the ethnic card," and pundits acknowledge that Lee's ouster from the KMT has hurt the party among the Hoklo Taiwanese electorate. Although KMT Organization Chief Chao Shou-po insisted that "those who left the party under Lee's chairmanship are now returning to the fold," those returnees are mainlanders who voted for James Soong.[27] Their return to the KMT takes votes from Soong's PFP. On the other hand, DPP Secretary General Wu Hai-jen said, "the result of the KMT's 'criticize Lee campaign' has been a hemorrhage of support in Southern Taiwan."

Coupled with a renewed attack on the KMT ill-gotten $3 billion (U.S.) warchest and the widely broadcast television clip of Chinese foreign minister Tang Jiaxuan interrupting and insulting Taiwan Economics Minister Lin Hsin-yi at the Asia Pacific Economic Cooperation leaders' conference on October 19, 2001, the KMT's ouster of Lee—and the increasingly pro-mainland complexion of the KMT—has eclipsed Taiwan's current economic depression as the dominant concern of the ethnic majority Hoklo in the upcoming election.

The DPP emerged as as the biggest party in the December 2001 elections, thanks, in part, to Lee's crossing over to bring his cofactionalists—the so-called Lee Wing of the KMT—with him.

Taiwan's Legislative Electoral System

The electoral structure for Taiwan's Legislative Yuan (LY) makes legislative elections a unique test of organization and precision electioneering. Although each electoral district elects several legislators, voters cast only a single vote for one candidate in a system called single vote, multiseat balloting. This system, therefore, requires that parties nominate only the right number of candidates for the party slate in each district and then mobilize their voters with the aim of very precisely distributing the votes among each of the candidates.

Small political parties and independents with strong personal networks can still compete in this environment, but for a major party, the system means that tactical mistakes could cost it just enough votes to lose potential seats to give their opposition much-prized control of the legislature. Still, upsets are unlikely because minority parties are unwilling to risk losing their few seats by nominating enough candidates to obtain an overall majority.

Under Taiwan's complex legislative electoral system, 176 of 225 seats in the LY are elected by the voters directly. Each voter casts a single vote for only one candidate. Each of Taiwan's 31 electoral districts elects several representatives to the LY with the exception of four small constituencies that have only one legislator. This means candidates compete not only against candidates from the opposition parties but also against others from their own party. Complicating this system further, in election districts that elect four or more legislators, one of every four elected must be a woman, even if a male candidate receives more votes. After the quota of reserved female seats is filled by the top females who received votes, female candidates compete head-to-head with their male counterparts.

The remaining 49 seats in the LY are allocated to political parties that receive at least 5 percent of the popular vote. These parties divide the seats on the basis of the percentage of valid votes they receive. For example, if the Democratic Progressive Party wins 30 percent of the popular vote, then it gets 30 percent of the appointed seats. Eight of these 49 appointed seats are seen as representing the overseas Chinese community while the rest are considered at-large representatives.[28]

Numbers Are Everything

To succeed in a Taiwan legislative election, each party must have a clear understanding before the election of approximately how many votes it will receive in each electoral district. This understanding helps determine how many candidates the party will run in that district. For example, if the KMT determines that in a 4-seat district of 160,000 voters, 80,000 will support the KMT, it is likely that it will choose to run only 2 candidates. If it runs three, it risks spreading its votes too thinly among its three candidates and risks losing all four seats. Conversely, if the KMT runs only 1 candidate in this district, that candidate might well win with 80,000 votes, but the party would give away another seat that it could have won easily. To maximize the number of seats, therefore, parties must closely examine each constituency and nominate candidates with extreme precision.

Gaining this understanding, however, is no small feat. During Taiwan's martial law era, the KMT used local police and identification card records to identify party members and others inclined to support KMT candidates in local elections. While this is no longer done, many mechanisms for voter mobilization used by the KMT remain in place. The rosters of farmer, fisherman, and irrigation associations tell parties (mainly the KMT) where potential blocks of like-minded voters reside. Township, village, and even neighborhood leaders also help the party organizations identify voters. Parties also employ political surveys to help them measure support in each area. Ultimately, a party's ability to predict the level of its support will go a long way toward ensuring it runs just the right number of candidates.

Mobilizing and Distributing Votes

Knowing how many votes a candidate receives in a given district and how many candidates to run is only half the battle. Because most districts elect several legislators, parties must not only run the right number of candidates but also must maximize distribution of the expected vote among all candidates. Successful vote distribution depends in large part on party ability to communicate with and mobilize voters. Local party leaders and middlemen, therefore, must communicate to voters for which of the party candidates they should vote. In rural areas, leaders of local political factions or social institutions such as farmers associations rally their members around specific candidates, making this job easier. In urban areas, however, mobilization and distribution of votes is becoming increasingly difficult because these organizations are less influential and voters are increasingly influenced by less manageable forces like the media.

Candidates also engage their own personal networks to help manage votes in certain areas. In fact, Taiwan's electoral system and personality-driven politics also make it possible for independent candidates with strong personal connections to win a seat. In Taoyuan county's 12-seat district, for example, a candidate needs only a little more than 8 percent of the vote to win a seat. This not only increases the competition for the major parties but also has allowed local faction leaders and even gangsters with deep pockets and strong networks to get elected.

Under Taiwan's Legislative Yuan election system, upsets are highly unlikely. Minority political parties will usually be unwilling to risk losing their few seats by nominating enough candidates to obtain an overall majority. Party nomination decisions are usually guided by past experience with voters and, therefore, the party will add and subtract candidates on the basis of slight shifts in support or improved capacity to mobilize.

However, in this respect, the December 2001 Legislative Yuan election may prove to be one of the most unusually dynamic in recent memory. The growth of the DPP and the emergence of the PFP since the last LY election have begun to undercut KMT historical organizational advantages, forcing it to try to reduce the number of candidates it runs. If the KMT cannot accurately measure shifts in support toward the PFP and DPP and cut its candidate roster accordingly, it may run too many candidates and pay the price of split votes and even more lost seats in December. Similarly, the DPP and PFP will have to be willing to gamble to take advantage of any cuts made by the KMT.

What this means is that every political party spends most of its effort trying to gauge just exactly what the support is for each of its candidates at the time of the nominations, which in 2001 came in March and April. The parties therefore rely on exhaustive polling, street canvassing, and in the final weeks, giving the party faithful very exact instructions on whom to vote for.

The December 2001 Election

The KMT's crushing defeat in the December 2001 midterm legislative elections was a major setback for Beijing, but it could have been worse. The KMT lost nearly half of its seats in the Legislative Yuan, while the DPP and its TSU allies increased the "Pan Green" representation by half. The election gave Chen a much-needed political boost, but not a mandate, so although the DPP became the largest party in the legislature (which has a total of 225 seats, 113 needed for control), it is still not the controlling party. The DPP (87 legislative seats, up from 66) ended the election with roughly the number of seats predicted in preelection estimates (80–85), but it was not the prime beneficiary of the KMT's collapse. At least 13 formerly KMT seats went to the infant pro-independence Taiwan Solidarity Union, giving the Pan Green a total of 100 legislative seats. But most of the KMT defections (the KMT dropped from 123 seats in the last election to 68 seats) went to the KMT splinter party (James Soong's People First Party), a group that did surprisingly well, ending up with 46 seats, versus expectations in the twenties. The PFP also gained several seats held by the pro-Beijing "China New Party," which lost 10 of its 11 seats in the December balloting. The KMT–PFP "Pan Blue" camp was therefore able to hold a razor-thin plurality of 113 and relied on various underworld-related "independent" parliamentarians to maintain a controlling margin. Both PFP and KMT views on cross-Strait issues tend to be similar: both draw large constituencies from people of mainlander descent who oppose Taiwan independence and others who are uncomfortable with Hoklo Taiwanese dominance in the political arena.

Rumors that the KMT hoped to woo James Soong back into the fold came to fruition on March 30, 2003, when the two parties announced a joint presidential Lien-Soong ticket for the March 2004 presidential election. But the personal animosities and political rivalries that exist among key players in both parties will make the marriage a rocky one. Upon the announcement of the joint ticket, Soong called for a "dual-leadership constitutional system" if the ticket wins in 2004.

But it is reasonable to assume that on cross-Strait issues the KMT and PFP will be natural allies in proposing deeper economic and transportation ties with China than President Chen or the Pan Green can stomach. The Pan Blue will also campaign on a One China platform designed to restrain Taiwan's continuing trend toward a separate identity from China. Should the Pan Blue KMT–PFP coalition win the presidency in 2004, it could arrest the pro-separation realignment of Taiwan's politics. A Green win in 2004 would likely continue the momentum for separation from China. Either way, Taiwan has a long way to go before reaching a consensus on its national identity.[29]

Conclusion

The important conclusion to draw is that ethnic identity—and consequently, national identity—is a permanent feature of Taiwan's political landscape.

Because national identity is at the core of the cross-Strait tensions, Taiwan's political process will not permit an accommodation of China's demands that Taiwan become subordinate to Beijing. So unless China changes, there is no near- to mid-term prospect of any cross-Strait rapprochement.

But the other side of the coin is that the political dynamics are such that the majority ethnic Hoklo-Taiwanese inclination toward an outright declaration of independence will be restrained by the uneasiness of the minority Hakka, mainlander, and aborigines.

Finally, although we might have justifiable concerns about the judgment of Taiwan's leadership, on the whole they are well educated, intelligent, resourceful, and very responsive to the electorate, which is more than can be said for China's leadership.

Notes

[1] From 1990 through 2000, Taiwan regularly imported 50 percent more in U.S. goods than the PRC. With the downturn in Taiwan's economy in 2001 and 2002, Taiwan's imports of U.S. goods fell to rough parity with the PRC. See U.S. International Trade Commission Web site, U.S. Trade Balance, by Partner Country 2001 in descending order of trade turnover (imports plus exports), accessed at <http://dataweb.usitc.gov/scripts/cy_m3_run.asp>.

[2] John Tkacik, "Taiwan's Presidential Countdown: What does it mean for the United States?" *China Brief* 3, no. 9 (May 6, 2003), accessed at <http://china.jamestown.org/pubs/view/cwe_003_009_001.htm>. See also Nancy Tucker, "If Taiwan Chooses Unification, Should the United States Care?" *The Washington Quarterly*, Summer 2002, 22. Tucker notes that Chinese control of Taiwan would alarm Japanese military planners, giving China a presence along Japan's shipping routes and abutting its Ryukyu Island chain. Control of Taiwan would "in fact lead to a more significant projection of Chinese naval and air power beyond coastal waters. Unpublished statistics collected by Taiwan's ministry of national defense in June 2002 show that roughly 246,015 commercial ships transited Taiwan waters in 2001, and 259,086 civilian airliners traversed the Taiwan Air Defense Identification Zone the same year."

[3] Sandy Huang, "Cross-Strait Ties: Surveys over the past year indicate that most Taiwanese favor the president's tough talk on China, but are cautious about opening direct links," *Taipei Times,* April 17, 2003, accessed at <http://www.taipeitimes.com/News/taiwan/archives/2003/04/17/202383>. Taiwan's public opinion has shown a steady warming to independence since 1994 when generally about 10 percent of respondents in public opinion polls were "pro-independence" and 25 percent were "pro-unification." At the height of Taiwan's 2000 presidential election campaign, pro-independence respondents were over 28 percent of samples, but pro-independence has leveled off at about 17 percent since then, with pro-unification sentiment running at 16 to 24 percent. See Taiwan's Mainland Affairs Council (MAC) tabulations, accessed at <http://www.mac.gov.tw/english/english/pos/9112/9112e_1.gif>. Taiwan's Mainland Affairs Council cites independence-unification surveys conducted by six separate agencies that appear not to ask precisely the same questions of respondents. Some agencies get consistently high sentiment for independence over time, while others get lesser interest. When the results are overlaid on a line graph (as appears at the MAC Web site), this phenomenon is visible. A more interesting poll was one conducted by Sun Yat-sen University in December 2000 that showed 57.8 percent of Taiwan elementary school pupils identified themselves as Taiwanese only, while 23.7 percent said they were both Chinese and Taiwanese. Only 6.4 percent of the children said they were Chinese only. See *"Zhongshan Daxue Diaocha Xianshi: Qi Cheng Xuetong Ji Ju Zhengdang Pian Hao"* ("Sun Yat-sen University Poll shows 70 percent of school pupils have partisan leanings"), *China Times,* December 10, 2000.

[4] Chen Shui-bian and Frank Chang-ting Hsieh, now respectively Taiwan's president and mayor of Kaohsiung, were the primary defense attorneys in the Martial Law Trial of the Kaohsiung Eight defendants. Also leading lights in the opposition movement then were Chang Chun-hsiung, now Taiwan's premier, and then-imprisoned Lu Hsiu-lien, now Taiwan's vice president.

[5] These include former U.S. citizen Mark Tang-shan Chen, former president of the World Federation of Taiwanese Associations, now magistrate of Tainan county; George Tsan-hung Chang, former chairman of the World United Formosans for Independence, now mayor of Tainan city; U.S. citizen Wang Hsing-nan, arrested and sentenced to life imprisonment in 1975 for the attempted assassination of Taiwan's vice president Hsien Tung-min, now member of the Legislative Yuan; former DPP Chairman Peng Ming-min, former chairman of the graduate school of political science at National Taiwan University, who was jailed on sedition charges in 1964, paroled, and in 1970, escaped by fishing boat to Japan, Canada, then the United States, where he taught international law until his return in November 1992. Among other prominent Taiwanese opposition politicians with U.S. training are DPP legislator Parris Chang and presidential aide Hsiao Mei-chin.

[6] Alan M. Wachman discusses the independence issue in several chapters of his *Taiwan, National Identity, and Democratization* (Armonk, NY: M.E. Sharpe, 1995), 79–87. Victor H. Li engages 15 Taiwanese and mainlanders in a discussion of Taiwan independence in his *Future of Taiwan, A Difference of Opinion* (Armonk, NY: M.E. Sharpe, 1980), 47–64. Shelly Rigger, however, points out advocates of Taiwan independence split from the Democratic Progressive Party in 1997 in frustration over the growing DPP embrace of the idea that Taiwan is already independent. See her *Politics in Taiwan, Voting for Democracy* (London: Routledge, 1999), 160.

[7] John Fuh-shen Hsieh and Emerson M.S. Niou, "Salient Issues in Taiwan's Electoral Politics," Conference Group on Taiwan Studies Working Papers in Taiwan Studies, 1995, accessed at <http://www.la.utexas.edu/research/cgots/Papers/03.pdf>

[8] This effect was somewhat dissipated by the convincing victory of the Democratic Progressive Party in the legislative of December 2001, but several media reports indicated that the elections ironically resulted in a deeper ethnic polarization of Taiwan's electorate. See Deborah Kuo, "KMT and PFP Decide Not To Take Part In Chen's Proposed Alliance," *Central News Agency,* December 6, 2001; and Stephanie Low, "KMT committee director abandons post," *Taipei Times,* December 8, 2001, accessed at <http://www.taipeitimes.com/news/2001/12/08/story/0000114876>.

[9] "*Fu Lao Ren*" in Mandarin or "Fujianese," who themselves can be further subdivided into those whose ancestors came from the Fujian cities of Quanzhou and Zhangzhou. A rivalry between the Hoklo from Quanzhou and those from Zhangzhou persists to this day. See also John Robert Shepherd,

Statecraft and Political Economy on the Taiwan Frontier 1600-1800 (Stanford: Stanford University Press, 1993), which describes in detail the local rivalries between Hakka, Quanzhou, and Zhangzhou Chinese during the 18th-century rebellions against the Qing dynasty.

[10] This chapter was originally written in November 2001 but has been updated. For a summary of the election results, see William Kristol, "Embrace Taiwan," *The Washington Post,* December 4, 2001.

[11] There is very little published survey data on voting patterns of Taiwan's ethnic subgroups. These conclusions are drawn from conversations with scholars at the Election Study Center of National Chengchi University in Taipei.

[12] Chen Lu-an also served as defense minister under President Chiang Ching-kuo and is the son of the late Chen Cheng, Taiwan's vice president under Chiang Kai-shek.

[13] Siba Ryotaro, "Lee Teng-hui's Candid Talk With Shiba," *Zili Zhoubao (Independence Post Weekly),* May 13, 1994, 4, interview with Li Teng-hui in Taipei, date of interview not given.

[14] See Zhou Yuguan, *Li Denghui de Yi Qian Tian (Lee Teng-hui's First Thousand Days 1988–1992),* (Taipei: Maitian Publishing, 1993), 145–147, 165, 180–182. In the power struggle between the KMT mainland faction and the emerging Taiwanese "Mainstream Faction" (*Zhuliu Pai*), Soong proved to be a stalwart Lee Teng-hui supporter and worked tirelessly to engineer Lee's election as KMT chairman.

[15] This anecdote comes from private conversations with sources in Taiwan. The author has not been able to track down a published citation.

[16] The most comprehensive history of the February 28, 1947, incident is found in George H. Kerr, *Formosa Betrayed* (Boston: Houghton Mifflin, 1965), 254–330.

[17] See John F. Copper, *Taiwan: Nation-State or Province?* (Boulder: Westview, 1990), 37–41; and Tun-jen Cheng and Stephan Haggard, *Political Change in Taiwan* (Boulder: Lynne Reinner, 1992), 190–194, for a discussion of the similarity in Hakka and mainlander voting patterns vis-à-vis Min-Nan (Hoklo) preferences.

[18] John Tkacik, "How A-bian Won," *China On Line,* March 26, 2000, accessed at <http://www.chinaonline.com/features/eyeontaiwan/eyeontaiwan/cs-protected/c0 032652.asp>.

[19] Liu Mei-chun, "Chen-Lee alliance steals the limelight," *The Taipei Times*; see also Xia Zhen, He Rongxing, and Yin Naiqing, "*Beishe Chengli, Li Bian tongtai Chuji, Lien Song Didiao Huiying*" ("North Association established, Lee and Chen launch attack on stage together, Lien and Soong play it down"), *China Times,* June 17, 2001.

[20] Liu Tiancai, "Li Zhengtuan Zhengming '*Taiwan Tuanjie Lianmeng'*" ("Lee Teng-hui Political Group rectifies its name as 'Taiwan Solidarity Union'"), *China Times,* July 25, 2001; Bu Mingwei, "Taiwan Tuanjie Lianmeng Cheng Jun" ("Taiwan Solidarity Union moves its troops"), *Commercial Times,* July 25, 2001.

[21] Lee did, in fact, midwife the emergence of the Taiwan Solidarity Union, a KMT splinter that supported the DPP and which won 6 percent of the vote and 13 seats in the Legislature in the December 1, 2001, elections.

[22] In several campaign stump speeches for TSU candidates in November 2001, Lee complained bitterly that a vote for the KMT would "let a flock of alien rulers once again plunge Taiwan back into dictatorship" ("*fouze jiu hui rang yipi wailai zhengquan tongzhi, rang Taiwan zaidu hui dao ducai*"). See "*Li Denghui: Rentong bi Tongyi Geng Zhongyao*" ("Lee Teng-hui, 'Recognition is more important than unification'"), *China Times,* November 19, 2001. In a separate stump speech in Hualien, Lee said he knew how the legislative elections would turn out, but he could not discuss it. He said that if "the election turns out good or bad, it will affect Taiwan's stability for the next twenty or thirty years, and if it's bad 'even I will kill myself,' this election is that important." See "*Li Denghui Da Yuyan Zhengju Jiang Bian*" ("Lee Tenghui makes a bold prediction, the political scene will change"), *China Times,* November 18, 2001.

[23] "*Guomindang Zhongchanghui Beicha Li Denghui An, Wu Boxiong: Hao Zhong hao san*" ("KMT Central Standing Committee will review Lee Teng-hui Case, Wu Po-hsiung says, 'we met as friends, let's part as friends'"), *China Times,* September 27, 2001.

[24] As of September 2002, Mayor Ma Ying-jeou was locked in a serious electoral battle with DPP candidate Lee Ying-yuan for the Taipei mayoralty. It is an election he should have had no trouble winning. But the DPP's Lee seems certain to have an "iron vote" of at least 43 percent. The highly popular former President Lee Teng-hui campaigned for Ma Ying-jeou in 1998, describing his as a "New Taiwanese" *(Xin Taiwanren)*. In the 2002 election campaign, however, the former president has attacked Ma and supported Lee Ying-yuan. It remains to be seen whether the former president can claim the additional 8 percentage points needed to put the DPP's Lee over the top.

[25] The DPP's major factions are "New Tide" *(Xin Chaoliu)*, led by Chiou I-jen and Wu Nai-jen; "Justice Alliance" *(Zhengyi Lianxian)*, led by President Chen Shui-bian; "Welfare State" *(Fuli Guo)*, led by Kaohsiung Mayor Chairman Frank Hsieh; "Formosa" *(Meilidao)*, of which Vice President Lu Hsiu-lien was one of the most prominent members; and the "Independence Alliance" *(Taidu Lianmeng)*, led by Tainan County mayor Mark Chen. For a discussion of how the factions work in election campaigns, see Joyce Huang, "DPP selects election candidates," *Taipei Times,* April 2, 2001, accessed at <http://www.taipeitimes.com/news/2001/04/02>.

[26] Hsu Hsin-liang ran against Chen Shui-bian for the presidency when he failed to gain the DPP presidential nomination for himself in the 2000 election.

[27] Chao resigned as KMT organization chief after the party's losses in the December 2001 legislative elections. Chao bemoaned the influence that local KMT had accreted to the detriment of the national party organization and said the fact that the KMT has urged the electorate to "vote for the person, not the party" indicates that the party lacked confidence in itself. Chao also admitted that because of the dependence on traditional vote captains and vote-buying politics, the DPP government's continual crackdown on vote buying, meant electoral losses for many KMT candidates. See Stephanie Low, "KMT committee director abandons post," *Taipei Times,* December 8, 2001, accessed at <http://www.taipeitimes.com/news/2001/12/08/story/0000114876>.

[28] The author is indebted to the American Institute in Taiwan for this analysis. Taiwan's Central Election Commission certified the results of the legislative elections on December 2, 2001: DPP received 38.67 percent of the vote and won 87 seats; the KMT received 30.22 percent of the vote and won 68 seats; the PFP received 20.44 percent of the vote and won 46 seats; the Taiwan Solidarity Union won 5.78 percent of the vote and took 13 seats; Independents received 4.45 percent of the vote and took 10 seats. The pro-China "New Party" got less than a half percent of the votes and won a single seat in Quemoy. See *Ziyou Shibao (Liberty Times)*, December 2, 2001, 2.

Chapter 13

Russian-Chinese Relations in the Brave New World

Eugene B. Rumer

Russian-Chinese relations, like most aspects of the international system, are not likely to escape the long shadow of the tragic events of September 11, 2001. What previously had seemed to many observers like one of the more important strategic relationships in the world will undoubtedly be recast as a function of both countries' reassessment of their foreign policy priorities, their respective relationships with the United States, as well as the potential impact of the September 11 events on their domestic policymaking environments.

Indeed, the notion of an emerging Russian-Chinese alliance or partnership was an exaggeration even prior to September 11. The two countries share considerable interests, but the relationship between them could be far more accurately described at best as a marriage of convenience, at worst as a latent geopolitical faultline in Eurasia.

Even a quick look at the balance sheet of Russian-Chinese relations leaves little doubt that this is a relationship in flux. The factors that draw the two countries together are quite well known: Russia has weapons to sell and needs to sell them, China needs weapons to modernize its arsenal; both Moscow and Beijing have grown tired of and irritated at Washington. Their shared resentment of the United States is fed by a whole range of factors, such as the U.S. global presence from Taiwan to the Caspian, lecturing about human rights and propensity toward unilateral action in the Balkans and Persian Gulf, and the Bush administration's commitment to missile defense, to name just a few.

Since the mid-1990s, Russia and China have also shared growing concerns about stability in Central Asia. Both have watched the United States expand its presence in Central Asia with suspicion. Both have been alarmed by the rise of the Taliban regime and the spread of militant Islam in the region. Both have sought to foster regional cooperation under the auspices of the Shanghai forum, while trying to keep the United States out of it and minimize its influence.

Less well known and often overlooked, but certainly increasingly prominent in the Russian debate about China, is the growing concern among Russia's foreign policy elite about the growing strategic imbalance between Russia and China and the uncertain geopolitical implications from this trend—Russia in decline, China on the rise—for the Russian position in the Far East. Suffice it to say that the leading Russian foreign policy association—the Council for Foreign and Defense Policy—has launched a debate about Russia's future in the Far East, inviting its members to discuss whether Moscow will be able to "hold on" to the region.

Concerns about the Russian position vis-à-vis China—regardless of any official pronouncements from Beijing—have spurred a number of leading Russian analysts to ponder the wisdom of the partnership, including the military-technical relationship with China. These recent concerns overlay the longstanding Russian suspicions about China,[1] which just as easily can be traced either to the relatively recent clashes of the late 1960s or the historic fears of the "yellow peril."

Have the events of September 11 changed this uneasy balance in Russian-Chinese relations and, if so, how? Any speculation so soon about the impact of an ongoing military campaign on Russian-Chinese relations involves some risk. That said, the risk is worth taking, if only to sketch out some of the possibilities.

The first impression is that China has come out the big loser in the aftermath of September 11. To the extent one could talk prior to that date about a nascent Russian-Chinese anti-U.S. partnership, it appears to be in even bigger trouble than before. Vladimir Putin's decisive stance in support of U.S. actions has triggered a new dynamic in U.S.-Russian relations. The Bush-Putin "agreement to agree" in Shanghai, regardless of the fine print, was an important signal of the high priority the two presidents placed on developing good U.S.-Russian relations. The prospect of a broad agreement on the national missile defense (NMD)-antiballistic missile (ABM) nexus of issues hinted at by the presidents' aides again raises the possibility of Russia breaking ranks with China and signing on to a strategic partnership with the United States.

In Central Asia, the post-September 11 situation looks very different as well. Making the best out of a potentially thorny situation, President Putin has endorsed U.S. deployment of troops in Uzbekistan and Tajikistan. U.S. troops are on the ground and by most accounts are there to stay for the long run. The fabled Shanghai forum sponsored by Moscow and Beijing, in large part to keep the United States out of Central Asia, has in effect collapsed—at China's expense. While Russia and the United States are collaborating in their common fight against terrorism and the Taliban regime, China has found itself on the sidelines.[2]

China has been sidelined in other ways, too. The marginal role accorded so far in the war on terrorism to the United Nations and its Security Council—Beijing's favorite forum for restraining U.S. global ambitions—has in effect marginalized China. Russia, by contrast, has gained from its bilateral relationship with the United States.

Evidently, President Putin hopes to reap substantial political benefits from his bold move in support of the war on terrorism. For Russia, with its diminished domestic circumstances and sagging international fortunes, the chief benefit would be a new level of political and strategic engagement with the West, most notably the United States, tilting the balance in internal Russian deliberations about the country's strategic orientation further away from China.

Should the United States and its allies offer Russia material rewards to encourage its westward integration, Putin might be emboldened to move against some of the most entrenched and powerful sources of internal opposition to deep structural reforms in the economy, in particular the defense-industrial complex, which has been an active proponent—and a major beneficiary of military-technical cooperation with China. Should this happen, some of China's strongest allies in Russian domestic politics would see their influence curtailed.

However, it would be unrealistic and naïve to expect Russia to cut off its arms sales to China or to make an abrupt shift in its political relations with it. Clearly, too much is at stake in this relationship for Moscow, and its position vis-à-vis China is still weak, leaving Putin and his team no room to antagonize Beijing. But the new rapprochement between Russia and the United States and its allies could well cast the relationship between Russia and China in a very different light. The fabled "strategic partnership" would then become what one China expert has described as the "lowest common denominator" below that neither side can afford to sink, rather than a cooperative relationship built on shared interests.

That said, even this relatively sanguine assessment of Sino-Russian relations after September 11 leaves many unanswered questions. For example, how will Russia maintain its "hold" on the Far East in the light of the shifting strategic balance in the region? What does this shift mean for the United States? Are we to fear, encourage, or remain indifferent to it? Are there threats to U.S. interests or are there opportunities in that strategic shift to be explored and exploited?

Notes

[1] It is not uncommon for Russian strategic analysts to remark casually that, of course, the missile defense system around Moscow has always been aimed at China, never at the United States.

[2] It is worth noting that in South Asia, too, China seems to have suffered a setback. Its traditional ally Pakistan has emerged as a pivotal U.S. partner in the war on terrorism, while India has reaffirmed its longstanding partnership with Russia and entered into a new relationship with the United States. Although most of these developments had been in train prior to September 11, the renewed U.S.-Pakistani relationship follows directly from it and confirms a trend that is generally unfavorable to China. The list goes on. The war on terrorism has produced some strange bedfellows. Perhaps most notable among them is the de facto realigning of the United States and Iran, both sworn enemies of the Taliban regime. Should this very tenuous rapprochement put an end to U.S.-Iranian rivalry in Central Asia, the U.S. position in the region would be further enhanced.

Chapter 14

The PLA, Trade, and U.S. Interests

Kevin G. Nealer

T he military capability of any country is shaped not only by policy and defense budget choices but also by the larger economic environment in which the country is operating. Therefore, this essay begins with an overview of the current macroeconomic environment facing China and other countries in the region.

The rate of growth of Chinese exports experienced some significant declines early last year. Since the beginning of 2001, exports that have enjoyed traditional strength (notably apparel) have declined. While exports growth returned in 2001, such downturns remind Chinese businesses that they are not immune from economic cycles in Asia and the United States.

In Japan, trade sensitivity regarding Chinese agricultural products and select manufactured goods from China has created turbulence between the two countries, and it is likely that China's other trading partners (including the United States) will be increasingly concerned about domestic import sensitivities resulting from Chinese products.

In addition, it appears that China is reaching the top of its labor cost advantage and will begin to face increased competition from other developing nations to be the low-cost producer of domestic and foreign products.

Coping with WTO Commitments

China is challenged by the fact that, after 15 years of negotiations, it is now a member of the World Trade Organization (WTO). The Chinese leadership has bet on WTO as an organizing principle for the final stage of reform of its state enterprises. While foreigners should be encouraged by China's commitment to live by international norms in conducting its global trade and investment policies, WTO obligations will test the limits of China's tolerance for deeper economic reforms.

WTO commitments will accelerate social adjustment brought about as the result of pressures from increased imports and a decreased obligation to locally source product input. This will exacerbate unemployment. Over 6.5 million urban workers lost their jobs in 1999, and there were an additional 2 million more through mid 2000, not including the rural jobless, who are not recorded in official tallies.

Modifications of over 1,000 domestic laws and regulations will put pressure on the Chinese legal system, which, as a civil law structure, is less adaptable than common law systems. (China's court system is unaccustomed to hearing challenges to existing laws and regulations, and provincial judicial systems are often unaware of changes made to existing laws for a significant period of time.)

China has seen breathtaking growth along the coastal region, but 7 out of 10 Chinese citizens still reside in rural communities, where they are less likely to find employment in growing sectors of exporting industries. WTO-induced growth is likely to widen the income disparity between coastal and inland residents.

Domestic Adjustment

Domestic growth of more than 6 percent seems sustainable; however, China is likely to face declining exports in the coming year, and there may also be a lessened appetite for Chinese corporate listings in Hong Kong and the United States. Much of the anticipated cleanup of the financial sector has been deferred; even access to the second largest pool of hard currency in the world cannot protect these firms from consolidation.

Issues relating to Chinese defense spending are common knowledge (see figure 14–1); however, these issues do need to be placed in a broader context (see figure 14–2). China announced a budget increase in March 2001 in education, science and technology, agriculture, and defense spending. The allocation of financial resources within the military is scheduled to be dispersed among China's 2.5 million troops and civil employees, as well as to finance the garrison in Macau. Conventional wisdom says that a large portion of the remaining money in the budget will be used to upgrade current military technology.

How is China sustaining this budget increase while trying to avoid contraction and declining demand (see figure 14–3)? The surprising thing about the list of policy options is their similarity to the toolbox used in fully marketized economies, such as America's. The cautionary tale here is that, as the devices for state planning have been relaxed over the past decade, the

Figure 14–1. **Military Spending, 1995–2000**

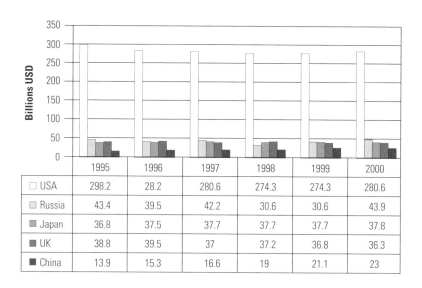

	1995	1996	1997	1998	1999	2000
☐ USA	298.2	28.2	280.6	274.3	274.3	280.6
▨ Russia	43.4	39.5	42.2	30.6	30.6	43.9
▦ Japan	36.8	37.5	37.7	37.7	37.7	37.8
▥ UK	38.8	39.5	37	37.2	36.8	36.3
■ China	13.9	15.3	16.6	19	21.1	23

Figure 14–2. **Increases in China's Budget Announced in March 2001**

Education	↑	27.9%
Agriculture	↑	21.4%
Defense spending	↑	17.7%
Science and technology	↑	14.5%
Social security	↑	
Agriculture	↑	
Three Gorges Dam	↑	
Development of Western China	↑	

central government's ability to adjust through market controls (such as wage and price adjustments and state purchasing) have diminished toward the vanishing point. Even fewer of these tools and administrative guides will be available after WTO implementation.

Figure 14–3. How China Is Paying for Fiscal Spending

Issuance of treasury bonds	Fiscal reform/better budget controls
Decrease corruption	Tax incentives as a macro tool
Possible fuel tax	

Figure 14–4. Partial List of Divested PLA and PAP Enterprises (in *ren min bi*)

Province	Units divested	Workers	Output value	Profits	Asset values	Debt values
Hebel	122				1.47b	1.07b
Guangdong	390	6700			2.0b	
Jiangsu	64				1.4b	
Beijing	68	2300			1.4b	
Shenyang	47	762	534m			
Hainan	29					
Shanghai	9	600		30m	300m	
Tianjin	67					
Jiangxi	8	687		45.75m		
Lanzhou	68					

Source: James C. Mulvenon, *Soldiers of Fortune—The Rise and Fall of the Chinese Military-Business Complex, 1978–1998* (New York: M.E. Sharpe, 2001), 185.

Trade Complexities

A decade ago, we were concerned about "trade as treason"—that is, trading with statist firms that passed knowledge and equipment on to the People's Liberation Army (PLA). With divestiture of PLA enterprises well under way (see figure 14–4), the risks are exquisitely subtler. The volumes of commerce we are talking about now are considerable (see figure 14–5). Total Sino-American trade this year will total nearly $140 billion. China's global imports and exports totaled about $600 billion last year. Increasingly, this reflects higher levels of technology on both sides. When China was selling us swizzle sticks and Barbie dolls a decade ago, technology

Figure 14–5. **U.S.-Chinese Bilateral Trade, 1998–2001**

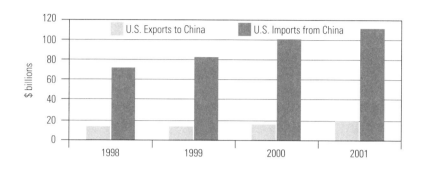

Source: Department of Commerce, Country Commercial Guide for FY–2002 (U.S. Customs Data).

transfer issues were easy to detect. Now the Chinese exports have moved downstream and are far more sophisticated (for example, digital cameras and videocassette recorders). Accordingly, the inputs needed to turn them out, including software, are far more sophisticated.

Analysts tend to focus on trade in goods in examining defense related contributions; however, there is a growing realization that money is fungible and that investment is strategically significant. To offer a sense of perspective, total global trade in goods amounts to an estimated $6 trillion annually. This contrasts with currency clearances every day of well over $800 billion, meaning that nearly as much money moves around the world every week as the total volume of goods trade in a year.

For China (see figure 14–6), $8 billion in U.S. inward investment is a very small part of the story. For most of the past decade, China has captured one out of every three dollars going into the developing world. This "big sucking sound" has a crowding effect on credit markets, reducing the funds available for investment in other developing markets.

The Investment Dilemma

There are increasing calls in the U.S. Congress for limits on China's access to American capital markets. At a first order, this is an effort to constrain the ability of Chinese companies to strengthen themselves as competitors by using equity and debt. In addition, the theory is that foreign investors are unwittingly capitalizing the PLA because access to foreign funding frees up Chinese assets to support military expansion. Assuming

Figure 14–6. **U.S. Foreign Direct Investment in China, 1979–2000**

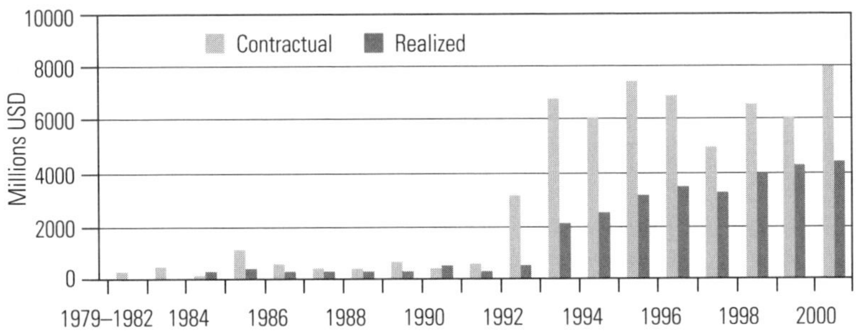

Source: Department of Commerce, Country Commercial Guide for FY–2002 (Ministry of Foreign Trade and Economic Cooperation, State Statistical Bureau).

a one-to-one correlation between Chinese corporate wealth and the PLA budget is unsupportable. The PLA competes for funds in the Chinese budget. While the military is clearly modernizing, it does not make sense to imagine that denying capital to either state sector or quasi-private ventures in any way inhibits PLA plans.

In fact, with increased access to the international securities market, there is a growing requirement for visibility and full disclosure about the structure and financing of these firms. In fact, we likely know more about the structure, functions, and relative health of Chinese companies as a result of reporting obligations associated with their increased reliance on foreign capital than from all of the sleuthing and conventional investigations of the past decade. The Bank of International Settlements, international accounting requirements, and reporting obligations are opening the books on Chinese companies and their practices. The picture is far from complete but comparable in many ways to Japan and South Korea. Shutting them off from capital shuts us off from participation and knowledge. Since capital markets are truly global, U.S. allies will not hesitate to participate in a good deal.

Export Control and Proliferation Concerns

If the United States accepts that trade leads the bilateral relationship, that it is broad and deep, and that it is likely to become more so, where does that leave how we think about diversion risks and export controls and exploitation of civilian technologies by the PLA?

Alfred Wilhelm has reviewed the terms of debate on military/military contacts. I cannot improve on what he wrote in considering the trade implications for dealing with the military, other than offer Larry Wortzel's cautionary criteria:

- Do not improve capability to fight the United States or Taiwan.
- Do not improve capacity to project force.
- Do not help them repress the Chinese people.

Larry Wortzel and others like Paul Godwin and Bernard Cole have made the case that the legitimate areas of concern are:

- AWACS
- air-to-air refueling
- satellites
- missiles and guidance
- *unique technologies* in which the United States provides a capacity that is otherwise unavailable.

As we consider renewal of the Export Administration Act, the direction of technology controls is clear. There is the need for fewer but higher fences around systems and capabilities that matter most to the United States in terms of risks to defensive and offensive capabilities. The notion of temporal speed bumps, essentially our current policy of keeping critical systems more than two generations behind in any sensitive exports of production technologies, should be considered also. The issue of what constitutes a generational shift is a matter of hot debate in the high-tech community. Bear in mind that American companies exercise a high degree of discipline over technology transfers for their own good commercial reasons. They are not unwilling participants in this process, and they often enjoy parrying the demands of Chinese partners for the best technology with demurrals based on U.S. law and policy.

Has PLA defense divestiture made it harder to tell legitimate commercial firms and purposes from those seeking military technologies? Yes, but in our experience with commercial transactions, it is fairly clear that most for-profit companies take care of their own interests with little regard for the military's wish list. This is not to say that covert programs are not filling PLA shopping lists, but for the most part, for-profit companies are unresponsive. They simply do not share the state sector's priorities or interests and are not willing to compromise essential business goals to help aggrandize PLA capabilities.

There are companies whose history and culture remain reliant on PLA contacts and purchases, which present more troublesome issues. Huawei has been cited as an example, as well as the Poly Group. With companies such as these, we see a need to do a finer-grain analysis and to look at what business units are involved and for what purposes. To a large extent, when we talk about improving Chinese military capability through trade, the risk points are Russia and Israel.

What about the other side of the coin, meaning China's record as an exporter of dangerous technologies and role as proliferator? The experience here is uneven. We have seen sanctions in 1991 and 1993 and Chemical Weapons Convention sanctions. We are now coping with the Helms sanctions, and there was to have been a fix at the recent Shanghai Summit, though the Chinese were unable to pick up the deal that was on the table so the decision may be deferred.

Finally, there are two trends: One is Chinese ability, and ours, to differentiate between acts of companies and state acts so that we are both identifying bad actors, not raising every issue to the level of state-to-state action. The other is a general trend, of which WTO membership is evidence, to seek the norms of the international system, not out of any sense of obligation, but because it is in China's self-interest.

Conclusions

The story of Ambassador Richard Armitage's meeting with the Pakistani Interior Minister is well known, as is Armitage's pronouncement that "History begins today." There is reason for hope that September 11, 2001, will become a catalyst for Chinese views on proliferation risk and that we can use this moment to encourage the instinct to restraint, to the extent it now exists in the Chinese view of self-interest.

By all events, Sino-American trade relations are condemned to become more complicated over time. While a high degree of caution is essential in protecting American security and commercial interests, the U.S. approach also must be part of a well-considered international effort, if it is to succeed.

Chapter 15

China's Trade Opening: Implications for Regional Stability and U.S.-China Relations

Howard M. Krawitz

C hina's entry into the World Trade Organization (WTO) could well have a decisive impact on that country's long-term economic, political, and military development, as well as on its relations with Asian neighbors and the United States. A best-case scenario posits a secure China, confident of its role in the region, valuing peace and stability as key to regional development and prosperity and, thus, in its interest. A Chinese middle class could arise. Prospects are good for mutually beneficial U.S.-China relations based on shared interests and for Chinese social reforms and political liberalizations.

Although a strong China could become a regional aggressor, there is, at present, little reason to expect this to happen, but it is also unrealistic to expect China will not modernize its military and use it to enhance international prestige. In any event, a strong, stable China is as likely as not to serve U.S. regional security interests and to cooperate with Asian neighbors to promote and maintain regional peace and stability.

A worst-case scenario has Beijing failing at stable, sustainable reform and finding itself hard-pressed to manage resulting economic and social ills and civil unrest. The leadership might encourage nationalism and military aggressiveness to ensure its survival. Internationally, China could become mired in a downward spiral of cheating, trade disputes, sanctions, and retaliation. U.S.-China relations overall, not just bilateral trade, would suffer, setting both nations on an increasingly tense and confrontational course, raising odds for direct conflict over sensitive issues such as Taiwan.

Whichever scenario prevails, China will show little change in the short run, but it will be a crucial time for Beijing. Encouraging domestic Chinese reforms ultimately serves U.S. interests, but productive U.S.-China relations will require strong doses of realism, clarity, consistency, and patience.

China's Big Move

In late 2001, China entered the WTO, a dramatic step that marks not only the end of a 15-year odyssey for Beijing but also the beginning of a new phase in the country's internal development and its relations with the outside world. It may sound odd to suggest that joining the WTO—an organization focused on rules of conduct for trade and commerce—will influence not only China's economy but also its political, military, and social development, as well as its interaction with the United States. Yet China's efforts to play by WTO rules could affect its internal development far more extensively than has been the case with many new member nations.

Most WTO entrants must grapple with difficult economic and social issues at accession. But China will have to come to grips with such issues on a massive scale. Geographic size, infrastructure, and population will make adjustments more difficult, as will the unbalanced nature of the Chinese economy. China will have to reconcile conflicting economic systems (socialist versus market-based) and varying levels of domestic development (technologically advanced, internationally competitive versus third-world) as it seeks to develop a new hybrid economy that can live by the rules of the global trading system.

Predicting how China will respond to domestic conditions created by WTO requirements is difficult. Beijing clearly will face numerous pressures from WTO benchmarks and timetables for achieving compliance; from the shocks that such compliance may create for the country's economic, financial, and social welfare systems; and from the near-certainty of rising domestic political opposition to WTO-mandated reforms, particularly at the regional and local levels.

Beijing's ability to manage the domestic politics of this turbulent phase will decisively influence its ultimate ability to transform China into a major economic power. Pockets of opposition to joining the WTO existed throughout the accession process, even among the leadership. Some opposition stemmed from political and ideological differences. But much was due to the regional grassroots economic and social issues dividing the "several Chinas" that exist in the People's Republic of China

(PRC) today—eastern/western China, urban/rural China, rapidly developing/stagnating China—and the fears that WTO membership will make things even worse for those trapped in these several Chinas.

As an aid to anticipating the future course of events, we should examine two possible lines of development—one a positive scenario, the other negative—and their associated implications for the United States. Such an exercise may help to bracket the range of possible, mixed positive-negative scenarios existing between these extremes.

China's Positive Scenario

In the best-case scenario, inflows of foreign management and legal expertise, foreign goods, foreign capital, and advanced technology will improve China's domestic economic and social infrastructure, improve the quality of life, and better prepare the nation's industries to face foreign competition at home and abroad.

WTO membership could graft an increasingly Western face onto China's economy and society. As China becomes more firmly integrated into the global trading community, foreign management practices, production expertise, and labor philosophies could be expected to diffuse gradually throughout the country, offering China tools for improving domestic infrastructure, restructuring its economy, and developing domestic investment and capital formation markets (now little more than sanctioned gambling). Ideally, wealth accrual would advance the reform of worker rights, improve social welfare systems, and generally bring about material improvements in the average person's quality of life.

China's neighbors and trade partners could benefit significantly. A prosperous China should be more receptive to opening markets to needed inputs, as it renovates old and installs new infrastructure. Moreover, integration into a global system that relies on law and legal precedent as the standard for conducting business should encourage China to adopt the rule of law as its own standard for governing business transactions and dispute resolution, at home as well as abroad. As the rule of law concept gains ground, it should promote development of a better-educated, more professional Chinese legal community (that is, law schools, judges, and lawyers). This, in turn, should stimulate application of the rule of law across a broader range of domestic civil and criminal matters, ultimately improving the general human rights situation within China.

A wealthier, technologically secure China should be more confident of its role in the region, more likely to weigh tradeoffs associated with specific courses of action or behavior. Odds are that a more prosperous China should come to believe that it stands to lose rather than gain from excessive nationalism and military adventurism and evolve into a regional power that sees maintaining regional peace and stability as the best means of promoting development and prosperity.

The Negative Scenario

On the other hand, there is no guarantee China will hew to a line of stable, sustainable reforms. In a worst-case scenario, implementing WTO-mandated changes could heighten political, social, and economic differences at home. China is already troubled by problems arising from perceived inequities between new classes of "haves" and "have-nots." These problems exist at macro (regional) and micro (neighborhood) levels. Efforts to meet WTO requirements could worsen geographic and urban/rural frictions, widen an already growing gulf between rich and poor, and generally make China more ungovernable. WTO-mandated reforms will almost certainly worsen existing problems with massive unemployment, increases in uncontrolled migrant populations, major public safety and public health issues, and rapid degradation of social welfare infrastructure.

There could be a significant potential downside for the global marketplace as well. China could try to twist WTO procedures to its own advantage—hiding behind time-consuming dispute resolution mechanisms and enjoying member benefits while protecting domestic markets by delaying implementation of required reforms. Such behavior by new entrants is not unknown. Indeed, some current members (for example, India) continue to exhibit problematic compliance with WTO rules. But in the case of China, the problem and its consequences could be greatly magnified, given China's sheer size and its already looming presence in the global marketplace.

Perceptions among Chinese that they are not benefiting from sacrifices made to enter the WTO could offer powerful arguments to conservative elements in China's leadership for opposing the country's current, more reform-minded government. Rising conservatism could feed nationalism. Perceptions that economic superpowers such as the United States, Japan, and the European Union are using complicated WTO rules and procedures either to exploit China or to contain it could cause a rethinking of China's current military philosophy (military development as subordinate to economic development) and could encourage Chinese military aggressiveness, as China turns to other means to establish its dominance in the region.

Impact on U.S.-China Relations

Arguably, the U.S.-China relationship is one of the most important bilateral relationships in existence today, with economics being very much part of the picture. The United States is China's second largest trade partner; China is America's fourth largest trade partner. Both countries are continental economies with plentiful human and natural resources. Both seek to maintain spheres of influence in the Asia-Pacific region and play key roles in regional affairs (America is already there; China aspires). America dominates through economic strength, technological superiority, and its ability to project military power. China relies on size, proximity, and personal relationships to exert influence; it seeks to expand its influence by developing economic and military strengths.

Without question, Chinese efforts to achieve regional strategic and political goals will create conditions that bring both nations into frequent and more intense contact. Avoidance is not an option; the question is whether the relationship will be one of conflict, competition, cooperation, or some mix.

If Things Go Well

Assuming China's development follows the best-case scenario, prospects seem fairly good for a cooperative, productive, and mutually beneficial U.S.-China relationship that is based on shared interests. They would probably be even better if China were to develop a solid middle class.

Economic benefits of WTO membership and WTO-related investment, intellectual property, and telecommunications agreements could create in China the proper environment for developing a broad services sector—one ranging from high-end telecommunications and financial and legal services to retail, entertainment, and personal services—and the starting point for creating a true middle class, often the source of a nation's social stability.

More importantly, while a true middle class is unlikely to arise in China's countryside, it is plausible that a new class of prosperous, non-farming peasants could emerge in areas that surround wealthy urban centers, to support these centers' needs. As "suburban peasants" grow wealthy in their own right, they will require goods and services, much of which will likely be supplied by rural residents even further from urban spheres of influence.

The concept is not new: the Pearl River Delta and Beijing's suburbs already evidence this process in action. The difference is that economic and trade benefits of WTO membership might help China more fully realize rural, as well as urban, development and, in doing so, more rapidly raise rural standards of living and education, improve the caliber of the workforce, and minimize migration, unemployment, and underemployment problems—in short, optimize prospects for rural, as well as urban, social stability.

A strong services sector, and the millions of jobs it will create, would not only support a real middle class but also slow growth in China's chronically unemployed underclass, a worrisome source of destabilizing social pressure. China must place over 10 million new workers into the economy every year. It must also find jobs for an estimated 150 million unemployed migrants, a number expected to swell by at least 5 to 6 million a year. Again, domestic stability is the issue.

Domestic stability in China benefits America. Comfortable, prosperous Chinese are more likely to share concerns similar to those Americans have and be more willing to cooperate on the range of issues relating to such concerns. For example, China already shows increased interest in working with U.S. officials and private experts on environmental problems (for example, pollution, hazardous waste, and transportation), drug trafficking, medicine, and public health. These are now issues of real concern for Chinese citizens in more prosperous areas of the country. They are also issues that transcend borders and have the potential to draw China into the international arena as a nation with a stake in making cooperation work. Dialogue on matters of mutual interest promotes communication, increased cooperation, and, ultimately, trust.

A wealthy, stable China serves U.S. regional security interests. A China that risks tangible loss from aggressive and confrontational behavior should be less likely to favor precipitous action and conflict. It should be more likely to be interested in preserving regional peace and stability, more open to consulting with Pacific Rim neighbors, and more willing to cooperate on regional security issues, strategies, and disputes. Speaking from a vantage point of growing economic strength and military capability would give Beijing the respect, prestige, and diplomatic stature it craves, making it easier for China to see itself as a player whose opinion is given serious weight by peers. This could calm Chinese fears of being marginalized or contained, making it easier for China to find common cause with the United States, Japan, and others in the region in maintaining calm and promoting dialogue on Korean Peninsula security issues, combating international terrorism and piracy, and perhaps even becoming more involved in curbing the proliferation of weapons of mass destruction.

Is a Wealthier China More Dangerous?

Ongoing debate holds that as economic power gives China the means to build military might, it will encourage military adventurism and feed the new nationalism already on the rise in China. Recent boosts in Chinese military spending hint this may already be happening.

This danger cannot be ignored. China's leaders are walking a tightrope. WTO-mandated changes and reform policy failures could engender widespread domestic discontent, nationwide strikes, riots, and other serious social disorder. Leaders, believing themselves in danger of losing control or of being marginalized by economic forces and social changes, might try to redirect domestic anger by rekindling Chinese xenophobic sentiments and turning to foreign adventurism as a means of recapturing power and reestablishing primacy. The new breed of Chinese capitalist could become the new breed of Chinese ultranationalist, equating wealth and power with the right to erase past national shame by establishing and enforcing a "Beijing Doctrine" in Asia. Or China might just interpret its own rise in terms of its neighbors' declines and simply push to see what it could get away with.

On balance, however, there is no compelling reason to believe the conditions favoring such a shift exist in strength in China today. China's government is neither weak nor easily exploited by splinter groups or radical elements. Its present leaders, and likely the next generation as well, are technocrats focused on economics and development. They are not overly close to the armed forces and are not particularly disposed to military adventurism. Indeed, China's armed services seek a greater role in political decisions and bigger budgets, but they do not seem to be pursuing their goals at the expense of the current order or by trying to undermine the civilian government. The People's Liberation Army, even while seeking a greater policymaking voice, has essentially adhered to its stated role of serving the party and its needs and putting China's economic development first.

There is little to support the argument that China seeks to modernize only to become an empire-builder or an armed bully in the region. Similarly, however, it is unrealistic to think that China would work to become a major economic power and regional policy player yet not take steps to modernize its armed forces, make them more professional, and turn them into a credible tool for enhancing international prestige. China considers its military strength less developed and capable, especially given its physical and economic size, than the armed forces of important Asian neighbors. Even taking recent large military spending increases into consideration (China views these spending boosts as attempts to catch up with militarily strong neighbors), China's defense spending has been generally moderate compared to spending by other nations in the region, even as a percentage of China's gross domestic product. Military spending increases can and should be expected, regardless of the path China takes. But the factor governing China's behavior is still the party, not the military.

In what may be a wonderfully ironic twist of history, under the optimistic scenario, the Chinese Communist Party (CCP) may become the main beneficiary of China's market-oriented changes, providing the United States and others with a stable, pragmatic counterpart with which to deal. Certainly, success with economic and social reforms and steady growth could give today's beleaguered reformers in the party the help that they need to hold China's military in check, keep neonationalist tendencies and latent anti-American sentiments under control, and address issues such as official corruption, a tarnished party image, and a lack of confidence among average Chinese.

The party itself could evolve as part of this process. At least, it will face increasing pressures to do so. More technocrats should begin filling more important positions in the party and the government. These future leaders are today being exposed to and learning the languages of international science, the global marketplace, and international organizations. Many will likely have studied in the West, probably in the United States. They will be more likely to understand the concerns and be sympathetic with the needs of an emerging middle class. They will be more likely to focus on goals similar to those that interest the United States and other developed nations. Over time, they should become easier to work with in the international arena.

A similar evolution could be expected in China's military as a younger generation of better-educated, more technologically savvy, more professional officers with more international exposure and experience learn that true military strength, which itself relies on economic power, is only one of the tools needed to achieve international eminence.

To be sure, WTO benefits and economic advancement will not squelch Chinese nationalism, slow China's drive toward military modernization, or cause CCP downfall, but they might help redirect China's nationalistic tendencies toward more positive expressions of pride and accomplishment and guide China's social and military evolution toward more internationally accepted ends—all of which, ultimately, will be to America's advantage.

If Things Go Poorly

The negative scenario, should it occur, promises its own very different consequences. Unable to move quickly enough to adapt to or enforce WTO rules and guidelines, China could become mired in a downward spiral of cheating, trade disputes, retaliatory behavior, and unilaterally imposed sanctions. The overall U.S.-China relationship, not just bilateral trade relations, would suffer.

Even if China can mollify foreign critics, Beijing is still certain to meet serious domestic resistance to implementing the WTO-required changes. Regional or class differences could stymie efforts to construct remedies for dealing with economic shocks and social dislocations caused by new, externally imposed rules. China could face serious national unity strains if wealthier provinces and economic regions were to seek more autonomy from the center and try to distance themselves from poorer areas. Such problems could worsen already serious public disillusionment with the party and loss of confidence in China's leadership as a whole. There could be a rise in xenophobic patriotism and a new, more aggressive Chinese nationalism.

Under these conditions, China's central government would be hard pressed to keep promises made to the United States and other WTO members. More likely, Beijing would retain or revive protectionist trade and investment measures and stall commitments to phase out trade barriers. More dangerously, the party and the government might come to see cultivating patriotic nationalism as the best means for retaining power. Hardliners, in league with aggressively patriotic military elements and an emerging class of civilian neonationalists, could regain political advantage over the present generation of relatively liberal-minded reformers, forcing them to change course or change jobs. (The leadership's cool relationship with the military, an asset in the positive scenario, would be a liability here.) Pressed by an ascendant military and egged on by such sentiments as "the China that can say no" and "wiping out 100 years of shame,"

China's leaders might feel compelled to push the envelope in "settling the Taiwan issue" and in pursuing policies in the South China Sea and along the northern/northwestern borders with more vigor than has been the case to date.

This would set the United States and China on an increasingly tense and confrontational course. Deteriorating U.S.-China relations would further justify, in the minds of a populace already suspicious that America intends to hold China back from its rightful place in Asia, China's need to build strong modern armed forces capable of defending China's sovereign interests and restoring Chinese pride. Military spending could power an increasingly mercantilist economy. Areas for possible U.S.-China confrontation might be the presence of U.S. forces in Asia; possible Chinese efforts to extend Chinese influence over the Korean Peninsula; a more aggressive PRC policy toward Japan; and Taiwan—the area most likely to lead to armed clashes.

Managing the Relationship

Ultimately, whichever scenario prevails, there may be few noticeable changes in China for the first few years after WTO accession. Even so, it will be a crucial period for Beijing. China will have to reduce tariffs, eliminate subsidies, dismantle market barriers, modify regulations to conform to WTO rules, enact implementing legislation, and train officials in the way of the WTO. In effect, China will be redefining its economic, perhaps even its political and military, future.

Helping China with its economic reforms ultimately serves U.S. interests. The United States can influence China's development along desired paths without giving away the store or harming national security. Promoting American management philosophies and expertise in labor relations, environmental and safety issues, banking, quality control, and conservation, to name a few areas, could help make China a cleaner, safer, more accountable, and more dependable trade partner, all of which work to U.S. purposes.

Even so, the American ability to influence China will depend on its success in establishing a framework that consistently furthers the relationship—first in economics, trade, and the legal mechanisms that support these activities and later in the broader context of the social development that stems from increasing wealth and stability. A successful U.S. effort to construct a productive relationship with China must pay heed to several factors.

First, the U.S.-China relationship must be realistic. Shaped by vastly different national experiences and philosophical traditions, American and Chinese worldviews differ greatly. Even when using the same words (for example, *democracy* and *freedom*), American and Chinese speakers may not be talking about the same things. It is unrealistic to expect that Chinese leaders, thinkers, and strategists will embrace American values merely because Americans say they are desirable. History may give Chinese good reason to think otherwise. It is equally unrealistic to expect Chinese will believe the United States means China well when it takes actions that Chinese interpret as designed to contain China.

But pragmatism is a strong trait in the Chinese character. China realistically can be expected to cooperate in relationships that bring tangible benefits to both nations and to expand this cooperation over time. Cooperation promotes better communication, which, in turn, builds trust.

Second, there must be clarity and consistency. Frequent U.S. policy shifts and ambiguously defined policy objectives have kept China's leadership off-balance and guessing for two decades. Definitional problems (saying what one means and meaning what one says) have added to bilateral tensions. Given the different nature of the two societies and cultures, clarity will always be a fundamental stumbling block in U.S.-China relations. This makes consistency an even more important element in managing the relationship.

Several types of inconsistent behavior have plagued U.S.-China relations. There is a history of inconsistency in the international arena in which the United States applies differing standards for certain issues (for example, human rights) to China than it does to other countries in which it has special interests. There is a history of inconsistency in the bilateral relationship itself; for example, one U.S. administration belaboring China for actions tacitly accepted by a different administration. Lastly, there is a Washington history of inconsistency in defining the very nature of U.S.-China relationship itself—calling China everything from a strategic partner to a rival.

This is by no means a one-way problem. Beijing also has a history of abruptly changing course as well, generally when it finds itself too far out in front on domestically sensitive and controversial issues. More disturbing is the prospect that Chinese inconsistency not only will continue but also even worsen as the next generation of Chinese leaders tries to find their footing, while the balance of domestic political power gradually passes from old-guard ideologues to the new technocrats.

Consistency in policy will be hard to achieve, given the ephemeral and ever-changing (by Chinese standards) nature of the American political landscape and Chinese unpredictability. Still, a relatively consistent approach should be feasible if a realistic policy is established at the outset: decide what is important and desirable; determine whether it is attainable; and stay the course.

Consistency and clarity in communication are both possible and the best way of ensuring a stable, productive bilateral relationship that could gradually guide China toward goals the United States finds desirable. Consistency means keeping communication lines open and maintaining academic, professional, and even military exchanges, regardless of the ups and downs of the overall relationship. It means maintaining funding and protocol levels for worthwhile programs such as rule of law exchanges even while both sides are arguing over some other aspect of the relationship. It also means managing the level and intensity of rhetoric aimed at China, positive and negative, and moderating U.S. responses to Chinese rhetoric. China tends to be surprisingly concerned with its public image. China is also very reactive, though often the response evoked is not the one sought.

Above all, there must be patience. Despite the not-inconsiderable influence Western thought has exerted on the Chinese psyche over the last 2 centuries, the Chinese worldview still remains firmly rooted in a belief that change is a product of evolutionary processes responding to events and conditions over time. Americans tend to approach things in a more linear fashion, based on a relatively direct cause-and-effect perspective and the belief that careful planning and a deliberate process bring the desired result. Given this gulf, mutual understanding has been and probably always will be difficult.

This is not to say that excuses must be made. It is to say that patience is paramount. It will always be difficult to avoid misunderstandings and clashes between two such widely differing worldviews. But setting a rational course, maintaining it with minimal variance, and proceeding in a steady manner over time will minimize mistakes. If one does it, the other is more likely to follow suit. Patience and consistency are the keys to a U.S.-China relationship that is successful over the long term.

Part V

U.S.-China Military Relations

PLA Doctrine and Strategy: Mutual Apprehension in Sino-American Military Planning

Paul H.B. Godwin

This chapter explores the evolving doctrine and strategy of the Chinese People's Liberation Army (PLA) as it prepares for a potential military conflict with the United States. It argues that although the primary near-term concern of the PLA is the use of force to prevent the permanent separation of Taiwan from the People's Republic, the United States is perceived as China's most dangerous potential adversary for two reasons. First, Beijing assumes that the United States will be militarily involved in any conflict over Taiwan. Second, because the United States perceives China as the single state in Asia likely to challenge American preeminence in maritime East Asia, U.S. security strategy is designed to contain China. PLA planners, therefore, have to prepare for two contingencies: a military conflict with the United States over Taiwan, and a probable long-term confrontation in which both Washington and Beijing view each other with mutual apprehension.

In exploring PLA doctrine and strategy, the focus is on the military issues involved. This is not to suggest that political issues are not relevant. They are clearly important. Indeed, they are probably more important than the military viewpoints that this essay explores. Nonetheless, to obtain as clear an image as possible of PLA preferences, the political issues are put aside.

Finally, the essay does not attempt to encompass doctrine and strategy for the entire PLA. It focuses specifically on the doctrine, strategy, and concepts of operations PLA researchers are contemplating as they analyze the formidable challenges presented by the capabilities of U.S. forces and their operational doctrine.

Definitions

Four core concepts are used in this chapter: military doctrine, strategy, operations, and operational doctrine. These terms encapsulate three different conceptual levels defining how military force is to be applied. *Military doctrine* consists of the fundamental principles by which those planning the application of military force guide their actions. These principles are developed from experience, analysis of past wars, and speculative analysis of future military conflicts. *Strategy* consists of the manner in which military force is applied to achieve the desired outcome of a potential or actual military conflict. *Operations* are the campaigns planned and conducted to achieve strategic objectives. *Operational doctrine* guides the employment of military forces in an operation. For the past two decades, Chinese military journals have focused primarily on operational doctrine.

The Context: Mutual Apprehension

Perception of China as a potential military threat to U.S. interests in East Asia emerged with the deterioration of Sino-American relations following the Tiananmen tragedy and the disintegration of the Soviet Union.[1] Apprehensions in the United States were matched by China's response to the radically changed post-Cold War international environment. Beijing's security assessments concluded that the United States was bent on using its unchallenged post-Cold War political and military strength to contain and encircle China with rejuvenated military alliances.[2] The Taiwan Strait crises of the mid-1990s confirmed apprehensions on both sides of the Pacific. Observers in the United States saw the PLA live-fire exercises and use of ballistic missiles as the centerpiece of coercive Beijing diplomacy as demonstrating China's dangerously increasing military capabilities.

The dispatch of two aircraft carrier battlegroups (CVBGs) to the Taiwan area was viewed in Beijing as more than demonstrating the American commitment to come to the island's defense. China saw this action as demonstrating U.S. covert commitment to an independent Republic of China. Despite the easing of Sino-American relations with the summits of 1997 and 1998, Beijing remained suspicious of U.S. intentions. Distrust of the United States was reinforced by the intent of the Bush administration to revise U.S. national military strategy and place greater emphasis on the Asia-Pacific region. Together with the new President's hard-line stance on

Taiwan, the administration was viewed as hostile toward China.[3] In the United States, the maturing Sino-Russian entente and Moscow's willingness to grant Beijing access to its most advanced conventional weapons systems was viewed with increasing suspicion.[4] Hence, on both sides of the Pacific, Sino-American relations are viewed with considerable apprehension.

Not all U.S. observers are so fearful of China's rise. Although recognizing China's increasing military and economic strength and Beijing's hostile reaction stemming from its suspicion of U.S. strategic intentions, less apprehensive assessments tend to stress two aspects of Beijing's external policies. First, despite tensions with some of its neighbors, Beijing's primary goal is to maintain an international environment permitting China to sustain its economic development and modernization goals. Foreign policies significantly reducing the high levels of foreign investment and international commerce that China needs to sustain its economic growth and modernization are seen by Beijing as undermining China's primary long-term interests. Second, notwithstanding their modernization programs and acquisition of advanced weaponry from Russia, China's armed forces are far from acquiring the capabilities required to challenge U.S. regional preeminence.[5] A potential military confrontation over Taiwan is viewed as a distinct possibility, but although demonstrating the clear intent to use military force to prevent the island achieving de jure independence, China seeks to avoid such a war if possible. Indeed, the publicity China grants the military exercises conducted adjacent to Taiwan, including the development of elite forces' joint and amphibious joint warfare capabilities, could well be designed in part to deter Taipei from taking steps that Beijing would likely view as the final move toward independence.

Harsh Realities

Most assessments agree that the pattern of mutual suspicion now characterizing the relationship between China and the United States contains the seeds of strategic competition. This does not imply that areas of Sino-American cooperation are unimportant but that the dominant dynamic is one of competition. In his discrete assessment of East Asia's power structure, Robert Ross introduced evaluations of importance to this competitive relationship.[6] First, China is now a great power—not a rising power. Second, although the United States is a global superpower, it is not the regional hegemon in East Asia. East Asia has become bipolar; the United States and China share the regional balance of power. China dominates continental Asia, and the United States is preeminent in maritime East Asia. In large part, this pattern of bipolarity was created by the disintegration of the Soviet Union. Not only did former Soviet military strength in East Asia disappear, but also Moscow's influence in Asian states was significantly diminished. Both consequences left an economically dynamic, politically active China with increasing military strength substantially more influential in continental Asia than had been the case before the Soviet demise. Sino-American security relations in East Asia are therefore those of a major continental power confronting the world's most powerful maritime power.

Strategic Competition?

If one postulates that Sino-American relations are strategically competitive, then it is necessary to state the potential objects of competition.[7] U.S. interests are twofold:

- to have military capability in or available to the region sufficient to prevent any power or combination of powers from dominating East Asia
- to ensure that the United States and its allies have unfettered access to regional markets and strategic resources, such as oil from the Middle East that transits the region's sea lanes.

China's primary external interests are threefold:

- to ensure secure borders on its periphery
- to sustain the regional stability and economic vitality essential to the regional trade and commerce so necessary for China's continued economic growth and modernization
- to ensure China's territorial integrity and sovereignty.

With the critically important exception of Taiwan, and secondarily the Spratly Islands, the past decade has seen Beijing achieve its primary interests. China is now militarily more secure than at any time in the past 150 years. There is no state on its borders threatening the security of continental China. The overwhelming nuclear and conventional military threat the former Soviet Union presented to China in the 1970s and 1980s has been replaced by a quasi-alliance with the new Russia. Moreover, Moscow has again become the principal source of PLA advanced military technologies and weaponry. China's rapprochement with Russia is paralleled by Beijing's diplomatic ties with its neighbors. For the first time since the People's Republic was established in 1949, China's relations with its neighbors have been normalized, and trade and commerce with the region is flourishing. Border issues with India are being carefully managed as both Beijing and New Delhi seek to avoid again militarizing their long-standing border disputes.[8]

China's lengthy frontiers with Russia and the new Central Asian states are similarly the focus of intense diplomacy and confidence-building measures. Thus, Inner Asia, historically the principal source of external threats to China, is no longer a primary security concern. Certainly, ethnic unrest in Tibet and Xinjiang remains a source of localized instability, but China does not confront a major threat to its security from Inner Asia.

In a similar manner, and again with the critical exception of Taiwan, primary U.S. regional interests are presently secure. U.S. security interests depend upon its ability to sustain an unwavering political, economic, and military presence in the region but do not require the United States to compete with China in continental Asia. Even so, politically and economically, no other state wields the degree of influence exercised by the United States in East Asia. Militarily, alliances and cooperative states provide American maritime, air, and ground forces access to extensive and excellent basing facilities on Asia's periphery extending from the Republic of Korea in Northeast Asia south to Australia and into the Indian Ocean. Whereas there may be questions about U.S. ability to bring sufficient military strength to the region under specific scenarios, there is no regional power with the capability to challenge successfully American military preeminence on Asia's maritime rim.

The extent to which China and the United States will become strategic competitors therefore depends on the desired futures sought by their respective capitals. At the core of U.S. apprehensions are two concerns, and both assume that China's economic, technological, and military modernization programs will be sustained over the coming decades. First and more immediately, as China's military capabilities increase, Beijing will be more willing to risk a military confrontation with the United States over Taiwan. Second, some decades hence as its economic, technological, and military strength increases, China will use its continental dominance as the foundation for challenging U.S. preeminence on the Asian periphery.[9] Furthermore, and as Ross observes, it is inevitable that the United States will focus more on China because it is the only regional power likely to challenge American preeminence.[10]

Chinese apprehension of U.S. strategic intentions stems back at least a decade. At its core, Beijing's suspicion is that American policy seeks not to engage (*jie chu*) but to contain (*e zhi*) China. Despite Washington's public commitment to a prosperous, unified People's Republic, America's strategic objective is to restrain China's emergence as a great power and uphold at least the de facto independence of Taiwan. Militarily, China's most recent defense white paper[11] makes no effort to mask Beijing's apprehension over the menace presented by U.S. military power and purpose. The "new negative developments" Beijing ascribes to the Asia-Pacific region are attributed to the United States. Strengthening the U.S. military presence and alliances, revising the U.S.-Japan defense guidelines, planning the deployment of missile defenses, and selling advanced weaponry to Taiwan are all seen as directed at China. In the white paper's reference to the South China Sea disputes, the United States is clearly the most important of the "extra-regional countries" seen as interfering in the issue. Following Beijing's assertion that it is China's policy to resolve international disputes peacefully, the white paper states:

> However, in view of the fact that hegemonism and power politics still exists [sic] and are further developing, and in particular, the basis for the country's peaceful reunification is seriously imperiled, China will have to enhance its capability to defend its sovereignty and security by military means.[12]

It is important to note how vigorously and directly Beijing stated its apprehension over the purpose of U.S. policy and military strategy in the Asia-Pacific region.[13] The 1998 white paper had limited its references to the United States to the code words "hegemonists" conducting "power politics." While retaining these oblique references, the 2000 white paper deliberately referred to the United States, indicating increasing apprehension over U.S. policy and strategy.

Mutual apprehension has created a condition in which both China and the United States view each other's military deployments, and the strategy behind them, as at least potentially threatening to their security interests. It is also probable that the degree of apprehension will vary within each country's security community, with the defense establishments of both having the harshest perception of the other's intentions and capabilities. Therefore, the context of Chinese military doctrine and strategy is no doubt developed around the most dangerous potential threat. Lesser threats to China's security will not be ignored, but the focus and priority will be on the most dangerous probable military threat. For the past decade, this threat has stemmed from the United States and the maritime approaches to China. Military concerns over China's Inner Asian periphery have not been eliminated, but they are currently and will be for the next decade far less a security concern than the potential threat presented by the United States.

Because the U.S. Armed Forces are the most technologically advanced, best equipped, and operationally competent in the world, preparing for a near-term clash with the United States over Taiwan and possibly even a long-term regional confrontation has placed China at a severe disadvantage. Furthermore, defending China's maritime approaches presents the PLA with a realm of warfare in which it has only extremely limited experience. PLA strength and experience is in land warfare. Even today, ground forces dominate the PLA, with the air and naval services functioning as their junior partners. The PLA is therefore confronting the United States in a theater of operations in which its weakest services have the heaviest operational responsibilities.

The Roots of Doctrine

To understand current and probable future PLA doctrine, it is necessary to look briefly at its roots in Mao Zedong's essays on military strategy and preparations prepared in the 1930s. These essays define the doctrine, strategy, and concepts of operations that the PLA and its predecessors were to apply when fighting Kuomintang (KMT) forces and the occupying army of Japan.[14] Mao's doctrinal principles were specifically developed to respond to the superior size, arms, and training of these adversaries. Because the military problem faced by Mao continues to confront China's military planners, these essays remain the touchstone of PLA thought. As such, the published writings of China's military theorists continue to use Mao's doctrinal precepts, even if applied in quite different types of operations.

Although a protracted war (*chijiuzhan*) of attrition was at the core of Mao's doctrine, at the operational level of war he stressed offensives conducted with speed and lethality to crush enemy combat effectiveness in the shortest possible time. Mao named this combination of protracted war joined with offensive operations "active defense" (*jijifangyu*). He feared that without the doctrinal tenet and operational principles of active defense, his forces could become bogged down in "passive defense" (*xiaoji fangyu*). Active defense forms the core of Chinese military thought today as the PLA assesses the doctrinal requirements for current and future warfare.

Active defense places utmost emphasis on gaining and retaining the battlefield initiative. Mao held that commanders holding the initiative would have the greatest flexibility in employing their forces. As he stated this principle, "flexibility is the concrete expression of the initiative in military operations."[15] A commander with the initiative will have freedom of action, which delivers him from passivity in the face of the enemy. Mao viewed deception as a useful tool in gaining the operational initiative. Deception creates "misconceptions" in the enemy commander's mind, leading to incorrect judgments and battlefield errors. By exploiting these mistakes, Mao's commanders could take the initiative away from the adversary.[16]

At the operational level of war, Mao's doctrine requires quick-decision engagements to annihilate enemy units. To ensure victory in battles of annihilation, superior forces were to be brought to bear on the enemy at the point of engagement. Moreover, because the opening engagements had a critical if not determining effect on the course of an offensive, Mao emphasized that "the first battle must be won."[17] The PLA has sought to apply Mao's operational doctrine in all the military conflicts China has fought since 1949.

China's Evolving Threat Environment

Revisions to PLA doctrine and strategy required by Beijing's response to China's changing threat environment have been significant. The principal organs of the PLA and the Chinese Communist Party (CCP) state that there have been two "strategic shifts" or "historic leaps" in Central Military Commission (CMC) guidance on national defense and war preparations.[18] First was the mid-1985 CMC decision that the defense of China no longer required preparation for a major, possibly nuclear, war with the Soviet Union. Because no major wars were anticipated, the PLA was directed to prepare for local, limited wars on China's periphery—essentially contingency planning.[19] In 1991, as the PLA was undergoing extensive reform and reorganization in response to its new guidance, the Persian Gulf War erupted. In many ways, the Gulf War was precisely the kind of military conflict PLA analysts had been assessing since the 1985 change in its strategic guidance. It was a short, high-intensity war fought for limited political objectives within a confined theater of operations. Chinese military researchers not only saw their earlier speculative analyses confirmed but were also stunned by the demonstrated effectiveness of high-technology warfare conducted by highly trained forces carrying out joint operations.

PLA deficiencies in arms and operational skills had been recognized for a decade, but the Gulf War demonstrated how far behind U.S.

capabilities China's armed forces actually were despite 12 years of re-form. These assessments led to an early 1993 enlarged meeting of the CMC where Jiang Zemin as chairman directed the PLA to henceforth prepare for "local war under high-tech conditions." This guidance was formalized in January 1999, when Jiang ordered a new "operational or-dinance" issued to establish "strategy and principle for the new period" intended to unify the operational doctrine of the PLA and to establish "an operational theoretical system fitting local wars under high-tech conditions."[20] Jiang's authoritative guidance came just a few months be-fore the North Atlantic Treaty Organization (NATO), led by the United States, conducted Operation *Allied Force* against Serbia. The intense use of precision guided munitions (PGMs) in that campaign heightened China's awareness of the deficiencies in its defenses and focused the PLA on the requirement to provide an adequate defense of its military facili-ties and critical civil infrastructure should China go to war with the United States.

Although a potential military conflict over Taiwan is Beijing's pri-mary near-term focus, the demands on the PLA have to be placed within a broader context. First, although defense of its maritime territories and claims is now the most salient near-term concern of the PLA, China re-mains a continental power and cannot neglect its extensive land borders. These borders extend some 13,729 miles and embrace 14 countries. His-torically, the principal threats to China have originated in Inner Asia. No matter how well Beijing has managed its border disputes over the past decade, it cannot ignore the possibility that these disputes will again flare up. Nor can China assume that Russia will forever be so economically, po-litically, and militarily weak that Moscow will continue to view Beijing as a useful foil to counterbalance American influence in Asia. The history of Sino-Russian and Sino-Soviet relations will certainly argue against any such confidence. Similarly, relations with a nuclear-armed India could enter a period of extreme tension in which unresolved border disputes could again be the source of military conflict.

Second, Chinese assessments of U.S. security strategy and intentions over the past decade suggest that Beijing does not view Sino-American tensions as limited to the Taiwan issue. Rather, the dispute over Taiwan is symptomatic of a broader American strategy to contain China and under-mine CCP authority and control of Chinese polity. Beijing recognizes U.S. fears that the growth of China's economic and military power will result in a challenge to American regional hegemony and that U.S. security policy is designed to sustain this preeminence against any challenger. These apprehensions over U.S. strategy were heightened by the new Bush administration's hard-line position on China. Beijing perceives the new administration's national military strategy as making two principal and threatening changes from the past. First, it sees the focus of U.S. military power shifting from Europe to Asia. Second, U.S. military planning is changing from preparing for two major regional contingencies to preparing for a large-scale regional war in East Asia, together with one extra-regional minor military operation. This major war would be with China.

These assessments see the emerging U.S. military strategy as offensive and the American perception of China as its single most important potential adversary lasting for some considerable time.[21] That the threatening posture toward China adopted by the United States is not a transient, short-term strategy is reinforced by the 2001 *Quadrennial Defense Review (QDR) Report*. Even if not by name, the QDR has clearly identified China as the most dangerous potential adversary of the United States in East Asia.[22] China's defense modernization and revisions of PLA doctrine and strategy have therefore to incorporate Beijing's expectation that China faces a long-term strategic confrontation with America.[23]

Responding to the U.S. Military Threat

PLA analysts have spent the last decade assessing the doctrine, strategy, and operations of the U.S. Armed Forces. They have conducted methodical assessments of American operations in the Gulf War and against Serbia in 1999, and they are certainly beginning their initial assessments of U.S. operations against Afghanistan. These evaluations have been accompanied by equally detailed assessments of American military strategy and objectives in the extensive U.S. Pacific Command area of responsibility. Furthermore, China's military researchers have conducted extensive analyses of U.S. approaches to future warfare and the implications of the revolution in military affairs for the conduct of these wars. From these extensive and detailed assessments, PLA researchers have developed what they believe to be a thorough understanding of how the United States will conduct military operations should war break out over Taiwan. They also believe they understand how U.S. strategy in East Asia will be implemented over the coming decade. In particular, the United States is strengthening its regional alliances and increasing its ability both to respond quickly to any military contingencies and to conduct sustained operations from regional bases. They are taking careful note of the American buildup in Guam and see the new large docking facility at Singapore's Changi naval base as pro-viding a "bridgehead" for U.S. naval operations in the South China Sea and Indian Ocean.[24] It is no exaggeration to suggest that PLA analysts perceive the United States as reinforcing an encircling set of alliances and military arrangements extending from Japan and South Korea in Northeast Asia through Southeast Asia and into the Indian Ocean, where the American rapprochement with India is viewed with deep suspicion.[25]

PLA analysts interpret the primary U.S. military threat as the ability to project and sustain high-intensity warfare on China's periphery and deep into its interior. Whereas operating out of its home bases does grant the PLA the advantage of proximity in a potential conflict with the United States, reliance on overseas bases buttresses the heart of U.S. doctrine, which places critical importance on significantly degrading if not crushing the adversary's defenses in the opening phase of a campaign. These ana-lysts therefore fully expect PLA command and control networks, air de-fenses, air, missile, and naval bases to come under intense attack in the opening hours of a war. The PLA is thus confronted with two distinct problems. U.S. operational doctrine demonstrated in the Gulf War and in the campaigns against Serbia and currently against Afghanistan requires an effective homeland defense. Such a defense, however, can become pas-sive. The problem for PLA planners is to join homeland defense with an active defense that quickly and effectively degrades the U.S. capability to sustain offensive operations.

Preparing to confront the United States required China's military planners to meet head on the deficiencies inherited from the final two decades of Mao Zedong's rule. When he died in 1976, Mao left a defense establishment in chaos. His domestic campaigns had so deeply involved the PLA in China's internecine politics that it had not undergone system-atic training for a decade or more. The defense industrial base and its re-search and development infrastructure had been similarly degraded by Mao's foreign and domestic policies. The Soviet Union had severed all support programs in 1959–1960. Mao's policies in the Great Leap For-ward, the Great Proletarian Cultural Revolution, and the so-called Third-Line strategy transferring defense industries and research centers to inner China compounded the consequences of Moscow's withdrawal. In essence, the aftermath of these policies was a military industrial complex that had eroded into chaotic obsolescence. Deng Xiaoping recognized the defense establishment's extensive deficiencies in the mid-1970s, but cor-recting them was properly seen as a long-term undertaking. There was no short-term fix for the problems created by two decades of neglect and ruinous policies.

Both the PLA and the Chinese military industrial complex (CMIC) have been under continuous reform and reorganization since the early 1980s as Beijing has sought to overcome the burden of Mao's legacies. Whereas progress has been made in both the armed forces and the defense industries, with few exceptions both remain dependent on foreign sources of supply. The most important exceptions are in technologies related to nuclear weapons, cruise and ballistic missiles, space, and communications. In each of these areas, the CMIC has reached capabilities adequate for basic military applications without extensive application of imported technologies. China's missile forces and space and communications technologies, although far from the level of sophistication found in U.S. programs, are therefore advancing with less dependence on foreign sources of technology. Nonetheless, China remains reliant on foreign acquisitions for the extensive range of weaponry and technologies required to transform the conventional general-purpose forces of the PLA into a late 20th-century defense force and prepare for 21st-century requirements.

For the most part, Chinese air, ground, and naval forces remain equipped with arms based on 1950s and 1960s technologies. Even China's small strategic deterrent remains dependent on missile technologies of the 1960s, although the weapons currently being developed have advanced the Second Artillery Corps into the 1970s. In essence, for the near term, PLA planners have taken into account the reality that the bulk of their force structure is composed of legacy forces. With their obsolescent arms and equipment, these forces cannot conduct the kinds of military operations China's military analysts observed in the Gulf War and over Serbia. Those few units equipped with the most advanced weapons and supporting systems available to the PLA can be defined as *contingency forces*. These units would have the most intense training, with their experience used as the basis for upgrading legacy forces as modern arms and equipment become available. Even contingency forces, however, would have great difficulty successfully conducting sustained operations against an adversary as powerful and competent as the U.S. Armed Forces. Against lesser potential adversaries, such as those that might appear on China's Inner Asian frontiers, the degree of modernization currently achieved and under way provides sufficient capability for any border conflicts that could occur.

In the long term, a period measured in five decades and more, the PLA seeks a multidimensional force structure capable of conducting military operations across a realm incorporating land, sea, air, space, and cyberspace. There is no sense, however, that China seeks the global reach seen in U.S. military capabilities. Rather, Beijing's objective is to attain sufficient regional capabilities such that no country, but specifically the United States, can threaten China with impunity. The PLA dilemma is how to respond to the potential U.S. threat over the next decade. What can be observed in China's military journals are systematic analyses of ways in which the PLA can compensate for its multiple deficiencies. It is this near-term problem that creates the most difficulties for PLA doctrine, strategy, and operations.

Doctrine and Strategy

Fully understanding that many years will pass before China's armed forces have the capability to conduct war effectively over the entire spectrum of conventional and nuclear military operations, PLA analysts have returned to their core doctrine. Nonetheless, defeating adversaries superior in the instruments of war is recognized as now much more difficult than it once was. In large part, this is because PLA planning is focused on short, high-intensity wars fought for limited political objectives within confined theaters of operations. In these types of conflicts, as the Gulf War convinced the PLA, forces equipped with advanced weaponry exploited by well-trained troops using appropriate joint operations have a potentially overwhelming advantage. While recognizing there are too few cases to draw a firm conclusion, a PLA analyst has observed, "There never has been an actual case of the weak defeating the strong or the inferior defeating the superior" in a high-intensity local war.[26] Despite these recognized deficiencies, PLA planners have to prepare for a confrontation with the United States embracing doctrine and strategy extending from strategic deterrence to conventional warfare.

Strategic Deterrence

Any near-term military conflict with the United States, and certainly the anticipated long-term confrontation, will take place under the shadow of nuclear weapons. As with the conventional general-purpose forces, doctrine and strategy for China's strategic deterrent face hazards from advanced military technologies. These hazards originate in the U.S. ballistic missile defense program. China's core strategic deterrence strategy has been based on the principle that even states with overwhelming nuclear power can be deterred from the threat or use of nuclear weapons when threatened with a punitive second strike. Such a strategy does not require nuclear parity. Rather, it requires that the state to be deterred believe that even after absorbing a first strike, China will retain the capability to inflict unacceptable damage in a second strike. Beijing did not see such a strategy requiring large numbers of warheads. Rather, the ability of some few strategic forces to survive a first strike was considered adequate. Since initial operational capability in 1981, China has deployed perhaps 20 DF–5 full-range (8,060 mile) intercontinental ballistic missiles (ICBMs). Twenty DF–4 limited-range (2,945 mile) ICBMs have been deployed since 1980. Beijing's single nuclear-powered ballistic missile submarine (SSBN) carries 12 JL–1 intermediate-range ballistic missiles with a range of 1,054 miles.[27] Despite a successful subsurface test launch in 1988, it is unlikely the SSBN ever entered operational service.

Beginning with the 1983 Reagan administration strategic defense initiative, Beijing has seen its deterrent strategy threatened by ballistic missile defense (BMD) technologies.[28] A national missile defense (NMD) system, even if designed to defeat only a small number of missiles launched by a rogue state or to defend against an accidental launch, would undercut the logic used by Beijing to limit its strategic force size. With NMD on the operational horizon, already existing pressures from China's strategists to change nuclear doctrine and strategy are granted greater influence within Beijing's security community.[29]

Apprehension that the credibility of its nuclear deterrent will be eroded presents Beijing with a number of choices. The most obvious choice is to increase the number of missiles in an effort to overwhelm thin national ballistic missile defenses. A second choice would be to develop and deploy multiple warheads to place penetration aids in the bus, thus diminishing BMD capabilities. A third and more difficult choice would be to change the strategy and operational doctrine for the use of nuclear forces.

Changing strategic doctrine from its relatively primitive punitive second strike "minimal deterrence" core will be the most problematic because moving beyond such strategy makes greater demands of China's research and development and defense industrial capabilities. Doctrine and strategy changes must be accompanied by operational capabilities to be effective. In many ways, therefore, the dilemmas facing China's strategic doctrine are the same as those confronting the conventional general-purpose forces. The strategy change most often considered is toward limited nuclear deterrence (*you xian he weishi*).[30] Such a strategy is designed to provide greater flexibility in the use of nuclear forces than a countervalue punitive second strike provides. Some analysts perceive minimum deterrence as being too sensitive to a disarming first strike. Limited deterrence is viewed as requiring the capability to deter strategic, theater, and conventional war.[31] Operationally, this demands the capability to respond effectively to any level of attack and provides an intrawar deterrent by demonstrating the ability to prevent escalation by managing the response to match different kinds of nuclear attack.

The range of targets is also more extensive than the countervalue "city busting" punitive strikes at the core of minimum deterrence.[32] Limited deterrence involves counterforce capabilities in addition to countervalue targets. Among those suggested by Chinese analysts are strategic missile bases, command and control centers, and communications hubs. Striking such targets while retaining sufficient forces to control possible escalation requires far more missiles than China currently deploys and far more sophisticated command and control and battle damage assessment capabilities than Beijing has at this time. In short, there is a significant gap between current capabilities and the operational demands of a limited deterrence strategy.

Force modernization under way since the early 1980s[33] will redress some of these deficiencies. Mobile, solid-fueled missiles, similar to the road- and rail-mobile DF–31 ICBM, have a much quicker response time and greater survivability than the liquid-fueled silo-based DF–5 that they will replace. The new weapons, however, do not redress a set of other requirements if Beijing were to shift to a strategy of limited deterrence, even if they are produced in much greater numbers than the current force.[34] First is the requirement to strike hardened targets, such as missile silos. With a circle error probable in the range of 1,000 meters, current accuracy of the DF–4/5 is insufficient for hardened targets. The DF–31 will have to demonstrate much greater accuracy. Second, there must be some kind of space-based early warning and reconnaissance system to warn of a coming attack and provide close to real-time assessment of targets. There is no point in shooting at empty silos. Third, to be effective at each rung of the escalation ladder, Beijing will need a significantly larger force structure of ICBMs. Fourth, in a BMD world, China would need some kind of missile defenses to ensure its own weapons survive. Currently, China has no such capabilities and is therefore not equipped to implement a revised nuclear strategy.

With the extensive constraints that it has to face, Beijing will most probably decide to sustain its minimum deterrent posture by increasing the number of ICBMs. With the new series of mobile, solid-fueled weapons that are almost certainly more accurate than the DF–5s they will replace, Beijing can be reasonably confident that its strategic deterrent will be survivable and thereby retain its credibility. It is also plausible that because these ground-based weapons are survivable, the cost of developing and deploying a new series of nuclear-powered ballistic missile submarines will limit the program to one or two in order to confirm operational effectiveness.

The Problem of Duplicate Operational Principles

With the exception of its doctrine for strategic deterrence, the PLA core doctrinal tenet for defeating militarily superior adversaries is to gain battlespace initiative through offensive and possibly preemptive operations. Winning the first battle of a campaign, however, is as central to American military doctrine as it is to that of the PLA. In any military conflict with the United States, therefore, the opposing forces will likely be attempting to apply identical operational principles.

Although PLA analysts had identified U.S. offensive doctrine as central to American operations in their assessments of the Gulf War, defense of China's homeland did not become a central issue for the PLA until late 1999, following the NATO air campaign against Serbia, in part because of Chinese estimates that the percentage of PGMs used against Serbia was so much greater than those used in the Gulf War. *Liberation Army Daily* states that only 8 percent of the weapons used in the Gulf War were PGMs, but 95 percent of those used against Serbia were precision munitions.[35] The PLA, therefore, assumes that the United States will open any military conflict with China by initiating an extremely intensive attack employing long-range cruise missiles and other types of PGMs launched from ships and aircraft. This opening attack would be designed to damage Chinese air defenses severely, as well as air, missile, and naval bases. Moreover, these hard attack weapons will be joined with the soft attack of electronic and information warfare to disrupt PLA communications, intelligence, and air defense networks. From its assessments of the air campaign against Serbia, it is also assumed that transportation networks, fuel reserves, oil refineries, and other economic targets will be attacked.[36] Chinese military analysts are clearly anticipating an opening phase of a war in which the United States seeks both to crush China's defenses and to cripple its ability to sustain offensive combat operations.

The incentive to preempt such a U.S. assault is high, but the PLA is also planning and developing tactics to defend against these attacks. These preparations have been given the rubric "three attacks and three defenses," referring to attacks against stealth aircraft, cruise missiles, and helicopter gunships, as well as defense against precision attacks, electronic warfare, reconnaissance, and surveillance.[37]

Because China lacks a national integrated air defense system, antiaircraft artillery and surface-to-air missiles are limited to point defense. This is not an effective defense when aircraft and missiles will be attacking targets from multiple directions. It also is unlikely that the People's Liberation Army Air Force will gain air superiority over U.S. airpower. Consequently, China is paying great attention to camouflaging installations, deception, dispersal, and hardening. Such passive defenses can limit the effectiveness of U.S. reconnaissance capabilities and the damage inflicted by weapons. Defense of military communications will depend in part upon redundancy. Command, control, communications, computers, and intelligence (C[4]I) modernization has been a longstanding PLA priority. In essence, China will use multiple transmission systems to build a national C[4]I infrastructure that is secure, mobile, and less susceptible to either hard or soft attack.[38] Defense against computer network attack is a clear PLA concern, but it is difficult to determine what, if any, progress has been made in this realm of defense.

China's military press has numerous references to the application of People's War methods to homeland defense. In addition to the expected mobilization of militia, reserve, and People's Air Defense units, the Chongqing military garrison introduced the "militia network warfare *fendui*." This unit, reportedly the first of its kind in the PLA, was formed out of graduate students, professors, and other computer specialists to conduct network warfare.[39] Additional People's War tactics suggested are the use of civil-defense installations to store military supplies and the use of local telecommunications, media and network systems, and civilian technological services to assist the military.[40] Major General Yao Youzhi of the Academy of Military Science credited Serbia with using People's War methods to preserve its military strength when under attack. He also declared that Mao's doctrine would remain a "magic weapon for prevailing over enemy forces in the future."[41]

An unidentified Group Army deputy commander sounded a far less optimistic note in the *Beijing Military Region* newspaper.[42] He charged that the training for the three attacks and three defenses was far too "idealistic." He criticized the training for underestimating the generation gap between the weapons employed by the attacking and defending forces, and that imagination was given precedence over reality. As examples, he cited the use of rifles to down Apache helicopters and artillery to attack Tomahawk cruise missiles. Misconceptions such as these, he declared, were not only wishful thinking but also using such misconceptions in training would produce bad results. He recognized that it is necessary to defeat the enemy using existing equipment, but to be effective, training must be realistic and "seek truth from facts."

Active Defense

Despite the much-publicized People's War methods used to implement the "three attacks and three defenses," these methods would be viewed as a passive defense and anathema to PLA doctrine. The ultimate homeland defense is to destroy enemy assets before they can directly threaten Chinese territory. In applying the tenets of active defense to a military conflict with the United States, PLA analysts have identified what they believe to be two critical American vulnerabilities. To conduct their high-tech offensive operations effectively, U.S. forces are critically dependent on information nodes for command, control, communications, and intelligence. These same forces are critically dependent on aircraft CVBGs and forward basing to sustain a high-intensity campaign.

Seriously degrading the communications nodes linking the systems acquiring, transmitting, and processing operational information is undertaken to erode if not disrupt U.S. hard attack capabilities. Attacking information nodes is therefore seen as a force multiplier because reducing the U.S. capacity to conduct offensive operations increases PLA offensive strength. It is also viewed as a form of "asymmetric warfare"[43] performing the same operational function as the short battles of annihilation conducted in the 1930s and 1940s.[44] This form of warfare, however, differs from Mao's tenets by replacing his principle of "accepting the first blow" (*houfa zhiren*) with gaining the initiative by striking first (*xianfa zhiren*).[45]

Both soft and hard weapons will be used to attack the U.S. information infrastructure. Soft attack employs jamming and other electronic warfare means and computer viruses.[46] The preferred hard attack weapons are standoff PGMs using information technologies for accuracy. Such munitions can be air-, land-, or sea-launched and are directed to their target by a variety of means, including terminal guidance, satellite guidance, and other information-based technologies. Of critical importance, given their targets, is the ability of PGMs to be launched outside the adversary's defenses.

American space-based surveillance, target acquisition, and communications capabilities are the targets of China's evolving antisatellite capabilities. Laser radars can be used to track satellites, and electronic jammers can be used against global positioning system receivers. China might already have the capability to damage or degrade satellite optical sensors, and ground-based high-energy lasers hold the promise of weapons that can destroy satellites themselves.[47]

Attacking U.S. foreign-hosted forward bases and the U.S. Navy CVBGs forms the second leg of active defense. China's space and un-manned aerial vehicle programs can dramatically improve PLA situational awareness and its ability to strike bases, ships, and aircraft carriers before they can launch their missiles and aircraft (although submarine-launched cruise missiles present a more difficult problem). Ballistic and cruise mis-siles are again the weapons of choice for hard attack.[48] There is, however, a disturbing facet of China's approach to limited war. Since the late 1980s, Beijing's military theorists have suggested that future high-intensity lim-ited wars will be fought in the shadow of nuclear weapons. Should this view become accepted, China's extensive arsenal theater-range missiles grant Beijing some dangerous options.

Theater nuclear missiles include the 2,900-mile-range DF–4, the 1,800-mile-range DF–3A, and the 1,100-mile-range DF–21A. Short-range ballistic missiles (SRBMs) include the conventionally armed but nuclear-capable 370-mile-range DF–15/M–9 and the 186-mile-range DF–11/M–11. With perhaps 20 DF–4s, 60 DF–3As, 50 DF–21As, 400 DF–15s, and 200 DF–11s, this diversity of missiles permits a choice of conventional and nuclear warheads to be employed in offensive operations.[49] It is also plau-sible that a theater missile, such as the DF–21A, could be armed with a conventional warhead, allowing a theater-range capability that avoids crossing the nuclear threshold.

Whereas SRBMs are clearly offensive weapons and their concen-trated deployment is directed at Taiwan, no doctrine for the employment of theater nuclear forces has been announced. Nonetheless, a strategy for their use can be inferred. As Bates Gill and James Mulvenon suggest,[50] Bei-jing could adopt the former Soviet Union's strategic objective for the SS–20 by using the threat of a nuclear attack to decouple the United States from its East Asian allies. It is also possible that conventionally armed the-ater weapons could be employed for the same purpose. Active defense con-sequently takes on a different image when ballistic missiles are introduced. Decoupling the United States from its allies and their base facilities would vastly complicate American force capability to conduct sustained opera-tions in the region.

China's theater and battlefield ballistic missile capabilities, however, are confronted with American theater missile defense (TMD) programs.

TMD will almost certainly be deployed in Japan and quite possibly in defense of Taiwan. Beijing's simplest response would be to overwhelm missile defenses with increased numbers of both theater and short-range ballistic missiles. One also must assume that the accuracy of these weapons will be improved and warheads designed to increase the lethality of the missiles against a variety of targets. Using missiles to saturate TMD will reduce the number of available weapons for follow-on attacks, making the accuracy and lethality of those remaining important to ensure that their targets can be damaged.

Parallel with increasing the numbers and accuracy of its theater and tactical ballistic missiles, it is certain that China will improve the range and accuracy of its cruise missiles and introduce a long-range land attack cruise missile. TMD is relatively ineffective against cruise missiles, making them an almost automatic choice to supplement SRBM and theater-range weapons. Improved range and accuracy of cruise missiles will also add lethality to the PLA navy's ship-to-ship missiles and the air-to-ship cruise missiles of naval aviation.

Active defense against forces as capable as those of the United States is clearly a demanding task. Indeed, it is a measure of the difficulties PLA planners understand they face that the operational concepts they are developing are dependent upon advanced military technologies for their success. Success in information warfare, antisatellite attacks, and missile offensives all require cutting edge technologies. It is most definitely the conclusion of PLA analysts that it now takes advanced technology to defeat advanced technology. This is far distant from Mao's pride in what his forces could achieve with "millet and rifles" 65 years ago.

Retrospect and Prospect

PLA doctrine originating in the 1930s holds that when facing militarily superior adversaries, it is critical to seize and sustain battlespace initiative. In preparing for a potential military conflict with the United States, China's military research centers have assessed American doctrine and the military operations conducted in the Gulf War and against Serbia asking two critical questions. First, what will be the intent of U.S. military operations in the opening phase of a war? Second, what are American vulnerabilities as they conduct these operations? The intent of these questions is to develop the operational capabilities to blunt U.S. offensive operations and simultaneously attack U.S. vulnerabilities. Linking operational doctrine with the answers to their questions, Chinese military researchers have concluded that to seize battlespace initiative and blunt U.S. offensive operations, it is necessary strike first—to preempt. Traditional PLA doctrine also contains the principle that an asymmetric strategy permits militarily inferior forces to defeat adversaries who are superior in arms and equipment. This longstanding doctrinal principle has been partially abandoned. Although the PLA trusts that its outdated weaponry will perform useful roles, advanced technology weapons and supporting systems will form the sharp point of the PLA spear. The information warfare, antisatellite operations, and missile attacks contemplated by Chinese military researchers rely on advanced technologies for their success.

Should the operational concepts and capabilities outlined by Chinese military authors come to fruition, then there is a clear danger of escalation. The high-technology approach to fighting a quick, decisive war suggests a contradiction between the doctrine and weapons used to conduct the war and the intent to keep such a war limited. How would the United States react if its forward-deployed forces and supporting space assets and base facilities came under a preemptive attack? What would the United States consider a "proportional response"? This uncertainty together with the complementary offensive doctrines of the U.S. and Chinese forces raises the distinct possibility of an escalation dynamic expanding the scope of the war beyond the intent of either adversary. The danger inherent in this dilemma is that the mutual apprehension guiding the military preparations of both China and the United States serves only to enhance the probability of escalation.

Notes

[1] See Thomas J. Christensen, "Posing Problems without Catching Up: China's Rise and Challenges for U.S. Security Policy," *International Security* 25, no. 4 (Spring 2001), for an assessment of this perception.

[2] See, for example, Yan Xuetong, "Forecasting International Politics at the Beginning of the Next Century," *Xiandai Guoji Guanxi*, no. 6 (June 20, 1995), in *Foreign Broadcast Information Service, Daily Report—China* (henceforth *FBIS–China*), September 20, 1995; and Wei Yang, "How Should We Understand and Face the World," *Liaowang*, no. 50 (December 11, 1995), in *FBIS–China*, December 18, 1995.

[3] See, for example, Wu Qingli, "At Whom Is the U.S. Asia-Pacific Strategic Spearhead Pointed," *Liaowang*, no. 21 (May 21, 2001), in *FBIS–China*, May 21, 2001.

[4] Among the many assessments of the threat that China presents to the United States are Nicholas Kristof, "The Rise of China," *Foreign Affairs* 72, no. 6 (November/December 1993), 59–74; and Richard Bernstein and Ross Munroe, "Coming Conflict With America," *Foreign Affairs* 76, no. 2 (March/April 1997), 18–31.

[5] See, for example, Michael C. Gallagher, "China's Illusory Threat to the South China Sea," *International Security* 19, no. 1 (Summer 1994), 169–194; Andrew J. Nathan and Robert S. Ross, *The*

Great Wall and the Empty Fortress: China's Search for Security (New York: Norton, 1997); and Avery Goldstein, "Great Expectations: Interpreting China's Arrival," *International Security* 22, no. 3 (Winter 1997–1998), 36–73.

⁶ Robert S. Ross, "The Geography of Peace: East Asia in the Twenty-first Century," *International Security* 23, no. 4 (Spring 1999), 81–118. Much of the author's discussion is taken from this chapter.

⁷ For a detailed assessment of Chinese and U.S. interests, see Ross, "The Geography of Peace," 99–108.

⁸ For a review of border developments, see Waheguru Pal Singh Sidhu and Jing-dong Yuan, "Resolving the Sino-Indian Border Dispute: Building Confidence through Cooperative Monitoring," *Asian Survey* 41, no. 2 (March/April 2001), 351–376.

⁹ For one recent example of this thesis, see Zalmay Khalilzad et al., *The United States and Asia: Toward a New U.S. Strategy and Force Structure* (Santa Monica, CA: RAND, 2001), 16.

¹⁰ Ross, "The Geography of Peace," 94.

¹¹ *China's National Defense 2000* (Beijing: Information Office of the State Council, October 2000).

¹² Ibid., 4.

¹³ Michael McDevitt and David Finkelstein stress this point in *Assessing China's Year 2000 White Paper: A Workshop Report* (Alexandria, VA: Center for Naval Analyses, November 16, 2000).

¹⁴ The two most complete essays outlining Mao's doctrinal principles are "Strategy in China's Revolutionary War" (December 1936) and "On Protracted War" (May 1938), both in *Selected Military Writings of Mao Tse-tung* (henceforth *Selected Military Writings*) (Peking: Foreign Languages Press, 1972).

¹⁵ Mao Tse-tung, "On Protracted War," 241.

¹⁶ Ibid., 239 and 252–254.

¹⁷ Mao Tse-tung, "Strategy in China's Revolutionary War," 129.

¹⁸ See Su Ruozhou, "A Great Military Reform—Roundup of Strategic Changes in Our Army Building," *Jiefangjun Bao*, December 18, 1998, in *FBIS–China*, January 20, 1999; Editorial, "Basic Guidelines for Our Army's Combat Drill in the New Period—Written on the Promulgation of Operational Ordinance of a New Generation," *Jiefangjun Bao*, January 25, 1999, in *FBIS–China*, February 1, 1999; and Xiao Yusheng and Chen Yu, "Historic Leaps in China's Military Scientific Study," *Renmin Ribao*, February 25, 1999, in *FBIS–China*, March 3, 1999.

¹⁹ For a detailed assessment of these changes, see Paul H.B. Godwin, "From Continent to Periphery: PLA Doctrine, Strategy and Capabilities Toward 2000," *The China Quarterly*, no. 146 (June 1996), 464–487.

²⁰ Editorial, "Basic Guidelines for Our Army's Combat Drill."

²¹ Among the many assessments presenting this argument, see "Renmin Ribao Analysis: China's State Security Considered from Perspective of U.S. Strategic Trend," *Renmin Ribao*, May 17, 2001; and Wu Xinbo, "How Should We View U.S. Policy of Military Containment of China," *Jiefang Ribao* (Shanghai), January 16, 2000, in *FBIS–China*, June 19, 2001.

²² Department of Defense, *Quadrennial Defense Review Report* (Washington, DC: Department of Defense, 2001).

²³ For a detailed assessment of Beijing's view of Sino-American relations, see Bonnie S. Glaser, "Trends in Chinese Assessments of the United States, 2000–2005," in *East Asia and the United States: Current Status and Five-Year Outlook* (Washington, DC: National Intelligence Council and the Federal Research Division, Library of Congress, CR 2000–02, September 2000), 21–35.

²⁴ Ni Wenxin, "U.S. Military Returns to Southeast Asia," *Jiefangjun Bao*, March 26, 2001.

²⁵ See, for example, "Weekly Talk" by Yang Li and Wang Ruolai, "The U.S. is Cooking Up an Asia 'Containment Net,'" *Renmin Ribao* (Guangzhou South China News Supplement), May 18, 2001, in *FBIS–China*, May 18, 2001.

[26] Colonel Yu Guohua, "On Turning Strong Forces into Weak and Vice Versa in a High-Tech Local War," *Zhongguo Junshi Kexue*, no. 2 (May 20, 1996), in *FBIS–China*, January 3, 1997.

[27] "Natural Resources Defense Council Nuclear Notebook, Chinese Nuclear Forces, 2001," *Bulletin of the Atomic Scientists* 57, no. 5 (September/October), accessed at <http://www.thebulletin.org/issues/nukenotes/so01nukenote.html>.

[28] For further analyses of China's response to SDI, see Bonnie S. Glaser and Banning N. Garrett, "Chinese Perspectives on the Strategic Defense Initiative," *Problems of Communism* 35, no. 2 (March/April 1986), 28–44; and John Garver, "China's Response to the Strategic Defense Initiative," *Asian Survey* 26, no. 11 (November 1986), 1220–1239.

[29] See Iain I. Johnston, "China's New 'Old Thinking': The Concept of Limited Deterrence," *International Security* 20, no. 3 (Winter 1995/1996), 5–42, for a thorough analysis of the pressure to change China's nuclear strategy.

[30] Johnston, "China's New 'Old Thinking,'" 17–23.

[31] See, for example, Major General Wu Jianguo, "The Nuclear Shadow in High-Tech Warfare Cannot Be Ignored," *Zhongguo Junshi Kexue*, no. 4 (November 20, 1995), in *FBIS–China*, April 18, 1996, 37–41.

[32] Johnston, "China's New 'Old Thinking,'" 19–20.

[33] See John Wilson Lewis and Hua Di, "China's Ballistic Missile Programs: Technologies, Strategies and Goals," *International Security* 17, no. 2 (Fall 1992), 5–39, for an assessment of these programs.

[34] Johnston, "China's New 'Old Thinking,'" 31–41.

[35] Xu Sheng, "Accurate Attack Will Dominate Future Battlefields," *Jiefangjun Bao*, June 22, 1999, in *FBIS–China*, July 15, 1999.

[36] See, for example, Xu Sining, "Analysis on New Characteristics of Rear Counter-Air-Strike Operations," *Jiefangjun Bao*, June 29, 2001, in *FBIS–China*, June 28, 2001.

[37] Chen Youyuan, "Deepen Training in the New 'Three Attacks and Three Defends,'" *Jiefangjun Bao*, November 14, 2000, in *FBIS–China*, June 22, 2000.

[38] For a detailed assessment of China's aerospace defense programs, see Mark A. Stokes, *China's Strategic Modernization: Implications for the United States* (Carlisle, PA: Strategic Studies Institute, U.S. Army War College, September 1999), chapter 5.

[39] *Zhongguo Guofang Bao*, August 28, 2000.

[40] Xu Sining, "Analysis on New Characteristics."

[41] Yao Youzhi and Zhao Dexi, "How Will China Handle War in the 21st Century?" *Liaowang*, no 2 (January 10, 2000) in *FBIS–China*, February 14, 2000.

[42] *Zhanyu Bao*, October 3, 2000, cited in *PLA Activities Report*, December 13, 2000.

[43] See, for example, an article (no title) presented by Professor Liu Kejun at the September 15, 1997, Defense Modernization Symposium organized by the Chinese Electronics Society, Beijing Yuguangtong Science and Technology Development Center, and *Zhongguo Dianzi Bao* held at the General Staff Department Research Institute 61, *Zhongguo Dianzi Bao*, October 24, 1997, in *FBIS–China*, January 14, 1998.

[44] Major General Zhang Bibo, People's Liberation Army Air Force (PLAAF), and Senior Colonel Zhang Song, PLAAF, "New Subjects of Study Brought about by Information Warfare—Summary of an Army Command Seminar on 'Confrontation of Command on Information Battlefield,' *Jiefangjun Bao*, November 11, 1997, in *FBIS–China*, January 14, 1998.

[45] Lu Linzhi, "Preemptive Strikes Crucial in Limited High Tech Wars," *Jiefangjun Bao*, February 14, 1996, in *FBIS–China*, February 14, 1996.

[46] Wang Baocun, "An Informal Discussion of Information Warfare," *Jiefangjun Bao*, June 13, 1995, in *FBIS–China*, August 25, 1995, 39–41.

[47] *Annual Report to Congress on the Military Power of the People's Republic of China* (Department of Defense, June 2000), 4.

⁴⁸ See Shirley A. Kan, *China: Ballistic and Cruise Missiles* (Congressional Research Service, Library of Congress, 97–391 F, updated August 10, 2000), for a valuable assessment of China's progress in these weapons.

⁴⁹ See Bates Gill and James Mulvenon, "The Chinese Strategic Rocket Forces: Transition to a Credible Deterrent," in *China and Weapons of Mass Destruction: Implications for the United States: Conference Report* (Washington, DC: National Intelligence Council, November 5, 1999), 11–57, for a more detailed discussion of this topic.

⁵⁰ Ibid., 40–41.

Chapter 17

The Military Component of the U.S.-China Relationship

Alfred D. Wilhelm, Jr.

In October 2001, Presidents George W. Bush and Jiang Zemin met in Shanghai to discuss the participation of the People's Republic of China (PRC) in the global antiterrorism campaign. This renewed interest in national security cooperation suggests a need for the U.S. Department of Defense (DOD) and the People's Liberation Army (PLA) to develop jointly a step-by-step plan for resuming the military component of the Sino-American bilateral relationship. Following the EP–3 incident in April 2001, the United States essentially cut off the remaining vestiges of the previous atrophying military relationship. Following the presidential discussions, the PRC awaited a U.S. invitation to talk.[1] Regular military-to-military exchanges finally resumed in 2002.

Beyond this immediate but potentially short-term mutual need, there is a critical, long-term need for national security cooperation, including substantive military-to-military relations, to enhance significantly prospects for enduring peace and prosperity, vital interests of both countries. Trying to build a cooperative, long-term economic, political, and social relationship without having a means to address the basic defense requirements and fears of each side is like building a house on a foundation of sand. Further complicating the growth of this relationship is the fact that neither side currently classifies the other as a friend and increasingly views the other with suspicion. The Quadrennial Defense Review (QDR), released at the end of September 2001 by DOD, points out that the United States and its Pacific allies and friends probably will have to deal with the emergence of a military competitor—no doubt reflecting fears of a rising PRC.[2] Similarly in China, fears that an unfriendly United States is attempting to surround and isolate China are reported regularly to the central leadership and are the subject of frequent news stories. Politically, the easier course of action is to respond to these fears by preparing for a hostile relationship rather than to exercise the political leadership necessary to maintain public support for a policy of forbearance while developing the trust and confidence essential to a cooperative relationship based on international law and convention between two major powers with very dissimilar views of the world and its dominant international order.

Experiences in Building a Military Relationship

A year after the normalization of diplomatic relations in January 1979, the first step was taken toward national security cooperation beyond intelligence collection against the Soviet Union. This step involved a series of high-level defense visits to pursue the normalization of military relations and to continue to reinforce perceptions in Moscow of an emerging condominium. Secretary of Defense Harold Brown visited Beijing in January 1980, followed by visits to the United States in May by General Liu Huaqing of the General Staff Department and in June by General Geng Biao, the next Minister of Defense. The overall framework for the relationship, as developed by Zhou Enlai and Henry Kissinger, envisioned building on common interests and setting aside differences. Foremost was the common security threat from the Soviet Union. For the United States, the new relationship meant further straining the Union of Soviet Socialist Republics (USSR) military capability toward its breaking point by turning its western flank; for the PRC, it meant greater security from global and regional military pressures within which to begin shifting resources to its newly evolving economic model and to acquiring Western technology in all sectors of society, including the military.

In the months and years that followed, the two sides stressed their common security interests, simultaneously causing the United States to have to assuage actively the resulting fears of its friends and allies in the region. These common security interests were getting Vietnam out of Cambodia; getting the USSR out of Afghanistan; limiting intermediate range nuclear missiles in Asia and Europe; reducing tensions on the Korean Peninsula; ensuring good relations with Japan; and maintaining a U.S. military presence in Asia that served the interest of peace and prosperity in the region.[3]

In support of these objectives, the military-to-military relationship was organized around three categories of exchanges: high-level visits, functional military exchanges (including education), and military technology cooperation. The last element in particular was designed to reward and provide incentives for the PRC to adapt its efforts to modernize the

PLA to international norms.[4] From the early experiences with the PLA, perspectives emerged within the U.S. military that these categories lacked bilateral understanding as to what was to be accomplished through these categories in support of bilateral and individual strategic objectives. Relatively few senior officers felt that the United States was getting as much from the relationship as the PRC. The PLA was not as forthcoming as the United States expected. Aside from intelligence cooperation, which was narrowly defined and focused on the Soviet Union and the PLA's ability to draw the Vietnamese out of Cambodia behind the inferred U.S.–PRC condominium against the Soviet Union, cooperation yielded few tangible results for the three services. Despite at least one major effort by each of the services and the Joint Staff, there was a growing concern that the relationship was not systematically producing any significant, long-term benefits to the missions of the individual services.[5]

Roughly parallel for a decade, U.S.–PRC mutual interests were never sufficiently coincidental to break through the years of distrust and other asymmetries in the relationship to establish a solid foundation for an "enduring military relationship," like those of the United States with North Atlantic Treaty Organization nations and with countries elsewhere in Asia. The mountain is higher for the PRC, whose experiences since 1949 have resulted in no similar relationships, only disappointment and distrust. An early indication of the difficulty of building such a foundation came when the PRC refused Secretary of Defense Brown's request for overflight rights to deliver weapons to the Afghan resistance, a seemingly logical step given the importance to both nations of getting the Soviet Union out of Afghanistan.

In China, the U.S. policy of encouraging change through "evolution," as interpreted by the Chinese Communist Party (CCP), reinforced suspicions among party leaders of U.S. motives. It was clear to many of these leaders that the United States was attempting to subvert China's independence and ability to provide reasonably for its own security—just as the other major powers provide for their security. In response to and by comparison with the U.S. approach to the relationship, the PRC approach was imminently practical, narrowly defined, and extractive. The PLA was organized to maximize the transfer of carefully determined technologies through selected arms purchases, training, and education. This approach gradually reinforced concerns in the United States that the relationship was a one-way and "thankless" giveaway that many PLA officers treated as their due—as payment for PLA cooperation against the Soviet Union.

Even during the relationship's euphoric high of 1987–1988, a growing number of U.S. military leaders found little in the relationship that they felt the United States needed or wanted in return. High-level return visits by senior U.S. military leaders increasingly involved little more substance than any other interesting representational visit and less for those who were carrying out obligatory return visits directed by the President.[6]

With some of the common security interests achieved by the late 1980s and others diminished in their urgency, as reflected in the reemergence of friendly Sino-Soviet relations in 1989, the differences between the United States and China had severely corroded their common national security bond—the critical underpinning of the overall relationship. Sino-American relations easily disintegrated into mutual rejection in the wake of the force of the televised tragedy that unfolded in Tiananmen Square in the summer of 1989. Despite a decade of cooperation, and at a time when communications were needed more than ever, military-to-military relations were severed by both sides.

Prior to 1989, military relations were a necessary component of an implicit strategic partnership to confront the Soviet Union. A certain amount of intelligence cooperation was a natural byproduct. Other exchanges were often viewed by both sides as rewards—the expected benefits of the relationship. Neither side trusted the other enough to place an explicit emphasis on building a friendship in the sense of "friends and allies." It was not a clearly defined objective of the relationship. Some on both sides hoped that the requisite trust and confidence in the intentions and capabilities of the other, as found in friendships or alliances, might evolve as a byproduct of the military exchanges. However, it did not.

In the early 1990s, Secretary of Defense William Perry began a revival of the military relationship with defense conversion as its core, but it quickly ground to a halt in the U.S. Congress, where the environment was one of rising fear of PRC military ambitions, espionage, and reactions to developments in Taiwan.[7] Despite the conclusion of the Military Maritime Consultative Agreement, by the time that the EP–3 incident occurred in April 2001, the ability of the military relationship to contribute to the avoidance of misunderstandings and crisis was virtually nonexistent. Since then, little constructive activity has occurred on either side in the military relationship.

The global antiterrorism campaign and the agreement in principle that was reached by Presidents Bush and Jiang in Shanghai offer both sides an opportunity to rethink the bilateral national security relationship and the role therein for a military relationship. As in 1980, intelligence cooperation against a common enemy will provide a greatly needed initial opening, but hopefully it will not be the core of the relationship.

The United States and the PRC are faced with a problem that may be unique in the history of major powers: How do two major powers—with adversarial ideologies,[8] a history of military conflict, a healthy dose of mutual distrust, a conflicting sense of whether the international system is fair, and publics with a strong sense of national pride—build a cooperative relationship grounded in international law and convention in which both must have trust and confidence? Escalating defense budgets, violence, and war have been the offspring of similar relationships in the past. Can the United States and the PRC build the defense aspects of the relationship based on long-term interests in peace and prosperity in lieu of war, or will it again be a temporary relationship of convenience—or, in the vernacular of the CCP, a united front campaign? Cutting through this Gordian knot will require more than commercial interests and diplomacy backed by the threat of encirclement.

Obstacles and Asymmetries to Overcome

If the two sides decide to restart the military relationship, a number of obstacles and asymmetries are likely to affect the relationship adversely, as they have in the past. To avoid a repetition of history, this time they need to be addressed openly with a joint, full-time staff to ensure that they are understood and overcome. As the Chinese are fond of saying, "Our histories are different," implying, among other things, that mirror-image analysis and expectations by either side can lead to serious disasters. The different histories have generated important asymmetries between the two military communities ranging across the larger societal differences of culture, language, and vocabulary to the role of intelligence, strategic and tactical concepts, military education objectives and methods, organization, and warfighting techniques. Learning more about theses differences and making them work for the relationship is essential if the two sides are to avoid mistakes based on the misinterpretation of intent and capability.

Distrust: The Fundamental Obstacle

The two sides have not trusted each other since General "Vinegar Joe" Stilwell left China at the end of World War II. Since then, the experiences of the U.S. military with the PLA during China's civil war (the remnants of which today are known as the Taiwan Question), the ill-fated PRC friendship agreement (alliance) with the Soviet Union, and the conflicts in

Korea, Vietnam, and various Asian insurgencies during the Cold War left memories and institutional legacies that made the initial overtures by the U.S. military to the PLA in the 1980s difficult, albeit, by Presidential fiat, manageable. This was as true, if not more so, for the PLA, in which every soldier knew from experience or training that the enemy was the United States. Throughout the 1980s, former bitter adversaries stepped forward out of conviction or duty to make the relationship work, often taking significant political heat and criticism from their colleagues and others. As a result of these efforts, an increasing number of friendly exchanges occurred during the 1980s (until the summer of 1989) that increased information and understanding about each other and began laying a modest foundation for future movement toward international security cooperation. However, this process stopped with the events of Tiananmen Square and President George H.W. Bush's termination of all aspects of the military-to-military relationship.[9] Despite subsequent efforts to resume the relationship, it never came close to achieving previous levels of cooperation or expectation when the United States again terminated it in the wake of the EP–3 incident of April 2001.

Today, many of those who stepped forward on both sides to make the relationship work feel betrayed or frustrated by political decisions made in the post-Tiananmen environment. Despite their significant investments of prestige, time, and effort, little of the relationship remains to show for it. Moreover, most of the individuals involved in the events of the1980s have been replaced in the ensuing 20 years, leaving the two sides with widely divergent and conflicting institutional memories and interpretations by current leaders of the PLA's role in Tiananmen Square in 1989 and of its missile firings near Taiwan, troop movements across from Taiwan, and foreign equipment purchases made throughout the 1990s. Then there are the memories of the bombing of the PRC Embassy in Belgrade and the EP–3 incident. The memories and emotions generated by these events also differ radically on each side and from those of their predecessors from the halcyon days of the 1980s. These recent experiences are exacerbated by longstanding U.S.–PRC disagreement over nuclear strategy, nuclear and missile technology transfers, and the apparent limited ability of the PRC to enforce its own policies and laws that are derivative of bilateral and international agreements.

PLA modernization in recent years, supported by a thriving economy and a parade of modern weapons purchased from Russia and others, has generated in the United States and elsewhere a growing number of forecasts about a rising China with a virulent or aggressive disposition.[10] Well before the arrival of the current Bush administration, a growing number of PRC strategists were interpreting U.S. national security policy as a hostile effort to surround and isolate the PRC and thereby deprive it of its legitimate right to self-defense. Even the most popular of the pulp literature in both countries that uses the relationship in the storyline contains a heavy dose of surrealistic appeals for macho responses to actions by the other.[11] Increasingly the military community on each side distrusts the intention of the other and lacks confidence in the public statements of the other government that effuse peaceful intentions and defensive needs.

Friendship or Partnership

Both the United States and China have somewhat different interpretations of what is meant by *friendship*. Most Americans who have visited China have been impressed with Chinese hospitality and the frequent use of the term "new friends or old friends," but seldom are the implications clear as to what is expected of either a new or an old friend.

Culture and history shape how both sides value, award, and bestow the title of friend. The differences generally are a matter of emphasis, as in both societies, friendship involves serious responsibilities and potential penalties if not fulfilled according to expectations. However, by tradition, Chinese friendships tend to be more hierarchical or unequal relationships that emphasize upward loyalty, downward responsibility, shared values, and obligations. Today, these obligations often translate into "backdoor" assistance, which many Westerners view as corruption but most Chinese (and Asians in general) view as an obligation and the grease that minimizes social friction. Breaches of the obligations of friendship result in a loss of face for the Chinese that is not usually matched in its severity among Westerners who depend more on legal sanctions.

The PRC government appears to have developed a preference for the use of partnerships with other nations, in most cases in lieu of friendship agreements and alliances with their extensive historical baggage. Partnerships[12] tend to be more focused in purpose, scope, and duration than the more open-ended friendship agreements and the obligations under Western law and tradition for alliances.

Within these general parameters, military-to-military relationships for both countries follow the flag, although military relations tend to be less automatic and less frequent for China.[13] The PLA tends to be the "last in" of the various bureaucracies that participate when the PRC opens diplomatic relations with another country and the "first out" later when there is stress in the state-to-state relationship. Permission for extensive contact with another country's military is not given easily by the Chinese Communist Party, to which the PLA owes its allegiance (not the government). The party tends to withdraw or reduce permission more quickly than does the U.S. Government when diplomatic relations are troubled. While a military relationship very seldom leads U.S. foreign policy, it is almost always a component of any relationship. It often involves forward-deployed forces and access to facilities—both practices the PRC rejects, with the exception of the assignment of military personnel in recent years to select United Nations military missions. For the United States, the world's largest purveyor of arms and military training, arms sales are a key component of military relations. In large part because of quality, the PRC is a much smaller supplier, albeit frequently to states with interests inimical to those of the United States. Conversely, the PRC is an important buyer of major, advanced technology weapons systems, especially at present from Russia and in the past from the United States.

Intelligence

The PLA intelligence community is the custodian of the military's international relations and of that element of Chinese strategy that says that the less others know about PLA capabilities, the more likely they are to overestimate its capabilities—which I have likened elsewhere to the protective strategy of a puffer fish. The result is that PLA intelligence staffs control access to other elements of the PLA, filter all information about the PLA, and provide most of the official interpretation of incoming information. This degree of control far exceeds any limitations placed on the U.S. military and, over the years, has generated considerable resentment, distrust, and, on occasion, significant misunderstanding between the sides.

In the U.S. military, activities and information are presumed to be unclassified unless specifically classified. The reverse is true in the PLA. As a result, PLA officers prepare carefully for meetings with foreigners and are very cautious about what they say. They are not trusted to meet with U.S. officers unless given specific permission to do so and even then are seldom allowed to meet alone. This practice even extends to retired senior officers. Private meetings in China easily can draw the unfavorable attention of the Ministry of State Security—a strong deterrent. The strict protocol that U.S. military attaches must follow to meet with PLA officials limits the opportunities to get to know the PLA beyond the narrow circle of officers designated for such contacts. As a matter of reciprocity, the U.S. military is now much more restrictive in permitting the PLA attaches in Washington to meet with U.S. officials than is normal. Unlike in China, however, such restrictions do not apply to retired military officers.

As contrasted with the openness of the U.S. system, articles by PRC analysts seldom cite original Chinese sources for their data, instead referring to such foreign sources as London's International Institute for Strategic Studies to describe PLA forces when necessary (but without confirming any information). The intelligence department's Foreign Affairs Bureau (FAB) must approve officers who travel abroad and any materials that they prepare. Retired senior officers also must have FAB approval, particularly for meetings and conferences—permission that is not easy to obtain. As a further protection, the maximum amount of time that a PLA researcher may spend in the United States was reduced several years ago from a year or more to 6 months or less.

During the mid-1980s, a significant two-way flow of information occurred between the PLA and the U.S. military, albeit in favor of the PLA. Nevertheless, both sides learned a great deal about each other. Those days are gone; today, the river of information is but a carefully controlled trickle, albeit still somewhat unbalanced in favor of the PRC by the more open nature of U.S. society.

Relationship to the Party and State

The PLA, as an instrument of the party, is charged by the constitution to provide a secure environment within which the Chinese people can achieve peace and prosperity. But in implementing this mission, the PLA allegiance is to the CCP, not the central government.[14] The party and thus the government's grand strategy (a Western term) for achieving peace and prosperity is the Four Modernizations as established by Zhou Enlai and refined by Deng Xiaoping. It is a strategy for ensuring that China can provide for its own security, as the other major powers do, and for the prosperity of its people. Each succeeding Chinese administration has put its own stamp on the implementation process, as has the PLA, which supports it completely. The key difference for the U.S. military is that the PLA allegiance to the party parallels that of the PRC government to the party, leaving room for significant differences in interpretation of the grand strategy. This relative equality has on occasions pitted the two bureaucracies against each other, but more frequently the relationship translates into irritating inefficiencies between them, especially when dealing with the United States.

Organization

The PLA is not organized around a tri-service structure as is the United States, in which all three services are relatively equal in all things ranging from budgets and organization to political and national policy influence. As its name implies, the *People's Liberation Army* is a continental army whose organizational heritage draws heavily on its own experiences with land warfare, sprinkled with a smattering of influence from the German general staff thinking of the early 20th century and a heavier dose from its period of tutelage by the Soviet Union. Like all militaries, its organization has changed to deal with current needs, but historical experiences shape how new ideas are integrated (or *sinicized*, in this case). Thus the PLA remains a single or unified military force in which the air force and navy are supporting arms, like its nuclear forces and its former armor and artillery commands.[15]

When in the early 1980s the PLA had to learn from the nonparty, nonunified militaries of the United States and the West, a position titled Minister of Defense was grafted onto the government so that there would be a counterpart to the U.S. Secretary of Defense. Supported by the PLA Intelligence Department, especially its Foreign Affairs Bureau, and currently as a senior member of the party's Central Military Commission (CMC), the minister is an influential member of the party's military community but primarily as the senior PLA "barbarian handler."[16] Consequently, he is not the functional equivalent of the Secretary of Defense, America's senior defense policymaker, but a go-between. The senior vice chairman of the CMC would be a more appropriate counterpart to the Secretary of Defense as the holders of both positions are policymakers who report directly to their country's senior political leader.

In the current relationship, senior policymakers are not talking to each other. The people who think about and decide how their respective military establishments will be equipped, trained, and utilized to implement their national strategies do not have to hammer out their differences directly with each other and thereby have an opportunity to gauge their mettle and sincerity. In addition, there may be times when a team of senior officials and commanders might better represent one side or the other.

In addition to the Secretary of Defense and the senior members of the CMC, the United States and the PRC should reexamine the current asymmetries in responsibilities in the counterpart relationships that involve the Chairman of the Joint Chiefs of Staff, the three service secretaries, the four chiefs of staff, and selected senior DOD deputy and under secretaries and, from the PRC, the chiefs of the General Staff, Political, Logistics, and Armament Departments, the navy, air force, Second Artillery, People's Armed Police, and the Academy of Military Science. There is a twice-established relationship between the two National Defense Universities that, if appropriately used, would benefit the military-to-military relationship enormously.

Party rules in the early 1980s did not permit party organs to have direct contact with comparable authorities in noncommunist states. In the late 1980s, Deng Xiaoping made an unsuccessful effort to establish a mirror-image, government version of the party's military commission in the government that would enable the PLA to be more transparent and efficient in its dealings with the outside world. In the post-Tiananmen era, the CCP decided that the party could have direct relations with foreign political parties other than communists and socialists. While this decision has yet to affect materially how the PLA deals with the outside world, it opens the door to redefining the counterpart relationships of the PLA and the U.S. defense community so that the policymakers of each community are working directly with each other and not through their respective intelligence communities.

An example of the difficulty that the asymmetries in organization create in identifying reasonably close counterparts is that there is no functional equivalent to the U.S. Army Chief of Staff, General Eric Shinseki. The functions of his general staff, as well as most of those of the air force and navy service chiefs, are performed primarily by the PLA General Staff Department (GSD). With the GSD as the keystone, the PLA general departments collect input from the various commands, collate, and build and direct the implementation of the military strategy of the PLA. Thus, there is no army (ground force) strategy; rather, there is a PLA strategy in which ground forces are the basic building blocks supported by air and naval forces and play the central role in most, but not all, warfighting scenarios. There are similar asymmetries in how doctrine is developed. Below the general staff level, China is divided into seven regional commands—where the warfighters are located (a sinicized version of the U.S. Joint Commands) and a series of support commands, including the PLA Air Force and Navy (less autonomous than a U.S. specified command; roughly comparable in authority to a U.S. Army major command). The official PLA counterparts of the U.S. Navy and Air Force command their services as major units with lower standing or levels of responsibility in the PLA than their counterparts in the United States.

During the 1980s, bilateral exchanges permitted the PLA and the United States to examine each other's organizational experiences for their potential import value, although Washington largely ignored the opportunity. Lessons from the U.S. joint system were used during the restructuring of the PLA regional commands beginning in the 1980s, as well as from the DOD personnel system when the PLA developed its civilian staff. The same is true for some logistics and education reforms. Nevertheless, there has been no wholesale importation of any system or matériel in lieu of domestic production. Importation is reserved for research, development, testing, and evaluation (RDT&E) and selected unit applications—the sinification of foreign knowledge.

The differences in organization are matched with differences in scope of responsibility of the two defense establishments. For example, most of the responsibilities of the U.S. Department of Energy for the development and production of nuclear weapons fall within the responsibilities of the PLA. Similarly, many of the arms sale and arms control and disarmament functions led by the U.S. Department of State are led by the PLA. As a result, the PLA, through its intelligence community, negotiates with a broad range of U.S. Government officials. Major differences in financial systems, beginning with budgets at both the national and defense levels, make it extremely difficult to compare expenditures and to extrapolate policy direction or intentions. Without a common understanding of the data, discussions become data debates. These and other asymmetries result in more preaching than discussion of ways to cooperate. Cooperation will depend on the development of a more effective process for understanding and negotiating solutions to critical differences.

Education and Sinification

The People's Liberation Army, like the Chinese military before it, studies the military experiences of other countries (particularly those of the United States in recent years) to identify the reasons for their success or failure (in essence a *principles of war* assessment) and to isolate those best practices or models for possible importation and sinification.[17] This approach to modernization exploits to its fullest the strengths of the Chinese (and thus the military's) education style, which emphasizes patterned learning, rote memorization, and the use of models for problemsolving. Until very recently, creativity and ingenuity have been neither the focus nor the purpose of education. Instead, creativity was relegated to the school of hard knocks, the purview of those who survive the arduous climb to the top.

China's short cut to modernization depends on identifying, adapting, and improving upon another country's creativity and ingenuity.

To support the adaptation approach to modernity, the PLA has developed a very competent system for examining firsthand what previously had been gleaned from the continuing and extensive study of foreign professional journals and books. Official PLA delegations are thoughtfully constructed to ensure a range of expertise is included so as to take full advantage of visits to U.S. military commands, units, and schools. Official delegations are supplemented by a limited number of delegations and research fellows sponsored by the U.S. corporate and education communities. Much of what is emerging in the PLA today was examined first (and later advocated) by top PLA leaders in delegations sent to the United States with their extraordinary capability to observe, listen, and report. Visits by U.S. delegations and individual experts to China also have been very beneficial. The Marxian scientific method component of the adaptation or sinification process results in the identification of important foreign concepts, *best practices* or technologies; the allocation of resources for the purchase of equipment sets; and the formation of a test platform (study group, unit, etc.) to research, test, and evaluate (RT&E) how the new concepts or equipment might be modified and applied in China's unique environment and military culture.

When new military or defense concepts arc identified in the West or elsewhere, appropriate civilian as well as military research institutes are requested to study them for their meaning and significance to China. If the concept is developed without much public debate in the West, such as the Missile Technology Control Regime (MTCR), China's researchers will be mute and China's top leaders uninformed. Such was the case when the United States sent its first delegation[18] to ask the PRC to abide by MTCR standards without having participated as a member in the development of the standards. The results were predictably negative. Conversely, if the debate is spirited and public, as it was in the United States over the revolution in military affairs (RMA), there will be a flurry of articles in professional Chinese military journals and increasingly in the public media making an array of recommendations for PLA and government action.[19] However, any decision by the PLA will be secret and essentially end or redirect the debate (the modern version of *the contending of a hundred flowers*—a dialectical thought process). The fact that a decision has been made may only be detectable by the lack of discussion. Because of the opaque nature of these processes, Western observers frequently mistake the views expressed during these debates as views widely held in the PLA and by its leaders.

From the PRC media, professional journals, and scholarly exchanges, we know that the experiences of the United States with 20th-century war from Vietnam to the Middle East, Africa, Panama, and Central Europe have been studied in great detail by the PLA and debated in numerous conferences to crystallize the analysis of these events and lessons drawn. However, the actual lineage of any PLA decisions that resulted in changes to strategy, tactics, and organization is much less clear. Most Western conclusions are conjecture based on perceptions of input and announced or observed changes and end products that emanate from China's decision-making black box. These conclusions, therefore, should be treated with caution. This was less true during the height of U.S.–PRC military-to-military relations in the mid 1980s.

Early PLA experience with the U.S. military, particularly when they examined the experiences of the U.S. Army in developing the 1st Air Cavalry Division,[20] greatly expanded their thinking about the use of test units in the RT&E process. The U.S. experience added an important dimension to their own thinking about how to absorb new or foreign technologies into PLA units. As a result, the PLA has developed a comparable rotary-wing test unit and has applied the test and evaluation process to other parts of the PLA. However, relatively little is known about the actual results of this process.

Technology Acquisition

The PLA purchases technologies, especially costly major foreign military systems, for RT&E purposes. Its priorities take into consideration a complicated set of objectives that go beyond enhancing military capability to include national technology priorities for development, industrial needs, regional needs for development (Hainan Island cannot be developed to its potential with either foreign or domestic investment if conflict with Vietnam is likely). China's military technology acquisition policy is to buy and experiment with the intent of avoiding large and sustained foreign currency expenditures and the creation of a foreign supply and maintenance dependency. Its early experience with the Soviet Union is not to be repeated with anyone. Occasionally, selected equipment will be purchased in sufficient quantity to aid with a specific mission shortfall, such as occurred against Vietnam and India and might occur vis-à-vis Taiwan, but not enough to equip more than a small number of PLA units.

Examples include the counterbattery radars purchased to defeat Vietnamese artillery in the late 1980s (or so it was argued to the United States); however, since then these radars have been the object of extensive RDT&E and have had application or been considered for use against Russia, India, the United States, and Taiwan.[21] The few purchased were insufficient for any sustained conflict. Similarly, a small number of helicopters were purchased from France, Italy, and the United States. In the latter case, the Sikorsky helicopters that the PLA purchased are a prime example of the unreliability of a foreign-based maintenance and logistic system—suspended by the United States in the wake of Tiananmen. Ideal for moving troops and supplies in China's vast roadless terrain, some of these helicopters were tested beyond their rated limits under extreme operating conditions in Tibet, Xinjiang, and elsewhere. However, others are being tested more systematically in the experimental aviation unit previously mentioned to determine how the PLA might more effectively use the helicopters that China will make and deploy. Destroyers for cross-strait and South China Sea operations have had more of an immediate psychological impact than an as-yet practical improvement in either immediate or long-term war fighting capability. However, all of these purchases are advancing China's RT&E ability, and in many cases its defense industry ability, to produce a better product—both commercially and militarily.

National Strategy

The United States and China are large, resource-rich countries with long borders, and both stretch across similar latitude with large extremes in terrain and weather. Both have clear national interests in a secure environment within which to achieve peace and prosperity for their people. Yet despite such macrosimilarities, the countries' geographical asymmetries, historical, cultural, and ideological differences, and different stages of development have resulted in national strategies that frequently conflict in implementation even when objectives may converge. This is especially true with the military component of national security.

Unlike the U.S. military with its global commitments and derivative need for matching maritime and air power strategies, the PLA is a continental military establishment with a matching strategy, despite 40 years of efforts by Mahan-influenced analysts in the West to prove otherwise. Since at least the early 1960s, members of the U.S. China-watching community have made several major efforts to prove that the PLA was pursuing a blue-water strategy that would threaten U.S. interests. However, so far the focus of GSD planners has been on the PLA mission to defend China's borders.

Their most critical requirements for the PLA Navy (PLAN) and the PLA Air Force (PLAAF) are to support this mission. The decision process is very wearing. The PLAN focus is the waters that lap China's shores—albeit at an increasing standoff distance and through the lens of the appropriate regional command. From the PLAN vantage point, the greatest potential threat is the United States, followed in changing order by Russia, Japan, and Vietnam. Taiwan is a variant of the U.S. threat equation. The PLAAF has a 360-degree support role, with its greatest concerns being the United States and Russia and the technology and equipment they provide to China's neighbors. Elements of both services have an eye on equipment that could enhance their mission capability further than most PLA seniors and GSD planners are willing to accept as necessary for national defense under current conditions.[22]

The PRC functional equivalent to the U.S. Program, Planning, and Budgeting System (PPBS) for implementing their strategy supports the continental orientation of the PLA by ensuring that internal security can be maintained and that the borders are adequately defended. Adequacy is driven by the key assumption that a global war remains unlikely in the foreseeable future. Troops (not just ground forces) are positioned to minimize transportation and logistics demands on the national budget. Civil aircraft, rail, and merchant marine stock are assigned civil reserve airfleet-type wartime missions, minimizing 5-year plan pressures to develop a large military equivalent capability. Every effort is made to take advantage of such compensating plans to minimize operational costs and to focus RDT&E and procurement efforts on the capabilities of highest priority.

PLA plans take into consideration the fact that virtually every foreign military establishment that shares a border with the PLA worries about PRC capabilities and sizes its force and diplomacy accordingly. The most likely, as well as the most recent, opposing forces are largely ground plus air and represent about every kind of terrain and type of warfare possible. As for many of China's other neighbors, its intentions have become a matter of increasing concern for planners in Central Asia plus Russia. Some Central Asians have even privately voiced their fear that the current Western development plans of China will directly threaten the sovereign interests of the Central Asian republics, particularly with respect to natural resources beginning with oil. A limited U.S. presence, a byproduct of the war on terrorism, provides balance and reduces concerns.

The PLA has a continental orientation, but not to the exclusion of its maritime interests. Given the large population and industrial centers of the East coast, and recalling the experiences of the Opium War, the PLA feels it is better to have barriers at sea (Great Wall)[23] than ashore, especially not on foreign soil. Recognizing the intrinsic value (if only political) in the various contending ideas for providing for China's security, the efforts of PLA planners to balance military modernization by building modern capabilities by mission area on a relatively small scale preempt relatively few significant options. Critical mission capabilities are being enhanced in support of China's still active grand national strategy, the Four Modernizations. The imbalances of the Cold War are being corrected gradually. This equation is sufficiently big and complicated (the big tent); it can enfold enough of the interests of those advocating a blue-water strategy, an anti- or pro-U.S. or Russia strategy, interests in Central Asia and resources, concerns about South Asia, the South China Sea, Taiwan, and even pure national development economics to keep each as a viable option and provide a working consensus. But the pace of modernization is less than optimum (or desired) by any of various advocates—and thus a source of continuous institutional and personal bickering.

The PLA ground forces of tomorrow will eventually be smaller and more capable, built around the results of today's experiments with special operations forces, rapid reaction units, helicopter units, and other "best practices" that they import or develop. The change or "PLA building" will be gradual and almost generational. There is not likely to be sufficient development of China's economic infrastructure, sufficient political stability, or enough resources available in the defense portion of the next three 5-year plans to obviate the need for large numbers of locally garrisoned forces and to allow the complete conversion of its ground forces into smaller, centralized forces that can be moved to the contingency area (border regions) by a modern military transportation system. The construction of such a force will require continued attention to making major advances, which are at the very least time-consuming, in its education system, military and defense civilian personnel systems (including the development of the functional equivalent of a noncommissioned officer corps), logistic and maintenance systems (including system-wide quality control—a huge headache in China), and militia and reserves structures, to mention a few.[24]

This national strategy is defensive by design, but the size and growing capability of the PLA is hegemonic by sheer presence. As a consequence, future differences in U.S.–PRC national interests and the accompanying differences in strategy could result in military conflict of increasing threat to both, if the two sides do not work to create an alternative that generates mutual trust and confidence.

Conclusions

Beginning with President Richard Nixon, every President has found early in his administration that the critical importance of the U.S.-China relationship and its tendencies to cyclical downturns require his personal commitment to stabilize and advance U.S. interests in the relationship. Each has had to commit the prestige of his office in the face of domestic criticism to advance economic, social, cultural, or military programs that contributed to each nation's sense of security. In part following this pattern, the Bush administration placed its initial emphasis on reinforcing economic cooperation, but was unable to find any way to reverse the downward spiraling sense of mutual insecurity. Irrespective of the cause of the Belgrade embassy bombing or of the EP–3 incident, this insecurity significantly worsened the impact of these accidents on the relationship. If both sides are to overcome their fears of each other and realize their critical interests in peace and prosperity through mutual security, their basic but evolving national security interests must be continuously and cooperatively addressed; the interests of one cannot be ignored or dictated by the other. Here both have failed. There is not now and never has been a bilateral means adequate to this task.

Following the September 11, 2001, terrorist attacks, there has emerged both an immediate need and an opportunity for the renewal of military-to-military relations in support of mutual security interests. This need, as in the past, is to further intelligence cooperation against a mutual threat—only this time, the threat is not the Soviet Union but the war against terrorism. However, the war is both a reminder and a start to addressing the longer-term need for a framework around which to build a cooperative defense relationship.

The implicit U.S.–PRC partnership of the 1980s was beneficial to the security of both countries as long as the common threat existed and the Soviets responded to the condominium in a manner that benefited both. The military component of the relationship was a major contributor to this success. However, any movement toward the development of a long-term military relationship based on cooperation and thrust was a casualty of Tiananmen, cross-strait events, and the virtual disappearance of the Soviet threat. Mutual fear and distrust of the other's intentions dominate the relationship.

To bring stability and security to the increasingly complex nature of the overall relationship today will require the commitment of the President and the Secretary of Defense to a cooperative defense relationship with China at a time when there is virtually no military relationship. The multiple Foreign Ministry–State Department exchanges (including such security issues as arms control), reemergent annual defense ministerial talks,[25] plus economic and trade commissions are insufficient to address the endless number, diversity, and complexity of problems that arise in implementing the results of such talks or insuring that new issues are promptly addressed. Embassies perform a variety of critical functions, including opening doors for new initiatives, but they are neither staffed nor designed to support the continuing, daily task of implementing the relationship. The primary mission of military attaches is intelligence—the collection of information—not building and orchestrating the many other aspects of a military-to-military relationship.

The earlier period of defense cooperation demonstrated that the asymmetries and obstacles in the relationship can be managed if there is a strong, focused partnership, but they will contribute to killing the partnership when mutual security is sacrificed to advance other less vital interests.

The bilateral agenda of national security issues should include the concerns of both sides and recognize that those that are mutual do not necessarily have the same importance to each side. Mutual concerns include the elimination of terrorism, but there are differences that must be addressed concerning what constitutes terrorism and appropriate preemptive actions as well as responses by either side that might degrade the ultimate value of the current cooperation and even contribute to Chinese concerns about encirclement. There are mutual concerns over arms control and technology proliferation that the West has enshrined in such instruments as the Non-Proliferation Treaty (NPT), the Missile Technology Control Regime, and the Chemical Weapons Convention. However, the PRC was not an architect in most cases and is suspicious of the implications of such agreements for China. Similar suspicions have kept China from any meaningful discussions of nuclear arms limitations and reductions or missile warning systems. The agenda should include ways to mitigate or neutralize Chinese concerns about U.S. deployments in the regions and improving relations, particularly defense, with its neighbors. The same holds for easing concerns in the region about the PRC as a destabilizing power and the concerns of others, including Taiwan, who feel that the U.S.–PRC relationship often works against them.

Recommendations

The administration should remove all remaining military-related sanctions imposed on the PRC since the events in Tiananmen Square and invite the PRC to reopen the bilateral military-to-military relationship with a clean slate.

The military relationship should have an explicit goal to build a long-term relationship of mutual trust, confidence, and respect that will enhance the security of both countries and their interest in peace and prosperity. In committing to this policy, the President should require that personal working relationships be attempted between policymakers in comparable positions of responsibility, similar to the example he has set in other forums.

Counterpart relations should be redefined so that they are between policymakers with comparable functional responsibilities and authority. The relationship should be supported by the respective intelligent communities but not operated through these communities. As a first step, the counterpart of the Secretary of Defense should be the most senior military member of the Central Military Commission after its Chairman, the General Secretary of the CCP, Jiang Zemin.

The two sides should establish a defense commission with a full-time staff to support the development of the bilateral agenda and the implementation of guidance and policy and to monitor and advise the commission on bilateral defense programs to include the adequacy of funding and support provided by the two governments. DOD should be the lead U.S. agency, parallel with the PLA, and should be charged to staff and fund the U.S. commitment to the commission. Other U.S. departments and agencies would provide representation and program funding and support according to their responsibilities, such as the Departments of State in the areas of arms control and arms sales and Energy regarding nuclear weapons design, production, and security.

The sides should expand on the pre-April 2001 very limited number and types of military exchanges and security dialogues—beyond those essential to the success of the global war on terrorism—so as to build trust, confidence, and understanding through practical efforts at cooperation. There are a host of areas, such as military medicine and nuclear surety, where jointly working on practical projects can be of mutual technological and scientific benefit while generating trust and confidence.

Every military department and command tasked to support the U.S.–PRC military relationship should be fully funded for any activities that they may be approved to implement. Creativity and commitment to the military-to-military relationship have been significantly constrained by the "take it out of your hide" approach to funding for most of the bilateral programs of the past.

The President should ensure that military-to-military relations are accepted as a critical means of communications with China and guarantee that they will not be sacrificed by the United States during a crisis or if sanctions are imposed. A defense commission could prove to be a vital means of communications during a crisis and an invaluable source of understanding and assistance in ensuring that sanctions are targeted so as to help achieve the desired objective—in stark contrast to past experiences.

Notes

[1] Conversations in mid-October 2001 with the defense attaché and political councilor at the PRC embassy in Washington, DC, made clear the PRC interest in the resumption of military-to-military relations. However, since the United States cut off the relationship, they pointed out that it is important that the United States initiate the expression of interest in the resumption of these relations.

[2] For a solid assessment of the role of East Asia in the Quadrennial Defense Review, see Michael McDevitt, "The Quadrennial Defense Review and East Asia," Center for Strategic and International Studies *PacNet* 43, October 26, 2001, accessed at <http://www.csis.org/pacfor/pac0143.htm>.

[3] Winston Lord (U.S. ambassador to China), "Sino-American Relations: No Time for Complacency," speech to the National Council of U.S.-China Trade, May 28, 1986. Cited in Edward W. Ross (Assistant for China, Office of the Assistant Secretary of Defense, International Security Affairs), "U.S.-China Military Relations and the Implications for ASEAN," Fourth U.S.-Association of Southeast Asian Nations (ASEAN) Conference on ASEAN and China, Kuala Lumpur, Malaysia, January 5–8, 1987.

[4] Ross, 4–17.

[5] Drawn from interviews and discussions with more than 100 senior U.S. military and civilian officials and key staff members involved in U.S.–PRC military-to-military relations.

[6] Based on author's interviews and conversation with participants.

[7] Edward Timperlake and William C. Triplett II, *Red Dragon Rising* (Washington, DC: Regnery, 1999).

[8] The major difference between any similar comparison with Russia is that extensive political reform came before economic reform in Russia, whereas the PRC has chosen to advance economic reform at a much faster rate than political reform with less human misery by most Asian calculations.

[9] President George H.W. Bush announced a list of retaliatory measures against the PRC that included the "suspension of all government-to-government sales and commercial exports of weapons, suspension of visits between U.S. and Chinese military leaders." George H. W. Bush and Brent Scowcroft, *A World Transformed* (New York: Knopf, 1998), 89–90. His statement initially left hope on both sides that only high-level military-to-military exchanges would be terminated; however, during the implementation of his instructions, all exchanges were terminated.

[10] Bill Gertz, *The China Threat, How the People's Republic Targets America* (Washington, DC: Regnery, 2000); Richard Bernstein and Ross H. Munro, *The Coming Conflict with China* (New York: Knopf, 1997).

[11] The best known in the United States is Tom Clancy, *The Bear and the Dragon* (New York: Berkley Books, 2000).

[12] In effect, a modern name for a united front action.

[13] Kenneth Allen and Eric McVadon, *China's Military Relations* (Washington, DC: The Henry L. Stimson Center, October 1999); Kenneth W. Allen, "Showing the Red Flag: The PLA Navy as an Instrument of China's Foreign Policy," paper presented at *PLA Navy Building at the Start of a New Century*, cosponsored by the Center for Naval Analyses and the Chinese Council for Advanced Policy Studies (Taipei), June 2001, Washington, DC.

[14] Constitution of the People's Republic of China, December 4, 1982. Also found in the party constitution.

[15] The description of the organizational differences is based on discussions with PLA staff officers and commanders from the various general departments and regional commands of the PLA from 1983–2001 about mutually frustrating experiences. For an understanding of many of the historical factors governing PLA organization, see William W. Whitson with Chen-hsia Huang, *The Chinese High Command, A History of Communist Military Politics, 1927-71* (New York: Praeger, 1973), and Michael D. Swaine, *The Military & Political Succession in China* (Santa Monica, CA: RAND, 1992).

[16] For a better understanding of the historical and social antecedents of this term, see Frederic Wakeman, Jr., *Strangers at the Gate* (Berkeley: University of California Press, 1966).

[17] Based on visits to most of the PLA universities, academies, and senior service schools and experience with approximately 150 U.S. or PLA delegations and more than 50 research fellowships, 1984–2001.

[18] Headed by Michael Armacost, Deputy Assistant Secretary of State, 1987.

[19] Michael Pillsbury has collected a selection of these articles in *Chinese Views of Future Warfare* (Washington, DC: National Defense University Press, 1997).

[20] Lectures about U.S. experiences in Vietnam and in developing its air cavalry concepts were given in China in the mid-1980s by a number of retired U.S. general officers while on tours sponsored by the United States Information Agency and others. These lectures have been studied and have played a role in shaping PLA policy. There was little interest in the United States in reciprocal visits.

[21] While Army attache, the author participated as a member of the team that negotiated the sale.

[22] Alfred D. Wilhelm, Jr., *China and Security in the Asian Pacific Region Through 2010* (Alexandria, VA: The CNA Corporation, 1996).

[23] Bernard D. Cole, *The Great Wall at Sea* (Annapolis, MD: Naval Institute Press, 2001).

[24] Paul H.B. Godwin, "The PLA Faces the Twenty-First Century: Reflections on Technology, Doctrine, Strategy, and Operations," in *China's Military Faces the Future*, ed. James R. Lilley and David Shambough (Washington, DC: American Enterprise Institute, 1999).

[25] Defense Consultative Conference talks.

Part VI

Options for U.S.-China Relations

Chapter 18

The United States and China: Time for a Change

Richard C. Thornton

I t is not enough to remember the past; it is imperative that one understands it. Before proposing a policy for the path ahead, this essay discusses the key decisions that have brought our relationship with
China to the point it is today.

The Evolution of U.S.-China Relations

From Richard Nixon's opening to China until the collapse of the Soviet Union in 1991, U.S. policy toward China was a function of strategy toward the Soviet Union. American leaders were of two minds, however, in
this regard. One faction, the *new world order* faction, saw policy toward
China and other states subordinate to the development of détente with
Moscow, the central axis of American strategy.

The other faction, the *containment* group, saw the Soviets as an adversary and sought to employ China as a counterweight to growing Soviet
power. China policy fluctuated by administration and the faction in control of American policy. In the past three decades, however, the containment faction prevailed only during two brief periods: Nixon's first term
and the first 6 years of the Reagan administration.

Nixon's opening to China was intended as a means of employing
China as a counterweight to the Soviet Union in the context of his Vietnam exit strategy, and Mao Zedong reciprocated by preparing to shift into
the American sphere as part of an anti-Soviet "alliance." But, when Nixon
faltered, Henry Kissinger turned American strategy away from containment and toward a search for détente with Moscow. A downturn in U.S.
relations with China was the result.

The turn in American strategy was matched by a shift in Chinese
strategy as Mao, too, faltered and was replaced by Deng. As Kissinger pursued détente with Moscow, Deng Xiaoping sought to play Washington off

Moscow, and from 1974 until the collapse of the Soviet Union in 1991, Deng attempted to occupy the middle position between the United States and the Soviet Union whenever feasible.

President Jimmy Carter continued the Kissinger strategy toward the Soviet Union and China until 1978, when he initiated the normalization process. Although Zbigniew Brzezinski hoped to employ normalization of relations with China as a means of strengthening the containment of the Soviet Union, Carter never fully abandoned the détente strategy.

It was not until Ronald Reagan became President and scrapped the failed strategy of détente that the United States once again sought to strengthen China as a counterweight to the Soviet Union. The 1982 August communiqué, whose surface aspect was a modus vivendi on Taiwan, marked a historic U.S. decision to increase the flow of technology, resources, investment, and trade to China. The essential bargain between Reagan and Deng Xiaoping was that in return for setting aside the issue of Taiwan as an obstacle to improvement of relations, the United States would assist China's economic development. Reagan hoped that this bargain would translate into the emergence of China as a counterweight to the Soviet Union, but it did not. Nevertheless, the bargain held through the Reagan administration, even though at its end Secretary of State George Shultz once again changed American strategy from Reagan's containment back to Kissinger's détente with Moscow.

The collapse of the Soviet Union fundamentally altered the strategic environment and led to further changes in both American and Chinese strategy. In a search for a new strategic partner, the United States, under George H.W. Bush, chose China to fill the vacuum created by the demise of the Soviet Union—a role that China in turn chose to fill. In short, if the collapse of the Soviet Union created a temporary strategic quandary for the United States, it offered Beijing the greatest unrequited opportunity in China's history to attempt to supplant Moscow and achieve a dominant position in the Far East.

The problem was, of course, that China was too weak to be a genuine partner. Therefore, the United States decided to help. Understand, too, the decision to build up China was not for it to be a counterweight to Russia but to replace Russia. In my humble opinion, we need a deeper inquiry into the circumstances surrounding this decision. It seems to be nothing less than a replay of the Kissinger strategy toward the Soviet Union of extending trade and technology in return for cooperation and the maintenance of stability. If that was the rationale, it failed in the China case the way it did in the Soviet. Regardless of the rationale, however, it was a decision that William Clinton carried to extraordinary lengths.

It is a truism that a country's foreign policy is a direct function of its economic power. And the extent and scale of American assistance in the development of China's economic base during the Clinton Presidency were enormous, as a few facts from the history of foreign direct investment (FDI) in China illustrate. Although Deng Xiaoping declared China's opening to the West in 1978, FDI was negligible between 1978 and 1982. Following the August 1982 agreement, however, that picture began to change, albeit still quite slowly. Between 1982 and 1991, FDI increased but never exceeded $3 billion in any given year, and the total was less than $20 billion.

The great surge in FDI began in 1992, when the decision had been made to build China into a strategic partner. The Chinese reciprocated by removing barriers and enacting enabling laws, but none of that would have mattered had the United States not made the decision to help. Between 1992 and 2000, FDI skyrocketed, reaching $40 billion in 2000 and possibly $46 billion in 2001, and to a cumulative total of some $400 billion in less than a decade. Combined with trade and technology transfer, this amounted to a truly massive shift of Western resources to China, greater and faster than any other shift of resources in the history of the world.

In other words, it was less than a decade ago that China truly began to develop the economic power on which it now bases an increasingly challenging strategy today. The adoption of this strategy has been premature, for the modern sector of the Chinese economy is quite vulnerable to external forces. China has not yet developed a self-sustaining, modern economy that can independently generate the level of wealth required to support the technological requirements of its strategy. Moreover, China's strategy is self-defeating, challenging the very country responsible for its present position. In short, the Chinese economy is too young, fragile, and dependent upon external inputs to support its current strategy. That is China's weakness. Its strategy can only succeed if we allow it to—and vice versa.

What is China's strategy? It is, of course, to make China into a great power, drawing upon the resources of both East and West to do it. The first requirement for success has been to strengthen the economic base and construct a hard-currency-generating economic system. The means to this end has been an export-led growth strategy, including the construction of Western export platforms containing the latest manufacturing technology, thus enabling Beijing to acquire wealth and technology from the West and to undertake what has truly been a Great Leap Forward. But the hard-currency-generating economic base has yet to be constructed.

China has accumulated an enormous hard currency reserve, estimated to reach $200 billion in 2001, the cumulative product of a large annual trade surplus with the United States. But instead of using this reserve of wealth to transform the Chinese economy, the Chinese have employed it to acquire a sophisticated arsenal of weaponry from the Russians. With Western wealth and Russian weapons, China now poses a challenge to the United States in Asia.

Enjoying this apparent best of both worlds, Chinese leaders anticipate that the growth in intimidating military power will enable them to restructure the Asian political balance to advantage, perhaps, as Sun Tsu would say, "winning the war without fighting a battle." The hoped-for outcome is abundantly clear: China will become the new power center of Asia, displacing the United States, absorbing Taiwan, coopting Russia, and drawing Japan and South Korea into its orbit. Were this strategy to succeed, China would indeed become a global power of the first rank, perhaps eclipsing the United States.

In retrospect, the general turn in Chinese strategy was signaled in the change in policy toward Taiwan in 1995. Some have mistaken the change as a regime survival issue, as Taiwan's move toward genuine democracy put its absorption farther out of reach, but that is not the case. Like the Chinese saying "*jr sang ma huai*" (to point at the small leaf but curse the big leaf), Chinese policy toward Taiwan represents a general challenge to the United States in the Far East.

Until 6 years ago, the Taiwan question had been dealt with according to the bargain reached with Reagan in 1982. The essence of that agreement was that the United States would gradually reduce the quantity and quality of armaments that it would provide Taiwan, but only as long as the Chinese pursued a peaceful approach toward resolution of their dispute. Were the Chinese to break that bargain, the United States would reassess its policy.

The Chinese made clear that Jiang Zemin's 8-point proposal for reunification in 1995 ended the bargain on Taiwan. Even though his proposal set no ultimatum, it was a signal that a tougher policy was coming in the absence of capitulation by Taipei. The subsequent missile shots bracketing the island before the 1996 election were an unmistakable signal, as was General Xiong Guangkai's nuclear threat that "Washington cares more about Los Angeles than about Taipei."

But Clinton had decided that he had too much invested in the strategic partnership to reassess China policy and so did what he vowed he would never do: he coddled dictators. The 1996 election year saw Clinton's policy of "engagement" move into high gear as export controls were removed on the sale of advanced computers and satellites and missile technology "transferred" to China. Even U.S. nuclear weapons laboratories opened for Chinese perusal.

In return, the Chinese pumped millions of dollars into Clinton's campaign coffers through various intermediaries. They could be forgiven for acting as if they had bought a President, if not the entire American leadership establishment. The Clinton rollover only encouraged the Chinese to believe that they could flaunt any agreements made with the United States.

And flaunt agreements they have. The list is long. For example, promising to open its markets, accession to the World Trade Organization (WTO) notwithstanding, China practices blatant neomercantilist protectionism. Claiming improved human rights practices, China continues to arrest and execute dissidents, even American citizens. Agreeing to protect intellectual property rights, China permits gross piracy of patented products and processes. Promising to curtail illegal emigration, China looks the other way as thousands seek sanctuary on American shores. Promising to use dual-use technology solely for civilian purposes, China diverts such technology for military purposes. Committed to adhere to the Missile Technology Control Regime, China continues to export missiles. Promising to adhere to the Comprehensive Test Ban Treaty, China continues to test nuclear weapons. Promising to desist from exporting nuclear technology, China exports nuclear technology all the same. Acquiescence has only emboldened Beijing in the belief that American capitalists care only for profits, not principle.

During the 1990s, the Chinese also became active in staking out positions beyond their borders, which indicates very ambitious future objectives. They have established relations with the former Soviet Central Asian republics, the Shanghai Five Agreement, not to mention reestablishing the Sino-Russian alliance. They are increasingly asserting their "maritime rights" in the Sea of Japan, mapping the sea floor. They have claimed the entire South China Sea as their own territorial waters, fortifying islands positions there, and are constructing a protective/coercive corridor from China to the Persian Gulf, through the supply of weaponry to nations along this waterway, including Burma. Indeed, the objective appears to be to take positions that would enable them to threaten to interdict the flow of goods from Japan, South Korea, and Taiwan to the west as well as the flow of oil from the Gulf.

In embarking upon this strategy, the Chinese have borrowed heavily from the former Soviet Union in regard to the employment of missile power, which explains their hostility to missile defense. No doubt the Russians have eagerly proffered their advice, for a Chinese challenge of the United States serves Russian long-term strategy.

The Soviet Union constructed a large, intermediate-range missile network that enabled Moscow to target virtually every nation in the Eastern Hemisphere. The Chinese appear to be in the early stages of doing the same. The ballistic missile network deployed along the coast enables the Chinese to target South Korea and Japan, in addition to Taiwan. China's support for North Korea's missile program also carries a thinly veiled threat to Japan and the U.S. position on Okinawa.

Of course, Chinese capability lags significantly behind that of the United States, but they do not need an equivalent capability to ours to be able to challenge us in the Far East. The heavy Chinese investment in ballistic and cruise missile systems, aircraft carriers, advanced fighter aircraft, attack and missile submarines, and antiship weapons clearly foreshadows a future intention to contest the United States for, at a minimum, maritime supremacy in the Far East.

The testing process has already begun, and the Chinese must be encouraged by the way the United States meekly responded to the latest challenge, the EP–3 incident. We possess but have not released tapes that I believe would show the Chinese deliberately provoked the incident and forced the aircraft down. By declining to expose their ploy, they must conclude that we are still fearful of causing a disruption of our relationship.

The United States and China

Thus far, I have tried to establish three propositions—that Chinese strategy has changed and now aims to displace the United States from East Asia; that the United States has played a crucial role in China's growth in power; and that China's power nevertheless rests on an extremely fragile economic base.

These three propositions form the context in which to address the issue of future American policy. After all, as American policy has been instrumental in establishing the conditions for the growth of Chinese power, it can also be instrumental in changing those conditions. I submit that it is within our power to tame the Chinese dragon and bring about a transition to peaceful relations in East Asia. Moreover, the time is ripe for change.

The success of Chinese strategy will require greater wealth than they now possess, good fortune, and American acquiescence. China depends fundamentally upon the good will of the United States to succeed, just as the Russians did. Atrophy of the link to the West will inevitably undermine, if not derail, the Chinese strategy, just as it did the Soviet one. The fundamental contradiction in Chinese (and Soviet) strategy is Beijing's dependence upon access to the wealth of the United States even as it attempts to challenge the United States.

The Soviet Union collapsed because the Russians did not have sufficient wealth to surmount their economic and technological backwardness when the United States decided to bring détente to an end. At the same time, their inability to match the Reagan administration's military modernization program exposed the fragility of the Soviet Union's technological-economic base and spelled the doom of Soviet strategy. Despite Mikhail Gorbachev's subsequent efforts to change strategy, constrict empire, and cut costs, the continuing inability to develop a viable economy led to collapse of the state.

China is in both a stronger and a weaker position than the Russians were in different ways. While the future may look rosy for China at the moment, it is facing a predicament at least as if not more difficult today than the Soviets faced in the early 1980s. For China, 2001 is like 1981 was for the Soviet Union. Like the Soviets, the Chinese have come to believe that rapid modernization is within their grasp, that the United States and the West will continue to pour wealth, technology, and human expertise into China indefinitely, that superpower status is inevitable, and that China will soon be equal or superior to the United States. Like the Russians, the Chinese believe that capitalist greed will insure that we sell the rope and tie the noose they will loop around our collective necks.

Like the Soviets in 1981, China has experienced the benefits of a lengthy period of détente and extensive trade with the West, accompanied by a heavy flow of wealth and high technology. Like the Soviets in 1981, the Chinese believe in the permanence of hard currency flows for the indefinite future to pay for this buildup. And like the Soviets in 1981, there is the soothing patois of businessmen, intellectuals, political leaders, and military leaders of all stripes urging the United States to continue along the path to engagement, the synonym for "détente."

I believe that we have reached the moment when we must turn the page on China policy, deflating overambitious Chinese aspirations, and disabusing them of any hope of displacing the United States as the hegemonic power in the Far East. The way to address the China problem, however, is not through military confrontation, although if the Chinese choose confrontation, we must be prepared and not shrink from it, as we did in the EP–3 incident.

The way to deal with China is the same way we dealt with the Soviet Union. We must apply the Reagan formula: constrict trade, staunch the flow of high technology and investment, and severely inhibit Chinese ability to acquire hard currency. At the same time, we must demonstrate our superiority by building a military capability they cannot match. Missile defense must occupy center stage in that effort because missile offense is the centerpiece of their strategy, just as it was the Soviet.

The essence of the solution to the China problem is to constrict severely Beijing's future ability to accumulate hard currency on anything like the scale accumulated in the past decade. Fortunately, three factors are converging that make this possible. First is the global economic recession, which began earlier this year. Second is the war on terrorism following the events of September 11, and third is the Chinese leadership's own decision to enter the World Trade Organization.

In theory, WTO entry over the next few years will throw open all of China's economic sectors to greater domestic and foreign competition, sharpening the contradictions between stagnant communism and modern capitalism. China stands at the point of no return, and only three things can happen. China will make the adjustments necessary and lay a strong foundation for future growth; stagnate in an attempt to cheat its way around WTO rules, essentially changing little; or falter and slide into turmoil.

The Chinese have said that they will try to maintain the best of all possible worlds, maximizing their profits, and delaying and minimizing their commitments. In a recent interview, vice-minister Long Youngtu said that during the 5-year accession period, China plans to delay commitments on market access for as long as possible while exporting the maximum. He indicated that they will only "gradually" reduce tariffs and export subsidies and will seek the West's agreement to restrain use of antidumping measures against China.

Most important, no matter which path they choose, it will be accompanied by increased social tension and repression as the regime attempts to suppress the inevitable dissent that the WTO process will produce inside

China itself. That dissent will be from both those who benefit from modernization—the demands of rising expectations, including demands for political democracy—and from those who do not benefit and despair at the price they will be forced to pay.

We must help this process along. Chinese exports had already begun to shrink and inventories grow as the global recession began to hit in early 2001. In fact, Chinese exports have already shrunk by a quarter compared to 2000. When recovery begins, as it inevitably will, we will have to find other means to discourage imports from China. These means are at hand.

For example, the Iran-Libya Sanctions Act, first passed in 1996 and renewed in August 2001, authorizes the U.S. Government to cut imports from any company making energy investments in Iran or Libya, both of which have been named by the United States as state sponsors of terrorism. Any contract over $20 million triggers sanctions. China has been heavily involved in Iran for some years. Indeed, Sinopec just signed a $160 million contract for energy development. Thus, China already qualifies under this law alone.

Also, the Iran-Iraq Arms Nonproliferation Act of 1992 calls for the imposition of sanctions on any state assisting either of these two in the development of their weapons programs. The Chinese qualify here, too, and under the Arms Export Control Act, the United States has imposed "wrist-slap" sanctions on a Chinese company for the sale of nuclear equipment to Pakistan. The Chinese already have broken their pledge of November 2000 that they would not export material designed to assist countries to develop nuclear missile systems.

In addition to discouraging trade, the U.S. Government should also encourage investors to look elsewhere. With sufficient incentives, investment into other areas and countries can be made profitable, offsetting China's low labor cost advantages. Our own hemisphere would be a productive area where the result is less likely to produce a challenge to American interests. If capitalists truly care only for profits, then investments will not be China-bound.

Would that strategy really work? China has a huge domestic economy. To a certain extent, it could compensate for any action we would take. And that is what Henry Kissinger believes. In a recent interview, he declared, "We cannot prevent China's growth. If we try, they will only grow a little slower, but we will guarantee that they will be an enemy." Since China already is an adversary, if not an enemy, we lose little and perhaps gain a great deal by having it grow a little slower.

But the hard facts are that trade and FDI combined account for over 40 percent of China's gross domestic product (GDP). The United States and Japan each take 20 percent of China's exports. It is China's Achilles' heel. A significant, prolonged decline in both of these areas would not only slow down China's growth rate, but it also would seriously impact its military spending, which is tied to hard currency earnings. In addition, the costs of managing WTO entry will impose further constraints on Beijing's ability to squeeze the domestic economy to pay for continued military modernization.

The Soviet Union took a decade to collapse. It may take longer to rein in China. Results will not be visible immediately because China's large currency reserve would enable it to cushion short-term effects. And they would complain both directly and through their agents of influence in the United States. But once the Chinese realize that we have become serious, their policies would change. And that is the object. In truth, the Chinese are in this way worse off than the Soviets were because their economic health is tied more directly to the United States than the Soviet Union's ever was.

The Chinese already see the problems coming and realize that the quality of their growth remains fragile. They are in the fifth year of a large fiscal stimulus program designed to expand their infrastructure base, but the problem is monumental and their resources too few. The Chinese economic base vis-à-vis its military structure is in better balance than the Soviet Union's was. The Soviet Union had a major military overhang, but the Chinese economic base is not as broad as many think. The effective base is relatively narrow. The high-tech sector of their military is not yet disproportionately large, but it is getting there.

China is a financial basket case. Officially, domestic debt is 15 percent of GDP, but when contingent liabilities—such as the bad debts of the state banks, the unfunded state pension system ($600 billion), and social welfare liabilities—are factored in, the figure quickly rises to nearly 100 percent of GDP. The nonperforming loan ratio in China's four largest banks alone—the Bank of China, China's Commercial Bank, the Agricultural Bank of China, and China's Construction Bank—is officially pegged at 30 percent of total assets, but many believe the true level to be closer to 50 percent. Even at 30 percent, however, China's banking system is bankrupt. Nonperforming debt is estimated to be half a trillion dollars, but if one counts China's rural credit cooperative banking network, nonperforming debt doubles to a figure that matches or even exceeds annual GDP.

The Chinese have failed to make the transition to a modern economy, notwithstanding all the changes in recent years. China remains a gigantic company town. The government owns the biggest banks and companies. Some 300,000 state-owned enterprises employ nearly half of all China's workers. The big banks lend to these companies, which receive two-thirds of all loans yet produce only one-third of all output. The regime absorbs the losses. The system is dysfunctional and money-losing.

Chinese leaders know that their only hope is to grow their way out of the hole they are in by phasing out the money-losing enterprises, selling off their debt, and phasing in the money-making enterprises. This process would take decades under the best of circumstances, and the Chinese are hesitating. In fact, Beijing recently prohibited large state-owned enterprises from declaring bankruptcy, one of the principal ways of liquidating money-losing companies. This decision is a strong indicator that the regime is further slowing economic reform in favor of warding off social unrest.

China needs capital and cannot raise enough domestically by increasing taxes, which it is doing at all levels, including on foreign enterprises, or expanding domestic demand through the sale of bonds to the people. The Chinese bond market is deformed by government control of interest rates, and the equity market is plagued by fraud, insider trading, and stock manipulation. In fact, Beijing recently suspended sales of shares owned by the government, reversing a policy begun earlier this year to raise funds for the bankrupt pension system.

The share sales are crucial to Beijing's market reform campaign. The government owns 70 percent of all shares outstanding in the Chinese stock market. The suspension of new share sales immediately boosted prices of existing shares in Shanghai and Shenzhen, but it comes at a stiff cost. It cuts off an important avenue of financing for the national pension fund designed to support tens of millions of unemployed people nearing retirement age who have no medical insurance or savings.

The Chinese also turn to our capital markets to raise money, but this is coming to an end. We cannot permit the Chinese to exploit our own financial system against us, and we have begun to tighten up by enforcing strict registration requirements, insisting on transparency, and requiring full disclosure. We are also gradually curtailing indirect access to our markets, such as by listing on the London stock exchange and selling to so-called qualified international buyers in the United States. And we are gradually uncovering the PLA hand in many ostensibly commercial Chinese companies operating in the United States.

China believes that it can foist its debt onto us. In the past 2 years, China created four asset management companies (AMCs), then shifted 1.4 billion *ren min bi* in state-owned enterprise debt from the books of the big four banks to the AMCs, which have sought to sell off to the West. Not surprisingly, there are few takers. Questions regarding legal rights foreign investors would have over land and other assets combined with China's less than transparent policy environment have frightened investors away. If the AMCs cannot find buyers for this debt, which they probably will not, the state itself will be saddled with the interest due on the bonds.

On top of all this will come the costs of entry into WTO, which will either transform China into the golden goose, as many Americans claim, or be the poison pill that kills it. The gap between rich and poor is now the largest in the world and far and away the largest since 1949. The urban economy seems robust, but the countryside, where 900 million people live, is mired in debt and inefficient farming practices. WTO impact on China's agriculture will be devastating. Already 120 million people are estimated to be living below the poverty line, and 150 million more are seasonally employed migrant workers. The countryside is a tinderbox waiting for a match, which may be the WTO.

WTO will effect a transformation of the countryside, but things will get much worse before they get better. China's agriculture sector is the weakest link in the entire economy, and farmers will be hit hardest by WTO entry at a time when rural incomes are falling and infant mortality rates are rising. Resistance is already strong; riots and demonstrations are frequent, especially in opposition to the heavy hand of government tax collectors. The Chinese will be damned if they conform to WTO rules and damned if they cheat. Enforcement will only raise the level of conflict, while the refusal to do so will confirm predictions that the Chinese are out to manipulate the world organization.

The Chinese have made a major mistake in showing their hand too soon, mounting a premature challenge to the United States in the Far East on the pretext of action against Taiwan. That challenge is based upon an economic system that is still too weak and dependent upon the very power being challenged to succeed. The United States can and must begin to curb Chinese ambitions by raising their costs of doing business, reducing their revenues, and building an unchallengeable military position. Furthermore, we must do this now before China becomes too strong to control and we find ourselves on the path to war, which will be the inevitable outcome of the continuation of current policy. Fundamentally, it is not up to them. It is up to us. The fate of the Far East, and more, is in our hands.

Chapter 19

U.S.-China Relations: A New Start?

David Lai

A war broke out 2,432 years ago in ancient Greece between the Spartans and the Athenians. Thucydides, an Athenian historian, took note of this bloody and protracted war (the war started in 431 BCE and lasted for 27 years) and turned his account and analysis into a book called *The Peloponnesian War*. At the beginning of this monumental work on war, Thucydides asserts that while there were many different factors contributing to the onset of this military conflict, what made this war inevitable was the growth of Athenian power and the fear this expanding power cast on the Spartans.

Since the Peloponnesian War, there have been many other major power wars resulting from similar situations (Germany's rise and World War I is a contemporary textbook example). Today, we may be witnessing the making of another power transition. This time, it is between China and the United States.

With the end of the Cold War and the fall of the Soviet Union, the United States stands as the lone superpower. In the past 10 years, riding the tides of the information revolution and globalization, the United States has raised its supremacy to an unprecedented level. Across the Pacific Ocean, however, China has embarked on industrialization. Rapid economic development in the past two decades has given China newfound power and influence.

History suggests that there is natural tension in the power transition process between the competing powers. Typically, the rising power is unhappy with the existing international order created and maintained by the hegemonic and status quo power. With its increased power, the rising state will try to alter the situation. Conflict will arise if the two powers cannot accommodate each other.[1]

The United States is watching with concern over this rising China—the world's youngest and oldest great powers have a precarious relationship that has gone through many ups and downs in the last 50 years. They are also currently at odds over a wide range of issues such as the way of government, Taiwan, human rights, arms sales, missile defense, military modernization, and many others. The rise of China has added more complexity to this troubled relationship. A pressing question for us is: Will this power transition result in another Peloponnesian War? No one can rule out such a possibility. We just have to recall how dangerous it was during the U.S.-China standoff over the military aircraft incident on April 1, 2001. In the long run, inherent tension generated out of the power transition process could prompt the two great powers for conflict. In the short term, the contentious Taiwan issue stands as a flashpoint.

However, if the relationship is properly handled, the United States and China will not have to go to war against each other. For better or for worse, the United States holds the keys to the issue of war and peace with China. Chinese leaders largely watch what the United States would do to China and make their responses and adjustments. Yet to put it jokingly, there is no guarantee that the "American sheriffs" would find the right keys to the demanding problems. More often than not, U.S. national leaders are influenced by an always divided policy advisory, checked by a divided government between the President and the Congress, and divided they mess up the keys.

Currently, there are mainly three schools of advocates, each proposing a different approach to deal with China. The Clinton administration pursued an engagement policy toward China. Conservatives attacked this approach for being too accommodating to the Chinese. They insist that the best way to change China is through discipline. Containment therefore is their proposed policy choice. Between these two camps comes a middle-of-the-road approach proposed by the RAND Corporation. It is a policy of *congagement*, a combination of engagement and containment.[2]

All three schools share a common goal: to change China in the U.S. image. They differ, however, on the means to this end. These approaches, after all, are not new. They are the traditional approaches of carrots and sticks. It is questionable that these old tricks are working on China. Indeed, John Mearsheimer bluntly warns that the United States should not expect too much from changing China. Instead, it would be better off to "do whatever it can to slow down China's rise."[3]

While the debate goes on, the United States appears to follow the RAND approach to deal with China. The engagement part is the continued economic, trade, and other exchanges. The containment part is the action taken by the United States to strengthen or promote bilateral security ties with China's neighboring countries. From the Chinese perspective, the United States is building a ring of encirclement around China that goes from Japan and Korea to China's northeast down around China's eastern and southeastern seaboards through Taiwan, the Philippines, Vietnam, Thailand, Singapore, Australia, and up to China's western frontier with India and Pakistan. The current war against terrorism in Afghanistan has brought the United States into Central Asia, right next to China's sensitive northwestern territory.

One cannot blame the Chinese for their concern. We just have to imagine how we would feel if we found the Chinese government making a presence around the United States. To a lesser extent, as David Shambaugh rightly puts it, even the U.S. engagement approach is perceived as a soft containment on China.[4] Distrust, as a result, still runs deep.

Contentious incidents in the last few years have made the tense relationship worse. The bombing of the Chinese embassy in Belgrade, Yugoslavia, in May 1999, the Cox report about Chinese stealing secret nuclear technology information, the continued American support for Taiwan, and the military aircraft crash on April 1, 2001, all served to reinforce the distrust between the two nations.

The Bush administration has not made this relationship any easier. During the 2000 Presidential election campaign, candidate George W. Bush criticized the Clinton administration's attempt to make China a strategic partner. He proposed to redefine China as a strategic competitor instead. No sooner had he moved into the White House than did President Bush and his foreign policy team start to translate this campaign rhetoric into policy consideration. Chinese leaders took note of this change and perceived it as a further deterioration in the already troubled U.S.-China relations.

Bush's attempt, however, quickly ran into snags. Shortly after the April 2001 military aircraft incident, the Bush administration started to modify its approach toward China. President Bush and his senior advisors quickly dropped the term *strategic competitor*. When Secretary of State Colin Powell went to Beijing on July 30, he was all smiles, calling the Chinese leaders friends. Secretary Powell was in Beijing to prepare for a summit meeting between President Bush and the Chinese president

Jiang Zemin in China in October 2001. U.S.-China relations appeared to be on the upswing.

Then came the unexpected terrorist attacks on the United States on September 11, 2001. The United States suddenly found China on the same side against terrorism. The scheduled meeting had become an opportunity for President Bush to solicit support from China (and other Asia Pacific national leaders who were attending the Asia Pacific Economic Cooperation annual meetings in Shanghai).

These changes ironically put President Bush much ahead of his predecessors in adjusting his approach toward China (David Lampton observes that it took Ronald Reagan more than a year and a half and Clinton more than 3 years to get back the main channel of U.S.-China policy[5]). However, it is becoming clearer that such an important relationship between the United States and China should not be like a constantly swinging pendulum. A more stable approach is badly needed to meet the long- and short-term challenges posed by the rising China.

A sound approach toward China should be based on a proper understanding of it. However, this understanding is still lacking. The lack of understanding of China is largely reflected in the following areas.

Overstating China Threat

There are several ways to see if China is a threat (to the United States and the international community). One is to determine if China has territorial design beyond its borders. This is certainly a disputable call. China's quest for unification with Taiwan and its claim on the South China Sea islands are cases in point. From China's perspective, these are historical losses waiting to be recovered. However, the other disputants insist that there must be room for negotiation and compromise. How the Taiwan question and South China Sea disputes will be settled is a topic for another analysis. A fair proposition can be made here that there is no reason to believe China would seek expansion beyond these disputes. A domino effect (in President Dwight Eisenhower's terms) is far fetched.

Realistically, any Chinese expansionist attempt will be easily offset by its geopolitical constraints. Unlike the United States, China has 15 formidable neighbors, some of whom it has unsettled border disputes with. Its approach is to mend fences and promote good neighbor relations. China has been quietly pursuing this policy for the last 20 years. One must agree that its accomplishment is rather impressive.

Another way to gauge if China is a threat is to see if it has ideological designs beyond its borders. China has abandoned its call to promote international communism long before the collapse of the communist camp (the alarming one was made by Lin Biao during China's Cultural Revolution in the late 1960s). Chinese leaders have no desire to revive the failed international communist movement. Aside from political ideology, China does not have a religious drive to conquer the souls of the world.

Still another way to see if China is a threat is to assess if it has the capability to threaten other nations. Chinese military power is the central focus. There have been numerous studies about the People's Liberation Army (PLA). Most see that China's priority and grand strategy is to develop the economy and to transform China into a great power in 50 to 100 years. Military modernization takes a backseat in China's modernization drive. However, new developments in the Taiwan question put much urgency on China's need to upgrade its military power. Much of the increase in China's military buildup in recent years has been largely driven by China's need to keep its reunification quest credible.

Moreover, many of China's neighbors have acquired impressive advanced weapon systems from the United States, Russia, and other Western major powers. The awesome American military power operations in the Gulf War, the Kosovo War, and the current war against terrorism in Afghanistan have put the Chinese on alert that they cannot let their military power fall too much behind.

The balance sheet should be clear: the China threat thesis has been overblown.

Overestimating China's Development

After a few false starts in the past, China finally embarked on a true process of industrialization in 1978. Its economic development in the last 23 years has been really impressive. However, a fair assessment of China's development has to take its huge population into account. The difference between China's gross domestic product (GDP) and its per capita GDP is a case in point.

China has come a long way in its quest for industrialization, but it has a long way to go. Chinese leaders rather modestly claim that China is still at the early stage of "socialism," and this early stage of socialism is going to be a long one, say, about 100 years. During this long period of time, China will remain a developing nation.

Overlooking Changes in China

As economic reform continues to thrive in China, many fundamental changes are also taking place. Most of the changes are taken for granted in the West and the United States. However, these changes are revolutionary to the Chinese. Indeed, from the list of change presented below, we see that the Chinese are actually Americanizing their life in many aspects. Specifically, the Chinese are:

- eating fast foods and drinking coffee (getting to be fast paced)
- moving on four wheels and highways (a car for each household in 20 years)
- housing single families (no more three generations under one roof)
- paying their own way in college education (it was practically free in the past)
- reforming government work assignments for college graduates (graduates are allowed to look for their own jobs)
- freeing up the labor market (a competitive labor force is on the move)
- loosening the household registration system (the Chinese government finally translates one constitutional right into action)
- transforming the state-run industries (it is privatization!)
- embracing free trade (becoming a member of the World Trade Organization)
- adopting American legal concepts and practices (presuming innocence rather than guilt and setting up law firms in China)
- having nationwide village level elections (grassroots democratization)
- modifying the Communist Party of China (capitalists are welcome to join the party).

This list can go on and on. These are fundamental changes that will eventually put China more and more in line with the advanced industrialized nations.

Underestimating Chinese Leaders' Ability to Move China Forward

The Chinese regime survived an internal uprising (the Tiananmen Square movement) and an external shock by the collapse of the communist camp in 1989 and 1990. Twelve years later, Chinese leaders continue to pay lip service to Marxism and Maoism in their effort to maintain the legitimacy of the Communist Party of China rule of the country. However, Chinese people know that Marxism and socialism are just talk. Capitalism is what everybody does in China. Socialism with Chinese characteristics is only the code word for capitalism in China.

Chinese leaders understand this. They clearly see that it is their efforts in moving the economy upward and improving the people's standard of living that help them win the support of the Chinese people. Their accomplishments in getting China into the World Trade Organization, winning the competition to host the 2008 Olympics, and maintaining a thriving economy have earned them much popularity and secured them in the driver's seat.

China is currently in the process of leadership transition. Jiang Zemin's successor apparent, Chinese Vice President Hu Jintao, took a "coming out" tour of five major European nations: Russia, Britain, France, Germany, and Spain (from October 27 to November 11, 2001) and made his first-ever official visit to the United States in April 2002. This high-profile exposure should help him prepare for his formal succession in the coming years.

With succession matters ostensibly in smooth progress, Chinese leaders appear to be more confident in dealing with both internal and external affairs. One new development in the Chinese leadership is the recent telephone diplomacy launched by President Jiang Zemin. Responding guardedly to the terrorist attacks on the United States and the U.S. war against terrorism, Jiang made calls to all the major power leaders (and answered a call from British Prime Minister Tony Blair) and quite a few leaders of other countries (for example, Egypt, Pakistan, and Sri Lanka). On another occasion, immediately after the conclusion of the Asia Pacific Economic Cooperation meetings in Shanghai, Jiang called French President Jacques Chirac to brief him on the key issues discussed at the meetings.

It is interesting to recall Deng Xiaoping's (Jiang's predecessor) remark that it was not in the Chinese tradition to have national leaders talk to foreign counterparts on the telephone. Deng made this remark to explain why he did not answer the call from President George H.W. Bush in the immediate aftermath of the June 4, 1989, suppression. That was during the old days when China had limited telephone users. China's telephone lines have since increased a million-fold (recent statistics report that China now has over 300 million telephone household accounts). It seems natural that current Chinese leaders would break this tradition. Nevertheless, it also shows that Chinese leaders are more confident and are taking a more proactive approach in international affairs.

U.S. Approach toward China

In the face of the misconceptions about China and the fundamental changes taking place there, the United States needs to reconsider its approaches toward China.

Engagement. The United States wants to integrate China into the U.S.-led international order through engagement. This is a non-issue now. China is already integrated in many parts of the world community and is actively trying to break into the remaining areas. Engagement with China will be more and more on equal terms.

Containment. It is a nonstarter (in David Shambaugh's term). There is no way to contain China. There is no need to, either.

Congagement. It is only a new bottle for the old wine.

To have a fresh new start in U.S.-China policy, American leaders would be better served to review the Nation's founding fathers' advice.

At his farewell address to the nation on September 17, 1796, President George Washington laid down the principle for future American foreign policy: "Observe good faith and justice towards all nations; cultivate peace and harmony with all." Washington also charted a course for America: "It will be worthy of a free, enlightened, and at no distant period a great nation to give to mankind the magnanimous and too novel example of a people always guided by an exalted justice and benevolence." However, Washington cautioned that:

> In the execution of such a plan nothing is more essential than that permanent, inveterate antipathies against particular nations and passionate attachments for others should be excluded, and that in place of them just and amicable feelings toward all be should cultivated. The nation which indulges toward another a habitual hatred or a habitual fondness is in some degree a slave. It is a slave to its animosity or to its affection, either of which is sufficient to lead it astray from its duty and its interest.[6]

There is ample evidence that contemporary American foreign policy leaders have forgotten Washington's advice and have indulged in both habitual hatred of some and fondness toward other nations. Our insistence on labeling some nations as rogue states is a perfect example. Defining China as a strategic partner or a competitor is another prime example. It has shackled our Government's attempt to promulgate a coherent China policy. Labeling China in any way will only lead us to deal with a China that we wish it to be.

Following Washington's advice, the United States should prepare to deal with all other nations with neither ill will nor illusion. Particularly, the United States should prepare to engage China frankly and squarely. We must see that some of the American approaches toward China are overbearing. The United States should take a more enlightened approach, especially with respect to China's internal problems. Many of the problems are best seen as growing pains of a developing nation. They are China's own problems, and they would be better off left to the Chinese to solve. Excessive intervention will only backfire. Moreover, our excessive meddling in China's internal affairs only gives the Chinese leaders an excuse to resist change. We also hand the Chinese leaders an opportunity to rally the Chinese behind them in their opposition to the United States. In short, facing the reality, not wishful thinking, is the key to many of the problems in U.S.-China relations.

In addition, a big failure in the American dealing with China is that many of the conflicts appear to be attacks on China rather than the Chinese leadership. This is typically the case with many of the resolutions passed by Congress against China. The annual threat to terminate most-favored-nation trade status, the resolutions to frustrate China's efforts to host the Olympic games, the attempt to get the United Nations to condemn China for its poor human rights conduct, the accidental bombing of the Chinese embassy in Belgrade, Yugoslavia, the Cox Report about Chinese stealing secret information from the United States, and flying spy planes along China's coasts all serve to reinforce the Chinese government's propaganda that the United States bullies China. The rise of nationalism in China has much to do with this failed U.S. approach toward China. The anti-American sentiment has gone to the extent that when terrorists attacked the United States on September 11, 2001, many Chinese hailed the attacks. Chinese Internet chat rooms were filled with comments that the United States deserved the attacks.

It Takes Two to Tango

If the United States is to take a fresh approach toward China, Chinese leaders must face reality in their policy toward the United States as well. Chinese leaders must see that they have their undeniable share of responsibility for the troubled relations between China and the United States. Particularly, Chinese leaders from Mao Zedong to Jiang Zemin have all looked at the United States as their archenemy. The root cause of the Chinese leaders' animosity toward the United States lies in their self-imposed

Marxist ideological outlook and in their cardinal interests derived from an outdated political system that was abolished in many other former communist countries.

Chinese leaders have been asking U.S. leaders to discard the Cold War mentality toward China. They do not see that they are the ones who live in contradiction, and they have much to discard on their side. It is their outdated views on a wide range of issues that get them into troubled relations with the United States. Specifically, Chinese leaders must see the fundamental problems in Marxism and the Chinese government, the inherent contradiction in China's economic development and political decay, their lack of understanding of democratic government and human rights, and their erroneous views on international relations. Chinese leaders also must see that the ideology and the political system they choose to run are not historically determined. However, until they remove these self-imposed ideological barriers, Chinese leaders will not share fundamental interests with the United States. There can be no true improvement of relations between the Chinese leaders and the United States.

Revolution versus Governance

Karl Marx is undisputedly one of the founding figures of contemporary sociology of social conflict and revolution. Marx's theory today continues to inform us about the tension between the haves and the have-nots, as well as the potential of deadly social upheavals. However, Marx had very little to say about governance. Thoughts and theories about governance are from other political thinkers, such as Aristotle, Thomas Hobbes, Hugo Grotius, John Locke, Charles de Montesquieu, Jean-Jacques Rousseau, James Madison, Alexis de Tocqueville, Max Weber, John Stuart Mill, and others. Unfortunately, Chinese leaders favor only Marxism and reject all others.

There is no evidence that Mao Zedong read any of these major Western works on representative government. Mao followed Marxism to launch a revolution in China and won the victory in 1949. However, Mao could not find answers from Marxism for governance. He then turned to the Chinese classics of palace power struggle such as *Zizhi Tongjian* for clues. The tragedy was that he ran the "People's Republic" as a revolution until he died in 1976.

Mao's successor, Deng Xiaoping, had his limitations as well. Deng was a little better than Mao in that he understood the importance of economics. While Mao emphasized the power of political authority, Deng relied on economic means. China under Deng took off in economic development. Unfortunately, Deng left behind an outmoded political system intact. Deng openly admitted that he hardly read any theoretical work. All he had offered was pragmatic experience talk. He believed that as long as the Chinese Communist Party (CCP) can improve Chinese people's standard of living, it can continue to control China. He refused to accept the idea that as China's economy develops, its political system has to change accordingly. Ironically, this is precisely what Marx's theory is all about.

Jiang Zemin inherited a Chinese government that is in the shadow of its suppression of the student movement in Tiananmen Square in 1989. The CCP and the PLA have no doubt lost much popularity. Jiang understood that the only way to continue the CCP rule of China was to continue China's economic reform. As Jiang and his associates put it, economic development is a necessity but not a choice. However, Chinese leaders also see that economic development carries the seed of political instability, a typical problem in changing societies. Therefore, they are trying everything they can to uphold their authoritarian control.

Chinese leaders also justified their continued economic reform by referring to Marx's theory about social development. Human society, according to this theory, develops in an evolutionary fashion from primitive tribes to agricultural communes, and then slavery, feudalism, and capitalist societies; eventually, capitalism gives way to socialism and finally the world becomes communist. China, as Jiang put it, jumped from feudalism and semicolonialism into socialism. It is clear that this rush was premature. So in the CCP 15th national convention in 1997, Jiang declared that China is still in the early stage of socialism; moreover, this early stage is going to be a long one, perhaps over 100 years. During this long period, China has to make up the lessons of capitalism.

We would leave aside this absurd theory about history developing in a predetermined and linear fashion. But we want to point out that since the corresponding political system to market economy (that is, capitalism) is democratic government, China would be better off making up the lessons of representative democratic government as well. In this respect, the thoughts and measures taken by the Founding Fathers of the United States have much to offer to the Chinese leaders in improving China's political machine. Specifically, the *Federalist Papers* should replace the "Mao Thought," "Deng Theory," and "Jiang Insight" to become the guiding principles of a new Chinese political system.

Lasting Stability

China has a recorded history of about 5,000 years. For thousands of years, Chinese leaders have been concerned with political stability. To date, China still does not have a political system that can guarantee lasting political and social stability.

For thousands of years, Chinese leaders have known and maintained only one form of government. It is a centralized authoritarian government without checks and balances on political power, especially the high-level rulers. As Lord Acton put it, power corrupts; absolute power corrupts absolutely. This system is unstable by design.

Adding to this fatal flaw is the absence of the mechanism for legitimate and peaceful transition of rulership. With no exception, every dynasty came to power through war or rebellion. When the CCP founded the People's Republic in 1949, the triumphant Chinese leaders claimed to have broken away from China's dynastic past. Unfortunately, the record of CCP rule of China in the last 50 years is essentially the same as the old dynasties. It was perhaps even worse during Mao's absolute dictatorial control.

Another major problem is the lack of political and civil liberty. Chinese top-level rulers are traditionally chosen through power struggle. Middle and lower level officials are all appointed from above. As a result, they all try to please their superiors, but none are responsive and accountable to the people under their control. Anyone who criticizes the government is charged with capital crime. For thousands of years, the Chinese government has kept perhaps the longest and worst record in the world for punishing people for what they think and say. One such example appears in one of China's earliest historical chronologies, *The Shiji*, by the great historian Sima Qian (145–90 BCE). According to *Shiji*, Emperor Li Wang of the Western Zhou dynasty (9th century BCE) brutally silenced dissidents and then bragged about his brutality. One of his senior advisers warned him that the emperor's heavy-handed suppression was like building a dam to withhold water; when the people's frustration built up, it would eventually break the dam. Unfortunately, Emperor Li Wang did not take this advice. Later generations of Chinese leaders all emulated Li Wang but paid no attention to the advice either.

Finally, it is the involvement of the military in the country's political life. Mao is credited for making the remark that power grows out of the barrel of a gun. However, the PLA mission, as its name suggests, has been long accomplished. It is high time the Chinese leaders turn it into the Armed Forces of China. Its new mission should be to defend China, but not as a tool of the CCP in handling China's internal political affairs. In the most recent *White Paper on Defense* (released in October 2000), Chinese leaders once again insisted that the PLA adhere to the absolute leadership of the CCP. Chinese leaders should realize how outdated the approach is to have the military under the control of the party rather than the government. The experience of military coups throughout the world in contemporary history should bear this argument out.

There are many other problems in the Chinese political system as well. However, the ones mentioned here are sufficient to ensure political instability in China. Once again, the American example is of much help to the Chinese leaders. The fiasco of the 2000 American Presidential election has become the laughing stock of Americans and other peoples alike (including the Chinese leaders). However, after the laughter, Chinese leaders should see the essence of democracy at work. The freedom in political debate, the respect for law, and Al Gore's graceful concession have no doubt impressed many Chinese. Unfortunately, these acts would all be inconceivable in China.

Chinese leaders are big fans of Harvard professor Samuel Huntington. They like his theory of economic development through authoritarian rule in changing societies. However, they have all skipped Huntington's comment about the Chinese government's lack of adaptability—a key element of mature political institution and political stability. So from 1921, the year when the CCP was founded, the Chinese have had only two generations of leaders. Although the CCP defines Deng as the second-generation leader, Deng and Mao are what Huntington calls the "intra-generation succession." The shift from Deng to Jiang is an "inter-generation succession." In the same time period, the Americans have seen 15 Presidents, from Warren Harding (1921–1923) to George W. Bush.

Peaceful transition of leadership in the United States is a routine matter. However, it is a crisis in China. The CCP and Chinese government will have a generational change of rulers in the years 2002 and 2003. Chinese leaders are still operating in their outdated black-box fashion to determine the fate of their party and the Chinese government. There are indications that they have managed this upcoming rulership change. However, Chinese leaders must see that they are only muddling through the crisis. They still do not have a mechanism in place to guarantee peaceful transition of rulership in China. Chinese leaders want to develop China into a great power. They must see that it takes more than economic power to become a great power in today's world. Chinese leaders must see that without a democratic government, there can be no lasting stability in China.

Westernization and Peaceful Evolution

Chinese leaders have been pursuing a campaign to resist Westernization in China for the last five decades. Unfortunately, they forget that the CCP leaders are the ones who first Westernized China when they imported Marxism from the West. There is really no reason for the CCP to favor only Marxism in China. Chinese leaders should not continue the useless attempt to resist ideas from the West. What they should do is to see if they have better ideas to offer. If Western ideas serve China's interest, why reject them? In fact, Chinese leaders should do the Chinese a great favor and build an electoral democracy that can ensure lasting peace in China. Deng Xiaoping said that if China did not pursue socialism, the best it could become would be a vassal state of the Western industrialized countries. This is completely absurd.

It is true that democracy and representative government are ideas of Western origin. However, these are ideas that have stood the test of both time and contests with other forms of government. As the Dalai Lama recently put it, no government is perfect, but electoral democracy offers the best government that can accommodate imperfect human nature.

In the 1950s, the late U.S. Secretary of State John Foster Dulles placed hope on the third and fourth generation Chinese to turn China into a democratic country. He also hoped that China would go through a peaceful evolution in the change from authoritarian rule to representative government. Chinese leaders hate this comment. They have been fighting hard to resist this change. Chinese leaders must see that attempts to resist peaceful evolution will breed only violent upheavals. They should take steps to make political change before it is too late.

The changes in Taiwan offer a great example of peaceful evolution. All Chinese should feel grateful that the change of leadership in Taiwan did not turn into a war. This is the first time in China's 5,000 years of history that there was a peaceful transition of leadership from one ruling party to its opposition. There are obviously many lessons to be learned from the Taiwan experience. Perhaps this is the most important one.

Lastly, Chinese leaders must stop their outmoded anti-U.S. propaganda. They must see that years of anti-American propaganda have given rise to a generation of hateful Chinese. It is really a shame to see the Chinese people take pleasure at the pains of the Americans following the

September 11, 2001, terrorist attacks. If the Chinese leaders do not stop this anti-U.S. practice, they will push the Chinese people toward confrontation with the Americans in the future.

A New Road to Peace

While the above-mentioned changes involve a change of mindset on both sides and will take time to implement, a quick fix is within our reach. This approach is to build a multilateral security regime in Asia. It is clear that the U.S. approach to pursue bilateral ties with the Asian nations around China does not serve the purpose to promote security and stability very well. It seems more reasonable that the United States should pursue a multilateral option.

An Organization of Security and Cooperation for Europe and Partnership for Peace-like political/security regime would offer the United States, China, and Asian nations an opportunity to minimize the chance of a future Peloponnesian War in Asia.

The reasons are multifold. First, this structure would offer continuous diplomatic contact and dialogue, currently absent in the region. Second, it would moderate China's fears of a U.S. containment strategy, as witnessed by U.S. bilateral alliances around China. Third, it would include an operational level structure, where one does not now exist, for military interaction to increase transparency, confidence, and predictability. Finally, a multilateral security regime would also induce stability that would stave off regional fears of a rising China through dialogue, confidence and security building measures, and preventive diplomacy.

To conclude, let us review George Washington's advice again. The United States and China should look into the mirror, reflect upon the past, and both take a refreshed new start toward each other. George Washington prophetically told us:

> The nation prompted by ill will and resentment sometimes impels to war the government contrary to the best calculations of policy. The government sometimes participates in the national propensity, and adopts through passion what reason would reject. At other times it makes the animosity of the nation subservient to projects of hostility, instigated by pride, ambition, and other sinister and pernicious motives. The peace often, sometimes perhaps the liberty, of nations has been the victim.[7]

Notes

[1] See A.F.K. Organski, *World Politics* (New York: Knopf, 1958), for a discussion of the power transition theory.

[2] Zalmay M. Khalilzad et al., *The United States and a Rising China* (Santa Monica, CA: The RAND Corporation, 1999).

[3] John J. Mearsheimer, "The Future of American Pacifier," *Foreign Affairs* (September/October 2001).

[4] David Shambaugh, "Containment or Engagement of China?" *International Security* 21, no. 2 (Fall 1996), 180.

[5] David Lampton, "Bush Is Ahead of the Game on China," *The Christian Science Monitor*, August 29, 2001.

[6] George Washington, "Farewell Address," *Two Centuries of U.S. Foreign Policy*, ed. Stephen J. Valone (Westport: Praeger, 1995).

[7] Ibid.

About the Authors

Stephen J. Flanagan is director of the Institute for National Strategic Studies and vice president for research at the National Defense University (NDU). Prior to joining NDU in January 2000, he served as special assistant to the President and senior director for Central and Eastern Europe at the National Security Council. Dr. Flanagan's earlier Government service includes senior positions with the Department of State, the National Intelligence Council, and the U.S. Senate. Dr. Flanagan also has held academic and research appointments at the Kennedy School of Government at Harvard University, the International Institute for Strategic Studies, the Council on Foreign Relations, and the Center for Strategic and International Studies. He has published widely on international security affairs and is co-author of *Challenges of the Global Century,* the report of the NDU Project on Globalization and National Security.

Michael E. Marti was a senior research fellow at the Center for the Study of Chinese Military Affairs in the Institute for National Strategic Studies from November 2000 to July 2002. Presently a senior analyst with the Department of Defense, he has over 27 years of military and civilian experience. He is a historian specializing in Chinese national security and foreign policy. He served a one-year tour in the Office of the Assistant Secretary of Defense for International Security Affairs as the assistant country director for China, Taiwan, and Mongolia. His most recent book is *China and the Legacy of Deng Xiaoping* (Brassey's, 2002).

Richard A. Bitzinger has been a defense industry analyst, specializing in the global defense industry and arms production, international armaments collaboration, and the international trade in weaponry and military technologies. He currently works for the U.S. Government. Mr. Bitzinger is the author or coauthor of over 40 monographs, articles, and book chapters, including "Globalization in the Post-Cold War Defense Industry: Challenges and Opportunities," in *Arming the Future* (Council on Foreign Relations Press, 1999); "Military Spending and Foreign Military Acquisitions by the PRC and Taiwan," in *Crisis in the Taiwan Strait* (National Defense University Press, 1997); and *Gearing Up for High-Tech Warfare? Chinese and Taiwanese Defense Modernization and Implications for Confrontation Across the Taiwan Strait* (Center for Strategic and Budgetary Analysis, 1996).

Bernard D. Cole is professor of military history in the National War College at the National Defense University, where he has served on the faculty since 1993. Dr. Cole's areas of expertise are Sino-American relations and maritime strategy. He has published many books, articles, book reviews, and essays, including *The Great Wall at Sea: China's Navy Enters the 21st Century* (Naval Institute Press, 2001).

David M. Finkelstein is a member of the Center for Strategic Studies at CNA Corporation. As the deputy director of Project Asia, he specializes in Asian security issues. He is a retired U.S. Army foreign area officer for China with extensive experience in joint political-military assignments at the national level.

Richard D. Fisher, Jr., is a senior fellow with The Jamestown Foundation in Washington, DC, where he monitors and comments on strategic issues pertaining to U.S. interests in Asia. He previously served as a senior analyst with the House Republican Committee. Fisher has published widely on U.S. interests in Asia from North Korea to New Zealand and in recent years has published several studies on the modernization of the People's Liberation Army of the People's Republic of China. He is the editor of *China Brief.*

Edward Friedman is the Hawkins Chair professor of political science at the University of Wisconsin, Madison, where he specializes in Chinese foreign policy. He has been the China specialist for the U.S. House of Representatives Committee on Foreign Affairs Subcommittee on Asia and the Pacific. His publications include *National Identity and Democratic Prospects in Socialist China* (M.E. Sharpe, 1995) and *What If China Doesn't Democratize? Implications for War and Peace* (M.E. Sharpe, 2000).

Bates Gill holds the Freeman Chair in China Studies at the Center for Strategic and International Studies in Washington, DC. Previously, he was a senior fellow in foreign policy studies and inaugural director of the Center for Northeast Asian Policy Studies at The Brookings Institution. A specialist in East Asian foreign policy and politics, his research focuses on Northeast Asian political, security, and military-technical issues. He is the author of *Contrasting Visions: U.S., China, and World Order* (The Brookings Institution Press, forthcoming); *Chinese Arms Transfers* (Praeger, 1992); and coauthor (with Taeho Kim) of *China's Arms Acquisitions from Abroad: A Quest for "Superb and Secret Weapons"* (Oxford University Press, 1995).

Paul H.B. Godwin is a consultant specializing in Chinese defense and security policies and serves as a nonresident scholar in the Atlantic Council's Asia-Pacific Program. He retired as professor of international affairs in the National War College at the National Defense University in 1998. Dr. Godwin's most recent publications are "China's Nuclear Forces: An Assessment," in *Current History* (September 1999); "China's Defense Modernization: Aspirations and Capabilities," in *Washington Journal of Modern China* (Spring 2000); and "China, America, and Missile Defense: Conflicting National Interests" (with Evan S. Medeiros), in *Current History* (September 2000).

Howard M. Krawitz has been a visiting fellow in the Institute of National Strategic Studies at the National Defense University since September 2001. He is a career Foreign Service officer with extensive East Asian experience. From 1999–2001, he was senior advisor on China and East Asia to Senator Dianne Feinstein. Mr. Krawitz has also been director for Chinese and Mongolian Affairs in the United States Trade Representative's Office and a Strategic Trade Controls negotiator for the Department of State.

David Lai joined the Department of Strategy and International Security at the Air War College in April 1999. His teaching and research interests are in international relations theory, war and peace studies, comparative foreign policy, and Asian and China politics. Prior to his graduate study at the University of Colorado, Dr. Lai was a diplomat in the Chinese Foreign Service. Dr. Lai has published articles in prominent international studies journals. He has also published a book on international relations and U.S. foreign policy and is currently writing on issues relating to the Taiwan-China question, U.S.-Asia relations, and Chinese strategic thinking.

Nan Li is senior fellow in the Institute for Defence and Strategic Studies at Nanyang Technological Institute in Singapore. He has also taught at the University of Cincinnati, Dartmouth College, University of

Massachusetts, Amherst, and Eastern Kentucky University. He has published on Chinese civil-military relations and military doctrine and organization in *Security Studies, China Quarterly*, and *Armed Forces & Society*, and has edited volumes for the RAND Corporation and Oxford University Press. His most recent publication is *From Revolutionary Internationalism to Conservative Nationalism: The Chinese Military's Discourse on National Security and Identity in the Post-Mao Era.*

James C. Mulvenon is an associate political scientist at the RAND Corporation in Washington, DC, and deputy director of the RAND Center for Asia-Pacific Policy. A specialist on the Chinese military, his current research focuses on Chinese strategic weapons doctrines (information warfare and nuclear warfare), theater ballistic missile defenses in Asia, Chinese military commercial divestiture, and the military and civilian implications of the information revolution in China. He recently completed a book on the Chinese military's business empire, entitled *Soldiers of Fortune* (M.E. Sharpe, 2001).

Kevin G. Nealer is a principal and partner in The Scowcroft Group, where he provides risk analysis and direct investment support to the group's multinational clients, specializing in financial services and trade policy issues. Before joining The Scowcroft Group, Mr. Nealer advised multinational clients on investment issues, project finance, and trade law/policy as a principal in the consulting affiliate of Washington's largest law firm and as vice president for corporate affairs with a leading government strategies practice. He is the author of numerous articles on political economy appearing in *The Asia Wall Street Journal, Journal of Commerce*, and other periodicals, books, and professional journals.

Eugene B. Rumer is a senior fellow in the Institute for National Strategic Studies at the National Defense University. He is a specialist on Russia and other states of the former Soviet Union. Dr. Rumer previously served as a visiting scholar at the Washington Institute for Near East Policy; a member of the Secretary's Policy Planning Staff at the Department of State; and director for Russian, Ukrainian, and Eurasian affairs at the National Security Council. Prior to government service, he worked for the RAND Corporation first as an analyst based in Santa Monica, California, and later as a senior staff member and resident representative in Moscow.

David Shambaugh is professor of Political Science and International Affairs and director of the China Policy Program in the Elliott School of International Affairs at The George Washington University. He is also a nonresident senior fellow in the Foreign Policy Studies Program at The Brookings Institution and a 2002–2003 residential fellow at the Woodrow Wilson International Center for Scholars in Washington, D.C. He is the author of numerous works on contemporary China and East Asian international relations, a consultant to various agencies of the U.S. Government, private sector foundations, corporations, and he is a frequent commentator in national and international media. He has recently published *Modernizing China's Military: Progress, Problems & Prospects* (University of California Press, 2002).

John Tkacik is a research fellow at the Asian Studies Center of The Heritage Foundation, where he studies policies and events concerning China, Taiwan, Hong Kong, and Macao. Previously, he was head of China Business Intelligence, a consulting firm, and publisher of the newsletter, *Taiwan Weekly Business Bulletin*. He also was a Foreign Service officer in the Department of State from 1971 to 1994, stationed in China, Hong Kong, and Taiwan.

Richard C. Thornton is professor of history and international affairs at the Elliot School of International Affairs at The George Washington University. His major works include *Odd Man Out: Truman, Stalin, Mao and the Origins of the Korean War* (Brassey's, 2000); *The Nixon-Kissinger Years: The Reshaping of American Foreign Policy* (Washington Institute Press, 1989); *The Carter Years: Toward a New Global Order* (Washington Institute Press, 1992); and *China: A Political History, 1917–1980* (Westview Press, 1982).

Cynthia A. Watson has been a faculty member in the National War College at the National Defense University since 1992, serving as associate dean from 1997–2000. She has also worked for the House of Representatives Subcommittee on Government Information Staff and the U.S. General Accounting Office. Dr. Watson's research has concentrated on nuclear and small arms proliferation, civil-military relations, and transnational issues across Third World states. She has recently published *U.S. National Security* (ABC–CLIO, 2002) and is completing a volume on the disintegration of Colombia.

Alfred D. Wilhelm, Jr., is managing director of Wilhelm and Associates, where he works to advance relations between the people of the United States, China, and Taiwan through education, finance, health care, and national security projects. From 1989 to 2001, as executive vice president and chief operating officer of The Atlantic Council of the United States, he developed programs to advance U.S. relations and academic exchanges throughout Asia. Earlier he served as the U.S. Army Attache in Beijing on the faculty of the National Defense University and in Vietnam. His publications include *China Policy for the Next Decade* (Oelgeschlager, Gunn, and Hain, 1984); *The Chinese at the Negotiating Table* (National Defense University Press, 1994); and *China and Security in the Asian Pacific Region through 2010* (Center for Naval Analyses, 1997).

U.S. Government Printing Office: 193–413 T&D 2003